LETTERS OF ARNOLD BENNETT

Volume III

1916–1931

Arnold Bennett in his last years

LETTERS OF ARNOLD BENNETT

Edited by

JAMES HEPBURN

VOLUME III

1916–1931

LONDON
OXFORD UNIVERSITY PRESS
NEW YORK TORONTO
1970

Oxford University Press, Ely House, London W.1
GLASGOW NEW YORK TORONTO MELBOURNE WELLINGTON
CAPE TOWN SALISBURY IBADAN NAIROBI DAR ES SALAAM LUSAKA
ADDIS ABABA BOMBAY CALCUTTA MADRAS KARACHI LAHORE
DACCA KUALA LUMPUR SINGAPORE HONG KONG TOKYO

SBN 19 212185 5

Printed in Great Britain by R. & R. Clark Ltd., Edinburgh

CONTENTS

LIST OF ILLUSTRATIONS

ACKNOWLEDGEMENTS

My thanks are due once again to the editors of the Oxford University Press for their helpfulness while this volume was being prepared, to the American Council of Learned Societies and the Penrose Fund of the American Philosophical Society for grants in support of the work, and to Dr. LaFayette Butler and Charles Tolhurst Butler for making manuscripts available that assisted in the locating of letters. The letters themselves are reproduced with the permission of the owner of the copyright, Mrs. D. C. Bennett. Mrs. Bennett also very kindly provided information about many of the letters.

I am obliged to a number of persons and institutions for allowing me to use the letters in their possession:

University of Arkansas, for letters to George Doran and Frank Swinnerton. I am particularly indebted to Professor Blair Rouse for his generous help in my obtaining permission to use these letters.

British Broadcasting Corporation, for a letter to the Corporation.

Trustees of the Beaverbrook Foundations, for letters to Lord and Lady Beaverbrook. I am very much obliged to Professor A. J. P. Taylor for bringing these letters to my attention and for providing information about many of them.

Mrs. Julia Birley, for a letter to Margaret Kennedy, and for information about Margaret Kennedy and Bennett.

University of Birmingham Library, and Rudolph Sauter, for letters to John Galsworthy.

Mrs. Thomas Bodkin, for letters to Thomas Bodkin. I am much obliged to Alan Denson for transcribing these letters and providing information about them.

Dr. LaFayette Butler, for letters to G. T. Bagguley, Jonathan Cape, Basil Dean, George Doran, John Drinkwater, James Hanley, Edward Knoblock, Rudolph Kommer, Beverley Nichols, Robert Nichols, Reginald Turner, Percy Withers, and an unidentified person.

University of California Library, Los Angeles, for letters to T. E. Caley, Jo Davidson, Adelaide Phillpotts, Eden Phillpotts, and J. B. Priestley.

The late Harriet Cohen, for letters to her.

Dorothy Collins, literary executor of the estate of G. K. Chesterton, for a letter to Chesterton, and for information.

Noel Coward, for a letter to him.

Donald S. Davis, for letters to his uncle Oswald H. Davis.

Professor Leon Edel, for a letter to him.

Dr. Desmond Flower, for letters to Newman Flower. I am especially grateful to Mrs. H. Ryder for her help in making these letters available to me.

Donald Gallup, for letters to T. S. Eliot.

Fonds Gide, Bibliothèque Littéraire Jacques Doucet, Paris, for letters to André Gide.

G. P. E. Griffin, for letters to Harriet Cohen, George Reeves-Smith, and Lord Rothermere, and for information.

Houghton Library, Harvard University (by permission of the Harvard College Library), and Sir John Rothenstein, for letters to William Rothenstein.

Paul M. Herzog, for letters to his father and mother, Paul and Elsie Herzog, and for information about them.

The late Gregory Hill, for letters to him, and for information about his friendship with Bennett.

The Countess of Iddlesleigh, for letters to Marie Belloc Lowndes and F. S. A. Lowndes.

University of Illinois Library, for letters to H. G. and Jane Wells. I am especially obliged to Professor Harris Wilson, editor of the Bennett–Wells correspondence, for allowing me to use these letters.

L. G. Johnson, for a letter to him, and for information.

James Keddie, Jr., for letters to E. V. Lucas. Mr. Keddie has very kindly provided me with information on several occasions.

King's School, Canterbury, for a letter to Edward Garnett.

Sir Allen Lane, for letters to John Lane.

Fonds Larbaud, Bibliothèque de la Ville de Vichy, for letters to Valery Larbaud.

Mrs. Geoffrey Madan, for letters to Geoffrey Madan.

University of Manchester Library, and Patrick Monkhouse, for a letter to A. N. Monkhouse.

Merton College Library, Oxford, for a letter to Max Beerbohm.

Mrs. D. Mewton-Wood, for letters to W. J. Turner. I am much obliged to Professor H. W. Häusermann for his help in making these letters available to me, and for providing information about them.

Mrs. Wainwright Morgan, for letters to Frederick Marriott.

The late Winifred Nerney, for a letter to her.

Henry W. and Albert A. Berg Collection, New York Public Library, Astor, Lenox, and Tilden Foundations, for letters to

G. T. Bagguley, E. M. Forster, John Freeman, Wilfred Hardie, J. M. Murry, Esmé Percy, Reginald Pound, Cedric Sharpe, J. C. Squire, Richmond Temple, and Gwladys Wheeler.

De Coursey Fales Collection, New York Public Library, for letters to Paul Nash. I am especially obliged to Robert W. Hill, Keeper of Manuscripts, for his courteous help.

Fales Collection, New York University, for letters to R. D. Blumenfeld, St. John and Leonora Ervine, J. W. Light, E. V. Lucas, Robert Nichols, William Nicholson, and Cedric Sharpe.

University of Rochester Library, for letters to Edward Knoblock.

J.-P. B. Ross, for letters to Alexander and Robert Ross. I am very much obliged to Sir Rupert Hart-Davis for transcribing these letters and for providing information about them.

Leonard Schuster, for letters to Edyth Goodall, and for information.

Mrs. Charles Shaw, for a letter to E. V. Lucas. I am particularly grateful to Martha A. Connor and Howard H. Williams, both of the Swarthmore College Library, for their help in making this letter available to me.

Society of Authors, for a letter to G. Herbert Thring.

Arnold Bennett Museum, Stoke-on-Trent, for letters to A. J. Caddie, George Doran, Thomas Lockyer, Hugh Walpole, and an unidentified person. I am especially obliged to K. D. Miller, City Librarian, John Ford, Deputy Librarian, and A. R. Mountford, Curator of the Museum, for their helpfulness on several matters.

Frank Swinnerton, for letters to Winifred Nerney. I am also very much obliged to Mr. Swinnerton for his kind and generous help on several occasions.

Manuscript Collections, Carnegie Library, Syracuse University, for letters to Sinclair Lewis.

Mayfield Library, Syracuse University, for letters to William Archer, Gerald Cumberland, His Majesty King George V, Louis Jouvet, Geoffrey Lapage, Grant Richards, C. Kennedy Scott, Sir William Weir, and the editors of the *Daily Express*, the *Evening Standard*, the *Nation*, *The Times*, and the *Times Literary Supplement*; and also for manuscripts concerned with the British Homesteads Association, a fiction competition, Louis Jouvet, and the Wounded Allies Relief Committee.

University of Texas Library, for letters to Maurice Baring, R. D. Blumenfeld, Jonathan Cape, Newman Flower, Hubert Griffith, Eugene Goossens, Francis Hackett, Frederick Keeble, Lillah McCarthy, William Lee Mathews, J. B. Priestley,

George Bernard Shaw, Jim Tully, and George Webster.

Professor Pierre Ullman, for a letter to Eugene Paul Ullman. Professor Ullman very kindly allowed me to use his father's memoir about Bennett, and provided information on several points.

University College Library, London University, for letters to Roger Fry and Radclyffe Hall, and for a letter from William Lee Mathews.

The late Sir Stanley Unwin, for a letter to him.

Beinecke Library, Yale University, for letters to Richard Curle, Louis Golding, Edith Sitwell, Osbert Sitwell, and John van Druten.

Her Majesty The Queen very kindly consented to the publication of the draft of the letter to George V.

I am very grateful to William D. Ridler for letting me see his collection of letters from Bennett to Anthony Ellis and for providing information about these letters. I am similarly obliged to Arthur D. Schlechter for the use of his collection of Bennett–Frank Swinnerton letters.

For help in locating letters and for other information I should like to thank Dudley Barker, Ernest Betts, G. J. Broadis of the Royal Institute of British Architects, Oliver Davies of the Royal College of Music, Alan Denson, Donald Gallup, Mrs. Olive Glendinning, Professor Alfred Havighurst, C. A. Johnson, Professor Dan Laurence, Patrick McCarthy, P. G. E. Nash of Broadcasting House, Professor Arthur Pollard, Reginald Pound, Miss S. Power-Kent of Canada House, Professor Eric Salmon, Professor Mark Schorer, Martin Secker, Professor Grover Smith, and the officials of the Victoria and Albert Museum.

I am very much obliged to June Osborne Bassett for transcribing a shorthand letterbook kept by Bennett.

Lastly I must thank my typist Mrs. E. L. Bird for her work, and Mlle. Claudie Clément for advice on Bennett's French.

Material from uncollected writings of Arnold Bennett is reprinted by permission of A. P. Watt & Son. Passages from *The Journal of Arnold Bennett*, copyright 1932, 1933, 1960, 1961 by the Viking Press, Inc., are reprinted by permission of the Viking Press, Inc., and also of A. P. Watt & Son. The quotation from a letter by Max Beerbohm is printed with the permission of the Beerbohm Estate. Passages from two letters by André Gide are reprinted with the permission of Madame Catherine Gide. Passages from two letters by George Bernard Shaw are reprinted with the permission of the Society of Authors, for the Bernard Shaw Estate. A few words from two letters by Hugh Walpole are printed with the permission of Sir Rupert Hart-Davis.

The photograph of Arnold Bennett is reproduced with the permission of the copyright holders, the City of Stoke-on-Trent Libraries, Museums and Information Committee. The facsimile of the first page of Chapter I of the manuscript of *The Roll-Call* is reproduced with the permission of the University of Illinois.

INTRODUCTION

This second volume of general correspondence contains more letters than the first and covers fewer years; it is compiled from a total number of surviving letters at least twice as large—upwards of four thousand. Twenty-three of the letters are printed with deletions. Some of the deletions have to do with the identity of the man with whom Marguerite Bennett was involved at the time of the breakdown of the Bennett marriage (letters 159, 160, 164, 165). Four withhold the names of other persons (letters 181, 223, 224, 385). The remainder are incidental deletions requested by Mrs. Bennett (letters 98, 131, 153, 164, 224, 235, 275, 277, 281, 283, 284, 288, 291, 308, 316, 331, 368). None of the deletions affects the character of the volume. One letter was omitted to protect persons still living. Marks of omission in one or two letters other than those listed above are Bennett's own.

A general account of the editorial forms used in preparing the volume will be found in the *Introduction* to Volume II. At the head of each letter is information on its owner or source. The following list identifies the owners or sources in full.

ARKANSAS (University of Arkansas Library)
ARNOLD BENNETT (*Arnold Bennett*, by Reginald Pound)
BBC (British Broadcasting Corporation)
BEAVERBROOK (Beaverbrook Library)
BERG (Henry W. and Albert A. Berg Collection, New York Public Library)
BIRLEY (Mrs. Julia Birley)
BIRMINGHAM (University of Birmingham Library)
BODKIN (Mrs. Thomas Bodkin)
BUTLER (Dr. LaFayette Butler)
CALIF (University of California Library, Los Angeles)
COHEN (the late Harriet Cohen)
COLLINS (Dorothy Collins)
COMMON SENSE

COWARD (Noel Coward)
DAILY EXPRESS
DAILY MAIL
DAILY NEWS
DAVIS (Donald S. Davis)
EDEL (Professor Leon Edel)
ETHEL SMYTH (*Ethel Smyth*, by Christopher St. John)
FALES, NYPL (De Coursey Fales Collection, New York Public Library)
FALES, NYU (Fales Collection, New York University)
FLOWER (Dr. Desmond Flower)
GALLUP (Donald Gallup)
GIDE (*Correspondance André Gide—Arnold Bennett*, ed. Linette F. Brugmans)
GRIFFIN (G. P. E. Griffin)
HARVARD (Houghton Library, Harvard University)
HEPBURN (James Hepburn)
HERZOG (Paul M. Herzog)
HILL (the late Gregory Hill)
IDDESLEIGH (Countess of Iddesleigh)
ILLINOIS (University of Illinois Library)
JOHNSON (L. G. Johnson)
KEDDIE (James Keddie, Jr.)
KING'S SCHOOL (King's School, Canterbury)
LANE (Sir Allen Lane)
LOCHERBIE-GOFF (*La Jeunesse d'Arnold Bennett*, by Margaret Locherbie-Goff)
LONDON MERCURY
MADAN (Mrs. Geoffrey Madan)
MANCHESTER (University of Manchester Library)
MANCHESTER GUARDIAN
MAYFIELD, SYRACUSE (Mayfield Library, Syracuse University)
MERTON (Merton College Library, Oxford)
MEWTON-WOOD (Mrs. D. Mewton-Wood)
NATION
NERNEY (the late Winifred Nerney)
NEW STATESMAN
OBSERVER
ROCHESTER (University of Rochester Library)

ROSS (J.-P. B. Ross)
S.A. (Society of Authors)
SCHUSTER (Leonard Schuster)
SHAW (Mrs. Charles Shaw)
STAR
STOKE (Arnold Bennett Museum, Stoke-on-Trent)
SUMMER'S LEASE (*Summer's Lease*, by Sir John Rothenstein)
SWINNERTON (Frank Swinnerton)
SYRACUSE, CARNEGIE (Carnegie Library, Syracuse University)
TEXAS (University of Texas Library)
U.C. (University College Library, London University)
ULLMAN (Professor Pierre Ullman)
UNITED METHODIST
UNWIN (the late Sir Stanley Unwin)
VICHY (Bibliothèque de la Ville de Vichy, Fonds Larbaud)
WESTMINSTER GAZETTE
W. MORGAN (Mrs. Wainwright Morgan)
YALE (Beinecke Library, Yale University)

The character of the text printed from, when it is not a book or periodical, is given thus: A.C. (autograph copy), A.D. (autograph draft), MS. (manuscript), S.TR. (shorthand transcript), T.C. (typed copy), T.C.C. (typed carbon copy), T.D. (typed draft), TR. (transcript), TS. (typescript). The single shorthand transcript comes from a shorthand letterbook kept by Bennett in 1930. Only the one letterbook is known to survive, although it is likely that Bennett filled two or three such books a year with several hundred letters from 1912 onward, when Winifred Nerney became his secretary. He apparently used these letterbooks at night when he could not sleep, mainly for business correspondence. The other transcripts were provided by owners or holders of original manuscripts, typescripts, or (in one case) a typed copy.

The letters to Harriet Cohen contain a regrettable number of fragments and unreadable and uncertain passages. Miss Cohen lent some of these letters to the editor to be photocopied, and the photocopies proved to be imperfect. Others she transcribed wholly or in part for her memoirs, and copies of the transcriptions were given to the editor. Then Miss Cohen died, and left her letters to the British Museum with the stipulation that they were not to be seen for thirty years. The authorities of the Museum felt unable to let the editor check his copies against them. For the sake of the reader, the editor has queried only the most doubtful of his readings of unclear passages in these letters.

MAYFIELD, SYRACUSE / MS. / 1
(*To C. Kennedy Scott*)

Comarques,
Thorpe-le-Soken,
Essex.
7th Jan 1916

Dear Sir,

I should be much obliged if you would read the enclosed pamphlet, written by myself, about the work of the Wounded Allies Relief Committee. I am getting up a really high-class concert in aid of the Committee's funds at the Haymarket Theatre on Sunday night 20th February, at 8 o'clock. I have asked only a few artists of the highest standing to help me. These include Mr. Ben Davies, Miss Ada Crossley, Madame Gleeson-White, Mr. Robert Radford, Mr. Walter Hyde, Miss Phyllis Lett and Miss Miriam Timothy.

Can I persuade you to bring the Oriana Madrigal Society to give us two or three items? Personally I am very interested in good music, & I know that the Oriana is the finest organisation of its kind in England if not in the world. Its presence would add immensely to the already great distinction of the programme. And I may promise, I think, that the audience will be worthy of the occasion. The war-charity to be helped is doing a very considerable & very varied work. It is patronized by Queen Alexandra, & has a number of eager & influential people behind it.

The matter is somewhat urgent, & I should be deeply obliged [illegible] might have your reply at once. An affirmative reply would not only earn the warm gratitude of the Committee and increase the success of the concert,—it would give deep pleasure to a number of musical enthusiasts.

Faithfully yours, Arnold Bennett

1. C. Kennedy Scott (b. 1876), choral conductor and composer, founded the Oriana Madrigal Society in 1904. Ben Davies (1858–1943) was a Welsh tenor, Ada Crossley (1874–1929) an Australian mezzo-soprano who had a highly successful career in London, Cicely Gleeson-White (1877–1968) a notable English soprano, Robert Radford (1874–1933) a bass singer, Walter Hyde (1875–1951) a tenor, Phyllis Lett (d. 1962) a well-known soprano, and Miriam Timothy a distinguished harpist and a professor at the Royal College of Music.

[illegible]n Bennett's work for the Wounded Allies Relief Committee see Vols. I and II. [illegible]he Haymarket concert he wrote an interview with himself by way of advertise-

[illegible] discovered Mr. Arnold Bennett in the offices of the Wounded Allies Relief [illegible]mittee. . . . "Now", said Mr. Bennett, "I can see at once you are a busy man.

So am I. Let us come to the point. You want to know something about the concert. . . . Your curiosity delights me. I will tell you simply everything."

"Well", I asked promptly, "How *does* one organise a war-concert?"

Mr. Bennett was certainly taken aback, but he seemed at once to recover his nerve.

"It is a highly difficult business," he said. "I have had to learn it. I am still learning. You first of all enquire from experts whether it is best to have the concert in the afternoon or in the evening. Thirty nine experts will strongly advise the afternoon. Thirty nine other experts will strongly advise the evening. I always take the advice of experts, so I gave myself the casting vote and decided for the evening. After all, theatres do a very great trade in the evening, and Sunday evening concerts are crowded."

"Yes, and what next?". . .

"Then there is a very important matter. Namely, measures to keep the concert from being too long. Most war-concerts are much too long, you know. Undue length has had a very bad effect on the enthusiasm of subscribers. Your measures must be drastic. Mine are. This concert of ours will begin at 8 and finish before 10.15. . . ."

"And after that?"

"Oh! After that there is nothing . . . nothing difficult, I mean. . . . All the rest is quite easy. You think of a first-class West End theatre, and you say to the lessee, 'Please sir, will you lend me your theatre free of charge for a Sunday night for our war-concert?' 'With the greatest pleasure', he says like a flash. You go to his various heads of departments and you say to them, 'Please sirs, will you work for nothing for our war-concert?' 'With the greatest pleasure', say they like a flash. This being arranged you think of eight or ten of your favourite artists, the best, the most renowned, the expensive ones, and you say to them, 'Please, sirs and mesdames, will you perform for nothing at our war-concert?' 'With the greatest pleasure', say they all like a flash. The rest is mere printing and postage."

"But the audience?"

"My dear colleague," said Mr. Bennett, leaning forward in his windsor chair, "I am organising the concert, not the audience. We are confidently expecting the audience. I don't wish to make any comparisons but I may tell you that there positively has not been and positively will not be a better war-concert than the Wounded Allies concert at the Haymarket Theatre on Sunday night the 20th at 8 sharp. It is not a concert from which a self-respecting musical amateur can stay away. . . ."

"But can't you tell me something about the audience?" I insisted.

"You mean the stalls and boxes?"

"Yes."

"Be not curious," said Mr. Bennett soothingly. "When you come you will have enough to do to look at the stage. But I don't mind letting you know that there will be many remarkable and well-known figures in the audience. And startling sights, too. For example you will be able to see West End theatre managers sitting in seats which they have paid for. I wrote to them and said: 'I want to offer you a new sensation—paying for seats in a theatre.' They took the offer."

"Organising a concert seems to be great fun," I ventured.

"It isn't," Mr. Bennett said firmly. "The whole thing is deadly serious. Money has to be collected, and it has to be collected every day. The Committee has enterprises in all Allied countries. It loses one occasionally. Not long since it lost a 600-bed hospital . . . to the enemy. . . . The Committee has to spend about £100 a day, every day. That money needs getting. There are no days off. Being wounded is just as disastrous and needs just as much sympathy, now, as at the

STOKE / MS. / 2
(*To Hugh Walpole*)

Comarques
5th Feby 1916

My dear Hugh,

Many thanks for the inscribed *D.F.* Overwork has delayed me much with it. I thought the opening rather vague and lacking in direction—due no doubt to 'recency' (a new word) of the impressions. However the book gathers force. By the time it finishes it is the best book of yours I have read since *Mr. P. & Mr. T.* This is certain. You have got hold of one of those themes that suit you, and the most important part of the story is very fine, simple, and sincere. The Audrey Vassilievitch stuff round about p. 220 is really moving. So is all the forest stuff and the war descriptive stuff, such as p. 196 etc., the best I have seen. Indeed the *only* really good descriptive stuff I have seen on this war. Such is the fact. I don't know to what constructional end you created two characters so similar as Trenchard and Audrey. I suppose I ought to know; but I just don't. Also I think the diaries lacking in *superficial* convincingness on account of the mere phrasing, which is too much like your own phrasing, and indeed a damn sight too good. So much for animadversion. The theme is fine; the effect sought for is got, and it is got gradually and surely. As a mere picture of life in a Red Cross unit the thing is of course very diverting & touching & convincing. But I regard all that as the background of the real business. As a mistake in grammar has been discovered by an American journalist in *These Twain*, I rejoice to find one in the *D.F.* See top of p. 310, the italicized words. You might at least have refrained from italicizing your sins. However, I shall say nothing to anybody. In my view you may make your mind easy about this book. You attempted an exceedingly dangerous feat, making fiction out of a mass of violent new impressions that could not possibly have settled down into any sort of right

---

beginning of the war. The public is apt to get tired. But the Committee dares not get tired. It is up against the facts. And so I want the Haymarket Theatre to be crammed on Sunday week." '

Some other comments by Bennett on the concert appear in Vol. I, p. 232.

perspective in your mind. (I had fears, despite your own conviction that the book was all right.) You have brought the affair very successfully off, with the help of an A1 central idea. So God be praised, and the aged and decrepitizing hereby sing Alleluia.

Curious streaks of Conrad and H. James in the vague opening pages. They then cease.

When come you here?

Yours, A. B.

VICHY / MS. / 3
(*To Valery Larbaud*)

Comarques
8th Feby 1916

My dear Larbaud,

Postcard & letter duly received—and with gladness. I have heard also from Viñes. I should like to be in Seville with you, very much. But I am tied up here, and much overworked. However, I will go to Spain after the war. Since Dec 1st I have done nothing but war work. But I have signed a contract to dramatise *Sacred & Profane Love* for Doris Keane (a really fine American actress), & I expect to begin to write the play about April 1st. It won't take very long I think. My novel *The Third Clayhanger* (*These Twain*) is a great success both here & in America, & has sold far better than any other of my novels. Prévost is going to publish *Hilda Lessways* in the *Revue de Paris* in April, and *These Twain* in March 1917. But of course he will cut them out of recognition. The man must be an ass. I have heard from André Gide. He is translating Mark Rutherford. He can of course 'adapt', but does he really know enough English to 'translate'? I doubt it. I very much doubt it. I hope you are keeping a diary in Seville. You ought to. I am so exceedingly busy that I cannot find time to write proper letters to my

2. For earlier letters to Hugh Walpole see Vols. I and II. *The Dark Forest* was published in February 1916. On p. 310 of the novel Walpole writes: 'I could see quite clearly how each of us—Marie, Semyonov, Nikitin, Durward, every one of us—had brought *their* private histories and scenes with *them*.' *Mr. Perrin and Mr. Traill* was published in 1911.

friends. Further, I am suffering severely from lumbago. So I close.

Marguerite sends you her kindest regards.

Ever yours, Arnold Bennett

P.S. Let us hear from you again, with your impressions. A. B.

HERZOG / MS. / 4
(*To Elsie Herzog*)

Comarques
23rd Feby 1916

Dear Mrs. Herzog,

Your return to right-handedness and general validity gives us very great pleasure. I should say, however, in regard to your excellent letter, that your account of your estimate of permanent weakness is wrong. Your real estimate is perhaps not so bad as you think it is. Anyhow you have come splendidly through this. The pity is that these things cannot be banished from the memory. I wish I had something to write about. I am still dulled with war work. If you had been well I should have had something to write about, as I should have asked you to help me to get money out of New York for my Wounded Allies Relief Committee, which helps all the allied wounded, & which is coming to the end of its tether for lack of funds, England being about squeezed dry. I have charge of the money-getting department of the Committee, and it is ageing me. I shall soon have quite grey hair. Grey*ing* hair, I am told, suits me. If I could get 75,000 dollars out of U.S.A. for my fund, my hair would resume its original heavenly brown. Next month I begin to write a play on the subject of *Sacred & Profane Love*, and after that another novel of which Munsey's will have the first bite. I suppose I shall do the best I can with these things in my odd moments. For we have now in England really begun to be at

3. For an earlier letter to Valery Larbaud see Vol. II, pp. 283–4. On Ricardo Viñes see Vol. II, pp. 215–16. Doris Keane and the dramatization of *Sacred and Profane Love* are mentioned at various points in Vol. I; Bennett began writing the play on 13 April. On Marcel Prévost see Vol. II, pp. 75–6. The *Revue de Paris* published *Hilda Lessways* in April–July 1917, and *These Twain* in October–December 1920. For letters to André Gide see below. On Mark Rutherford (William Hale White, 1831–1913) see below, pp. 201–2.

war. I gather that Germany is anxious for the end of the war. But she is always so previous. She will be much more anxious before she gets it. I imagine the situation in England will be much more trying than it actually is, by the autumn. Indeed, except for casualties & income tax, it hasn't been at all trying yet. But I think we shall be ready for it. Nothing else to say. Your letter was much better than this one. Still, our powerful good wishes go in this envelope, & I shall like to know that they have had effect. My wife's kindest thoughts to you.

Always yours sincerely, Arnold Bennett

P.S. Your letter arrived 3 hours ago. A. B.

DAVIS / TR. / 5
(*To Oswald H. Davis*)

Comarques
6th March 1916

Dear Mr. Davis,

Your letter is really very interesting and I am glad to have it. This new world of yours is entirely strange to me, though the village is always full of soldiers. My own observations are confined to officers, with whom I am in constant intimate relations, and as to whom I reckon to have learnt something in the last 18 months. As regards perception of beauty and intellectual interests they seem to be very like their men; but they are in the main excellent fellows and their manners are extremely satisfactory. I seem to be unable to get on terms with the men; indeed I feel no real desire to do so, though both my grandfathers were working-men—or perhaps because of that! I know Dunstable pretty well. Between 1900 and 1902 I had a house called Trinity Hall Farm, a little to the left of Watling Street, about 2½ miles north of Dunstable. You can see it, rather bare and funereal, on the opposite slope, immediately you come out of the cutting north of Dunstable. The country is beautiful, especially up in the Chilterns. There is a village called Ivinghoe up there that is worth seeing. The name of my village was

4. For earlier letters to Mrs. Herzog see Vol. II. The novel intended for the Munsey Syndicate in New York was *The Roll-Call*. See Vol. I for Bennett's quarrel with the Syndicate over it.

Hockliffe. I can't resolve your doubts about *These Twain*. The popular reception has been very satisfactory. Some people call it tired and dull; some who ought to know say that it is not first-rate; but others who equally ought to know say that it is the best of the three. I am a great believer in leaving these judgments to time. I do hope that you will keep notes of all your impressions of military life.

With best wishes,

Yours sincerely, Arnold Bennett

HERZOG / MS. / 6
(*To Elsie Herzog*)

Comarques
25th Mch 1916

Dear Mrs. Herzog,

You will not get this letter on the 25th, but I am writing it on the 25th.

I was *most particularly obliged* for your letter & your efforts on behalf of the Wounded Allies Relief Committee, & the cheque. You say these efforts will continue, & I hope they will. It is my business to keep the W.A.R.C. in funds, & the difficulty of so doing increases every week. In fact general appeals to the British public are now become almost useless. I have obtained over £5,000 out of the U.S.A. public, but if I could find the way I ought surely to be able to get a great deal more than that! I am sending you some other pamphlets calculated to open purses. Anything that you can do will be very highly esteemed and will be of real value. What you say about pro-Ally Americans of German descent is especially interesting, & I have acquainted the British public with the fact through the medium of the *Westminster Gazette*. I expect you won't mind, as I haven't mentioned your name. I have only been able to see Messmore Kendall once. Most of the time he has been in Paris. I found him very interesting, and apparently much more alert and developed than four years ago. For myself I am like a vast

5. Oswald H. Davis (1882–1962), author and journalist, met Bennett in 1915, and corresponded with him for ten years. He wrote a small book about Bennett, the title of which—*The Master*—indicates its character.

The Bennetts billeted a number of officers at their home during the war.

number of other people here, in that my own work has been practically stopped by the war, & I don't see much hope for it until the war is over. I have absolutely to write a play, however. The war has turned me into a political writer, & I have somehow created a new notoriety for myself in this department of my Wanamaker store. But immediately after the war I shall close it down. I may tell you that I should have written beseeching you to attempt something for my W.A.R.C., but really I did not think you could be anything like well enough for such activities. Hence I am surprised & doubly pleased. The war itself seems to be going on well. There are lots of things I could say as to the East coast, but recently the censorship has been very active among American private correspondence; hence I shall respect the wishes of the War Office. We are all right. My wife is in admirable health, & much occupied with her soldiers' club in our garden (beyond the lakelet). I am well, except for liver. The proof of your good recovery delights us. Our kindest regards to you both.

Yours sincerely, Arnold Bennett

UNITED METHODIST, 6 April 1916 / 7
(*To the editor*)

[Comarques]
[about 1 April 1916]

Dear Sir,

Thank you for sending me a copy of the *United Methodist* containing the article 'Books and Bookmen', which deals with the close resemblances between an episode in Charles Shaw's anonymous book, *When I was a Child* and an episode in *Clayhanger*. Let me remark that I am a fairly regular student of the columns of the *United Methodist* and other denominational organs, and I only wish that certain papers of a different stamp showed as keen an interest in literature as you do.

6. Mrs. Herzog's letter enclosed a cheque for £25, £23 of which she said was given by pro-Ally Americans of German descent, the other £2 by an Englishman. Bennett mentioned the fact in a letter to the *Westminster Gazette* published on 24 March.

Messmore Kendall (1872–1959) was the law partner of Mrs. Herzog's husband; he was also a vice-president of the George H. Doran Co., Bennett's American publisher.

I dare say that I have already affirmatively answered the question whether I was indebted to *When I was a Child* for the basis of the similar episode in *Clayhanger* about ten thousand times.

You yourself hit the nail on the head when you say: 'He may regard it as justifiable to use information derived from a printed book regarding the conditions of life in the hungry forties.'

Charles Shaw did not invent the episode. He lived it. He did not publish his book as a work of fiction, but, presumably, as a serious and valuable contribution to social history; which it assuredly is. As soon as I heard of it I bought the book with the full intention of using it if I could, as I have bought and used scores of historical books bearing on the district or period in which I happened as a novelist to be interested. In so doing I believe that I followed the customary practice of novelists attempting to portray a past epoch. It is a practice which I propose to continue. If anybody wishes to realize what the novelist's function is, and to understand the difference between history and fiction, let him read in its entirety the episode as related by Charles Shaw and then the episode in its entirety as related by me.

A little time ago I had some correspondence on this subject with Charles Shaw's son, who appeared to feel a grievance against me. I then offered to help Mr. Shaw to obtain publication of his implied charge in some suitable paper. The offer was not accepted. Your enterprise has rendered unnecessary any repetition of the offer.

Yours faithfully, Arnold Bennett

7. Chapter V of *Clayhanger* describes a day that Darius Clayhanger spends in a workhouse, one of the so-called Bastiles. The time is the 1830s.

'In the low room where the boys were assembled there fell a silence, and Darius heard someone whisper that the celebrated boy who had run away and been caught would be flogged before supper. Down the long room ran a long table. Someone brought in three candles in tin candlesticks and set them near the end of this table. Then somebody else brought in a pickled birch-rod, dripping with the salt water from which it had been taken, and also a small square table. Then came some officials, and a clergyman, and then, surpassing the rest in majesty, the governor of the Bastile, a terrible man. The governor made a speech about the crime of running away from the Bastile, and when he had spoken for a fair time, the clergyman talked in the same sense; and then a captured tiger, dressed like a boy, with darting fierce eyes, was dragged in by two men, and laid face down on the square table, and four boys were commanded to step forward and hold tightly the four members of this tiger. And, his clothes having previously been removed as far as his waist, his breeches were next pulled down his legs. Then the rod was raised and it descended swishing, and blood began to flow; but far more startling than the blood were the shrill screams of the tiger; they were so loud and deafening that the spectators could safely converse under their shelter. The boys in charge of the victim had to cling hard and grind their teeth in the effort to keep him prone. As the blows succeeded each other, Darius became more and more ashamed. The physical spectacle did not sicken nor horrify him, for he was a man of wide experience; but he had never before seen a flogging by lawful authority. Flogging in the workshop was different, a private if sanguinary affair between free human beings. This ritualistic and cold-blooded torture was infinitely more appalling in its humiliation. The screaming grew feebler, then ceased; then the blows ceased, and the unconscious infant (cured of being a tiger) was carried away, leaving a trail of red drops along the floor.'

Charles Shaw came of a poor family in the Potteries, and he grew up as a potter's boy. Eventually he became a minister, and in 1903 he published his account of his youth. Two brief chapters are devoted to a description of the Bastile in about 1840. The second is devoted to 'a case of discipline'.

'The case I am now going to refer to was that of a boy of lively temperament and unflagging energy. His activity was always bringing him into trouble. The theory formed by the officials seemed to be that his activity was essentially vicious, and so, instead of trying to guide it into wise and useful developments, it must be sternly repressed. Such a policy goaded the lad. He became defiant and reckless. Punish him they might, but he could not be repressed. One day, after being unusually provoked and punished, he scaled the workhouse wall, and bolted. Soon a hue and cry was raised, searchers were sent out, and after a few hours the lad was captured and brought back. This incident made an awful flutter in our little dove-cote. All were sorry for the lad, for he had made no enemies among us. All sorts of punishment were imagined as likely to be inflicted, but the boys who had been longest in the workhouse said he would be flogged in the presence of the other boys with a pickled birch rod—that is a rod which has been kept soaking in salt water. After the usual skilly supper that night we were all told to remain in the room. None were to go out on any account. The long table was cleared, and a smaller square table was brought in and placed in the middle of the room. The knowing ones whispered that the flogging would take place on this table, and this news made us all curious, eager, yet fearful. Several persons came in whom we did not usually see. Then the governor came in. To us poor lads he was the incarnation of every dread power which a mortal could possess. He was to us the Bastile in its most repulsive embodiment. Personally he may have been an amiable man, I don't know. He never gave one look or touch which led me to feel he was a man. He was only "the governor", and as such, in those days when the New Poor Laws meant making a workhouse a dread and a horror to be avoided, he was perhaps only acting the part he felt to be due to his office. . . . We were duly informed by him what was to take place, the bad qualities of the runaway were ponderously and slowly described, and we were exhorted in menacing tones to take warning by his "awful example". This homily was enough of itself to make us shiver, and shiver most of us did with fear of those present and fear of the sight we were about to witness. When the solemn harangue was finished, the poor boy was pushed into the room like a sheep for the slaughter. He had a wild, eager look. His eyes flashed, and searched the room and all present with rapid glances. His body was stripped down to his waist and in the yellow and sickly candlelight of the room his heart could be seen beating rapidly against his poor thin ribs. To punish such a boy as that, half nourished, and trembling with fear, was a monstrous cruelty. However, discipline was sacred,

STOKE / TR. / 8
(*To George Doran*)

[Comarques]
2nd May 1916

My dear Doran,

In the issue for December 23rd, 1915 of the New York *Nation* there is an extremely fine article on me by Stuart P. Sherman. On the whole I regard it as the best article I have ever seen on the subject. I should very much like to have seen this article reprinted, either with other by the same hand or alone, but I suppose that there is no chance of this. I should judge it to be about 5,000 words in length.

---

and could do no wrong in a Bastile sixty years ago. The boy was lifted upon the table, and four of the biggest boys were called out to hold each a leg or an arm. The boy was laid flat on the table, his breeches well pushed down, so as to give as much play as possible for the birch rod. The lad struggled and screamed. Swish went the pickled birch on his back, administered by the schoolmaster, who was too flinty to show any emotion. Thin red strips were seen across the poor lad's back after the first stroke. They then increased in number and thickness as blow after blow fell on his back. Then there were seen tiny red tricklings following the course of the stripes, and ultimately his back was a red inflamed surface, contrasting strongly with the skin on his sides. How long the flogging went on I cannot say, but the screaming became less and less piercing, and at last the boy was taken out, giving vent only to heavy sobs at intervals. If he was conscious, I should think only partially so. The common rumour was that he would have his back washed with salt water. Of this I don't know. I do know there had been cruelty enough. A living horror, hateful in every aspect, had been put before the eyes of the boys present. To see a poor lad with red rivulets running down his back and sides, as I see it all again even yet, among strangers, with the governor's awful presence, with the schoolmaster's fiercely gleaming eyes, away from father, mother and home;—all this when our late gracious Queen was a young queen. The spirit of the New Poor Law and of the Corn Laws was present in that torture-room that night. Lord Brougham, not many years before this, had said that "charity is an interference with a healing process of nature, which acts by increasing the rate of mortality, and thereby raising wages". . . . How that poor little wretch got on that night I never knew. He did not come to his usual bed in our room. . . . I never saw him again, for in a few days came the joyful news that my father had got a situation.'

In 1918 Bennett wrote in his *Journal*: 'I have read 100 pages or so of the Hammonds' *Town Labourer*. There is undoubtedly a pleasure in reading recitals of horrible injustice and tyranny.' And the next day: 'I didn't like reading the child-labour chapter in the Hammonds' *Town Labourer*. It exceeded the limits in its physicalness. I wish I had read it before I wrote the child chapter in *Clayhanger* to which the Hammonds refer. I could have made that chapter even more appalling than it is.' Other details of the relationship of *Clayhanger* to *When I was a Child* are discussed in *Studies in the Sources of Arnold Bennett's Novels*, by Louis Tillier (1969).

I am still exceedingly busy on all sorts of things, but the Carlotta play is steadily progressing.

Our affectionate regards to you all,

Yours, [Arnold Bennett]

MAYFIELD, SYRACUSE / A.D. / 9
(*To His Majesty King George V*)

[Comarques]
4th May 1916

May it please Your Majesty,

I am desired by the Wounded Allies Relief Committee to solicit Your Majesty's gracious attention to the following facts.

The Wounded Allies Relief Committee was established in nucleus on the day of the declaration of war, and it has helped and is still helping the wounded of all Your Majesty's European allies without exception. In this work it has already expended a sum approaching £50,000, and the value of its labours is shown by warm testimonials received from various Allied Governments.

Being now in serious need of further funds, the Wounded Allies Relief Committee has arranged to hold a gigantic War-Fair in the Caledonian Market (Metropolitan Cattle Market), Islington, on Tuesday & Wednesday, 6th & 7th June next. For this purpose the City of London has very kindly granted the use of the Market free of charge, and the Lord Mayor has promised his active cooperation. The very substantial help already received from and promised by all classes of Your Majesty's subjects renders a success practically certain.

Many enterprises have been undertaken on behalf of war

8. For earlier letters to George Doran, Bennett's American publisher, see Vols. I and II.

Stuart Pratt Sherman (1881–1927) was one of the most distinguished American critics of his day. He was the first critic, and has remained almost the only one, to take serious account of Bennett's pocket philosophies in relation to his novels. He did so in response to the Jamesian view—widely held—that Bennett's novels lacked any sort of framework, and were mere slices of life. His article concluded: 'I do not undertake to speak critically of his philosophy. I only know that it seems to support an altogether decent theory of human conduct. And this in turn underlies an artistic representation of life remarkable for its fullness, its energy, its gusto, its pathos, its play of tragic and comic lights, its dramatic clashes, its catastrophes, and its reconciliations—in short, for its adequacy.' His article was followed by an extended correspondence in succeeding issues, and was reprinted in his collection of essays *On Contemporary Literature* in 1917.

charities, but the Caledonian War-Fair is the first thing of the sort to be organised on a thoroughly popular basis. It will constitute a true gathering of the people of London, in the interests of a war-charity whose ramifications extend from Belgium to Portuguese Africa, & from northern Russia to Corfu. The Caledonian Market, which was opened by Your Majesty's grandfather, the late Prince Albert in 1855, comprises 15 acres of ground, and gives accommodation for 1,500 separate stalls. The popular interest in the affair is already such that expert authorities have insisted to the Committee upon the necessity of making a charge for admission on at any rate the first day.

These being the circumstances, I am desired by the Committee to transmit to Your Majesty their humble appeal that Your Majesty should deign to pay a visit to the Caledonian War-Fair on one of the two days on which it will be open. The Committee feel strongly that Your Majesty's subjects the citizens of London would in a quite special degree appreciate the deep significance of the presence of Your Majesty at this great popular manifestation of practical sympathy with the wounded soldiers of all Your Majesty's European allies, and they approach Your Majesty with the more confidence in that Your Majesty has consistently shown a determination to encourage truly democratic enterprises of benevolence in the august and supremely effective manner reserved to the sovereign alone.

I venture to enclose with this for Your Majesty's gracious attention two pamphlets, together with a circular as to the Caledonian scheme, all written by myself as chairman of the Publication Sub-Committee of the Wounded Allies Relief Committee.

And I am always,

Your Majesty's loyal and dutiful subject, [Arnold Bennett]

HERZOG / MS. / 10

(*To Elsie Herzog*)

Comarques
12th May 1916

Dear Mrs. Herzog,

The cheque gratefully received. Also the 'letter'. Your enquiries about hair deserve a faithful answer. Mine is greying,

9. King George did not attend the fair.

I believe, but its lush vitality still costs me a lot in barbers' fees. I shall not be a human being again until after June 7th. See enclosure. Heaven alone knows whether this affair will be the success I have prophesied for it. Personally, I am not managing it. But it is managing me. However, I am still slowly but surely proceeding with the 'Carlotta' play for Doris Keane. Middle of second act now. And before the War-Fair the second act will be finished. Today I am additionally worried, by a neighbour who threatens to put me into court because my dachshund, a fine German temperament, persists in killing his fowls. Also my wife is in London on War-Fair business, & will be till tomorrow. But the lawn tennis season opens on our lawn tomorrow, & I shall play. I should like to play F.P.A. I think I could give him a goodish game. I don't know whether the translation from the Russian, *The Golovleff Family*, (published by Knopf out your way) is any good, but the book is *great*. I read it twice in French. This is about all that the unhuman being, his head full of full-page advertisements for the *Daily Mail*, can write to you just now.

Our kindest wishes to you both.

Yours sincerely, Arnold Bennett

MAYFIELD, SYRACUSE / T.C. / 11

Sardinia House
Kingsway
London, W.C.
[? May 1916]

Dear Madam or Sir,

I have the honour to enclose a circular about the great War-Fair organised by the Wounded Allies Relief Committee at the Caledonian Market Islington for Tuesday and Wednesday June 6th and 7th. And to solicit your immediate help.

You can help in five different ways.

I. By sending anything and everything you don't want, or can do without, to the great War-Fair, at once. Ransack your attics and your cupboards. Nothing is too trifling, too worn out,

10. Bennett finished writing *Sacred and Profane Love* on 16 July. Franklin P. Adams (1881–1960) later conducted a famous column in the New York *Herald Tribune*. *The Golovleff Family* is the best-known work of Mikhail Evgrafovich Saltuikov (1826–89).

or too valuable for the War-Fair. When you are looking for something to send, do not say: 'That is not worth sending.' It is. And do not say: 'That is too valuable to send.' It isn't. Valuables will be competently handled by experts.

All gifts should be sent, packed, and carriage paid to:—

The Wounded Allies Warehouse,
Caledonian Market,
Islington.

The Wounded Allies Relief Committee cannot pay for carriage. Its great principle is to pay for nothing. But if you have bulky and valuable gifts for us, and are in difficulties as to the carriage, please communicate with the Caledonian Secretary, Wounded Allies Relief Committee, Sardinia House, Kingsway, London. (Telephone Holborn 2608, 2609)

II. By acting as principal or assistant saleswoman or salesman at a stall. Those who are willing to do this are requested at once to write to, or call upon, the Caledonian Secretary, as above.

III. By collecting goods for, and entirely equipping, and taking sole responsibility for a stall or for several stalls. Intending benefactors under this head are requested at once to write, or call upon, the Caledonian Secretary, as above.

IV. *By sending copies of the present appeal and its enclosure to your friends.* A postcard from you to the Caledonian Secretary will ensure the delivery to yourself by return of post, of as many copies as you may require for this purpose.

V. In the very unlikely event of your not being able to help under I, II, III, or IV you can send a gift of money to the Committee, and you are implored to do so.

We want everything, and we can use everything, except delay.

Your assistance will be highly appreciated.

Faithfully yours, Arnold Bennett
Publicity Manager

DAVIS / TR. / 12
(*To Oswald H. Davis*)

Comarques
June 11th 1916

Dear Mr. Oswald Davis,

I was very glad indeed to have your long and very interesting letter. It is full of useful glimpses. I suppose you will soon be leaving Dunstable again.—I hear so from a friend of mine who is in the motor-cyclists at Dunstable: a man named Leslie Green. He is the son of a Colonial judge and was an officer at the front for some time. He came home for a bad heart. Then he saw he didn't like being an officer, resigned his commission, and enlisted with your lot in the ranks. He is a very interesting boy. If you come across him you might mention the link between you and him. He told me that you might all leave for Mesopotamia any day. We have been through a considerable invasion scare here, but I fancy that the Jutland Battle has ended it in the minds of the principal scared, namely the military authorities.

You have not seen my articles in the *Daily News* because I haven't been writing any. The *D.N.* signified that they couldn't continue my articles. Whether it was the financial question or something else I don't know. The Irish article was semi-official, and written chiefly for America. I do a certain amount of semi-official work at the instance of various Departments. Thus I have just been asked to write a music-hall sketch to inculcate the fine principle of economy into the breasts of spendthrift citizens! I think this must almost constitute a record in government activity.

Unless I have got everything mixed up it was at the Dunstable farmhouse that I wrote *The Truth About an Author* also *Teresa* also *Anna of the Five Towns*. I am in excellent health, but overworked. I had charge of the great 'War Fair' at the Caledonian Market in aid of the funds of the Wounded Allies Relief Committee. It was a colossal enterprise, but I took care to delegate most of the work. Neither Kitchener's death nor the weather could spoil it, and we netted at least £20,000.

If and when you go to the Front I shall be particularly interested to hear your impressions. I hope you are writing some verse.

Yours sincerely, Arnold Bennett

12. Leslie Green is not otherwise known. On Bennett's articles for the *Daily News*, and the Irish article, see Vol. I. The music-hall sketch is not known.

The writing of *Anna of the Five Towns* was begun long before Bennett went to live at Trinity Hall Farm; see Vol. II.

Bennett reported on the War Fair in the *Journal*: 'Great success. I sold books at M's stall. After 5.30, crowds of young women came to look at books and some to buy. One well-dressed man had never heard of Balzac. Demand for Kipling,

ILLINOIS / MS. / 13
(*To H. G. Wells*)

Comarques
8 July 1916

My dear Herbert,

I like this book very much. It is extremely original & sympathetic, & the scenes that ought to be the best are the best. In fact it is an impressive work. (I doubt if Direck is anything like upon the level of the other characters as a creation.) Also as a tract it is jolly fine. It would have been even finer if old Brit had made the slightest attempt imaginatively to understand the difficulties of the British Government, or what it *did* do. If he had given to this business a quarter of the skill and force which he gives to understanding what it failed to do, he would have been liker God. Also his notions about the 'steely resolution' of the French nation are a bit *Morning-Postish.* I say this because I know it would anger him. There is much more steely resolution in England than in France. The spirit of Paris has not been good. The spirit of the Midi has been rotten. This I know of my own knowledge. What has saved France is nothing but the accident of first-rate generalship. If the Battle of the Marne had been lost there wouldn't have been even a semblance of steely resolution in France. Even after the Marne every military setback has been instantly followed by a civil crisis. Much more might be said on these two points, but old Brit shall not be harried.

Thine, A. B.

P.S. You will doubtless find some of the corrections quite inadmissible. They are all simply suggestions. A. B.

Chesterton, Conrad, and me. Difficulty of selling autographs. . . . Various estimates of profits of 2 days, but you can see that the men keep estimates lower than their hopes. Thus Mr. Henry—£8,000 to £15,000. Selfridge estimated attendance first day at from 25 to 30,000. I agree. Yet one man in charge of a gate said that through that gate alone he estimated 30,000 people had passed. And so on. There were not enough goods, nor stalls. . . . News of Kitchener's drowning came at noon on first day. . . . The rumour in the afternoon that Kitchener was saved roused cheers, again and again.' Lord Kitchener (b. 1850) was embarked on a mission to Russia when his ship struck a German mine.

13. On H. G. Wells see Vols. I and II. Earlier letters to him appear in Vol. II. His new novel was *Mr. Britling Sees It Through.*

HERZOG / MS. / 14
(*To Elsie Herzog*)

Comarques
10th Sept 1916

Dear Mrs. Herzog,

Very many thanks for letter & cheque for £20. This continues to be very noble of you. I guarantee that your summer weather has not been worse than ours. Tennis has been greatly interfered with. We have been to Scotland, but only for 12 days. It was exhausting but improving. I am having a slack month, before tackling Hilda's son in October. I think my chief interest at present is water colour painting. Progress, though slight, is indicated. I have come across one of the best water colour painters in England, a very wise man, & as I go out painting with him, the result cannot ultimately be bad. The war proves more & more that those who based their calculations on the ultimate resources of the combatants, & on nothing else, are going to be right. For me, the most striking item in the war, is the failure of German generalship. The observation car of a Zeppelin was dropped within 4½ miles of this spot early last Sunday morning. The Zep was wounded & had to lighten itself. The shrapnel of our own anti-aircraft guns dropped within 1½ miles. This is getting close. But nobody seems to tremble. Touching air warfare I am sending you a little book that I have edited. Remembrances to you both.

Yours sincerely, Arnold Bennett

P.S. I cannot possibly say anything as to Elsie's novel till it is finished. When it is finished the talking will be entitled to begin. A. B.

14. Hilda's son, George Cannon, is the hero of *The Roll-Call*, which Bennett began on 16 October.

On Bennett's water-colour friend, John Wright, see Vol. I, p. 277.

In the Royal Naval Air Service, by Harold Rosher, was edited with an introduction by Bennett in 1916.

Mrs. Herzog wrote poetry, and published a few volumes privately. The novel, presumably hers, is unknown.

WESTMINSTER GAZETTE, 19 September 1916 / 15
(*To the editor*)

The Berkeley Hotel
Piccadilly, W.
September 18 [1916]

Sir,

Critics of stage morals might perhaps be listened to with more respect if their language was less wild. The Bishop of London has just withdrawn or disowned an indefensible phrase attributed to him, and now 'Tawwaf', untaught by the misfortunes of others, comes along with a fresh one. 'Tawwaf' abandons the attack on dialogue and songs, and talks about 'the lust of the eye'. He refers to 'the parade of women in all degrees of nudity which is an apparently indispensable feature in any modern revue'. Either he has little sense of the value of words, in which case silence would become him, or his evidence is worthless. 'All degrees of nudity' must, of course, include absolute nudity. Of late years absolutely nude women have been seen on the stage in Paris, but I have never heard of one on the London stage, and I doubt very much whether 'Tawwaf' has witnessed such a phenomenon. My addiction to revues is limited, but revues are not unknown to me. I have not yet observed in a revue any woman whose 'degree of nudity' appreciably exceeded that which was insisted upon by the late Queen Victoria at her own dinner-table, and which is visible nightly in the drawing-rooms of London. The point at issue is confined to décolletage. 'Tawwaf' is entitled to think that women are too décolletées, but he is not entitled to libel women who take part in spectacles which conform to rules established by the custom of whole nations. His remarks about 'costumes approaching that of Mother Eve', 'the cult of woman and the beauty of woman', and the coming 'substitution of modesty for nudity', are, to speak mildly, ridiculous. For myself, I regard the increase during this century of 'the cult of woman and beauty of woman' as one of the most satisfactory and promising features of British national life, and I am glad to see the music-halls reflecting it. Music-halls will reflect, and happily nothing can stop them from reflecting.

Yours faithfully, Arnold Bennett

15. During the first two years of the war Bennett often stayed at the Berkeley Hotel when he came to London for war work.

BERG / MS. / 16
(*To J. C. Squire*)

Comarques
27 Nov 1916

Dear Squire,

I have at length had an opportunity to read *The Farm Servant*. At first I thought it wasn't going to be anything very particular, but it began to hold me soon afterwards. The pregnancy & so on of Anna are really very good indeed. Authentic! I doubt whether the same level is reached again until the scene between Frank & Anna almost at the end of the book. Throughout, it is very sound. Horrible thing to say of any work that it is a quite remarkable first novel. Mais que voulez-vous? It *is*. There is no *big* fault to be found with it unless on the extremely debatable point of the main construction. The most sympathetic character is Anna, & during a stretch of about 140 pages she is absolutely out of the story. To replace her into the story after all the Paris stuff is very difficult. It might be argued that there is something wrong with a construction that brings about this strain on both author & reader. On the other hand the use of Australia, Australia being an excellent place for Anna, is exceeding neat. Touching the Paris stuff, I think there is a certain lack of intimate knowledge of detail in it. I felt it slightly all through. For instance, the tea dialogue on p. 260. I don't know what E. H. Anstruther's experience of Paris is, but I do know that A1 tea is extremely easy to get in Paris, & that the Anglo-Saxon colony always does get it. In fact tea-parties with admirable tea, are the leading feature of respectable existence in the Anglo-Saxon colony. You can get very good tea all over France. Does E. H. Anstruther know that the Boulevard des Italiens runs on *both* sides of the Place de l'Opéra? I never heard the Champs Élysées called the 'Champs', anywhere. These are samples, but of course I can't remember the best ones. Further, I think some of the writing is maladroit. Yet I assume you looked through the proofs! Do you defend this:—'She loathed intensely, the sugges-

---

The Bishop of London, the Rt. Rev. A. F. Winnington-Ingram (1858–1946), had recently asserted that there were one hundred and fifty immoral women in every music hall every night; but he seems to have been free with indefensible assertions, and this may not have been the one Bennett was referring to.

tion of the *stairs* that she had *come down* in the world.' To my mind there is something most ingeniously clumsy in such a phrase. This also is only a sample. I bet I could find 50—if someone would give me 5/- apiece for them. I think this kind of thing wants looking after. Mrs. Hyde is the best visualised character. Then Mrs. Murrell & old Harding. Also Letitia. Heroes & heroines are seldom if ever visualised. I have given up trying to visualise them myself. One is too close to them & too much inside them. Old writers succeed best with young characters & young writers with old characters,—because they can't get too close to them. Such is my opinion. This doesn't prevent me from sharply appreciating Anna, who is much better than Frank. It was very daring, if not rash, to give Frank both artistic talent *and* a weak heart. Naturally, I am criticizing on a very exacting standard. The book is a *book*. You know what I mean. So the author ought to be well satisfied with herself, & go on. It is *second* books, however, that are the devil. We shall see. I hope to meet E. H. Anstruther one day & have a yarn. I shall ask her.

Yours, Ungerald Gould

HERZOG / MS. / 17
(*To Elsie Herzog*)

Comarques
4th Dec 1916

Dear Mrs. Herzog,

Two letters I have received without answering. I did write one letter, but I doubt if you will ever receive it. It was to introduce to you a friend of mine, a Frenchman, Jacques Copeau, the directeur of *La Nouvelle Revue Française*. I doubt if he is coming to New York now at all. The government may stop him, though not long since it wanted him to undertake a tour with a theatrical company in U.S.A.! Still, I felt as though I had written to you, as indeed I had. My wife will be delighted to swallow up your money for her club, which still flourishes in

16. For earlier letters to J. C. Squire see Vol. II.

E. H. Anstruther became Mrs. Squire. *The Farm Servant* was the first of three novels published between 1916 and 1924.

On Gerald Gould see below, p. 28.

the plantation at the end of our garden. We now have no officers actually staying in the house, though they dine & lunch often. This is a great change for me. I have learnt more about what are called 'ordinary people' during the war than ever I knew before. By 'ordinary' I simply mean people with the sense of art practically undeveloped, people without any subtlety, who don't understand what you are talking about unless you translate for them. As an experience it was interesting, but really very trying sometimes. For me, part of the war! Still there were some strange surprises. One officer (medical) mentioned the fourth dimension. So I began to talk about the fourth dimension. In my opinion the 4th d. is the most awful rot, save as an intellectual pastime. However, he was enchanted. He then got on to spiritualism, etc., & enquired if I had thought of it. I gave him a copy of *The Glimpse*. He has not yet recovered from *The Glimpse*, which I believe he regards as the most brilliant work of genius yet produced by the human mind. Well, he was a highly advanced specimen of the military intelligence! So you may guess. I now have a second home in my yacht club in London, & am seeing more of my old sets. And I have been 3 times to the opera! And I have read Dreiser's *The Financier*, which I could never get hold of till the other day. This book, despite its dreadful slovenliness in details of phrase, is an extremely remarkable affair indeed. It gave me intense pleasure. This is praise. I wish I knew Dreiser intimately. Wells's new novel is very fine. I doubt if mine (a quarter written up to date) is. We are supposed just now to be rather gloomy in England, but it will pass. We have about cleaned up the Zepps, I think. One superb specimen of them lies naked a few miles from here. I hope this will reach you before Christmas. Your letter was very interesting. Best wishes from us both.

Yours sincerely, Arnold Bennett

17. Jacques Copeau (1879–1949) left the *NRF* in 1913 to found his Théâtre du Vieux-Colombier.

Bennett published *The Glimpse* in 1909. See Vol. II. On Theodore Dreiser see Vol. II.

WESTMINSTER GAZETTE, 3 January 1917 / 18
(*To the editor*)

Comarques
January 2 [1917]

Sir,

In your 'Literary Notes and News' of Monday you state that George Smith paid Browning £12,500 for the first five years' rights in *The Ring and the Book*. It is just as well that this munificent printer's error should be set right at once. The sum was £1,250.

The occasion may serve to point out a curious discrepancy in *The Dictionary of National Biography*. Mr. Edmund Gosse, in his article on Browning, says, 'The reception of *The Ring and the Book* was a triumph for the author. . . . A second edition of the entire *Ring and the Book* was called for in 1869.' (The first edition, in four volumes, was published between November 1868 and February 1869.)

But Mr. Sidney Lee, in his 'Memoir of George Smith', prefixed to the volume of the *D.N.B.* which contains Mr. Gosse's article on Browning, says: 'Of the first two volumes (of *The Ring and the Book*) the edition consisted of three thousand copies each; but the sale was not rapid, and of the last two volumes only two thousand were printed.'

Still, I doubt not that George Smith did very well over the transaction.

Yours faithfully, Arnold Bennett

LANE / TS. / 19
(*To John Lane*)

Comarques
6th January 1917

Dear John Lane,

I am on the Executive of the Wounded Allies Relief Committee of No. 8 Grosvenor Gardens. This Committee maintains several hospitals on the continent, including one at Vodena in

18. George Smith (1824–1901) was founder and proprietor of the *Dictionary of National Biography*. He did sufficiently well in his publishing career, except with the *DNB* itself, to leave an estate of several hundred thousand pounds. Sidney Lee (1859–1926) edited the *DNB*. For a letter to Edmund Gosse see Vol. II, p. 194.

the Balkans. The staff there have absolutely nothing to read, and I have promised to do what I can to obtain for them a number of books which will be sent out under the auspices of the Committee. I should really be very much obliged to you if you could see your way to letting me have a parcel of cheap books for this purpose. If you are able to comply, you will be doing a good turn to a number of English people who are working under extremely hard conditions.

The parcel, if any, should be sent direct to the offices of the Wounded Allies Relief Committee, 8, Grosvenor Gardens, S.W.

Yours sincerely, Arnold Bennett

HERZOG / MS. / 20
(*To Elsie Herzog*)

Comarques
4th February 1917

Dear Mrs. Herzog,

With reference to your amiable & tintinnabulating typewriter, the most common letter in the English language is not S, but E. You would know this if you wrote the MSS. of your novels as I do mine.

In a printed hand E is very handsome. The temptation is always to do it E, but the most beautiful way is e, which seems easier but is really more difficult. I have now written 35,000 words like this of my new novel.

So Wilson has broken off relations. I must tell you that though I have little regard for Wilson's power of self-expression, I have been slowly coming to the conclusion during the last few months that he is no fool, but rather a statesman. And it is quite possible that some of you excellent & admirable pro-Allies may change your minds about him. The startling thing is that in Foreign Affairs he should be an autocrat, & no one objecting seriously to his power. I am now exceedingly busy and exceedingly worried. This kind of situation seems always to suit me. My health is better than for a long time. My wife & I spend 3½ days in London, 3½ here, practically every week. I am going out more. One day I went out to lunch, tea, & dinner, sat on a

19. For other letters to the publisher John Lane see Vols. I and II.

I

In the clerks' room of the offices of Lucas and Enwright, architects, Russell Square, Bloomsbury, George Edwin Cannon, an articled pupil, leaned over a large drawing-board and looked up at Mr. Enwright, the head of the firm, who with cigarette and stick was on his way out after what he called a good day's work. It was ~~something~~ past six o'clock on an evening in early July 1901. To George's ~~l~~ right was ~~a~~ an open door leading to the principals' room, and to his left another open door leading to more rooms and to the staircase. The lofty chambers were full of lassitude; but round about George, who was working late, there floated ~~like a vapour~~ the tonic vapour of conscious ~~rectitude~~ virtue. Haim, the factotum, could be seen and heard moving in his cubicle which guarded the offices from the stairs. ~~The three men~~ In the rooms shortly to be deserted and locked up, and in the decline of the day, the three men were drawn together like survivors.

"I gather you're going to change your abode," said Mr. Enwright, ~~stopping~~ having stopped.

"Did Mr. Orgreave tell you then?" George asked.

"Well, he didn't exactly tell me..."

~~Mr~~ John Orgreave was Mr. Enwright's junior partner; and for nearly two years, since his advent in London from the Five Towns, George had lived with Mr. and Mrs. Orgreave, at Bedford Park. The Orgreaves, too, sprang from the Five Towns. John's people and George's people were closely intertwined in the local annals.

1

Facsimile of the first page of Chapter 1 of the manuscript of *The Roll Call*

committee, and wrote 1,800 words of my novel. I am worried about the *New Statesman*, of which I am a director. The editor has been called up for military service. Awful rot. The War Office is adamant. We can exert influence, but not enough to get him off! In U.S.A. we could have done it. His departure means extra work for me, and also a constant effort on my part to keep the policy of the paper straight. He & I think alike. Further I am very worried about my brother, a lawyer, whom the war & other things have spectacularly ruined. Still, I don't seem to mind. Have you read Frank Harris's privately published *Life & Confessions of Oscar Wilde*? It is a strange & powerful book, written by a man who is a curious mixture of impulses noble and ignoble. I am just finishing it. The best things I have read for ages are the Chekhov short stories in the new complete edition (2 vols out) published here by Chatto & Windus, translated by the eternal Constance Garnett. These stories are unmatched. I shall publish later in the spring (wars permitting) a selection from my old 'Jacob Tonson' literary criticisms in the *New Age*. They are extremely rollicking & will infuriate many while diverting the judicious (I hope). I expect Marguerite has written to you about the cheque. I'll ask her. Anyhow she was much touched by it.

Yours sincerely, Arnold Bennett

NEW STATESMAN, 24 February 1917 / 21
(*To the editor*)

Comarques
February 19th [1917]

Sir,

In reference to Mr. F. W. Willcox's letter objecting to your musical critic's attack on Charpentier's *Louise*, I should like to

20. Woodrow Wilson (1856–1924) was leading the American nation slowly into war with Germany. In January the Germans informed the American government that unrestricted submarine warfare was being resumed, and in April the Americans declared war.

Bennett became a director of the *New Statesman* in 1915. Clifford Sharp (1883–1935) was editor from 1913 to 1931.

On Bennett's brother Frank see Vols. I and II.

For letters to Frank Harris see Vol. II.

Books and Persons, Bennett's *New Age* criticisms, originally written under the pseudonym of Jacob Tonson, appeared in July. See further, Vols. I and II.

say that, as an amateur of music and a member of the public, I agree warmly with your musical critic though I somewhat regret the crudity of his phrasing. Further, and much more important, I have known many composers, musical critics, and keen musical amateurs in Paris, but I never met one who did not regard the music of *Louise* as utterly ridiculous. When *Louise* was produced at Covent Garden I was astonished that some of my friends, professional musicians, were at first inclined to like it. After a few hearings, however, they entirely ceased to like it.

As regrads the libretto of the opera, it is very feeble, very clumsy, and very mawkish—but happily full of rich unconscious humour. I can never forget my joy, at the Opéra Comique many years ago, when the stout lady so dramatically burst forth with the important annunciation: 'La soupe est prête'.

Mr. F. W. Willcox is rather difficult to satisfy. *Louise* has received the highest commendation from your regular scientific contributor. He cannot reasonably expect this surprising opera to be lauded in every department of the *New Statesman*.

Yours, etc., Arnold Bennett

HERZOG / MS. / 22
(*To Elsie Herzog*)

Comarques
4 Mch 1917

Dear Mrs. Herzog,

I received 3 letters,—the contents of 3 envelopes, from you on Friday last. I am glad that you are being kind to de Lanux, & I hope the same thing will occur in the case of Copeau. These two are certain to know each other. It appears to me that Wilson is going along all right. In fact I think he is showing great skill. I remember that long ago Henry James told me that Ambassador Page told him of his own knowledge that Wilson was definitely pro-Ally. I imagine that history will justify

21. The music critic of the *New Statesman* was W. J. Turner. He described the music of *Louise* as 'absolute bunkum'. For letters to him see below. The scientific contributor, who wrote under the name of 'Lens', praised the opera a few weeks earlier.

Wilson's course of conduct. The editor of the *New Statesman* has now been gathered into the Army, & staff rearrangements throw a certain amount of extra work on me,—at any rate more attendances in London. I now live half in town & half in the country. I should like it if I hadn't got to work. I am two-thirds through my novel. My secretary is delighted with it; but I don't think I am. Still, it is something to be able to write novels at all. I gather that you are afraid of mails being interrupted. They won't be, except by occasional sinkings. I am not well. I have had 4 days in bed with chill on the colon. I am up again, & have been to London; but the East wind is blowing on this coast. My wife has also been ill in bed with bronchial trouble. She too is up again. So that we are all right. We send our best wishes for that birthday of yours. I have been meeting a good few women lately who are disgusted because they aren't men. A grave sign!

Please remember us to your men persons & to M de Lanux, & Copeau too if he is there.

Yours sincerely, Arnold Bennett

BERG / MS. / 23
(*To J. C. Squire*)

[Comarques]
2.4.17.

For Mr. Squire.

I congratulate you on getting in a Thursday night par. Pity that in the hurry the end of it was disfigured by two 'Buts'. I think the first par. beginning on p. 602 is the best of the notes.

Right Side of Fence. This is good. I don't know the arguments against proportional Rep. But if they have been fully stated in the paper already I think Webb ought to state them fully again as soon as possible.

Home Grown Food. Scarcely as good as first article. Carelessly written. Repetition of 'least' in 1st col. and the sentence at top of 2nd col. of p. 606 has no meaning.

Cure For Parents. This contains a lot of real stuff & is on the whole

22. On Pierre de Lanux see Vol. II, pp. 345–7.
For other references to Henry James see below and also Vols. I and II.
Walter Hines Page (1855–1918) was American ambassador to England during the war and helped to bring America into it on the Allied side.

excellent. But you can see the writer is a compulsionist for the poor. He would compel operations on the children of the poor, were it not for public opinion. Yet he admits that education is the right cure for stupidity. This tendency towards compulsion (which the Webbs will encourage rather than check) has to be watched in the policy of the paper. It is so much easier to compel than to wait for the results of education. There is a trace of the same thing at the end of 'Home Grown Food'. I mean that the writer would probably let the State dictate the use of the land before the State bought the land.

The Weather. This is pretty good, but like most such articles in this paper it would be improved by cutting out the opening sentences. If it had begun at 'Every Summer in London' it would have been much better.

Old [?] is pretty good this week. In fact I should have boomed this article a bit more.

Observations. I told you the copy wasn't short.

Adolescent. This is a very good article.

MacCarthy is all right. He is very intelligent.

New Novels. Let me know if G.G. drops down dead one day.

The other reviews seem quite all right.

No answer required.

A. B.

STOKE / A.C. / 24
(*To Thomas Lockyer*)

80, Piccadilly
12 April 1917

Dear Lockyer,

I understand that Mrs. Bennett asked you for some keys and that you refused to give them to her. If you cannot see that this kind of thing is absolutely inexcusable you must be mad.

23. In the absence of Clifford Sharp, John Squire acted as editor of the *New Statesman*, and for more than a year Bennett wrote weekly criticisms of the paper for him. Sidney Webb (1859–1927) and Beatrice Webb (1859–1943) founded the *New Statesman* and were Bennett's co-directors. Most of the contributions were anonymous, including Bennett's own 'Observations', by 'Sardonyx', a weekly column he began on 18 October 1916. (Sir) Desmond MacCarthy (1877–1952) was the drama critic. Gerald Gould (1885–1936) was the book reviewer. 'An Adolescent' was a review by Lytton Strachey.

Unless you apologise to Mrs. Bennett immediately and in the most complete manner, I shall have to deprive myself of your services.

I hope this is clear,

Yours truly, Arnold Bennett

STOKE / MS. / 25
(*To Hugh Walpole*)

80, Piccadilly
1st May 1917

My dear Hughie,

I finished my damned novel yesterday, & now I take up your two letters. The novel is entitled *The Roll-Call*, 114,000 words. I am glad you are alive. I heard of your desire to bathe in a dock or harbour, but you might have removed your eyeglasses before plunging. Also I read your letter to Swinnerton (whose new novel seems to be good—I just glanced at the proofs). Touching Russia, on behalf of the *New Statesman* I desire you most particularly to write me an article, or get someone to write an article, or send me the full material for me to work up into an article, showing the present groupings, relative strength and the character, of parties & individualities. We want something *absolutely true* & first-hand. It would of course be published anonymously or pseudonymously. You will perform a real service in attending to this for us at once. Squire (now editor—Sharp being a gunner) said he would write to you, but I said he might as well leave it to me, which he did. I went to the Russian Exhibition yesterday, not for pleasure, but to put the

24. Eighty Piccadilly was the address of the Royal Thames Yacht Club. Bennett usually stayed here on his visits to London in 1917.

Thomas Lockyer was Bennett's gardener. He was presumably the model for Aguilar in *The Lion's Share*. Mrs. Bennett recorded some of her difficulties with him in *My Arnold Bennett*: '. . . the head gardener made us feel the garden belonged to him first. It was to me unbelievable that a man paid for his work could prevent me from picking my own flowers, from picking fruit, green peas or whatever I wished to pick. By his attitude he spoilt the joy I derived from the garden. Happily he could not deprive me of the joy that the house gave me. Arnold found no fault with the gardener, in common with many owners of gardens requiring head gardeners. However, he ended by finding out, after many years, that he trusted the man too blindly. I must say, till his discharge, he kept the place in beautiful order and was very industrious. He knew that his master could not tell the name of a plant and he took advantage of his ignorance.'

sacred autograph in books, & to answer questions by Lady Muriel P. & other toffs about how to make these enterprises hum. (Of course such questions are perfectly futile.) I liked Lady M.P. much. Never met her before. I could get on with her. I vote that when you return we organize a dinner, & have her in it. The Russian theatre in the basement of the Grafton Galleries is most excellent. To see a play with ideas in it was like having a bath. It made me want to sit down & write more plays at once. The Russian pictures were terrible. It would have been better to have had none. This is universally admitted. I haven't tried the Russian restaurant, but I shall. The chief factor in English life at the present moment is the weather, which is suddenly lovely. There will doubtless be a great mess over submarines, but the weather seems likely to continue grand. I am sick of work, & am working for 3 government departments. I meant to take a holiday this week, being completely exhausted. I came up to my beautiful Club yesterday & it is a solemn fact that I hadn't been here ten minutes before I had undertaken to write a government article for the *Strand Magazine* in three days. A bit thick. Then I ran off to lunch with the Sidney Webbs, who live in a house entirely constructed of Blue bricks, a marvel of ingenuity recalling the labours of beavers & coral insects. I get on very well with the Webbs (my co-directors), but they do not understand (what I call) life. Squire is an A1 chap. But he is a vegetarian & *he* doesn't understand life either. And either he or his wife doesn't understand shirts. I am 50 on 27th current, &, considering that, I am very well. Marguerite is now what she calls 'toppole'. She has the gilded nephew in town for 3 days before returning him to school. This raw 5-Towns boy is a wit. He will have a brutal, sardonic wit in the nature of his benevolent uncle's. Now don't forget about the *New Statesman*. And be assured that if we do not say much about your adventures they are properly esteemed. Marguerite sends her best love.

Thine ever, A. B.

Proofs of *B. & Persons* now corrected. Swinnerton has 'written the index'. We rather like the book.

25. Walpole had recently returned to Russia as head of the Anglo-Russian propaganda bureau in Leningrad. While boarding his ship in Liverpool he missed his footing and fell into the harbour.

BUTLER / MS. / 26
(*To an unidentified person*)

Comarques
6th May 1917

My dear Sir,

Your letter has great interest. I won't use your story in fiction, but I have been glad to hear from you. You seem to be doing pretty well for yourself! I cannot tell you what you ought to do after the war. If you really want to write, you will write. But if I were you I shouldn't depend on it for a living until I knew what it was going to bring in. Nothing is worse for a writer than poverty, and, with few exceptions, writing does not pay a living wage until it has been practised for a long time. I suppose you know that it is advisable for a writer to be able to spell correctly. In guessing that I am fully occupied you are slightly under the mark. Nevertheless it is a pleasure to me to answer, even briefly, your letter.

Yours sincerely, Arnold Bennett

TEXAS / T.C. / 27
(*To Newman Flower*)

[80, Piccadilly]
19th May, 1917

My dear Flower,

I am very glad I so charmed your flu, and I hope it is now quite over. I am delighted to have your opinion of *The Old Wives' Tale*. As regards the next book I will make the following observations:—

I ain't going to write any more about the 5 Towns.

The Old Wives' Tale is 200,000 words long, and its length makes part of its effect. Do you see yourself handling a serial 200,000 words long? I doubt it. Anyhow it is most comforting

---

Frank Swinnerton's new novel was *Nocturne*. He and Walpole together persuaded Bennett to gather his 'Books and Persons' essays into a volume. For other information on him see Vols. I and II, and for letters to him see below.

On Lady Muriel Paget see Vol. II, p. 362.

Bennett's club was the Reform. His article for the *Strand*, 'Are We a Thrifty Race?', was ultimately taken by the *Fortnightly Review*. See further, Vol. I, p. 249.

Richard Bennett, son of brother Frank, was adopted by Arnold and Marguerite in 1916.

to me to be asked for a *serious* serial. The next novel I write will be short, and will emphatically be unfit for serial use. This you may take from me as a fact, seeing that the principal person in it is a professional courtesan. It is a war-novel and I anticipate that it will startle the public. Please treat this item as confidential.

Yours sincerely, Arnold Bennett

DAVIS / TR. / 28
(*To Oswald H. Davis*)

[Comarques]
8th June 1917

Dear Mr. Oswald Davis,

I am very glad to have your letter of 2nd June on my return home from Paris. It is most interesting. You wrote it, by the way, on my fiftieth birthday. It is excellent that despatch-riding suits you so well.

If you knew G. B. S. as I know him, you would understand why he is not taken more seriously. I quite agree that he often says very wise things, and things that need to be said. The press-correspondents are not a very brilliant lot perhaps: but have you ever seen them at work? They are kept together all the time, practically under lock and key, always under the eye of a Staff officer. They are told what they can say and what they can't say, and you will find that they all say practically the same things. Often they are deliberately hoodwinked by soldiers whom they meet. P. Gibbs is a very conscientious man; I know him and I like him; but his reputation is a mystery to me. I think he is incurably sentimental and therefore false. The best of the correspondents, easily, is Tomlinson.

You did not see any article by me on the Russian Rev. in the *Daily News*, because it is impossible to put down facts without getting into a row. I have gone as far as I could in the *New Statesman*. Moreover the facts are very difficult to get at, though I am in touch with a good man in Petrograd. Perhaps you may

27. (Sir) Newman Flower (1879–1964) was head of the Cassell firm, who were now publishing most of Bennett's work. The new novel was *The Pretty Lady*, begun on 24 May. Bennett later had some difficulty with Flower over the proposed serialization of *Riceyman Steps*; see Vol. I, pp. 326–30. For letters to Flower see below and also Vol. I.

know that over 5,000 people were killed in the first days of the Rev. in Petrograd. In London there is a fairly strong undercurrent of feeling in Tory circles in favour of the overthrown regime! I have girded at this several times in the *New Statesman.* I have written several things specially for Petrograd papers that have been cabled over to them, in order to make clear what democratic England really thinks.

I think MacGill has written one or two excellent things on the Push. I do want you to realise that intelligent people here, though civilian, well understand that most of the stuff printed in the dailies about the army is largely tosh. I do not agree with you about the aristocratic element, though I agree that it is excellent in some ways. Seldom in any large way. From my own observation and from statements by very good observant civilians-turned-soldiers, I am convinced that on the whole the finest element in the Army is the N.C.O. of the old regular Army. As for the aristocratic element, I am inclined to say that every improvement of importance in military methods has been made in the teeth of its opposition.

I should like to hear from you again.

Best wishes,

Yours sincerely, Arnold Bennett

HERZOG / MS. / 29
(*To Elsie Herzog*)

Comarques
15 June 1917

My dear Lady,

In reply to yours of the 8th May, your agreeable cable was duly received and suitably acknowledged. In spite of what you

28. Davis was now a despatch rider in the X Corps of the B.E.F.

Bennett and George Bernard Shaw were at odds about the conduct of the war from its earliest days. See Vol. I, p. 215, for Bennett's views on Shaw's essay 'Common-Sense About the War'. For letters to Shaw see below. On (Sir) Philip Gibbs see Vol. II, pp. 167–8. On H. M. Tomlinson see Vol. I, p. 336. Patrick MacGill, author and journalist, published several books about the war, including *The Great Push*, 1916.

On 26 May appeared an article on the Russian press, signed 'J. W.', and on 28 July appeared 'Sketches in Petrograd', likewise signed 'J. W.' The latter article is presumably by Hugh Walpole, and the former apparently by Bennett as advised by Walpole.

say I remain of my original opinion about Wilson. The men who will come well out of this war—apart from soldiers—are Wilson, Asquith, Painlevé, Smuts, Branting, & Bethmann-Hollweg. I think Smuts is about the best man we have in the B. Empire. He combines principles & caution with real cleverness. In fact I am quite struck by Smuts. Your letter reached me on Monday last. It is now Saturday. At least I forget whether it was Monday or Tuesday it came. The weather is the most consistently magnificent I ever remember it this time of year. But it is much too hot for industry. I have begun a new novel. In summer, however, I am more interested in water colour painting than in writing. I am still improving, & have been asked to give one of my sketches to the Tate Gallery! John R. Raphael was an intimate acquaintance of mine (not friend). He is dead. He had a mistress in Paris whom I knew very well, & then I think he married her which was rather daring of him. Anyhow he had no talent whatever, but never knew it. You ought to read *He looked in my Window* by Robert Halifax (publ. by Chatto & Windus). It is really remarkable. I doubt if it will be published in U.S.A., being too good for publishers to see any good in it. But in fairness I must state that I never mentioned it to George Doran. How on earth can you call a play by Hartley Manners 'appealing'? I cannot conceive H.M. doing anything that would not inspire me with the idea of flight. There are no plays in England. I have written an article about war work for the *Cosmopolitan*; but it won't appear just yet. It is very sarcastic. I am just now in a deep sardonic vein.

Our best wishes to you both & kind remembrances.

Yours sincerely, Arnold Bennett

29. Herbert Henry Asquith (1st Earl of Oxford and Asquith, 1852–1928) was Prime Minister 1908–16. Paul Painlevé (1863–1933) was French Prime Minister briefly in 1917. Jan Christiaan Smuts (1870–1950) was one of the originators of the League of Nations. Karl Branting (1860–1925) was a Swedish statesman. Theobald von Bethman-Hollweg (1856–1921) was the German Imperial Chancellor before and during the war.

On John Raphael see Vol. II, p. 284.

Robert Halifax published a dozen novels from 1899 to 1917. *He Looked in My Window* was a love story.

Hartley Manners (1870–1928) was author of *Peg O' My Heart* and other plays.

Bennett's article 'Some Axioms of War-Work' appeared in the *Cosmopolitan* in December 1917.

FALES, NYU / MS. / 30
(*To J. W. Light*)

Comarques
17–6–17

Dear Sir,

What can *I* say by way of a message to Canadians? I saw their maple leaves when I was at the front, & it gave a richness to their transport which matched the general splendour of their manner of existing. I have met only one Canadian officer in my life, and he was one of the modestest men I ever did meet. I like to see Canadians walking about London. There is freedom & independence in their very gait and in the way they hold their shoulders. I like to see this because I am intensely a democrat, & I am sure that men could not walk as they walk if their principles were not fundamentally right. I wish I could say more. But I have not even been to Canada. I used to hold some Canadian Pacific shares, but the British Government took them from me by force, at much less than I had paid for them! Another link gone! The fracture, however, has by no means weakened my appreciation of your Canadian warriors, to whom & to their friends, I wish the best luck.

Yours sincerely, Arnold Bennett

ARKANSAS / T.C. / 31
(*To Frank Swinnerton*)

The Reform Club
5th July, 1917

My dear Henry,

A slight work, but just about perfect. In fact I do not know how to find fault with it. The construction is most beautiful, and entirely satisfactory from end to end. The characterisation is thoroughly sound, and in places made me say, 'I should never have noticed *that*.' The dramatic quality is also thoroughly sound. In fact the thing is beyond criticism. If the medal had been stamped more deeply—i.e. the emotional quality had

30. J. W. Light was associated with the *Maple Leaf*, the journal of the Canadian contingent of the B.E.F. Bennett's letter apparently appeared in the journal in September 1917.

been more powerful—I dare say I should have been more pleased, but I think the emotional power just about fits the theme. I have had a pretty rare feeling of satisfaction in contemplating this work. And I left off *Wuthering Heights* in order to read it, which was a fairly clear test. (Never read *W.H.* before. Very fine.) Dashed if I don't congratulate you on the book.

I am off to-morrow morning to the Charlton Arms Hotel, Ludford Bridge, Ludlow, to paint water colours for six days, and I need it, being very short of sleep. Marguerite is now reading *Nocturne*, confound her!, and she has already read far more of it than of *B. and P.*—good reviews of that last in *Land and Water* and *Times*.

Yes, you have done a devilish pretty thing. One or two misprints, I think, which I will point out to you in due course. I propose taking the 4-57 on Friday 13th.

Yours, [A. B.]

ROSS / TR. / 32
(*To Robert Ross*)

80, Piccadilly
17.7.17

[no salutation]

The fact is, my dear Robert, I am much concerned about Sassoon. He wrote & told me, & I replied with what I thought to be a judicious letter. You see I do not know him well enough to write very intimately without seeming impertinent. I agree with you that he must be a little deranged. If I knew who his C.O. was, and you thought it proper, I would send a line to his C.O. But if he has not already gone & made a fool of himself the best thing would be for you & any other of his more intimate friends solemnly to see him.

I well understand & admire your pious regard for the works of Wilde, but the fact is that, though I have an immense esteem

31. The Reform Club was Bennett's chief London club in these and later years. 'Henry' was a name first given to Swinnerton by some officers billeted at Comarques during the war. His novel, *Nocturne*, and Bennett's *Books and Persons* were both published in July 1917.

for him, I do not place his works *in the same order* as you do, & I do not consider that *De Profundis* is among his best. I may well be wrong, but this is my settled opinion, & I am not prepared to let you take on your shoulders what I am quite sure is attributable to Wilde himself. Some day I will point out to you such sentences as I mean, & I shall be greatly astonished if you can explain them on your present theory. Needless to say I make these remarks with due submission to & respect for the greatest Wilde expert in the world.

I am very distressed about that F. Harris review. Squire is always asking me for it now. But the fact is I simply have not been able to do it, & I have got into such a row with my doctor & my wife for alleged overwork that I have been obliged to swear not to do *any literary* work during August, & till August I have more than I can do. And the book is steadily growing older! But it has not been my fault, I assure thee.

Please give my kindest regards to your sister and niece. I have the most pleasant souvenir of them. In fact, if I couldn't have my—however, I will not complete that sentence. I am very glad Mrs. Sprigge liked *B & P.*

Yours ever, Arnold Bennett

32. For earlier letters to Robert Ross see Vol. II, pp. 332–3.

Siegfried Sassoon (1886–1967) met Bennett in May 1917, when Sassoon was just home from France and beginning to think about his public protest against the war. Some of the contradictory feelings that were later elaborated in *Memoirs of an Infantry Officer* were noted by Bennett in his *Journal* after the two men had a lunch together in June: 'Sassoon was uncertain about accepting a home billet if he got the offer of one. I advised him to accept it. He is evidently one of the reckless ones. He said his pals said he always gave the Germans every chance to pot him. He said he would like to go out once more and give them another chance to get him, and come home unscathed. He seemed jealous for the military reputation of poets. He said most of the war was a tedious nuisance, but there were great moments, and he would like them again.' In succeeding weeks the view that the Allies were turning what was originally a war of defence into a war of aggrandisement became uppermost in Sassoon's mind, and he announced his refusal to serve and threw his Military Cross into the Severn. In *Siegfried's Journey, 1916–1920*, written fifteen years after the *Memoirs*, he says: 'When I sent my statement to Arnold Bennett he replied at some length, with typical tolerance and good sense. He pointed out that I was not in a position to judge the situation, and was arrogating to myself a right to which I was not entitled—the right to be free from my obligations as an officer whenever I happened to conclude that the War ought to be over. "What is the matter with you is spiritual pride," he affirmed.'

Bennett did not review Frank Harris's *Oscar Wilde* for the *New Statesman*.

Mrs. Sprigge—the second wife of Sir Squire Sprigge (1860–1937), editor of the *Lancet*. She was the daughter of Robert Ross's sister.

MAYIFELD, SYRACUSE / A.D. / 33
(*To Sir William Weir*)

[? Comarques]
[? July 1917]

My dear Weir,

I wonder whether you can help me, & do a virtuous action in the following matter.

Last year the War Office asked the Royal Institute of British Architects for good architects speaking French, for new and important work behind the front. They got two men, E. A. Rickards and Henry Hare, both with a brilliant reputation, both Fellows of the Institute, & both over military age. Having been made full lieutenants in the A.S.C., these men were sent to France and set to do jobs, such as making inventories, which their own clerks could have done better and which any clerks could have done. The job had no relation at all to architecture. Further, they had to work under such conditions of exposure that in four months they were both invalided home. You may judge of their civilian status by the fact that Mr. Hare has just been elected President of the Royal Institute of British Architects. I think he now has a post in Munitions. Mr. Rickards is a great friend of mine, & he is also known to Richmond, who once described him as one of the most interesting men he had ever met. He is now nominally at a Requisitions job in Motor Transport, which he cannot possibly do. He is an absolutely first-class draughtsman, & is specially famous as such throughout the profession. In particular he is wonderful at making perspective views from plans,—and all that sort of thing. Have you not got some opening for such a man? Or your brother the Major? Mr. Rickards is now passed for Home Service. He is 44, and will have a warm recommendation from Colonel Foster, Assistant Director of Motor Transport. He could easily obtain his discharge from the Army, but he has a natural objection to doing so. On the other hand he does not want to be wasted if he stays in the Army.

If you have a moment I should much esteem a word from you. But I should still more esteem another evening with you. It is the turn of you & the Major to dine with me, & I hope you will do so. If I got Rickards to meet you, you would at any rate be entertained. Any Tuesday, Wednesday, or Thursday will suit me, & as you know, my address on those days is the R.T.Y.C.

Yours sincerely, [Arnold Bennett]

MADAN / MS. / 34
(*To Geoffrey Madan*)

Comarques
12–8–17

Dear Mr Madan,

We are very glad to hear from you. I feared you were in Italy holding up Austrians. I *can't* come over & see you. Good God! Haven't you realised that I am civilly running the country? I alone keep Northcliffe from becoming Prime Minister. Your general is very characteristic, but his remark was not better than that of Dallas. I am horribly busy, but my busy-ness is different from yours. I have 49 jobs, & among them is the job of dining out with politicians and big wigs & having too much to drink. I like it sensually, but you will be aware that it runs counter to the genuine austerity of my higher nature. In between I am struggling with my highly improper novel. In fact it is wondrous that I write any letters at all. I shouldn't, except that if I didn't I shouldn't get any letters. This is why I am writing to you, in my cold calculating way.

Best wishes from us both, & when you are on leave, let us know, & when you aren't, let us know too.

Yours sincerely, Arnold Bennett

33. Sir William Weir (1877–1959) was Director of Air Supply. His brother was on the Flying Staff of the War Office. For a letter to E. A. Rickards and information on him see Vols. I and II. For letters to Richmond Temple see below.

Henry Thomas Hare (1844–1921). Colonel (later Major-General) Henry Nedham Foster (1878–1951).

A.S.C.—Army Service Corps. R.T.Y.C.—the Royal Thames Yacht Club, at 80, Piccadilly.

34. Geoffrey Madan (d. 1947) left Balliol to join the army. He was wounded three times during the war. In later years he was notable as a scholar and bibliophile.

Lord Northcliffe (1862–1922) owned *The Times* and other newspapers, and his press campaign against Asquith the previous year was in some part responsible for the fall of the Asquith government. For one of Bennett's attacks on him see below, p. 53 n.

Dallas—presumably Major-General Alister Grant Dallas (1866–1931). In March 1917 he took his division into action at Gaza, captured the place, and was then told by the Higher Command to withdraw—an order he protested against.

HERZOG / MS. / 35
(*To Elsie Herzog*)

Comarques
10–11–17

Dear Lady,

Many thanks for two letters of yours—19th Sept & 14th Oct. The latter took a deuce of a time to arrive, & I was away in Ireland on war work when it *did* arrive, so there has been no chance of me getting something ready for you in time for the bazaar. Moreover, I don't really care to send a water colour for sale, as I am improving in that art & hate amateurishness more & more, even in water colours. I expect you to comprehend. I am not an amateur by temperament. I have now taken to dry points, at which I hope to do better. But I get no time at them. War work, instead of decreasing, has begun to increase again, & I am more & more mixed up in politics; which I do not like, but there is no escape. I am extremely busy & my novel isn't getting a fair chance. I solace myself with the 'note books' of Samuel Butler.

This is all for the present.

Yours sincerely, Arnold Bennett

HERZOG / MS. / 36
(*To Elsie Herzog*)

Comarques
18–11–17

Dear Mrs. Herzog,

Your letter took 25 days. I forgot in my last letter to say that I found Beer's book very good, certainly useful to me. It is very sound. I forget now what I said about it. The *Call* could only have got my article by lifting it.

You will scarcely believe that I get letters from people asking me why I, with my critical taste, am so enthusiastic about Elinor Glyn.

I am now well & very busy in multifarious things. I think I'm going to be brutal & not send you anything for your bazaars & Fairs. No drawings of mine are going forth, & my stock of author's copies of my books is dangerously low, & the

35. The *Notebooks* of Samuel Butler (1835–1902) were edited in 1912 by Henry Festing Jones.

autographed copy stunt is played out. I hope the *Mr. Britling* has reached you. Remembrances to the males.

Yours sincerely, Arnold Bennett

P.S. I am very glad you really liked *B. & P.*

The Frocks Theory is unanswerable.

By the way, have you read *A Theory of the Leisure Class?* It is a wonderful book, damnably written. A. B.

BEAVERBROOK / MS. / 37
(*To Lord Beaverbrook*)

80, Piccadilly
20–11–17

Dear Beaverbrook,

I was at the Carfax Gallery today at the private view of Roger Fry's pictures. I only had a few words with Clifton, the proprietor, but I will venture the opinion that if you offer 1,200 guineas for that Augustus John, Clifton will break like the Italian army.

It was exceedingly nice of you to give me the Rops.

Yours sincerely, Arnold Bennett

36. Clifford Beer (1876–1943) was one of the originators of the notion of 'mental health' in America. His autobiography, *A Mind That Found Itself*, had considerable influence.

Elinor Glyn (1864–1943), popular novelist, was the subject of a diverting attack by Bennett in *Books and Persons*. He praised her 'splendour of subject and elevation of style' and went on to quote some ludicrous passages from *His Hour*.

Bennett published 'The Meaning of Frocks' in *Cosmopolitan* in November 1917. Along with 'Some Axioms of War-Work' it was collected in *Self and Self-Management* in 1918. Bennett was an informal observer of the phenomenon of dress, and Thorstein Veblen (1857–1929) a professorial one. They both proved the old point that clothes make the man and woman.

37. Lord Beaverbrook (1879–1964), the newspaper proprietor, arranged a first meeting with Bennett earlier in November. In an article on Bennett in 1927, Beaverbrook said that before he would sit down with him, Bennett read out an article attacking him and his politics. The article was to be published the following day. Beaverbrook still invited him to sit down, and the article duly appeared, and the two men became great friends. Bennett, says Beaverbrook, was 'extraordinarily lovable and supremely honest'. Bennett recorded a second meeting a few days later in his *Journal*. 'At this second meeting he asked me to take him to Leicester Gallery, where I had mentioned there was a good etching of Rops. I did so, with [Robert] Ross. He asked which was the etching, bought it (20 guineas), and gave it me on the spot. This was at only our 2nd meeting. *Un peu brusqué*.' In some recollections of Beaverbrook years later, the novelist William Gerhardi said: 'I have known only Arnold Bennett, whom he loved, to shake him, so to speak, by the collar.'

For letters to Roger Fry see below. Augustus John (1878–1961). Félicien Rops (1833–98). Arthur Clifton ran the Carfax Gallery for several years in association with Robert Ross. Ross severed the connection in 1908.

BODKIN / TR. / 38
(*To Thomas Bodkin*)

Comarques
22.11.17.

Dear Mr. Bodkin,

This is very kind of you—both in regard to all your trouble about the garde-de-vin, and for the A1 Daumiers. All my thanks. I am now bitterly regretting my offer to send you one of my own dry-points. They are so rotten. However, I am nothing if not valorous. I am at present doing a new one; if it turns out better than the last one, I will send you an example; in case it doesn't I am keeping an example of the last one for you to sneeze at. Touching the Rebellion, of course I got all my statements at second-hand. Both the head of the R.I.C. & the head of the D.M.P. were very strong about the unfair fighting of the Sinn Feiners. So was O'Connor. To put myself on the safe side, I asked for details, & O'Connor gave me details in writing of nearly forty cases of unfair fighting. As regards many of these I am of opinion that, unless they have no basis in fact, they prove what I so briefly said in my articles. I have several times heard very strong complaints in England from officers who fought in the Rebellion, on this point. I write this, not to pit my view against yours, but simply to show that I did not state my view without reasonable prima facie grounds first hand & obtained. If I was challenged in print, which thank heaven I have not been, I should give particulars of a few cases & say that I took no further responsibility! I greatly appreciated your amiable care of me in Dublin. Like you, I have no first-rate interest in politics, but I have a first-rate interest in the arts. I will send you a translation I did many years ago of a Maeterlinck song you have translated.

My kindest regards to Mrs. Bodkin & best wishes to you both.

Yours sincerely, Arnold Bennett

38. Thomas Bodkin (1881–1961), later Director of the National Gallery of Ireland, was a practising barrister until 1916. James O'Connor (1872–1931) was Attorney-General of Ireland from 1916 to 1918. Bennett published three articles on Irish affairs in the *Daily News* on 8, 12, and 15 November. He thought that the English authority in Ireland (represented in part by the Royal Irish Constabulary and the Dublin Military Police) was sympathetic to Home Rule, and that the Sinn Fein consisted of 'misguided and utterly impractical men who . . . did not even fight fairly'.

Honoré Daumier (1808–79); Maurice Maeterlinck (1862–1949).

BERG / MS. / 39
(*To G. T. Bagguley*)

Comarques
8–12–17

Dear Mr. Bagguley,

I am sending you 4 vols for binding. The three Claudels should be uniformly half bound, at a reasonable price. For some reason they are of different heights. Perhaps you could correct this in cutting the top edges for the gilding. I fear the side edges of at least one volume will have to be clipped, but I leave this to you.

The *Ballads* is a beautiful book. You might see what you can do with it, without ruining me. I have shown the binding I lately bought from you to some bibliophiles among my friends, and they have been thereby staggered, having supposed that this kind of thing can only be done in London. I have explained that London is just the place where it can't be done!

With kind regards,

Yours sincerely, Arnold Bennett

BUTLER / MS. / 40
(*To G. T. Bagguley*)

Comarques
22–12–17

Dear Mr. Bagguley,

The book has reached me. It is the most superb gift I have ever received in my life, and gives me intense satisfaction. But I am still wondering why you should have been moved to such generosity. I have spent most of my time in gazing at this work of art. It leaves my friends speechless. Please accept my insufficient but very sincere thanks.

Believe me,

Always yours sincerely, Arnold Bennett

P.S. I have written to Mr. C. & am delighted to have had the opportunity of doing so. A. B.

39. For an earlier letter to George Thomas Bagguley see Vol. II, p. 282. On Paul Claudel see II, 245–6, 287.

CALIF / MS. / 41
(*To T. E. Caley*)

Comarques
22–12–17

My dear Sir,

I understand from Mr. Bagguley that it is you who are the craftsman of the binding of the *Candide* which he has been so kind as to give me. Will you allow me to offer you my most sincere congratulations on your extraordinary art? And also on your patience? The binding is magnificent, & I am proud to have come from the part of the world from which it came.

Believe me,
Cordially yours, Arnold Bennett

DAVIS / TR. / 42
(*To Oswald H. Davis*)

Comarques
24 Dec 1917

Dear Mr. Davis,

Your letter was very interesting, and I have used some sentences from it (of course without giving away the origin) in connection with some remarks of mine on the army in the *New Statesman*. I shall be very glad to hear from you again—this time as to the military virtues. I spoke of the old Army N.C.O.s from my own knowledge of them. I dare say that what you say of them is true also, but their good points are undeniable. Your charges against them could be true of similar people in any business organisation of immense size. I heartily congratulate you on getting the M.M.

I think G.K.C. has been a giant. I doubt if he has not much shrunken. The juxtaposition of him and E. V. L. was accidental. Still, E.V.L. has written some admirable sarcasm. His account of an evening at The Pines, Putney, was masterly. Merrick has written some pretty good stuff, notably in *The Actor Manager*, but he is dreadfully uneven, and has been overpraised to the point of absurdity, solely because Barrie once happened to say that he was a master of narrative. A complete edition of his works was contemplated, and a number of authors were asked

41. Thomas Caley is not otherwise known, except in that he lived for several years in Newcastle-under-Lyme where Bagguley had his business.

to write introductions for various volumes. I was asked, and agreed to do so. Merrick is a Jew, and his breadth of mind is such that he refused to consent to me writing a preface, on the score of a single phrase in, I think, *The Old Wives' Tale*, in which I referred—*ironically at the expense of Nonconformists*—to the Jews as the murderers of Christ! I thought this rather funny. I believe the project of the complete edition then fell through! I like W. H. Davies very much. I think Ralph Hodgson is about the best young poet we have.

Best wishes,

Yours sincerely, Arnold Bennett

IDDESLEIGH / MS. / 43
(*To F. S. A. Lowndes*)

Comarques
8–1–18

My dear Lowndes,

Well, I don't think Scribe is anything like so good as Labiche, and if I were you I should read Labiche. He makes you laugh. What you mean about Lillah I don't cotton to. True we have been rather friendly lately, & she has read one of my plays and says she likes it. But I have heard nothing as to her buying it for production! In fact I told Pinker the other day to demand the return of the play. I am staying at home all this week, so as to get a good period of 10 days at my cocotte novel. I hope to finish the debauched thing by the end of the month. I doubt whether I ever said to you: 'Any fool can write a play.' What I probably did say was: 'Any fool can write a first act.' We have seen *Dear Brutus*, & despite its dreadful method of production—it is continuously offensive to the eye—I greatly enjoyed it. The best Barrie I remember. I quite expected to be bored. Packed

42. Davis won the Military Medal. He was probably reading *Books and Persons* in which was reprinted an essay on G. K. Chesterton (1874–1936) and E. V. Lucas written in 1909. Bennett remarks in it that 'not all Mr. Chesterton's immense cleverness and charm will ever erase from the minds of his best readers this impression—caused by his mistimed religious dogmatism—that there is something seriously deficient in the very basis of his mind'. For other references to E. V. Lucas see Vols. I and II; for letters to him see Vol. II and below. The Pines—A. C. Swinburne's home in Putney. Leonard Merrick (1864–1939) wrote *Conrad in Quest of His Youth*, which J. M. Barrie described as the best sentimental journey since the first one. W. H. Davies (1871–1940) was famous for his *Autobiography of a Super-Tramp*. Ralph Hodgson (1871–1962) published his first volume of verse ten years earlier.

theatre. I wish good luck to your play. I expect I shall write another one myself before I am much older.

Best respex to you both, & good wishes for the boy.

Yours, A. B.

DAILY NEWS, 25 January 1918 / 44
(*To the editor*)

[80, Piccadilly]
Jan. 24 [1918]

Sir,

I wish to take up one detail in Mr. Belloc's able letter to you today. Mr. Belloc refers to 'individual publicists' who write from time to time for the Harmsworth Press, but 'apologise in private for their action'. On more than one occasion during the war I have written for the Harmsworth Press, but I have never apologised for my action. I doubt whether even Mr. Belloc has written more severely about the methods of the Harmsworth Press than I have. If in the face of what I have written the Harmsworth Press invites me to express in it my own opinions on important and highly controversial subjects, over my own signature, I see various good reasons why I should not refuse the invitation. It appears to me an excellent thing that the opinions broadly held by the *Daily News* should be prominently printed in the Harmsworth Press. That the advisability of my action is arguable I freely admit, but the advantages of it, such as they are, seem to me greatly to outweigh the disadvantages, such as they are.

A. B.

43. For an earlier letter to F. S. A. Lowndes see Vol. II, p. 330.

Bennett's remarks on Augustin Eugène Scribe (1791–1861) and Eugène Marin Labiche (1815–88) call to mind Bernard Shaw's remark to Bennett apropos of *The Bright Island* a few years later: 'You have nothing to learn from Scribe & Co., and everything to learn from Beethoven'.

Lillah McCarthy was interested in producing *Don Juan de Marana*; see also the letter to Miss McCarthy below, pp. 94–5, and the footnote.

For letters, to J. B. Pinker, Bennett's literary agent, see Vol. I.

Dear Brutus opened in London the preceding October.

44. On Hilaire Belloc see Vol. II, pp. 366–7. His letter concerned the attempt by various newspapers of the Harmsworth group to alter the military conduct of the war, and he asserted that 'many individual publicists, some of the most distinguished, write from time to time in the Harmsworth papers rather than run the risk of their enmity'. In 1915 Belloc wanted Lord Northcliffe arrested under the 'Defence of the Realm' act.

HILL / MS. / 45
(*To Gregory Hill*)

Comarques
7-2-18

My dear Gregory,

I am delighted to hear from you, & that you are well, even if not comfortable! I well understand what you mean when you talk of the discomforts felt by anyone who has been used to an ordered existence. They must be exceedingly trying, & you have all my sympathies. But for my age, I should probably be in the same boat, which boat I should most strongly object to. Still I would sooner be in siege than in anything else. The chief ruined towns I saw were Arras and Ypres. I forget the names of a lot of the smaller ones. I think that the war is now drawing to a close, & I should be rather surprised if it didn't end this year. When you see the newspapers more occupied with social & political news of the war than with military news of the war, you may bet a great change has come over the scene. The food situation here is grave. In Germany & Austria it is appalling. The strikes in Germany & Austria were very real and alarming, and all this is to the good. You see, it would be sufficient for us if Austria caved in. If Austria did, Germany would have to. As Austria is easily the weakest, the most interesting thing is what is happening in *Austria*, & yet people seem to be always more interested in what happens in Germany. The chain is no stronger than its weakest link, & Austria is the weakest link. (I don't count Turkey & Bulgaria.) The United States have now 400,000 men in France, & the number is increasing all the time. Up to the present, however, the U.S.A. have not displayed much talent for turning men into a coherent fighting machine. They are not conceited, and they admit this. So far, they are far inferior to us in this respect. I see a good many people of all sorts who are in a position to know the facts and who talk freely to me. Russian news is scarce, & much of it is censored. An English manufacturer in Russia who has escaped told a friend of mine, who told me, that he was tried for his life by his own workmen, & got off by a majority of 2! Also that he himself saw people being burned alive in barrels of kerosene in the Nevsky Prospect, the principal street of Petrograd, & that nobody seemed to be particularly upset about it. So you see there are worse things than the Western Front. An intimate friend of mine, Hugh Walpole, has been at Petrograd on behalf of the Foreign Office during most of the war. He has the most astounding stories to tell of robbery & violence & so on.

I hope you will go on all right, & I hope to hear from you again quite soon. My wife & I are all right. I have just finished a book, but it doesn't leave me much freer, as I am always worried with articles & oddments for this tedious war.

Our best wishes,

Yours, Arnold Bennett

FALES, NYU / MS. / 46
(*To William Nicholson*)

Comarques
9–2–18

My dear Nicholson,

We received a little while ago an invitation from some people named Nicholson living in Apple Tree Yard to the wedding of their daughter with R. Graves. Just before that I had met Graves somewhere at lunch, & I thought that possibly the invitation had come through him (though he had said naught of marriage). My wife said to me: 'Who are these Nicholsons?' I said: 'Dashed if I know!' It was not till Thursday last when Sybil Colefax told me that you had a daughter married that it occurred to me that *you* must be the Nicholsons. How the deuce do you expect people to guess that *your* daughter is old enough to get married? And why in hades when you change your address don't you notify the same? I had not the faintest idea that William & Mabel's daughter was joining herself to this admirable youthful poet, or I should have written in a different strain in response to the invitation.

45. Gregory Hill (1884–1967) was the son of Bennett's friend Joseph Hill (see Vol. II). In some notes written shortly before his death, Hill remarked upon Bennett's kindness. When Hill was ten years old, his father died, and in the following two years Bennett took him on month-long holidays abroad. In 1899 or 1900, when Hill was still a schoolboy, Bennett had him do some reporting for *Woman*. In the First World War Hill was attached to an artillery battery. On Bennett's visit to the Front see Vol. II.

Bennett finished writing *The Pretty Lady* on 28 January.

I shall call on you one night *after* dinner to lay my excuses at the feet of mamma-in-law.

And best wishes to you both,

Yours sincerely, Arnold Bennett

BERG / MS. / 47
(*To Richmond Temple*)

Comarques
20–2–18

Dear Mr. Temple,

It is within the facts to say that I have intended every day to answer your letter at once. But instead of gliding over the Bay of Taranto I have been up to my neck in the mud of work—especially proof correcting. I have now got my improper novel entirely off my mind, & don't want to hear anything more about it except highly favourable reviews and immense cheques. You talk of the young air-ministry that has never flown. But the only young man *I* know in the Air Ministry is a real flier, *and* a first-class engineering expert, *and* an excellent fellow. To whit Colonel Weir, brother of Sir Wm. Weir. Also let me tell you that at the Lloyd George dinner at Gray's Inn at the end of last year I sat between two *young* R.F.C. Brigadier-Generals, and they were both fliers. One of them had a wound stripe up. They were very nice, anti-Ll.G. and moderately pro-Lansdowne. But the best fellow at that affair was Colonel Scott, who sat opposite me, and whom I liked enormously. I expect you know whom I mean. You will never be asked to lunch at the Reform Club any more until after the war—not because you have committed any crime, but because the idiotic old committee has forbidden guests to lunch. But perhaps after all you *will* be asked, as I think exception is made for officers on leave. The Club is greatly changed—but there is more room. Bomb on St. Pancras

46. (Sir) William Nicholson (1872–1949), the artist, did some work for the British War Memorial Committee, of which Bennett was a member. Bennett first met Robert Graves (1895–) at the Reform Club in December 1917, along with another young poet, and he wrote in his *Journal*: 'I was very pleased with both these youths. Lately I am more and more struck by the certainty, strength, and unconscious self-confidence of young men, so different from my middle-aged uncertainty.' Sybil Colefax was wife of Sir Arthur Colefax (d. 1936).

Hotel on Sunday night, and on Chelsea hospital on Saturday night. The clouds here today are not 25,000 but about 25 foot altitude. Yesterday there was a fog. We now like fogs and rain —except on moonless nights. I suppose you know that Robert Graves has got married to Nancy Nicholson. His in-laws are friends of mine. I am well aware that there is nothing at all in this letter except good will.

With best wishes,

Yours sincerely, Arnold Bennett

STOKE / MS. / 48
(*To Hugh Walpole*)

80, Piccadilly
23–2–18

My dear Hughie,

Many thanks. I will dine with you & P. A. on Thursday 7th March, if that suits you. I am exceedingly distressed about your eyes, & wish to be informed of what is being done for them. Needless to say, I know, like everybody else, *the* oculist in London.

re Lucas, what amuses me is that *he* should make the charge, seeing that nobody could guess the realities of *his* character from *his* books. I may tell you there is nothing whatever in it. Your talk may be more dashing than your literature, in appearance, but I think that that springs from your tremendous physical 'go' and youthfulness, & I attach no importance to it. In my opinion your writing is better than your talking, though less showy. For example in talking you constantly use clichés—such as 'any sort *or kind*'—which would pass in a fashionable barrister such as Marshall Hall, but do not redound to the credit, as a talker, of Hugh Walpole the author of *Mr. P. & Mr. T.*, *The Dark F.* or *The G. Mirror*. (Has the candid E.V.L.

47. Richmond Temple was in the Air Force. When he returned from the war, he became publicity chief of the Savoy Hotel.

On the Weirs see above, pp. 38–9.

David Lloyd George (1863–1945) and the Marquess of Landsowne (1845–1927) fell out in 1917 over the latter's publication of his recommendations on a peace of accommodation with Germany.

Colonel Scott is not otherwise known.

ever told you this? I bet not.) In your writing you instinctively avoid clichés—not *always* with success; but then none of us *always* avoids them with success. Now the frequency or infrequency of clichés is for me a sure symptom invented by an omnipotent God to enable us to come to conclusions about style. I don't think I have concealed from you my opinion that *Fortitude* and *The Duchess* are not on a level with the other three. But this unlevelness does not worry me in the least. It is constantly found in the greatest novelists, and is natural & inevitable. No artist really knows what he is doing till long after he has done it. You can tell my views about you to anybody you like. *I* always do.

Thine, A. B.

P.S. I saw thee in St. James's Sq. Friday I think about 3 p.m. But thou tookst about as much notice of me as a taxi driver going home to his dinner.

HERZOG / MS. / 49
(*To Elsie Herzog*)

Comarques
2–3–18

Dear Mrs. Herzog,

You know about William Nicholson, one of the best English painters. He and his wife are great friends of mine; & in virtue of his painting & her painting & their general niceness I want you to do something for them. Their son Ben has been discharged totally unfit from the army, & has gone to California to try to get cured of asthma. His name & address are Ben Nicholson, 943 North Los Robles, Pasadena, Los Angeles. He is a painter too. His age is 24 & he is extremely lonely. You are bound to know some suitable people in Los Angeles, or to know someone who knows some. Will you put them on to Ben & tell them to assuage Ben's loneliness? I haven't seen Ben since he

48. P. A.—presumably Percy Anderson (d. 1928), artist and designer, and Walpole's closest friend for some while.

E. V. Lucas seems to have accused Walpole of losing all individuality when he wrote. Walpole's novels were *Mr. Perrin and Mr. Traill* (1911), *The Dark Forest* (1916), *The Green Mirror* (1918), *Fortitude* (1913), and *The Duchess of Wrexe* (1914).

Marshall Hall—Sir Edward (1858–1929).

was a schoolboy; but if he is anything like his parents he is a highly distinguished person. Thank you.

I am very busy.

Best wishes from us both to you both.

Yours sincerely, Arnold Bennett

DAVIS / TR. / 50
(*To Oswald H. Davis*)

Comarques
2–3–1918

Dear Mr. Oswald Davis,

I've kept your letter in hand for some time because I thought the notes and impressions which it includes might form the basis of journalistic stuff. However I find—what I did not know before—that a great deal of such notes etc. was printed in the early part of the war in the sixpenny political weeklies. Anyhow your stuff is very interesting, and possibly later on you might use it in a more ambitious way. I *do* write each week in the *New Statesman*, under the signature 'Sardonyx', but all my paragraphs are not always printed because sometimes the editor shies at them. I do not think that *Victory* is anything like equal to *Chance*. In fact it is not first-rate Conrad, *Chance* is. *Bealby* I have never read. Wells sends me all his books; but he didn't send *Bealby* along, and I lost the list and didn't get it. I have just finished a book and shall begin a play as soon as I have got over the neuralgia which is now seriously impairing my epistolary performances.

Best wishes,

Yours sincerely, Arnold Bennett

MADAN / MS. / 51
(*To Geoffrey Madan*)

Comarques
10–3–18

Dear Mr. Madan,

Your defence of Dallas is too thin. Despite this, I (or we) shall be delighted to see you when you are in London on leave.

49. Ben Nicholson (1894–).

50. *Victory* and *Bealby* were published in 1915, *Chance* in 1914. The new play was *The Title*, begun 24 March.

No guests are allowed for lunch at the Reform Club now *except officers on leave from the Front.* The novel will be out at the end of the month. It is *not* new. I thought it was, but it isn't. The heroine is a cocotte. To my intense disgust Compton Mackenzie is publishing a novel about a cocotte almost simultaneously. I am still hammering at Northcliffe. He is now much shaken. I have become so friendly with the other bête noire of the public, Beaverbrook, that I can't attack him. In fact I am sitting, with *Rothermere* & Masterman, on one of his committees—a Committee which has charge of the task of having the war recorded in paint and marble. Great larks. I defend the artists. Masterman alone has the slightest idea of what an artist is. As for Asquith, I am seeing him, & I hope drinking with him, on Tuesday night.

This letter is highly indiscreet—therefore private.

I will keep an eye on Macdowell.

Spender has recently introduced me to Thucydides, & I think he is the greatest of all historians. Indeed I need say no more than that if I wrote history this is the way I should write it.

Let me know before you arrive in town. And I hope your book is well written. I feel sure it is.

Our best wishes.

Yours sincerely, Arnold Bennett

BODKIN / TR. / 52
(*To Thomas Bodkin*)

Comarques
4.4.18.

My dear Mr. Bodkin,

Keep calm for the shock. The garde-vin has arrived. While I was in correspondence with Broad Street and with Euston

51. *The Pretty Lady* was published in April; *The Early Life and Adventures of Sylvia Scarlett*, by (Sir) Compton Mackenzie (1883–), in August.

In an article in the *Daily News* on 3 March Bennett referred to Lord Northcliffe's services to the government as those of a circus horse. Lord Beaverbrook became head of the newly formed Ministry of Information in February. Lord Rothermere (1868–1940), proprietor of the *Daily Mirror*, was Air-Minister in 1917–18. C. F. G. Masterman (1873–1927) was Director of Wellington House (propaganda department), which was now a part of the Ministry of Information. For a letter to Masterman see Vol. I, pp. 237–8; see also below. Macdowell is unidentified.

J. A. Spender (1862–1942) edited the *Westminster Gazette.*

Station, I received a notice from Camden Station that the crate had been there 15 weeks and that there was 15/- to pay for carriage etc. I just paid. The thing arrived broken and damaged, owing to bad packing. However, on my return to London I hope to see it all in order again. The amiable rascal Morrison said he would attend to the lock. He did not do so. Still, it is a nice piece, and I am exceedingly obliged for your most Christian conduct in regard to the same. I never hoped to see the thing again, and that's a fact. I wish we could meet in order to discuss. I bought a Brabazon for 20 guineas a few days before Brabazons went up to 40 and more at Christie's. They had never till then been 'quoted' at Christie's. There is a new war artist named Roberts whose sketches are fine. I've got 2 of those; and etchings by Picasso, Rops, and Sickert. I am now on the Imperial War Memorial Committee, and as the other members are Charles Masterman and Rothermere I'm the only one with a first-class interest in the subject. Rothermere collects, but he employs P. J. Konody to collect for him! Can you imagine it? The object of the Committee is to procure a complete record of the whole blooming war in paint, ink and sculpture. I have succeeded in turning down *all* R.A. painters, except Clausen. Some feat, believe me! Yes, I have turned down even the inevitable Brangwyn. My kindest regards to all 3 of you. I seem to know that child.

Yours sincerely, Arnold Bennett

STOKE / MS. / 53
(*To Hugh Walpole*)

Comarques
4.4.18.

My dear Hughie,

This is excellent tidings, & does me much good in the midst of a chill on the entrails which has laid me low—just as I am in the middle of the 1st act of my new play! I feel really relieved that you admire the book. One can't judge, oneself, under

52. Morrison is unidentified.

Hercules Brabazon (1821–1906), Cyril Roberts (1871–1949), Pablo Picasso (1881–), Walter Sickert (1860–1942), (Sir) George Clausen (1852–1944), and Sir Frank Brangwyn (1867–1956). P. J. Konody (1872–1933) was art critic for the *Observer*.

about 2 years. It is possible you are right about Concepcion. I must do her again, that's all. It is a rare Shakespearean scheme to draw the same character again & again till you get it. I am just correcting proofs of *The Roll-Call*. Now when I was writing this I didn't think much of it—from 30 to 16 months ago. But at the present moment it seems to me to be quite all right, & very interesting. Most of the reviews of the *P.L.* so far are specially footling. Astonishing, the number of critics who daren't *mention* that the chief character is a whore! You don't say anything about your eyesight & so on.

By the way, the spermatozoa phrase has surely by this time passed into the language. It is Butlerian, & has probably been used by about 7 million writers. I should class it for used-ness with such a phrase as 'see life steadily & see it whole'. Robert Ross was in great form the other night. He said that it might well be said of Edward VII that he saw life unsteadily but saw it whole.

I must now close as I am much enfeebled. On your return that Alhambra affair has to take place.

Thine with thanksgivings, A. B.

IDDESLEIGH / MS. / 54
(*To F. S. A. Lowndes*)

Comarques
6–4–18

My dear Lowndes,

On the contrary, it is quite the 'right spirit' in you to be pleased about Charles's ankle wound. If the consequences of doing duty are better than was feared and not much worse than was hoped, the people chiefly concerned *ought* to be quite pleased, & to display their joy & add it to the meagre national stock of that commodity. My best wishes to Charles. I am sorry you have returned to P.H. Sq. (which is really G.H.Q.). I am scathing some of this lot in *my* new play, which, granting as I willingly do the 'superbness' of *your* play, also has points, I

53. Concepcion is the second heroine of *The Pretty Lady*. The hero of the novel, bent upon the mysteries of love, fails to reflect that he and his mistress are 'huge contrivances of certain active spermatozoa for producing other active spermatozoa'.

Bennett did the actual writing of *The Roll-Call* from 16 October 1916 to 30 April 1917.

believe. May yours be produced instantly. Mine won't. The review in the *Globe*, enthusiastic but not any good, was well balanced by Jimmy Douglas's outpouring in the *Star* last night. I regard the situation as [? daring]. I am much too deeply plunged in work. The play, aforesaid! Sitting on one of Beaverbrook's chief committees, which means a hades of a lot of cerebration, as the whole of the work is done by Charlie Masterman & me! And more & more journalism. I have just beaten all journalistic records (except Horatio's). *Lloyd's Weekly News* have just contracted to pay me £100 a week for a weekly 1,500 word article. I offered to bet Pinker he wouldn't get £100 a week. He wouldn't bet, but he said if he didn't get it he wouldn't agree to me taking the contract at all. Other people can say what they like, but I say: Give me Pinker.

Our kindest regards to you all.

Ever yours, A. B.

BERG / MS. / 55
(*To Richmond Temple*)

Comarques
27–4–18

Dear Mr Temple,

Many thanks for yours of the 6th March. You dated it 6th May, but I surmise that cannot be correct. As you know, there have been great ructions at the [?] lately. I had a conversation with Rothermere the other day. I won't describe it to you—the description would be libellous. Anyhow you have got a first-class Air Minister in William Weir. He is a friend of mine, & I have the highest opinion of his abilities, modesty, and 'fundamental decency'. I saw him at the Yacht Club yesterday. He was with an Air general, who looked very mild, & he astonished me by introducing 'General Sykes'! I only had one word with these twain but I must say I liked the look of Sykes. I am told he is something of an intriguer, but as to that I know naught. I must say something about those 'penguins' in the

54. Lowndes was on the staff of *The Times* (Printing House Square). On James Douglas's review of *The Pretty Lady* and on *Lloyd's Weekly News* see Vol. I. Horatio—presumably Horatio Bottomley (1860–1933), the flamboyant journalist and financier.

New Statesman. I have heard of their mountebanking before. It may astonish you to learn that—by six weeks—I am now in the Army Reserve. Wells just isn't! However, as I work for various Govt departments, & have been for some time regularly labouring for the Ministry of Information, I hope to be spared from the ranks & even from a commission. Still I may have to salute you yet. If I have to, I shall do so with pleasure. My novel has made a hades of a racket in the press, & also in what is known as the 'West End'. It has several times been called 'pornographic', 'the last word in decadence', 'shameful', 'abominable', etc.; still I survive.

My best wishes,

Yours sincerely, Arnold Bennett

MERTON / MS. / 56
(*To Max Beerbohm*)

Comarques
2nd May 1918

My dear Max,

I am instructed by the British War Memorial Committee (of which I am a member & which is engaged in making a collection of paintings & drawings about the war by *really* modern artists) to approach you about doing some cartoons about the war. You may remember that several years ago I got you to lunch with the secret purpose of finding out whether you meant to do any war stuff. The excuses you then gave were terribly inefficient. I do want you to understand that the absence of war-cartoons by you is generally *felt*, & that there is a general feeling that you *ought* to do war-cartoons & that you certainly can, & are only being withheld from so doing by a certain diffidence charming but criminal. I do want you to understand that you are about to be *strongly* urged to do some war-cartoons & that your life will be made a hell for you if you prove obdurate. I doubt if you realise what the feeling is in favour of your cartoons.

The Committee will be willing to enter into some arrangement

55. The 'penguins' are unidentified.
Sykes—Brigadier-General Clement Arthur (1871–1938).
H. G. Wells was just a few months older than Bennett.

with you by which they would take your whole output for an agreed period for a reasonably fixed sum. All the best painters are working for the Committee, from Cameron to Nevinson. The only R.A.'s on the Committee's list are good men. You will be in as good company as there is in England.

I want you to come and lunch with me again, & perhaps you will let me suggest a day.

My position, when it comes to business, is strictly official, but of course the general terms & effrontery of this letter are strictly unofficial.

Kindest regards to Mrs. Max.

Yours, Arnold Bennett

ARNOLD BENNETT / 57
(*To George Doran*)

80, Piccadilly
May 13th, 1918

My dear Doran,

I suppose you are about to publish, or have just published, *The Pretty Lady*. Here, a few of the lower class papers have gone for it rather heavily as being pornographic and unsuitable for war-time, etc., etc. The higher class papers, however, with the exception of *The Star*, have treated it very well indeed, and I expect that next week it will have reached a sale of 20,000 copies at least.

Some of the good reviews have said that it is decadent and cynical, and that it gives an entirely ruthless picture of heartless people in London. This is not so, and I particularly want you to note that the war has a good effect on the three principal characters, namely, Christine, Concepcion and G. J., all of whom do what they can. The book is emphatically not cynical. Nor does it portray heartless people, and I should like this to be insisted upon.

56. For an earlier letter to Max Beerbohm see Vol. II, p. 372. He replied to Bennett's urgings on the other occasion: 'No, I don't think I shall do any war cartoons. My drawing is too *funny*. A tremendous grimness seems to me the only way; and *I* can't be grim or tremendous.'

Cameron and Nevinson—(Sir) David Young (1865–1945) and Christopher Richard Wynne (1889–1946).

I have just taken charge of British Propaganda for France, so that I have rather more than I can do.

Affectionate regards to all of you,

Yours, Arnold Bennett

TEXAS / T.C.C. / 58
(*To Newman Flower*)

80, Piccadilly
May 14th, 1918

My dear Flower,

Many thanks for your letter of the 13th and the enclosed copy letter from Mr. Mara.

I greatly regret that Roman Catholics should find offence in *The Pretty Lady*, and the more so as I have greater sympathy with their religion than with any other.

It is surely unnecessary for me to point out, first, that in so far as the book deals with Catholicism it does so exclusively from the point of view of an ignorant and superstitious courtesan anxious to justify her own conduct to herself, and, second, that all the details given as to legends of the Virgin Mary can be found, with hundreds of others, in devout Catholic literature.

As to the detail that Christine goes out into the streets at the supposed call of the Virgin Mary, the story makes quite clear that she went out to find one particular man and to succour him,—really to save him from the consequences of his drunkenness.

Seeing that the objection of the Catholic Federation is a purely religious objection, I am afraid that no purpose would be served by arguing it further. Nor do I perceive that you or I could do anything. Does the Catholic Federation wish us to suppress the book, or to suppress certain parts of it, because in their opinion it offends Catholic susceptibilities? If so, I can only reply, with respect and regret, that such a course is absolutely out of the question, and that I personally should oppose it by every means in my power. The book is a serious and considered work; it has received very high praise from many

57. Bennett began formal work as Director of British Propaganda in France on 9 May. For other details about his appointment see Vol. I, p. 262–3.

periodicals and critics of the highest reputation; and I shall most assuredly stand by it.

To show, however, my respect for opinions which do not agree with my own, I am quite willing to write a special preface for the new edition, indicating the nature of the Catholic objection and specifically stating that I do not wish any passages in the book to be interpreted as the Catholic Federation fears they may be interpreted.

More than this I cannot do, and, having made this offer, I must leave the Catholic Federation to employ the 'remedies' to which Mr. Mara refers.

Yours sincerely, [Arnold Bennett]

MADAN / MS. / 59
(*To Geoffrey Madan*)

80, Piccadilly
24 May 1918

Dear Captain Madan,

I doubt if you ought to call France & Flaubert 'dry'. *L'Éducation Sentimentale* ought to be read with ease. Ditto *Thaïs*, & *La Rôtisserie*. Personally, though, I think France over-rated. You ought to read *Bubu de Montparnasse* of Charles Louis Philippe. This is a great little novel, one of the finest modern French novels. I think *Cœur simple* is the best thing Flaubert ever wrote, except his correspondence, which *is* his best work, & ought to be read. I tell you that Lytton Strachey's *Eminent Victorians* is a most juicy & devastating affair. I thoroughly enjoyed it. The Chekhov tales are still coming out (Chatto & Windus), two new volumes just issued, & no self respecting trench-mortarist could miss them.

The Pretty Lady is not a moralising or a shaft against moralising or against anybody or anything. It is just *a* novel about the war. And I leave it at that. Never had it occurred to me that 'Iquist' resembled 'Asquith'! I made the name up, as I occasionally do, & I thought it a very fine made-up name. This book is getting me into a hades of a row with the Catholics. Various

58. W. P. Mara was Lay Secretary of the Catholic Federation of the Archdiocese of Westminster. The Catholic Truth Society made a similar complaint. Neither got anywhere.

attempts have been made to suppress it. Smiths, after doing exceedingly well out of it, have decided to ban it. Boots of course wouldn't touch it. I doubt whether the attempts to suppress it are yet over. However, I have influences in high places which ought to be able to counteract such moves. The book sells like hot cakes.

I have now given up literature. I am a man of business. I have clerks, offices, agents, tentacles, & God knows what. I was requested to take charge of British Propaganda in France, & I could not refuse. It is most amusing—the work. Not half so fatiguing as writing novels; but more tie-ing—much more. I don't know how soon I shall get sick of it, or how soon something splendid that I do will get me the sack. I insisted on giving my services, & so I simply don't care.

We hope you are keeping your soul in your body. My wife has a nervous affection of the foot & is, I think, going to Harrogate or somewhere. Otherwise all is well. Best wishes.

Yours sincerely, Arnold Bennett

COMMON SENSE, 15 June 1918 / 60
(*To the editor*)

Ministry of Information
June 12, 1918

Dear Sir,

In your issue of the 8th instant, there is a paragraph which mentions my name as having accepted an important post at the Ministry of Information, and immediately afterwards asks: 'How far is propaganda expenditure (at the expense of the taxpayers) used for the purpose of supporting the Government and increasing its adherents?' The implication, though it was probably unintentional, is only too clear. I therefore wish to say that I give the Ministry of Information a regular eight-hour day and receive no salary whatever nor any payment of any kind. What is more, my appointment involves me in considerable financial loss. It is extremely unpleasant to say such things in these days when soldiers are risking and losing their lives for a shilling a

59. For other comments on Anatole France, Gustave Flaubert, and C. L. Philippe see Vol. II. Lytton Strachey (1880–1932) published *Eminent Victorians* in May 1918.

day; but in fairness to the Ministry and myself, I am obliged to correct the impression given by your paragraph by stating the facts.

Yours faithfully, Arnold Bennett

HILL / MS. / 61
(*To Gregory Hill*)

Comarques
30–6–18

My dear Gregory,

I was glad to have your letter, and especially to read certain things in it. Nowadays I have scarcely any time to write private letters. I have been appointed Director of British Propaganda for France, and it is some job. I am Lord God (from London) over a bureau in Paris & over I don't know how many provincial committees in the said France. I only come home on Saturday evenings, & I leave by the 8.20 train on Monday mornings. I thought my cup was full, & just now, lo! I am having a play produced! I wrote it some months ago. It is a satire on the Government (of which I am now the servant—unpaid) & will create some row,—that is certain. I will have a copy of my new novel sent to you. It is supposed to be highly daring and obscene; & prosecutions have been threatened. (It isn't really obscene.) We have had two gardeners killed in the war, and now the head gardener (aged 45) is being called up. As the whole place rests on him, & he is thoroughly capable & thoroughly trustworthy, I don't know what will happen. Did I tell you the Ledwards are living here now. They keep the house warm for us. That is to say, Mrs. Ledward, Enid Jowett, and Olive Valentine. All 3 delightful. Also a kid. It is about time you had some leave. When you get it, let me know. You will have to go through London on your way home. Everybody I have seen from the Front speaks in the *very highest* terms of the American soldiers. So the prospects are good. But Paris is very much shaken up. Marguerite is in town.

Best wishes. Good luck.

Yours ever, A. B.

61. *The Title* opened at the Royalty Theatre on 20 July.

The Ledwards were a Burslem family. Mrs. Ledward was an aunt of William Kennerley, who married Bennett's sister Tertia. Her daughter Enid married Percy

MADAN / MS. / 62
(*To Geoffrey Madan*)

80, Piccadilly
6–7–18

My dear Geoffrey Madan,

No I don't know any such book as you want that is worth a damn. Nor do I much believe in such books. I prefer miscellaneous browsings. I told F. Swinnerton all the French novels he ought to read, & he has read them all, & is now writing a book on the *English* novel. He said he couldn't deal with the English novel without knowing the main French novels. A good position to take. I am too busy for anything. I have no time at all for my own affairs, & yet have a play coming forth on the 20th at the Royalty. I haven't yet been to a rehearsal—not one. But I'm told that Eva Moore is frightfully good in the chief female role. I left London last night (Friday) & shall be at Comarques till Monday morn, & am spending much time in getting level with my private correspondence & arranging the arrangements for my head gardener to go into the Army. He is 45. I had 4 gardeners. Two have been killed at the Front. One died last week, and the fourth, the head gardener, the base of the pyramid of this establishment, will go next week. This is what people like me call 'suffering in the war'. Still, it is the best I can do in the suffering line. I have only one nephew old enough for the army, he is in the R.A.F., & hasn't yet flown alone.

Marguerite is in bed with flu.

I have 3 books coming out this summer & autumn.

1: The aforesaid play.

2: A book of moral essays for the young of both sexes.

Jowett, who eventually became Principal of the Royal College of Art. Daughter Olive (now Mrs. Olive Glendinning) was the widow of Guy Nossiter, son of the actor 'Sydney Valentine'; see also Vol. I, p. 130. She writes: 'I spent two of my school summer holidays with Arnold and Marguerite at Fontainebleau. I was actually with them in 1908 when he finished *The Old Wives' Tale* and he asked me to proof-read some of the early chapters which were in galley form in July. He advised me at that time to leave school early and to take a full secretarial course in order to be his private secretary. . . . I sometimes think and very much hope it was a definite fact, that my being there gave him more relaxation during that period of terrific concentration on the final chapters of *The Old Wives' Tale* because we went on long walks in the Forest and sketched together most afternoons, and played piano duets invariably after dinner.'

3: A novel I wrote 2 years ago. *The Roll-Call*; much better than *The Pretty Lady*, but people won't like it so well.

Our best wishes to thee

Yours ever, A. B.

BIRMINGHAM / MS. / 63
(*To John Galsworthy*)

Ministry of Information
Norfolk Street
Strand
16–7–18

My dear Galsworthy,

I return the cover. I should have been delighted to write you something gratis, but you may believe me when I tell you I am so rushed that I cannot attend to my private correspondence even. Here, I do more than attend to French propaganda—with an entirely inadequate staff. I can't imagine how the story got about that I had written my Red Cross experiences for Irene to recite. I enclose a copy of what I actually did write. You will see that it is of no use to you. I never had any Red Cross experiences. I see no prospect of any relief from my present business until the end of the war. So that's that. I have only been to half of 2 rehearsals of my play. Marguerite is in the country.

Best affections to you both.

Yours, Arnold Bennett

DAILY NEWS, 19 July 1918 / 64
(*To the editor*)

[80, Piccadilly]
[17 or 18 July 1918]

Sir,

It would, I think, be easy for me to show that Mr. Maurice Hewlett has misunderstood, and (no doubt innocently) misrepresented my article.

62. Eva Moore (1870–1955) co-starred in *The Title* with C. Aubrey Smith.

The nephew was Alan Beardmore, eldest son of sister Fanny Gertrude.

Self and Self-Management, one of the pocket philosophies, was published in December. *The Roll-Call* did not appear until January 1919.

63. For an earlier letter to John Galsworthy see Vol. II, p. 255. He was involved in relief work throughout the war. The actress Irene Vanbrugh (d. 1949) spoke a 'Message to the Audience' written by Bennett for a concert in aid of the British Committee of the French Red Cross at the Coliseum on 14 July 1918. The manuscript of the 'Message' was then sold at auction, and fetched £800.

I do not, however, propose to attempt to do so, because I object to the tone of his letter. It seems to me that controversy, as between people whose ideals are after all extremely similar, cannot be satisfactorily carried on in the tone which Mr. Hewlett adopts. Phrases such as 'lightning cartoonist', 'dashing article', 'amiable dream', 'I don't suppose Mr. Bennett has a notion', 'stoop from his high politics', 'too airy by half', 'perhaps he will take the trouble to consider', etc., etc., are in my opinion out of place in an argument between serious persons.

If Mr. Hewlett considers me to be a serious person, his letter is indefensible in manner. If he does not, I have nothing to say. Long ago I determined that I would decline controversy from which the elements of fundamental politeness were absent, unless public considerations forced me to take it up.

Arnold Bennett

STOKE / MS. / 65
(*To Hugh Walpole*)

80, Piccadilly
22–7–18

My dear Hughie,

Your hopes were fully justified by the 1st night, which according to all accounts was a very great success. But as to the future, God alone knoweth. However, so far so good. I hope you are getting better & that you are keeping in good spirits. I am not at all well; but I don't care, somehow. In spite of the fact that the play is off my chest, I am still very busy. Have no time even to correct proofs of my books, of which there will be three in the autumn. The weather is damnable, especially when one has neither car nor taxi. I read ¼ of *Nicholas Nickleby* yesterday

64. Maurice Hewlett (1861–1923), the author, wrote to the *Daily News* to protest against Bennett's article 'The Embargo *v.* the Gun', which appeared on the 16th. The article considered the arguments against a league of nations and rejected them. The view that since the Allies were already a league and could not stop the war and hence would not be able to keep the peace was hardly worth taking seriously; for the present league was specifically a war-making enterprise. The view that a new league would consist of rival factions, Central Powers *v.* Allies, did not take into account the fact that the Central Powers would be crushed and that most of the Central Powers were at present reluctant instruments of Prussia and would not be later. And if Prussia chose to remain outside the new league, and chose to re-arm, the league could defeat her by embargo. 'As a method of subduing an enemy the gun is an extremely clumsy, barbaric, and ineffective weapon compared with the moral and economic embargo.'

because I had no brain left. It wasn't so bad in its crude, posterish way. Anyhow, it could be read. House full of people. I met a Staff officer in the train this morn who asked after you. He once dined at Comarques when you were there. He said he should never forget you & me pulling one another's legs. Tut tut!

Thine ever, A. B.

The postcard of Polperro is very appetising. A. B.

HEPBURN / TR. / 66
(*To the War Office*)

80, Piccadilly
August 26th 1918

[no salutation]

I have pleasure in stating that Mr. T. S. Eliot (whom I understand to be a candidate for a commission in the Quartermasters or Interpreters Corps) has an intimate knowledge of the French language. Also that he is a writer of distinguished merit, for whose work personally I have a great admiration. I may mention that it was my admiration for Mr. Eliot's work which led to my acquaintance with him, and not vice versa.

Arnold Bennett

HILL / MS. / 67
(*To Gregory Hill*)

Comarques
1st Sept 1918

My dear Gregory,

Your letter is full of sagacity. Walpole's best book is *Mr. Perrin and Mr. Traill*. Much better than *Fortitude*. Walpole is a great friend of mine; but he is certainly not improving. Are you aware that *Love & Mr. L* is about 20 years old? Strange you had not read it before! Yes, the war news is all right. The police strike has at any rate done 2 good things. It has got Edward Henry out of the Police Force & it has got General Macready

65. *The Title* was Bennett's last considerable theatrical success.
Walpole lived at Polperro from 1913 to 1921.

66. T. S. Eliot (1888–1965) published his first volume of poetry the preceding year. In the *Journal* in December 1917, Bennett wrote: 'Poetry recital at Mrs. Colefax's. . . . The best thing for me was "Hippopotamus" by T. S. Eliot. Had I been the house, this would have brought the house down.'

out of the army. I met Macready at the Front in 1915, & I saw him again at the War Office on my business a few weeks ago. He is the personification of the old gang, & must have been a tremendous obstructive force as A. G. I could see at once from his face & demeanour that he had learnt nothing in 3 years, and was determined to learn nothing. The gang system in the British Army has certainly prolonged this war by about a year, cost about a million casualties, & about a 1000 millions £. So much for that. Do you read the *Sunday Times*? It is a poor paper, but has great military articles by Spenser Wilkinson, one of the foremost European authorities. This man does not in the least hide his notions about the running of the British Army by the old cavalry crew at the War Office. I am never in Paris, & don't want to go. When you get your Blighty leave I hope you will let me know. Lord Rothermere is a hopeless pessimist. Nice chap, but thoroughly biassed on the war. On the 17th July last he bet me £25 to my £50 that the war would still be on on the 31st Dec 1920! So you can imagine! He is going to lose that £25. He wanted to bet £250, but I seldom gamble, & when I do it is not in hundreds. I *don't* think. Such is life. Look here, if I can do anything about your commission, let me know. I know Macpherson, J. Cowans, and R. Brade, than whom there are no greater mandarins in the W.O.

Marguerite joins with me in very best wishes.

Yours, Arnold Bennett

HERZOG / MS. / 68
(*To Elsie Herzog*)

Comarques
7 Sept 1918

Dear Friend,

I have been intending for about 3 months to tell you that J. C. Squire *is* Solomon Eagle, & to thank you for what you did

67. H. G. Wells's *Love and Mr. Lewisham* was published in 1900.

Sir Edward Henry (1850–1931) was Commissioner of the Metropolitan Police, and resigned when he failed to prevent the police strike. Sir Nevil Macready (1862–1946) was Adjutant-General to the Forces, 1916–18. Spenser Wilkinson (1853–1937) was Chichele Professor of Military History at Oxford. Ian Macpherson (First Baron Strathcarron, 1880–1937) was Under-Secretary for War, 1916–18. General Sir John Steven Cowans (1862–1921) was General of the Forces, War Office, 1912–19. Reginald Brade (1864–1933) was Secretary at the War Office, 1914–20.

about Ben Nicholson. That young man's mother died rather suddenly not long since. She had Spanish influenza & did not recover from it. She smoked a cigarette and went away. She was a good painter; & a good friend of mine & of many other people—chiefly of her husband's. I have been too busy & important to write. Also ill, as a result: gastro-enteritis, the usual thing. Having lived on the edge of a collapse for 3 weeks, I am now going for a holiday with Marguerite for a fortnight. In my Ministry I have led a bureaucratic life & acquired the most marvellous material for a book. I don't reckon I have done anything but establish order. Nevertheless I hear that I am about to be promoted to a still higher grade of autocratic departmentalism. The fact is, my minister adores me. I may inform you that *The Roll-Call* is a much better book than *The Pretty Lady*. The latter is too brilliant. No really first-class book is ever glittering. With regard to verse, I am going to acquire & run a quarterly started by one Frank Rutter, *Art & Letters*. He cannot keep it up. You have an American poet, T. S. Eliot. I was so struck by his work that I made his acquaintance. He came to see me, & I was well content. I should like to see some of the women's war-work in New York & Chicago. There is a vast amount of genuine work done in England, but the female artistic snobs are terrible here. I mean to be still more sarcastic about them later on. They are at every function. I was at the first night of the Russian ballet on Thursday. They were all there; I knew they would be: headed by Lady Cunard. Yet I believe they all believe they are seriously helping the war along. I doubt if any of them do surgical dressing. I was rather startled the other day by the reception given to certain articles of mine that (without my knowledge or consent) were cabled over to the *N.Y. Times*. Comment by me would be inept. I thought of writing to Lane Allen to reason with him about his inelegant protest & to tell him that in England we had nothing to learn from any part of the earth about the business of sticking-to-it. But I refrained. George still writes me excellent letters in the right spirit. Best wishes to all of you from us both.

Yours sincerely, Arnold Bennett

Your typewriting has immensely improved. A. B.

68. Solomon Eagle was J. C. Squire's pseudonym for his weekly article on 'Books in General' in the *New Statesman*.

STOKE / MS. / 69
(*To Hugh Walpole*)

Walton Park Hotel
Clevedon
Somerset
19.9.18.

My dear Hughie,

Thanks for the glimpse. I return it. A thoughtful act on your part. Remember me to J.C.

Recovery slow.

Weather appalling.

But I don't care.

Have you read Dolly Richardson's *Backwater*? If not, do. It is a book. Our loves.

Yours, A. B.

BERG / MS. / 70
(*To J. C. Squire*)

80, Piccadilly
29–9–18

My dear Squire,

This is a very good number. The Wells review seems most just, but I haven't yet finished the book. I foresee difficulties in my relations with the *N.S.* I have only been at the Ministry of Information five months, and have risen to be the head of it, with supreme authority over all departments, under Beaverbrook, who leaves decisions to me. You will understand that the work is terrific. I mind that less than the responsibility. Of course I am not cut out for the job by nature at all. I can only keep my head. It is my fatal gift for inspiring confidence & never saying anything that lands me into these messes. I am

---

Bennett became Director of Propaganda in September.

On Frank Rutter and *Art and Letters* see Vol. I, pp. 265–6, and below, pp. 71–2.

Lady Cunard was the wife of Sir Bache Cunard (d. 1925).

In the New York *Times* on 14 July and 4 August and also apparently on 21 July appeared articles by Bennett that took the line that the Allies had failed to respond adequately to German peace overtures. Several persons, among them the author James Lane Allen (1849–1925), wrote, letters to the editors accusing him of being an instrument of German policy.

69. Bennett was at Clevedon from 10 to 26 September.

Walpole first met Joseph Conrad in January 1918. Earlier he had written a small book on him. Dorothy Richardson (d. 1957) published *Backwater* in 1916.

not yet sure whether I can continue to turn out the Sardonyx stuff but anyhow I will begin for the next issue. I have sworn on oath never to work on Sundays.

The funniest thing is that at the end of the year I shall have the distribution of honours to the staff in my hands! And I think every damn one of them has been to see my play.

About Turkish Baths I haven't yet seen Masterman.

Yours, A. B.

BEAVERBROOK / MS. / 71
(*To Lord Beaverbrook*)

Ministry of Information
6–10–18

My dear Max,

American journalists

I have arranged as follows with Sims:—

2nd party. Returns to U.S.A. on the 20th.

3rd party (*religious*). Will go to France on 25th & will be kept there till Dec 9th.

4th party. Will be out of Glasgow by 20th instant & between then & Dec 2nd will be kept busy with a very full programme in England. Shipped to France Dec 2nd & kept there till 17th.

South Africans. Leave here 3rd week of this month.

This is the best that can be done to keep American journalists out of our elections. It assumes Dec 7th as the fatal date.

Sims cables New York today to suspend further departures for at least 3 weeks; so that in practice nobody will arrive till after Christmas. And by that time the capitalist regime may be at an end.

We have hitherto been doing our best to keep American editors as much as possible off the French & American fronts, the argument being that we are paying for them to see *our* Front. They have, however, seen something of the French & American Fronts, & we find that they are so disgusted with the attitude towards them of the French & American Fronts, & so delighted with the attitude of our Front, that future parties will

70. The new Wells book was *The Soul of a Bishop*.

After 17 August 1918 'Sardonyx' appeared irregularly in the *New Statesman*, and the 'Observations' were often made by 'Onyx'. In the Chronology, Vol. I, p. xix, Bennett is identified as 'Onyx', but he was not.

be *encouraged* by us to see all they want of the French and American Fronts. It amounts to the finest propaganda for us.

You will receive from Hatchards a list of the unobtainable Wells books, & you can then advertise for them.

Kindest regards to Lady Beaverbrook.

Thine, A. B.

ROSS / TS. / 72
(*To Alexander Ross*)

80, Piccadilly
7.10.18.

Dear Mr. Alec Ross,

Robbie & I dined together on Friday night. I had to go to Brighton on business on Saturday, & not until this afternoon at 4 o'clock had I the slightest idea that anything had happened to him. I need not talk to *you* about the shock. I think that Meiklejohn & I were Robbie's greatest friends at the Reform. I cannot say anything. I do beg of you not to ask me to go to the funeral. I could not stand it. Please accept my most profound sympathies & give them also to his sister & niece, whom I know slightly. Many people in London will have been desolated today.

Yours sincerely, Arnold Bennett

YALE / T.C.C. / 73
(*To Osbert Sitwell*)

[80, Piccadilly]
October 12th, 1918

Dear Osbert Sitwell,

I could not talk to you on Thursday night. I had been expecting to hear from you for a long time, and I had made arrangements, as you know, that you should see Mr. Pinker and that he

71. Sims—Brigadier-General R. F. Manley (1878–1951); he was Controller of Personal Propaganda.

The 'coupon' election in December was an overwhelming triumph for the continuation of the Coalition government. Nearly all the Asquith liberals lost their seats.

72. Alexander G. Ross (d. 1927) was one of Robert's two older brothers. He was a partner in the bill-broking firm of Allen, Harvey and Ross. Robert Ross died in his sleep on 5 October. (Sir) Roderick Sinclair Meiklejohn (1876–1962) was private secretary to Asquith for some years.

should see to the business side of the affair. You will remember that I told you very clearly that in my opinion the next number ought to come out not later than the end of October. This is quite impossible now. In fact I doubt whether now you could get anything satisfactory out before Christmas. A periodical, even a quarterly, needs a great deal of time and attention, and absolute promptitude is essential. The lack of promptness has ruined many quarterlies. I think therefore that the matter should be allowed to drop, or that the present proprietor should be persuaded to continue for the present. I have less hesitation in suggesting this as I know you are very busy indeed with political matters.

Yours sincerely, [Arnold Bennett]

BEAVERBROOK / MS. / 74
(*To Lord Beaverbrook*)

80, Piccadilly
19–10–18

My dear Max,

Holt gave me your message this morning. He said you hadn't come to a decision, but I naturally assume that you *have* come to a decision. I am only sorry about your health, & hope that an operation, if you have one, will put you quite right. Doctor's advice about resigning makes little impression on me, though doubtless genuine enough. I lay any money that, doctors or no doctors, if you resign you will be even more deeply occupied with politics than you would have been had you remained Minister. This is my reading of the affair.

If you resign, I do. I came into the show through you originally, and most assuredly no one but you would have got me to assume the directorship. I don't see myself director under anybody else—Northcliffe, for instance! You told me to use my own policy, so long as I kept a decent balance between your views and mine. No other Minister would have said as much. I would stick to the show (assuming I was asked to do so) if I

73. Early in September Bennett promised Osbert Sitwell (1892–1969) to purchase Frank Rutter's *Art and Letters* (see above, pp. 68–9) and to back it for Sitwell and others. The venture fell through and Rutter continued with the journal until 1920. Bennett was aware that Sitwell had several interests apart from poetry. See further, Vol. I, pp. 265–6.

thought the Ministry would be given a fair chance of being an efficient machine. But I don't think so. I know perfectly well, and all the responsible heads of departments know, that the hand of every other Ministry is against it. This of course is notorious. I quite believe you when you say that Bonar Law is benevolent. He no doubt is, but his reasons are purely personal. And Bonar Law is not the Treasury. The Treasury is unquestionably hostile, despite anything that you and Needham may say. The explanation of the general hostility is plain. That there ought to be a Ministry of Information is certain; there ought to have been one much earlier. But the belief widely exists that the Ministry was brought into being for the sake of the Minister, and not vice-versa. That is the general belief. It may be quite wrong, but it is the origin of the hostility which does and must impair the efficiency of the machine. I don't think for a moment that I can be of much use in the Ministry without you, and I am quite sure that I can do vastly more to push my ideas outside the Ministry than in it. I needn't tell you it is very trying to me not to be at liberty to write articles at this period when there is so much scope for a journalist, and when I am being implored to write articles.

If you are going to be anyhow visible on Monday, you had better ask me to come along & we will discuss. In the meantime I beseech you to take care of yourself.

Thine, A. B.

ARKANSAS / MS. / 75
(*To Frank Swinnerton*)

80, Piccadilly
21–10–18

My dear Henry,

I should have read *S. & H.* earlier, despite *J. & P.*, but I couldn't get the book off Marguerite. Conjugal unpleasantness

74. Beaverbrook threatened several times to resign his post as Minister of Information on account of dissatisfaction with the attitude of the Foreign Office towards his work. He was now ill, and did resign on 21 October. Holt—presumably Major A. P. Holt, one of Beaverbrook's private secretaries. Northcliffe was Director of Propaganda in Enemy Countries at this time. Bonar Law (1858–1923) was Chancellor of the Exchequer. (Sir) Raymond Needham, a friend of Bennett's, was Beaverbrook's other private secretary. For other references to Needham see Vols. I and II.

became so acute on the point that I was obliged to buy a second copy. I think this book shows marked development on the part of the author. There are about 150 pp. as good as the very best few pages of *On the Staircase*, & some much better. (I leave out *Nocturne*, because it was a long short story and easier to do.) The plot is very happily worked out, & the young women and men jolly well done. In fact it is an *individual contribution*; and the emotional quality is at least equal to the invention. The whole thing decidedly more mature. I think you have a 'down' on Beckwith, and though all the details you give are true, you choose the details rather unfairly, & your generalisations from *your* details are too drastic. This is the only important fault, in my opinion, but it *is* important. I think chaps. 20, 21, 22 & 23 are not emotionally equal to the rest, but the last chapter bucks up all right. I fail to see the point of the Epilogue. The writing is often not so elegant as in *Nocturne*, especially in the early part. Look, e.g., at the top of p. 62, where you have 'a piece of nougat', 'a piece of reckless greediness' and 'a piece of justice', all in a few lines. I could quote other examples. I don't want to insist unduly on such trifles, & I fully admit that a style must be human, i.e. erring; or it would be intolerable.

This is about all. I gather Hughie's rev. is less favourable of the book than mine. He is merely wrong. You have good reason to be well satisfied with the production, which is easily your best.

Thine, A. B.

BEAVERBROOK / MS. / 76
(*To Lord Beaverbrook*)

Ministry of Information
24–10–18

My dear Max,

Very many thanks for your note. I hear you may have an operation tomorrow. Well, I hope the best from it.

I have come to an arrangement with Sims about the P.P. Dept. Whether it can be carried out is another matter. But he is agreeable to it, & we arrived at it without the slightest friction.

75. Swinnerton's novel *Shops and Houses* was published in October. *On the Staircase* appeared in 1914. *J. & P.* is unidentified.

I had an interview with Charlie today about the reduction of his department. He was very gloomy & upset & had a bad cold —perhaps flu. But he accepts the situation.

You won't catch me working under Arthur James, unless I had a clear charter to run the show. I am opposed to him in nearly everything, & I strongly object to both his ideals & his mentality. A much better arrangement would be to put the show under Fisher—is not propaganda education?—a man of modern ideas with whom it would be possible to work.

Very best wishes,
& regrets I couldn't write a book for you tonight,
Thine, A. B.

BEAVERBROOK / MS. / 77
(*To Lord Beaverbrook*)

80, Piccadilly
25–10–18

My dear Max,

In further reference to your letter of yesterday, it only occurred to me this morning that the 'considerable opposition' which you mention might be to myself. As such opposition, in view of my lurid past, would be very natural, it is surprising that I never thought of myself as a stumbling-block until after the lapse of 14 hours!

If this is so, I imagine that you will be much more free to act with my resignation in your hands. Please therefore accept this letter as my tender of resignation, and use it exactly as you like. You may believe me when I affirm that I have not the very faintest desire to remain in the Ministry after your departure.

Best wishes for your body & soul,
Thine, A. B.

76. Charlie—Charles Masterman. Arthur James (1876–1959) served in the Ministry of National Service in 1917–18. H. A. L. Fisher (1865–1940) was President of the Board of Education, 1916–22.

BEAVERBROOK / TS. / 78
(*To Lord Beaverbrook*)
MINUTE PAPER

Ministry of Information
4/11/18

[no salutation]

At the present time the machinery for propaganda exists, and is working satisfactorily. The most successful propaganda, as shown by visible results, has been personal propaganda, that is to say, the arranging of visits by foreigners to this country and to the centres of British activity at and behind the Front. Such visits are now in progress, and a continuous series of them is definitely contemplated. Before a decision is taken to put an end to this form of activity, the following points deserve careful consideration.

1. The excellent results of such propaganda in promoting good relations between foreign countries and Great Britain cannot be denied. The need for it is clear. The cost of it is relatively trifling. The reasons for stopping it can therefore only be reasons having their root in domestic politics. Ought such reasons to weigh?

2. That such propaganda would be useful up to the signing of the Treaty of peace is undeniable, and the War Cabinet in sanctioning the issue of a semi-official document containing its peace terms, for the use of British propaganda agencies, has admitted this. Few people will dispute that even after the signature of the Treaty of peace there will still be an urgent need to place before the world by propaganda methods, the British point of view on the inseparable subjects of politics and commerce.

3. Much is said about the immense material advantages which American propaganda has over ours, and arguments have been advanced to show that in propaganda we could not possibly compete with the United States on anything like equal terms. I do not accept these arguments. Against enormous difficulties the Ministry of Information has made great and unmistakable progress in a very short space of time, and I have no doubt whatever that with a somewhat larger vote British propaganda on any subject would compete successfully with any propaganda in the world.

4. In view of all this, surely it is inadvisable to scrap the most important part of our propaganda machinery, or to interrupt the working of such machinery (which is elastic and can be turned to any desired purpose), unless and until the Allies mutually agree to abandon propaganda as a form of national activity. Surely to destroy or gravely impair the existing organisation at the present juncture would be to incur a very serious responsibility.

The question is not: Shall the Ministry of Information continue to exist? The question is a much larger one: Shall the already existing satisfactory working machinery of propaganda be destroyed or even stopped before it is known whether or not British propaganda has a future? The Cabinet might well decide to abrogate the Ministry of Information while continuing propaganda. In face of such a possibility, is it right or expedient or defensible for the Ministry of Information at once to render itself wholly or partly futile?

A. B.

HILL / MS. / 79
(*To Gregory Hill*)

Ministry of Information
7–11–18

My dear Gregory,

I am very sorry indeed to hear of your rheumatism. I do hope you will continue to improve. I have had some rheumatism myself, though never acute, so I can judge somewhat. I don't think your 'commission business' has the slightest importance now. The war will almost certainly be over within a week. You needn't trouble about Germany not accepting the armistice terms. If she doesn't accept instantly (but I feel sure she will) she will accept even worse terms after a short time. So many people seem incapable of believing that Germany can be humiliated to this point. But why not! When you are beaten you are beaten. It will not be the first time that Germany has been smashed—not by any means. She will lick the dust (and the boots) just like other vanquished & hopeless persons. I am now the head of this Ministry, & have command over Generals, Colonels, Majors, M.P.'s, *Bank directors*, Railway directors, millionaires, baronets, peers, & I don't know what. It is a highly responsible position but a great lark—especially giving orders to generals, as you will appreciate. In spite of the greatness of the lark, my one idea is to chuck it, and get back to my own work.

Best wishes for your recovery, & for your return speedily to civil life. And I do hope bank-clerks will form a Union, & get decent treatment for themselves at last.

Yours, Arnold Bennett

BEAVERBROOK / TS. / 80
(*To Lord Beaverbrook*)

Ministry of Information
November 13th, 1918

Dear Max,

I have made more than one application to the War Cabinet for instructions as to the future of this Ministry, but I have received no answer of any kind. Under these circumstances I resign my position here, and I shall be much obliged if you will forward my resignation to the proper quarter. I have the less hesitation in resigning as I had previously asked Needham to mention to you that I wished to leave as soon as possible, and you had expressed the opinion that this might be arranged without detriment to the Ministry.

Yours, Arnold Bennett

80. Lord Beaverbrook replied to Bennett's letter:
'My dear Arnold,

I am sorry that the War Cabinet have been so dilatory in answering your communications. Under the circumstances I think that you are perfectly right in resigning, and that you can do so without detriment to the Ministry. I will, therefore, communicate your resignation to the proper quarter.

I am sorry in a way that it is all over. My association with you in the Ministry will always be a memorable incident in my life, and I feel sure that our personal friendship will survive the mere dissolution of official ties. Just for this reason you will perhaps allow me to say something on the work that you did at the Ministry. I was much struck with the way in which you conducted the French Department. It seemed to me to show a real genius for administration. As a consequence I felt that you were the man to act as my second in command, and I praise myself by saying that I was perfectly correct in my judgement. When illness compelled me to throw up my work, and resign, I knew I was perfectly safe in leaving everything to you as Deputy Minister, and that you would do the job, quite as well, if not better, than myself. This thought saved me a lot of worry, so you will see that I owe you a real debt of gratitude.

I must thank you for the great service you have rendered to the State, at a critical period and for the way in which you sacrificed your private inclinations and interest to perform that service.

Yours faithfully, Beaverbrook'

BEAVERBROOK / MS. / 81
(*To Lord Beaverbrook*)

Ministry of Information
14–11–18

My dear Max,

I have now pieced all the tales together, & I conclude that the future of the Ministry was discussed & decided yesterday in the Cabinet without the slightest reference to the Director of Propaganda. I don't think Stuart had conspired, but I am fairly sure that Buchan had. He went there without saying a word to me, & my letters to the Cabinet asking for a decision have had no answer. Snagge showed a tendency to quarrel with Buchan; but I have smoothed that over, & they have gone through the formality of burying the hatchet (in each other's ribs). I shall stay on here for the present—chiefly because my house is closed up, & I have no other office in which to transact my own complicated private business, which will now re-open. I have of course told Buchan that I will help him all I can.

I hope you make progress.

Thine, A. B.

KEDDIE / MS. / 82
(*To E. V. Lucas*)

80, Piccadilly
22–11–18

My dear Lucas,

Pardon my frankness. This is most distinctly an idea for a play. And you have put everything into it except the play. Bits of the play have got into it, in spite of you, here and there; but I think only by accident. It is not dramatic. I wouldn't mind that. What is worse is that I think you *mean* it to be not dramatic. A lot of the dialogue is really first-class. Ditto jokes. The last scene between Kate & Herbert is masterly—in my opinion. But the basis of a play is the plot, & your plot is just the part of the work

81. (Sir) Campbell Stuart was Deputy Director of Propaganda in Enemy Countries. John Buchan, the novelist, was serving in the Ministry of Information; see also Vols. I and II for comments on him. (Sir) Harold Snagge (1872–1949), later Director of Barclay's Bank, was Secretary of the Ministry of Information.

that you have scorned. You don't care a damn about it. You regard it only as any old peg on which to hang your dialogue. In the first scene, e.g. nothing whatever happens. And indeed there is no drama till scene iii & not much then. Some of the incidents sin by excessive improbability, & some of the dialogue is very stilted—as though you had forgotten who was writing the play. The atmosphere, original & amusing, of a play is there, and if the first stages of composition had been handled in an entirely different creative spirit, something immense could have been accomplished. I repeat: pardon my frankness. If you have any more ideas as good as this, & care to impart them, do impart them, & we will perpend thereupon. But I am definitely, finally, & forever up against your attitude towards plot. And so that's that. Come & dine with me. You prefer lunches. I prefer dinners. We have had a whole series of lunches. It is now my turn. I write this in bed, waiting for my august bath.

Yours, A. B.

Play returned herewith. A. B.

BEAVERBROOK / MS. / 83
(*To Lord Beaverbrook*)

80, Piccadilly
26–11–18

My dear Max,

I am very sorry to hear today that you are in bed. You are unquestionably getting better—on that I bank!—so these brief relapses are highly unnecessary. You were in excellent form at the weekend, and I profited accordingly. The secret book really does you very high credit indeed. God knows my opinion of your powers was high; but it has raised my opinion higher. If you want to see Newman Flower here, telephone to Miss Nerney at the Ministry, or to me here, and I will arrange it. I can't get you that copy of *Paris Nights* till I go home, & I'm not

82. For earlier letters to E. V. Lucas see Vol. II. *The Sane Star* was eventually produced by the Leeds Repertory Theatre, and it was published in 1924. It was the only full-length play by Lucas to be produced.

going home just yet. The English edition is out of print, but I think I have the American edition, which is just as good.

Thine, A. B.

BEAVERBROOK / MS. / 84
(*To Lord Beaverbrook*)

80, Piccadilly
4–12–18

My dear Max,

I enclose the application form for your 2,000 shares in the London & Local Playhouses Ltd. Will you please see that the *Secretary* has the form & your cheque at once. We want money to spend. Prospects seem good.

Will you have me to lunch next Tuesday or Wednesday?

I hear you are considering a scheme for a Canadian War Memorial out at the Front, & that Mestrovic's name is mentioned as sculptor. Mestrovic is a very great man; but the general control & design of the memorial as a whole ought to be those of an architect, & the sculptor ought to take his proper place in the architectural scheme. I have seen too many memorials spoilt through entrusting to a sculptor what ought to be in the province of an architect. All sculptural memorials are essentially architectural, and the sculptor, while remaining of course supreme in the actual work of sculpture, should not be allowed to be an amateur architect. I make this intrusion on the strength of my great interest in you & in architecture & in sculpture.

I hope you are maintaining a philosophic calm during your tedious convalescence.

Thine, A. B.

83. Beaverbrook's book was *Politicians and the War*, eventually published in 1928. Letters to Winifred Nerney, Bennett's secretary, appear below. Bennett's travel book, *Paris Nights*, was published in 1913.

84. London and Local Playhouses Ltd. was formed in 1918 by Bennett, Nigel Playfair, and Alistair Tayler to run the Lyric Theatre, Hammersmith. See Vol. I, pp. 275–6, for further details.

Mestrovic—Ivan (1883–1962), the Yugoslav sculptor.

FALES, NYU / MS. / 85
(*To R. D. Blumenfeld*)

80, Piccadilly
21–12–18

Dear Blumenfeld,

Any publicity you can give to my Hammersmith Lyric Opera House scheme during the next few days in the *Express* will be appreciated by two shareholders, Max & myself. The thing opens next Tuesday afternoon.

You have been producing a great paper these days.

I hope to see you early in the New Year.

Yours sincerely, Arnold Bennett

ARKANSAS / MS. / 86
(*To Frank Swinnerton*)

80 Piccadilly
3.1.19.

My dear Henry,

Doran consulted me yesterday about his *Bookman* & about things generally. He had a scheme for getting you to go over & settle in the States. I told him I thought you would refuse, & that if you asked my advice I should certainly urge you to refuse. He also wants you to contribute criticism or personalia to the *Bookman*. I am now writing to remind you that the sum he will offer (I haven't the least idea what it is) will not be the sum he is prepared to pay. You ought to stick out for *good* terms, & you should discuss the thing with Pinker beforehand. Don't let Doran think you are ready to jump at his offer. Doran gave me the news that over 8,000 of *Nocturne* had already been sold & that he would certainly touch 10,000. He took the line that this sale was due to H.G. & me. I informed him firmly that no introductions or articles would sell 10,000 of a book that the public didn't really enjoy. It will be difficult for you to take quite the same line with him; but you can hint at it & make him understand that you know exactly where you are. I go to Comarques early tomorrow. Whether Marguerite goeth or not God alone knows. When I have found my feet there I should

85. Ralph David Blumenfeld (1864–1948) edited the *Daily Express* from 1904 to 1932. The paper was now owned by Beaverbrook.

like you to come down. Perhaps Doran too, if food difficulties can be arranged.

Yours, A. B.

MAYFIELD, SYRACUSE / A.D. / 87
(*To Grant Richards*)

[Comarques]
[about 6 January 1919]

Dear Mr. Grant Richards,

I have just seen (quoted in the *National News*) the following extract from 'Gerald Cumberland's' *A Book of Reminiscences.*

['That Arnold Bennett is almost painfully conscious of his own cleverness there is no manner of doubt. He is stupendously aware of the figure he cuts in contemporary literature. He is for ever standing outside himself and enjoying the spectacle of his own greatness, and he whispers ten times a day: "Oh, what a great boy am I!" I was once shown a series of privately printed booklets written by Bennett—booklets that he sent to his intimates at Christmas time. They consisted of extracts from his diary—a diary that, one feels, would never have been written if the de Goncourts had not lived. One self-conscious extract lingers in the mind; the spirit of it, though not the words (and perhaps not the facts), is embodied in the following: "It is 3 a.m. I have been working fourteen hours at a stretch. In these fourteen hours I have written ten thousand words. My book is finished—finished in excitement, in exaltation. Surely not even Balzac went one better than this!" ']

Assuming the quotation in the *National News* to be correct, I have to object to this paragraph. I do not want to take it too seriously, & in particular I do not want to inconvenience the publisher, but the extent to which I take it seriously will depend on Mr. Cumberland's behaviour.

In the first place, surely it is improper to quote without permission, for ordinary publication, from a privately printed book issued by the author only to intimate personal friends!

In the second place no such entry as that given by Mr.

86. George Doran bought the *Bookman* (New York) from Dodd, Mead in 1918. Swinnerton wrote a column for the journal under the pseudonym 'Simon Pure', but at a distance.

Cumberland is to be found in either of the booklets to which he refers. The only entry which he could have had in mind runs as follows:—

'I finished *Anna of the Five Towns* this morning at 2.45 a.m., after seventeen hours continuous work, save for meals, on the last five thousand words. I was very pleased with it.'

I leave you to judge whether Mr. Cumberland's version of what I wrote is other than a maliciously fabricated and utterly misleading perversion, consciously or unconsciously designed to fit in with his remarks on me.

I suggest that Mr. Cumberland should write a letter (to be approved by me) to the *Times Literary Supplement* expressing his regret for having quoted from a privately printed book without permission, and admitting that his quotation, in addition to being verbally and factually quite inaccurate, was a gross perversion (partly mere invention) of the spirit of what I wrote; and that in default of the *Times Literary Supplement* publishing the letter as correspondence it should be published as an advertisement under the heading 'An Apology'.

I suggest further that no further copies of Mr. Cumberland's book should be issued until printed slips have been affixed, to the following effect: 'The author regrets that the whole reference to Mr. Arnold Bennett's private journal on pp. [70-71] is inaccurate and utterly misleading.'

I write to you as I do not know Mr. Cumberland's real name nor his address, and also because I think that by doing so I may save trouble for both of us.

Best Wishes for the New Year,

Yours sincerely, [Arnold Bennett]

MAYFIELD, SYRACUSE / A.D. / 88
(*To Gerald Cumberland*)

[Comarques]
[about 12 January 1919]

Dear Sir,

In your letter to Messrs. Grant Richards you write: 'I cannot understand why any public character of Mr. Arnold Bennett's

87. For an earlier letter to the publisher Grant Richards see Vol. II. Gerald Cumberland was the pseudonym of the critic and author Charles Frederick

eminence should object to a caricature of himself, however clumsily done, being placed in full view of the public.'

I do not object to a caricature of myself. I have been caricatured as much as most writers and I have never objected.

What I object to is the attempt to confirm the truth of a portrait admittedly malicious by means of spurious documentary evidence falsely attributed to my own pen.

Yours truly, [Arnold Bennett]

MAYFIELD, SYRACUSE / A.D. / 89
(*To the editor of the* TIMES LITERARY SUPPLEMENT)

[Comarques]
[about 20 January 1919]

Sir,

I hope you will allow me to mention in the chief literary organ a matter which, though personal, involves questions of principle that may be of interest to the reading public at large.

In his book *Set Down in Malice* Mr. Gerald Cumberland, whom I once met in a concert hall for three minutes, purports to quote an extract from a journal of mine privately printed for a few intimate friends. He did not ask my permission to quote and I do not know from whom he obtained a sight of the booklet. He introduces his extract with these words: 'one self-conscious extract lingers in the mind; the spirit of it, though not the words (and perhaps not the facts) is embodied in the following.' Mr. Cumberland's version of the extract ends thus: 'My book is finished—finished in excitement, in exaltation. Surely not even Balzac went one better than this!' If I had presented such sentences to my friends, or even written them solely for my own eye, the fact would give some confirmation of the admittedly malicious portrait of me drawn by Mr. Cumberland. But I did not write them, nor anything in any way resembling them. They are totally and absolutely the invention of Mr. Gerald

---

Kenyon (1879–1926). His book, whose main title was *Set Down in Malice*, was reviewed in the *National News* on 5 January. The exact journal passage quoted by Bennett appears in *Things Which Have Interested Me*, Burslem, 1907, the second of three privately printed booklets. See Vol. II for other references to these booklets and for comments on the origin of Bennett's journal.

Cumberland, who moreover is both verbally and factually wrong in his version of the opening of the extract.

The questions of principle involved are these:—Is an author justified in quoting publicly from a privately-printed book without permission? Is a critic justified in attempting to convict an author out of his own mouth by inventing documentary evidence and attributing it to the author himself?

Mr. Cumberland puts forward the excuse (a) that he wrote his book in Greece and Serbia and (b) that he had not seen my booklet for eight years.

Mr. Cumberland and his publishers, Messrs. Grant Richards & Co., have been good enough to agree to insert a corrective slip into all copies of *Set Down in Malice* not yet sold.

Yours faithfully, [Arnold Bennett]

STOKE / MS. / 90
(*To Hugh Walpole*)

Comarques
22–1–19

My dear Hughie,

It appeareth to me that you have attempted the impossible in *The Secret City*. Therefore be not surprised if I think you have not achieved the same. I am of course judging the book by the highest standards. I do not see how even Joseph Conrad or Jesus Christ himself could hope to deal with recent events concerning a land and people with whom he had an acquaintance of only 2 or 3 years, and bring the thing off satisfactorily on the topmost emotional plane. These feats simply are not done. (I am aware of your defence in the first section.) You may say that you did it in *The Dark Forest*, but that book was much less ambitious & comprehensive. Further, you have deliberately added to your difficulties by thinking of a plot (the Markovitch-Semyonov idea) which is of the very highest psychological interest but also fantastically ticklish to handle convincingly. How you have come out of the affair alive I'm hanged if I know. But that you have done so is to your credit as a professional man. Of course a great deal of the material is very interesting. But I reckon that when you have run up against the

89. The letter was printed with negligible changes in the *Times Literary Supplement* on 30 January.

impossible you have had to get clear of the problem by slanting off into something akin to conventionality. This is my view, and, dash it, you have got to know that my view exists, whether you respect it or not. Apropos of your last book, I indicted you about some of the writing thereof. There are a number of grammatical errors (not printer's slips) in this book. What do I care about grammar? Great men have failed to understand it. Still, there is such a thing. Also, loose writing exists in the book. Do you or do you not defend the top of p. 32 down to the end of the 4th line? If you do, I say no more on the point of loose writing. This letter has a brutal air after your noble epistle which I have this moment received & which delighteth me much. But seeing that I am a brute I am determined to *be* one. So there you are. Marguerite has not yet finished *The Roll-Call.* When she has she will read *The S.C.* & will probably differ from her spouse. She sends her affection.

Thine, A. B.

I am delighted about the sales.

U.C. / T.C.C. / 91
(*To Roger Fry*)

17 Berkeley Street, W.1.
18th February 1919

Dear Fry,

Many thanks. By this time you will have received my excuses. Knowing your Machiavellian nature I of course assumed a plot. (I don't think!)

I am very sorry to hear about Wolfe. You may rely on me for £20, and in any similar case you may rely on me.

You have been misinformed, I think, about my attitude towards your designs. I certainly did not like the sketches which were shown to me. I thought them too realistic. At the same interview I was told that the commission had been given to Ricketts. (This of course is strictly private.) I had previously been asked whether I objected to Ricketts, and had replied that I did not, but that I expected something more original from you.

90. Both *The Secret City* and *The Roll-Call* were published in January 1919.

I do not know yet whether or not I have got a flat, but I have my eye on a very good one. However, all my plans have been altered, and I have had to give up the scheme of having offices separate from our flat. The thing cannot be done. I hope to come up and see you quite soon. You will probably be in bed, but I can get you up.

Yours sincerely, [Arnold Bennett]

ILLINOIS / MS. / 92
(*To H. G. Wells*)

17 Berkeley Street
22–2–19

My dear H.G.,

I've been looking for you for days. So has all the Reform Club. I have been 'approached' with a request to 'approach' you on the matter of the correspondence between you & Henry James apropos of *Boon*. Admirers & fanatics of H.J. regard his letters in this affair as the greatest statement of his artistic 'case' that he ever gave. In your place, if it pleased them, I would let them print the whole thing, without suppressing a phrase; and in fact there is only one short phrase (about 'bad manners') to which any objection could be taken. If they printed his letters (with the above-indicated suppression), and your replies, the matter would be perfect. Can't you agree to this, and content the vast H.J. world?

Yours, A. B.

91. The Bennetts used Mexborough House, 17 Berkeley Street, when they visited London together during these months.

Edward Wolfe the artist (1896–) was a protégé of Fry's. He was ill with pneumonia.

On Charles Ricketts see Vol. I, pp. 387–8.

92. Wells made a devastating attack on James in his novel *Boon* in 1914, and there followed an exchange of letters in which James exhibited wounded dignity and Wells some repentance. Part of the exchange appeared in Percy Lubbock's edition of James's *Letters* in 1920, and a larger history of the affair in *Henry James and H. G. Wells*, edited by Leon Edel and Gordon Ray in 1958. How vast the H. J. world has grown since 1919 is indicated in the editorial bias of the Edel–Ray book. Bennett did not share this bias, and he wrote of the *Letters* when they appeared: 'I think they are taken too solemnly and that the editor has taken them too piously. . . . Very many of the letters are admirable, but very many of them grate on the sensibility by reason of the tone of ecstatic friendship, and of the ecstatic appreciation of the work of friends, which abound in them.'

BEAVERBROOK / TS. / 93
(*To Lord Beaverbrook*)

[Comarques]
March 3rd, 1919

My dear Max,

In reply to his letter, I have written to your secretary that I will lunch with you on Thursday at 1.30 if that suits.

For a man with two telephones in his room you are singularly difficult to get at. I have tried to reach your abode on the 'phone nearly every day when I have been in London, but have only succeeded in establishing communication *once*, when the report was quite favourable. I am very glad indeed that you have come well out of the second operation and I hope there won't be a third.

In addition to the James Douglas affair, I want to discuss with you the affair of the Hammersmith Theatre lease. The facts are as follows. Will my chief financial adviser reflect upon them and advise me?

Alderson Horne, a friend of Nigel Playfair's, bought the lease of the theatre and promised to let it to us for 7 years at £700 a year. Lady Chetwynd, another friend of the excellent Nigel, promised to guarantee the rent for the 7 years. Both these alleged friends entirely let us down. Lady Chetwynd took to her bed and refused any guarantee. Horne took umbrage (mysteriously), and refused to let the theatre at £700. As we were in possession and actually playing, he held us to ransom for £1,000 a year, and our solicitors, Langton and Passmore (the chief theatrical solicitors), could do nothing with him. More than that, he insisted on a personal guarantee. I gave it. However, as soon as the lease was signed I sent a diplomatic intermediary to Horne to excite his dulled conscience, with the result that Horne now very decently offers to sell the superior lease at the price he gave for it. I am determined to buy this lease, either for myself or for the Company, but the matter has to be concluded immediately or the capricious gentleman may draw back.

The figures run thus:—

Ground rent:	£425
Length of superior lease:	60 years
Price paid by Horne:	£3,900

If I don't get hold of the lease Horne will assuredly sell it to one of the theatrical rings, who, I think, would give him an appreciable profit.

It seems to me that Horne's original offer to let to the Company at £700 was rather quixotic. I don't perceive how he could pay the ground rent and provide for a sinking fund and for interest on his capital, all out of £700.

There are three ways of getting the lease:

1. I could buy it.
2. The Company could call up more capital and buy it.
3. Debentures could be issued to buy it, and the shareholders would be bullied into taking them up.

I don't want to buy it, but my objection to being done in the eye is such that I would buy it if 2 and 3 proved unsuitable.

Advise me between 2 and 3.

The freehold could be bought for less than £12,000.

I consider the theatre as cheap at even £1,000 a year, seeing that the bars and programmes are actually bringing in more than that on a quarterly contract with a first-class firm.

As regards the enterprise generally, I have now, to my intense chagrin, become passionately interested in it. I have a directors' meeting every week, and I personally supervise the whole of the management both artistic and financial. Vedrenne of the Royalty Theatre, who is Chairman of the West End Managers Association, has put all his experience absolutely at my disposal, and I am on the way to become an expert.

Touching the productions:—

1. *Make Believe* played to more money than any small suburban theatre with 5/- stalls has the right to hope for; namely £3,770 in four weeks and two days. The production, however, had to be done in a tremendous hurry and therefore cost a lot extra on that account, and moreover money was wasted. Nigel is not powerful in finance, and I had not then begun to supervise. It barely covered expenses. It was nevertheless a great popular success, and a considerable artistic success—though rough in many details.

2. *The Younger Generation* and *The Maid turned Mistress* was an unmitigated artistic success. Financially it was killed by the Tube strike.

3. *Abraham Lincoln* is the best artistic success of all, and in spite of the 'flu, which is ravaging theatres, it is making money.

The theatre had been closed for over a year, and before that it had a bad melodramatic reputation. We have undoubtedly put it on the map, and unless the wild sensationalism of the *Daily Express*, the *Daily Sketch* and the *Daily Mirror* plunges this millionaire-ridden country into anarchy, we have an excellent chance of accomplishing something permanent and valuable. The artistic credit will be Nigel's. The credit on the practical side will be mine and Alistair Tayler's (the other director). The press has been exceedingly kind on the whole, and already our prestige is unquestionable. Our prestige is indeed such that we have been invited to take sole charge of the Shakespeare Memorial Week at Stratford-on-Avon.

Thine, Arnold Bennett

HERZOG / MS. / 94
(*To Paul Herzog*)

Comarques
8–3–19

My dear Herzog,

What am I to say to you? And what are the feelings of your young son? Professional users of words have a special duty of decency to say little on these occasions. I am very sorry. The news was a great shock to me. You & the boy have all my sympathies. I should like to hear something from you, if you feel inclined to write. It was touching of her to remember that I wear a fob, & I am glad to have the memento.

Always yours sincerely, Arnold Bennett

93. A. P. Horne, a former actor, was secretary and treasurer of the St. James's Theatre for some years under Sir George Alexander, and he became business manager of the Lyric Hammersmith. Alistair (Duff) Tayler (d. 1935) was a good friend of Bennett's. He was a person of private means. He co-authored and edited several books on Scottish history with his sister.

On J. E. Vedrenne see Vols. I and II. *Make Believe*, by A. A. Milne, was the first production at the Lyric Hammersmith. *The Younger Generation*, by Stanley Houghton, and *The Maid Turned Mistress*, an operetta by Pergolesi, formed a double bill. John Drinkwater's *Abraham Lincoln* established the success of the theatre.

94. On Paul Herzog see Vol. II, p. 293. Mrs. Herzog died of cancer on 7 February.

LANE / TS. / 95
(*To John Lane*)

Comarques
March 17th, 1919

My dear Lane,

I do not know Dell personally, but I have come to the conclusion that he is an extremely able and well informed man, if somewhat wrong-headed. I thoroughly agree with his diagnosis of the bad elements in French life which he gives to you in his proposal for a book, and I feel pretty sure that he would write an excellent book on the lines indicated. I also think that such a book ought to be written.

The only objection is Dell's reputation. The attitude which got him into trouble during the war was in my opinion perverse. He defended himself afterwards with great skill and scored many points off his opponents, but in various important ways I think he was wrong, not only in his general judgment but in his judgment of individuals. He was undoubtedly wrong, for instance, about Caillaux.

The question of the disadvantage of Dell's name is one which only you can decide, and you are just as good a judge of it as anybody else.

We are very glad to hear that you are making such a fine recovery. I should imagine that Weston is more agreeable in the off-season than in the season.

My wife joins with me in kindest regards to you both.

Yours sincerely, Arnold Bennett

P.S. I return Dell's letter. A. B.

BEAVERBROOK / TS. / 96
(*To Lord Beaverbrook*)

Comarques
March 20th, 1919

My dear Max,

I hope you are going on all right. I am also hoping to have an answer to my last letter.

95. Robert Dell was the author of several books on social and political affairs. Lane published the book *My Second Country* in 1920. Of J. M. A. Caillaux (1863–1944) Bennett wrote in 1917: 'I doubt whether there exists in European statesmanship today another man so completely bereft of common sense as Caillaux.'

Your Sidney Dark is a terrible fellow. He always was. I have known his work for twenty years or so, and it was invariably incompetent. Why he should have been sent to Paris to represent the *Express* at such an important time is one of the mysteries of up-to-date journalism. I know nothing of the inside circumstances in Paris, and I am quite willing to believe that Wilson is using Paris for purposes of American politics, but whatever his motives, his position is right and the only position that has the slightest chance of countering the idiotic notions of France and Italy and 'Poland'. Further, even admitting that a case could be made out for Dark's attitude, he might at any rate express his point of view with some force and distinction. He achieves neither. However, I could have foretold what he would do.

I don't know him.

He almost always praises my books.

Lastly, why did you let the *Express* attribute the West Leyton result to public resentment against the No Returns order? It was too funny.

I offer these remarks out of fatherly interest in your paper. I also told Blumenfeld I would criticise it whenever I felt inclined.

Thine, A. B.

P.S. Hulton has been very nice and agrees to come in, re Hammersmith. A. B.

MAYFIELD, SYRACUSE / A.D. / 97
(*To the editor of* THE TIMES)

[? 17 Berkeley Street]
[about 5 April 1919]

Sir,

Mr. Justice Darling in his judgment, so charmingly ornamented with recondite historical allusions, said 'To my mind we have heard a great deal too much of what was in the articles'. Now to my mind we had not heard enough. With deference to the learned and literary judge, I submit that the point lay in the contents of the articles. And as my name was vainly tossed about

96. Sidney Dark (1874–1947) was special correspondent for the *Daily Express* at the Paris Peace Congress. He had been associated with the *Express* since 1902.

The West Leyton by-election was a stunning reversal after the Coalition triumph in the General Election in December.

Hulton—presumably Sir Edward (1869–1925), newspaper proprietor.

quite a good deal during the trial I wish to state that the article which I wrote for Sir Hedley Le Bas contained no attack of any kind on Mr. Lloyd George. Indeed it made only a passing reference to this gifted man. It was nothing but the outline of a legislative programme for the Liberal Party, and it certainly did not entirely please some of the high lights of the Liberal Party. When I wrote it I had not the slightest idea that it was to be used as an advertisement. (Nor, I think, had Sir Hedley Le Bas.) But if Sir Hedley had told me that he intended to pay for the insertion of the article as an advertisement I should have made no objection at all. The more any news about the future of Liberalism is advertised the more I shall be pleased. The Government itself is the greatest political advertiser in existence. No private organisation has or could rival its matchless skill in the use of both open and disguised advertisement. And I can perceive in the ethics of journalism no reason why the Government should have a monopoly of this mighty instrument.

[Arnold Bennett]

TEXAS / TS. / 98
(*To Lillah McCarthy*)

Comarques
April 10th, 1919

My dear Lillah,

I hate to praise star-actresses. They get too much praise as a rule, especially when they are beautiful. I must, however, say that your performance wholly, entirely, completely, and rather more than completely, fulfils my expectations. It is a very great and very finished performance. Don't go and tinker with it. Let this be clearly understood henceforward between us. Whatever

97. The letter was printed with a few changes in *The Times* on 7 April 1919. Justice Darling (Charles John Darling, 1852–1931) presided over a suit for libel brought by the publisher and publicist Sir Hedley Le Bas (1868–1926) against Associated Newspapers. Le Bas, who had stood as a Liberal candidate in 1914, founded the Westminster News Agency in 1919 as a means of providing the Liberal press with news. His original intention was for such newspapers to pay for the material, but that scheme fell through, and Le Bas himself then paid to have signed articles put in as advertisements. Bennett's, on 'The Future of Liberalism', was the first one, and appeared on 13 February 1918 in the Liverpool *Daily Post* and elsewhere. The *Daily Mail* attacked Le Bas as a turncoat politician paying to advertise his views and disguising the advertisements as articles. Justice Darling returned a verdict for the defendants.

may happen to the play in London a tremendous personal triumph for you is certain.

So that's that.

I seem to notice beneath your polite remarks a certain dissatisfaction with Eaton. If I am right, this is very naughty of you. You will never get a better or a more reliable producer than Eaton. Can you name one . . .? What you are looking for in a producer you won't get. I mean to say that you won't get from him the poetic interpretative ideas that persons like you and me are able to furnish. A producer capable of furnishing them is an extreme rarity, because the chances are 1,000 to 1 that, if he had the ideas, he would be either an actor or an author and would scorn mere producing. Eaton missed many important rehearsals, but this was due to accident; and that the accident might occur was quite plainly stated to us. We accepted the risks and must abide by them. Eaton is a great worker, very loyal, very quick in the uptake, and very good on the mechanical side, and he has a fundamental commonsense which will save him from fatal errors. Further he will faithfully abide by instructions.

All instructions to the company ought to go through him or be given in his presence.

I enclose some notes, of which I am sending him a duplicate.

Yours ever, Arnold Bennett

P.S. By the way I noticed on Tuesday a slight tendency to over-stress the sentence of which the end is: 'And touch not the goblet.' (I forget the beginning.) You did it more effectively at the dress-rehearsal. A. B.

LOCHERBIE-GOFF / 99
(*To Ernest Hales*)

Comarques
April 14th 1919

My dear Ernest,

I am very sorry to hear of your mother's death and offer you all my sympathy. I do not remember ever having met your

98. For an earlier letter and other references to Lillah McCarthy see Vols. I and II. She was starring in *Judith*, then in rehearsal. It had its provincial opening in Eastbourne on 17 April. Wilfred Eaton is not otherwise known.

mother. If I have met her it could not have been more than once, and only when I was a very small boy. You may accept my positive assurance that there is no foundation whatever for the idea that Sophia was drawn from or suggested in any way by your mother. Such is not the case. I can see now that you point it out that there is a certain resemblance between your mother and Sophia, but the idea had never occurred to me before.

Yours sincerely, Arnold Bennett

TEXAS / MS. / 100
(*To Lillah McCarthy*)

80, Piccadilly
30–4–19

Dear Lillah,

Your dressing-room was too much of a reception room last night for me to get at you.

Good luck be with you. You *immensely* deserve it.

Please note:

1. Move as little as possible during the speech after the murder. Speak the words *low* but very clear. If possible do *not* move until the last sentence: 'The grave shall be thy house'. It has struck me several times that this speech is a bit long. I enclose a cut, which you will use or not as you like.

2. You used the knife all right last night. You kept the point downwards as you raised the knife. This is correct. Don't raise the point.

3. Let there be *no pause whatever* between the murder & the speech.

4. Tell Holofernes to keep still after one single convulsive movement. If he is not still, attention is distracted from the speech & you.

5. Make a pause between the two parts of your speech to Haggith. Say the second part, 'Take the head in a cloth & let us depart' in a very firm self-controlled dominating tone. Tell

99. Ernest Hales was a schoolboy friend of Bennett's and the brother of H. K. Hales, the model for Denry Machin in *The Card*. In *The Old Wives' Tale* Sophia Baines runs off with Gerald Scales, and the family is publicly shamed.

Haggith that when you have said 'The power of Assyria is fallen' & pointed, she must look *at the blood* & *not* at you. She must start back, with the least possible cry, & certainly not a cry like a new born lamb. Then the second part of the speech will pull her together again, & she must pull herself together.

The curtain must be very quick.

Peace be upon you.

Yours, A. B.

P.S. You must keep yourself entirely covered in Act III. Last night we could see not merely the green tunic but a great deal of your admirable body. A. B.

STOKE / MS. / 101
(*To Hugh Walpole*)

80, Piccadilly
14.5.19.

My sweet Hughie,

I have yours & am glad thereof. If you will still be in Polperro at Whitsuntide, & I can have a bedroom to myself somewhere, I will honour myself by coming down, for a week. I greatly need a change & young cheerful society. Insomnia has been upon me for weeks. I expect to finish my Female book before Whitsuntide. I have had immense trouble over *Judith*, but also I have had the, to me, tremendous satisfaction that Hardy has seen it & is unreservedly enthusiastic about it. (Ditto Barrie.) Nothing has pleased me so much for years. I have not believed in its popular success since the first night in London, & now the positive optimists are coming round to my pessimistic view. Unlike me, they are finding fault with everything except the play. The whole fault is in the play which contains too much psychological realism for the public.

You are not the only person who is interested & optimistic about the Cathedral book. I am.

Marguerite is giving a lecture on Baudelaire today at the

100. *Judith* opened at the Kingsway Theatre on the evening of the 30th. On Miss McCarthy's costume see also Vol. I, pp. 387–8.

Anglo-French Society, illustrated with examples of his poems. Great excitement.

I am reading *Mr. Sponge's Sporting Tour*. Rather good.

Yours, A. B.

MAYFIELD, SYRACUSE /A.D. /102
(*To William Archer*)

[?, 80 Piccadilly]
[27 May 1919]

My dear Archer,

I much regret that it is impossible for me to be with you all tonight, especially as the day is my birthday. Forgive me for being personal, but I am 52 years of age, and I have been a rationalist (so far as it is permitted to human beings to be so) for 52 years. That is to say, I cannot remember the time when I had any use whatever for religious dogma, or when I felt the need of 'religion' in the Christian sense—or in any other sense that I can define. Rationalism has made immense progress during recent years, and it will undoubtedly make still greater progress in the immediate future. The danger is that it may become respectable. This would be a pity. When to be a rationalist is to be truly correct, then the living fire of rationalism will be exhausted. However, we need not fear such a calamity just yet. In the meantime let us rationalists amid the triumphs which are awaiting us resolve to maintain that breadth of mind and that charitableness the lack of which we so much deplore in our dogmatical opponents. I drink, in

101. *Our Women* was published in 1920. For other comments on Thomas Hardy see Vols. I and II.

Walpole took three years to write *The Cathedral*.

The Anglo-French Poetry Society was organized in 1919 with Bennett as President, and Marguerite and Edith Sitwell on the managing committee. Its main activity was a monthly recital.

Mr. Sponge's Sporting Tour (1853) was R. S. Surtees's first successful novel. Bennett remarks elsewhere that it 'seems to me to be a rather remarkable novel. It is very badly written. In texture it is monotonous, and its colour is dull. But it is a genuinely realistic work; true to life; free from sentimentality. It shows a notable feeling for certain sorts of landscape and a ruthlessly firm grasp of character. The picture which it gives of English sporting society is as dreadful as it is convincing.'

spirit, to the prosperity of the R.P.A., to which I am proud to belong.

Yours sincerely, [Arnold Bennett]

ARKANSAS / T.S. / 103
(*To Frank Swinnerton*)

Comarques
June 16th 1919

My dear Henry,

I return *The Moon and Sixpence* and your criticism. I agree with your criticism, but I do not think that you have laid sufficient [? stress] on the positive qualities of the book. Anyhow, I read it with interest, and I think the Tahiti chapters are really very good. Also the man has a sardonic crude humour which pleaseth me.

Yours, A. B.

FALES, NYPL / T.C.C. / 104
(*To Paul Nash*)

[? 80, Piccadilly]
June 16th 1919

Dear Paul Nash,

Let me say that I am delighted with the drawing you have given me. I wonder whether you would be kind enough to have it mounted and framed for me, and tell the framer to deliver it at 12B George Street, with the bill. If you could find time for this I should be greatly obliged. It would then be impossible for you to say, when you saw the drawing in my flat, that I had spoilt it by my barbaric ignorance of the principles of framing.

Further, could you find out if that straight-backed tiger of Rupert Lee's is for sale, and if so, what the price is.

If you have any *real* project for an illustrated periodical devoted to the arts—I suppose especially the graphic arts—I

102. William Archer presided over a dinner of the Rationalist Press Association on 27 May. Bennett, an agnostic, was an Honorary Associate. His letter declining the invitation appeared in the *Literary Guide and Rationalist Review* for July. For other information on Archer see Vol. II.

103. W. Somerset Maugham's *The Moon and the Sixpence* was published in April 1919. For other comments on Maugham see Vols. I and II.

should be glad to interest myself in it. This does not mean that I should want to interfere in any way in the artistic direction of the thing. I should not.

Kind regards to Mrs. Nash.

Yours sincerely, [Arnold Bennett]

P.S. I am at 80 Piccadilly in the middles of the weeks, and at Thorpe-le-Soken at the week-ends.

ULLMAN / MS. / 105
(*To Eugene Paul Ullman*)

Comarques
21–6–19

My dear Ullman,

I am glad to have your letter. The rumour that I am coming soon to Paris is untrue. I prefer England for the present. I have had some correspondence with Alice, but not with George for a very long time. I have been in politics for some longish period, & even head of a ministry for some months. But now I have retired again to the pursuit of my various arts. (I have exhibited 3 aquarelles & illustrated a book.) I don't know how many books I have written during the war. But I have only had two plays produced; one was a success & the other a total frost. Rickards has been nearly dead with tuberculosis (accelerated by military duties (not otherwise dangerous) in France). He is slowly recovering, but I don't think he will ever recover entirely. In the meantime I am looking after his affairs for him. About 3 years ago he married a most beautiful girl ½ his age. The marriage is a success—except for this tuberculosis. He has been in a hospital for months. Marguerite now gives recitals of French poetry, with great éclat. We are just taking a new flat in London, though I should prefer to live here entirely. I think most of my translatable novels are arranged for. Just at the moment Marguerite is in bed indisposed internally. But she will

104. Paul Nash (1889–1946) was one of the artists commissioned by the British War Memorial Committee, and Bennett wrote an introduction to an exhibition of his paintings, 'Void of War', that was held at the Leicester Galleries in 1918.

Rupert Lee is not otherwise known.

soon be all right again. She is in London & I am here. I rejoin her on Tuesday. Remember me to everyone.

Yours, Arnold Bennett

FALES, NYPL / T.C.C. / 106
(*To Paul Nash*)

[? 12B George Street]
[Hanover Square W.1.]
July 2nd 1919

My dear Paul Nash,

It is agreed by your expert advisers that if a thousand copies are sold of a 5/- quarterly devoted to the arts a miracle will have occurred. Also that the utmost total cash sum receivable from the public if 1,000 copies are sold will be £150.

For myself I do not believe that the miracle will occur, but I am ready to take the risk of it not occurring and for one year from the first issue of the said quarterly. That is to say, I will be responsible in any case for all proper expenditure on the

105. Eugene Paul Ullman (1877–1953) was an American painter who spent many of his mature years in France. He and his brother George met Bennett there in 1903 or 1904. Ullman's first wife was Alice Woods (b. 1871), an American author of some popularity. Ullman wrote a brief memoir about Bennett in France. He recalls a party that Bennett gave at which a female friend of Bennett's was to sing. 'There were not so very many people there as his place was small but the guests were carefully selected. When we arrived we were not presented to this lady but she was presented to us, and this is how it went as his guests came in: "Allow me to present you to my mistress." He certainly knew that he was not behaving like a Frenchman. But the great idea was to show everybody very formally and very cynically (perhaps) that he had reached a goal. People who said that he didn't know any better were both right and wrong. He knew perfectly well that this kind of thing "wasn't done" but those who know his books will recognize that his every description of things and places has this same spirit.' The identity of the woman is of interest. Ullman describes her as Bennett's 'friend, his very close friend'. One such friend appears in the *Journal* in 1903 as 'C'; she was a musical comedy actress, and Bennett drew the portrait of Cosette in *A Great Man* after her. The only other known possibility, and an unlikely one, is Eleanor Green, Bennett's fiancée for a few months, who had operatic ambitions. Whoever the woman was, the episode casts further doubt upon the notion that Bennett's relationship with Miss Green in 1906 was a naive one. (See Vol. II, pp. 205–11.) Ullman also recalls a visit to Bennett and Marguerite soon after their marriage. He found Marguerite and the maid in tears. It appeared that ten francs of the household money was unaccounted for. Bennett admitted privately to Ullman that it was easier to handle a woman in a book than in life. At lunch Bennett bit into his prunes and cracked his teeth on a ten franc piece.

Bennett illustrated *A Floating Home*, by Cyril Ionides and J. B. Atkins, published in 1918.

For a letter and other references to E. A. Rickards see Vols. I and II.

production and publishing of the first four numbers. I assume of course that the total expenditure on each number must not exceed £150, since it would be absurd, irrational, and socially inartistic to spend more than you could get back even in the event of a miracle.

Your business will of course be to cut the coat according to the cloth. How you will do it I do not know. That is an affair for you and your creative friends. Personally I shall not be able to *de*vise: I can only *ad*vise—if I am asked. I already take an active share in the running of a theatre and a weekly paper, and this is about as much as I can do in the way of active propaganda. (May I mention, incidentally, in view of the rumours about me acquiring vast fortunes out of these things, that I receive nothing from them whatever.)

I want to offer you some advice unasked.

1. You cannot possibly set out to improve the distribution machinery of books in this country. Only a millionaire and a born organiser who lived solely for organising could do that.
2. This affair that you are taking on is not your main job. It is only a secondary job for you. You ought not therefore to expect more from it than is warranted by the energy you can put into it.
3. If the quarterly succeeds I can produce capitalists; but it would be useless to approach them with no accomplishment to show. The contemplated experiment will be quite adequate to show whether your ideas correspond with the reality of things, and if it is successful it will be enough to obtain the necessary money for a larger scheme.

Yours sincerely, [Arnold Bennett]

SCHUSTER / TR. / 107
(*To Edyth Goodall*)

Comarques
5.7.19

My sweet & martyrised niece,

It is all right. You will have a much more riotous part in the play I am now writing, and if you don't open with it you will

106. The Bennetts were just now moving into their new flat at 12B George Street.

make a grave error. As a fact, when Dean told me he had mentioned the *Sac. & Prof.* part to you, I showed no enthusiasm. You and yours had the refusal of that play. You and yours refused it. I know it wasn't your fault, but a management is all one, and the innocent must suffer with the guilty. Beneath a modest and diffident exterior, I hide powerful feelings about my plays. Was it likely that I should agree willingly to you taking on *Sac. & Prof.*, which might run 1, 2, 3 God knows how many years, while a part specially written for you was waiting in a drawer? I opine not. No. Either you are going into management or you aren't. In declining *Sac. & Prof.* you and I are agreed that your mysterious advisers were wrong. In declining to let you play in it under another management I think they were quite right. So that's that.

I adore you as aforetime.

Marguerite is somewhat indisposed but from her restless couch sends you her love and to Mr. T. (Tinker not Turner) her duty. Me too.

Yours, Arnold Bennett

FALES, NYU / MS. / 108
(*To Cedric Sharpe*)

Comarques
10–7–19

My dear Cedric,

This news about your father is very grave. I had already written to your mother. I take it there is nothing whatever to be done. I want to persuade you against the Paris concerts. Very few concerts in Paris do succeed, especially foreign concerts. I have sat in scores of nearly empty auditoriums. I think you would be absolutely certain to lose a great deal of money over the venture, & I do not perceive where the advantage comes in.

107. Edyth Goodall (1886–1929) had played in *Cupid and Commonsense* and *Milestones*; her notable success was as Fanny Hawthorn in *Hindle Wakes*. Bennett wrote *Sacred and Profane Love* in 1916; the new play was *Body and Soul*, begun on 3 July. Basil Dean (1888–) was manager of the Aldwych, and he produced *Sacred and Profane Love* there later in the year. For a letter to him see below. Mr. T. refers to the nickname of Miss Goodall's husband, Leonard Schuster, an engineer. Turner was Alfred Turner (1870–1941), who was manager for Miss Goodall at the Court and Kingsway theatres.

I can see the advantage of London concerts; but a mere escapade to Paris, with nothing to follow it up, does not seem to me to mean much, practically. Moreover, I anticipate that Paris will soon be in a highly unsettled state—much more so than London.

Martin is a complete invalid & quite unable to do anything at all. I have never heard of the Salle [?]. So it must be either a new hall or an old one re-named. There *were* only 3 halls in Paris worth a damn for chamber-concerts. The Salles Erard, Pleyel, and Gaveau. The Gaveau is the newest of the three & in some ways the best of the three. You had better reconsider this project before you go any further. Write me again. I had meant to see you before you left, but my indispositions, & Marguerite's, & trying to move into a new flat & to write a new play simultaneously, have put me in the background. Loves to you both.

Yours, A. B.

Murdoch was pretty rotten at your concert. In fact neither of the other 2 was in the same street with you. A. B.

FALES, NYPL / T.C.C. / 109
(*To Paul Nash*)

[? 12B George Street]
July 16th 1919

Dear Paul Nash,

Many thanks for your letter. Your scheme seems very good. I am not prepared to pay the whole cost of the four numbers, and at the same time to leave the whole of the proceeds to you. I am prepared to stand all the loss, which I am fairly sure will be considerable. I do not want any glory out of this scheme. I do not want even to be mentioned in regard to it. The scheme will be yours, and if it succeeds yours will be the renown. I think therefore that if you wish to go on with it you must be ready to work for nothing at the start—unless of course you can arrange

108. For earlier letters to Cedric Sharpe see Vol. II. Émile Martin was a Parisian friend of Bennett's.

Murdoch—William David (1888–1942), Australian-born pianist notable as a player of chamber music.

to pay yourself out of the £150. I need not restate the financial principles which I stated in my previous letter and with which you agreed.

Kindest regards to you both.

Yours sincerely, [Arnold Bennett]

YALE / T.C.C. / 110
(*To Osbert Sitwell*)

[Comarques]
July 31st 1919

My dear Osbert Sitwell,

I enclose the note for the catalogue. If it is too long cut it.

It would be very good of you to tell Zborowski that I will give him £55 for the Vlaminck sailing boat. The present rate of exchange is 31.10. This makes it over 1,700 frs. He asked 2000 frs. I will give him £20 for Soutine's red fiddle, and £60 for any of Modigliani's three women, but I prefer the one in the black cloak. £50 for Kisling's yellow dancer (he asked the equivalent of £59—1,800 frs.) £40 for any of the three principal Vlaminck landscapes. He can choose among these—I do not want to spend more than £120 altogether—but my choice would be among the Modiglianis and the Vlamincks (especially the sailing boat).

Yours sincerely, [Arnold Bennett]

110. Bennett's note, which follows, was for an exhibition at the Mansard Gallery, August 1919, brought together by the Sitwell brothers. Leopold Zborowski was a dealer in modern paintings, and one of the Modiglianis graced Bennett's home for several years.

'For artists, an island is especially an island. And it is so, not because of the surrounding water, but because it cannot possibly be near the centre of things. Britain, really, is a colony of queer and obstinate and romantic people lying on a scrap of earth in the ocean somewhere to the west of the continent. And thus Britain is certainly regarded by the continent. British artists suffer from their seclusion in a way in which British writers, for example, do not. The transport of books is a simple affair. The transport of pictures and sculpture is quite an enterprise—not to mention framing, glazing and pedestals. British artists do not travel enough,—for five years they have travelled enough, but with rifles and other impediments unconducive to the study of art. And even when they do travel, in normal times, they usually travel at seasons when the truly interesting continental art-exhibitions are not open. Hence they are thrown inwards upon themselves. Their talents therefore are apt to intermarry too much, with the customary results. Hence their need, and the need of the smaller passionate public which encourages

BERG / MS. / III
(*To Gwladys Wheeler*)

Comarques
5-8-19

Dear Gwladys,

Many thanks. I should think that nothing is easier than to buy warposters. If you spent a few shillings on an advt in *The Times*, *Mail*, or *Bazaar*, you would get offers of far more than you wanted. Believe me, I really *want* to come & stay with you, & we shall come if a date mutually agreeable can be found. I consider it most touching of you to desire the presence of non-sport in your home. I regret that you have given up the *New Statesman*. The old editor has returned from the war & the paper is in its best form. It is no use being 'tired of Trade Unions'.

---

evolution among them, is to see more and still more illustrations of foreign evolution in art.

I do not mean that they need to see the pictures and sculpture of the arrived, successful, and accepted continental artists. The works of the latter always travel with ease. I mean that they need to see the works of the younger pioneers, those who are clearing new paths, those whose reputations are yet unachieved, those of whom the English dowagers cry out in their raucous imperious voices: "But you mustn't try to persuade me that he is not deliberately pulling our legs!" (As if anybody would dream of pulling their legs!)

The present exhibition fulfils a felt want, both for young artists and young public. It is widely continental, and has been collected from France, Spain, Poland, Russia, Italy and Norway. It is the first of its kind since the war; and in my opinion it is the best of its kind at any rate since the celebrated exhibition at the Grafton many years ago.

It is chiefly an exhibition of young artists. Modigliani (Spanish) is 29, Survage (French) is 25, Utrillo (Italian) is 32, Kisling (French) is 28, Bara (French) is 26, Krohg (Norway) is 26, Fournier, Dufy, and Soutine are probably all under thirty. And I have mentioned only a representative few. The exhibition is steadied by such "veterans" as Picasso (who still looks about 23), Derain (who looks little more), Matisse, Vlaminck, and the excellent Lhote. As an amateur who ignorantly excites himself about all the arts I have no intention of differentiating between these pictures (the sculpture had not turned up when I wrote this note). But I am determined to say that the four figure subjects of Modigliani seem to me to have a suspicious resemblance to masterpieces; that in particular Soutine's red fiddle, Kisling's yellow dancer, Dufy's amusing paddock scene, Fournier's blue river, and Bara's landscape with the scarlet centre remain provocatively and delightfully in my mind; that the Matisses are very good Matisses, and the Picassos and Derains very advanced indeed; and finally that the adorable Vlaminck, who in spite of his reputation is scarcely better *appreciated* than Gauguin was before he went to the South Seas, is steadily rising.

This exhibition ought, in its degree, to do as much good as the lately departed Russian ballet. It is an education to the islanders; and of course it is equally a joy.'

The one useful thing is an honest attempt to understand them. This you cannot possibly do from any daily paper—of any colour. It is as unwise to be 'tired of Unions' now as it would have been to be 'tired of the war' in April 1918.

Marguerite has gone to London to meet her French relatives. I am struggling with my last act. Respex to A.W.

Yours, A. B.

FALES, NYPL / T.C.C. / 112
(*To Paul Nash*)

[12B George Street]
August 25th 1919

Dear Paul Nash,

I have now seen Swinnerton. He seems to think your amended project has some chance of not failing, provided the contents are not too uncompromisingly unpopular. If you can convince him as a publisher, that they are not, by all means go ahead, on the assumption that with a sale of 2,000 no loss will be incurred.

Let me repeat what I said to you at your studio.

I am quite willing for other people to come into the affair.

But I personally am not prepared to come into it unless you can show to Swinnerton's satisfaction that it is not absolutely bound to fail commercially. That other people are willing to join me in the risks does not at all affect my attitude on this point. However, I think, from what Swinnerton said, that you may be able to satisfy him.

I am going away tomorrow and shall not be back for three weeks.

Yours sincerely, [Arnold Bennett]

111. Gwladys Wheeler was the wife of Dr. Alec Wheeler, who was active in the Stage Society for many years.

112. Bennett sought Swinnerton's advice on Nash's proposal, and Swinnerton was sufficiently interested to suggest that Chatto and Windus might do the publishing. The proposal was eventually abandoned, apparently because of lack of sustained interest by Nash himself.

Bennett went on a trip to Ireland and Liverpool. He spent a fortnight in Liverpool attending rehearsals of *Sacred and Profane Love*, which opened at the Playhouse Theatre there on 15 September.

NATION, 20 September 1919 / 113
(*To the editor*)

12B George Street
September 17, 1919

Sir,

With reference to Mr. William Archer's refusal to believe that certain plays can be 'intelligibly recited—much less acted— in two hours and a half', he may be interested to know that about fifteen years ago Antoine gave at the Théâtre Antoine an absolutely unabridged performance of *King Lear* (in French) with all the changes of scene. There were, I think, two intervals. The actual playing time, as carefully taken by me, was 2 hours and 10 minutes. The performance was perfectly intelligible. In fact, it was the most intelligible performance of *King Lear* that I have ever witnessed.

Yours etc., Arnold Bennett

SCHUSTER / TR. / 114
(*To Edyth Goodall*)

12B George Street
17.9.19.

Dear & sweet niece,

The Romney telegram was much appreciated. So please tell the august directors. The affair came off very well. Iris will be all right. Being in Liverpool and not in London, I was locally compelled, forced, and obliged to respond to a call. I was then vociferously re-demanded, and had to grace the stage once more, this time holding Iris's trembling hand. An affecting scene! Respex to Tinker.

Your unique uncle, Arnold Bennett

113. Antoine—André-Leonard (1858–1943).

114. Edyth Goodall's management was called the Romney Street Syndicate, after her and her husband's address. *Sacred and Profane Love* had its first showing at the Playhouse in Liverpool on 15 September. Iris Hoey (1885–) played the leading role. Bennett wrote in his *Journal*. 'The audience laughed when Iris Hoey called out "I cannot bear it" as the hero was playing the piano. True, the playing was appallingly bad. This ruined the first act, Sc. I. Act I, Sc. 2 went perfectly. The hold of the play on the audience gradually increased, and at the close an emphatic success was undeniable. I took a call because I had to. Then I had to take a second call. A thing I never did before.'

BODKIN / TR. / 115
(*To Thomas Bodkin*)

12B George Street
18.9.19.

My dear Bodkin,

It is regrettable that I should have to charge the beautiful Mrs. Bodkin with inaccuracy. I did not 'volunteer' to see those infants. I specifically asked to see them. I said that I was always allowed to see the children, asleep or awake, at houses which I visited, and I gave corroborative (and amusing) evidence of this. Such are the facts, and no vague denials from Ll. G. or Philip Kerr can upset them. So that's that.

I am infinitely obliged to you for all your trouble, and I attend the goods with impatience. I hope the picture-show from Heals is maturing. It won't anyhow be complete, because I have 3 of the best pictures here—Modigliani, Vlaminck and Soutine. I suggested to Heals that the collection should not be broken up till after Dublin, but they insisted on delivering the stuff.

Kindly tell James O'C., L.J., that my play was a furious success in Liverpool. What it will be in London God knows.

Mes hommages à cette mère si belle mais si dure.

Yours, A. B.

U.C. / T.C.C. / 116
(*To Roger Fry*)

[Comarques]
September 19th 1919

My dear Roger Fry,

Many thanks for your letter. I should be only too pleased to have my portrait painted by Wolfe, but it is a fact that I have no time. I do hope that after the production of my new play, on or about the 14th October, I shall be much more free, but I suppose that Wolfe will have to leave England before then. If he is not leaving England before the end of October I will guarantee to give him six sittings before that date. I could not honestly guarantee more. And even so I am afraid that he

115. Philip Henry Kerr (Marquis of Lothian, 1882–1940) was private secretary to Lloyd George, 1916–21. James O'Connor was now Lord Justice of Appeal.

would have to suit my time. You may believe me, I am a very busy man.

As regards the £20, it is absolutely at your disposal. I too hate the idea of charity to an artist, but surely you could arrange this in some way. I do not want my name to appear in any way. If there are any other paintings to be sold he could give me a painting in exchange for the £20, and he could have it back at the same price afterwards if he wanted it. Any arrangement that you make would be satisfactory to me, and I will send you the cheque at once on hearing from you. It would be a great pleasure to me to help a man like Wolfe.

Yours sincerely, [Arnold Bennett]

ARKANSAS / MS. / 117
(*To Frank Swinnerton*)

Comarques
28–9–19

Sir,

re: *September*

This work is admirably conceived and just about perfectly constructed. The characterisation is quite level with the conception & construction. Cherry is to my mind the best drawn character; she coincides exactly with my observations. The interest never slackens, and towards the close it gathers itself together as it should. The book is easily the author's best—better than *Nocturne* page by page, and of course far superior to it in scale and importance. Its general authenticity and distinction cannot be questioned, at any rate by me.

The animadversions which I have to make on it are as follows:—

The mechanical details of construction are occasionally too facile, and show a certain idleness of invention and artifice. Thus I think the end of p. 116 is a bit thick. Ditto the end of section V on p. 204. There are several of these things.

The writing is sometimes too damnably adroit in what appears to be a superficial way. So that though actual clichés are avoided they are not always avoided by the thought but by mere verbal cleverness, and the discerning person can see where they 'lurk concealed'.

Some of the descriptive stuff is also a bit facile, if not otiose. Thus, the beginning of the first paragraph on p. 62.

Some of the scenes are not properly 'set'; indeed some of them are not set at all. Doubtless this was generally intentioned, but it seems to me to be a gratuitous handicap. There is an instance where the scene obviously has been set, but where the business of setting seems to me to have been done perfunctorily & ineffectively. This is the dance scene beginning on p. 200. My notion is that the book might have been about twice as long with advantage. I am not denying that your intention was otherwise or that you are not within your rights to dispense with scenery.

I attach little weight to any of the foregoing animadversions. My one real criticism is that I think the emotional power might have been stronger. The best examples of emotional quality are the scene between Marian and Cherry (p. 76); the scene between Marian and Nigel ending on p. 224; the scene between Marian & Cherry on pp. 251–3; and all the closing pages. I think that there might have [been] many more pages of the quality of these very fine things, & that these might have been even more powerful. This is of course to apply the highest standard to the book, by which I mean the Dostoevsky or Balzac standard.

I am exceedingly well satisfied with the book, & it will stand any criticism except such as I have just applied. It is incomparably the best novel by an author under 40 that I have read since *The Rainbow*, and of course vastly superior to that in technical qualities.

Damned if there isn't a play already made in it.

Yours, A. B.

P.S. I note that Robert, if not his sister, calls Howard & Marian 'uncle' and 'aunt' in the opening pages, whereas Cherry is calling them freely by their Christian names at the end. This is not explained. And I am reminded that Robert is not utilised in the latter half; he merely drops out through a hole in the bottom. This is inefficient waste of material. A. B.

117. D. H. Lawrence's *The Rainbow* was published in 1915.

FALES, NYU / MS. / 118
(*To R. D. Blumenfeld*)

Comarques
6–10–19

My dear Blumenfeld,

Many thanks for so kindly sending me the two telegrams. I think that the *Express* did not begin very well, but that after the first 2 or 3 days its leaders & general attitude were on the whole admirable. The Cadbury crew wired me on Monday to wire them a series of 1,500 word articles containing my priceless views; but I declined, partly because I couldn't get at the facts nor argue with knowledgeable people, & partly because now that Gardiner has gone my original distaste for the Cadburys has a free rein!

I think that you might now usefully get up an agitation for the removal of everybody named Geddes. They may be devilish good railway organisers, but they are bloody bad politicians.

Have you read the *New Statesman* this week? If not, read it. I take pride in the fact that I more than anybody else kept that paper alive during the war. It is now a property.

Lastly I consider it damnable that the only paper that could be bought in this village during the strike was the *Chronicle*. I had to send daily to Clacton for my papers.

Yours sincerely, Arnold Bennett

BEAVERBROOK / MS. / 119
(*To Lord Beaverbrook*)

12B George Street
5–11–19

My dear Max,

It is very nice of you to think of arranging a supper party after the first night for us, but the fact is our physical resources will not run to it. So that we shall respectfully & gratefully

118. A national railwaymen's strike began on 27 September. The brothers Cadbury (Edward, 1873–1948, and George, d. 1922) controlled the *Daily News*, which A. G. Gardiner (1865–1946) edited from 1902 to 1919. Gardiner wrote an appreciative article on Bennett for the *Daily News*, in 1925; it was reprinted in his collection of essays *Certain People of Importance*. Auckland Campbell Geddes (Baron Geddes, 1879–1954) was Minister of National Service, 1917–19; his brother, Sir Eric Campbell Geddes (1875–1937), was a Unionist M.P., 1917–22.

decline. My one notion when I have heard an account of a first night of a play of my own is to go to bed. (I shall not be present myself.) We will foregather later. I will send you 2 stalls at the end of the week.

Speaking of the drama, you should read the preface to Shaw's new book of plays. As a journalistic performance it is of the very highest order. *Nobody* can state a case like this fellow.

Thine, A. B.

FALES, NYPL / T.C.C. / 120
(*To Paul Nash*)

[12B George Street]
November 5th 1919

Dear Paul Nash,

There is very shortly to be an exhibition of modern pictures in the Five Towns, and I am doing what I can to get some really modern work into it. The thing is being done under the auspices of the Fine Art Section of the Ceramic Society. Can you and your brother let me have something for the show. If you can, I shall be greatly obliged. Transport is in the hands of Messrs. P. & D. Colnaghi & Obach, 144 New Bond Street, so that you will have no trouble or expense. In this district of 250,000 people there has never been a picture show.

Yours sincerely, [Arnold Bennett]

BERG / MS. / 121
(*To J. C. Squire*)

12B George Street
6–11–19

Dear Squire,

I have now perused the *L.M.*I. & will inflict my views on you. It is on the whole what I should call a 'sound' number—good, considering that it is a first number. In spite of the disclaimer in the last par. of the Editorial notes, I seem to detect in these a slight pontificality, & a slight ignoring of the fact that to distinguish between sound art & the other thing is the greatest of all difficulties, in all questions of criticism. Of the verse I shall

119. *Sacred and Profane Love* opened on 10 November at the Aldwych. Shaw's *Heartbreak House, Great Catherine, and Playlets About the War* was published in October.

not presume to speak, but I think some of the poems are highly good. Nichols's story is fair. The most to be said for it is that it can be read. It lacks style (not that I object at all to the freedoms), and it is too diffuse in construction. Of the articles, leaving out present company, I assume that the insertion of the Gosse article was chiefly politic. It does not seem to me to possess any positive merit. The Lynd & the Stobart are both A1. Alice leaves me cold. I think you did a lot of the poetry reviews, & I expect they are quite all right. I do not like the attitude of the fiction reviewer. In particular I object to his 3 times repeated remark about Swinnerton producing for the autumn season, or once a year, or whatever it is. What has this got to do with the matter? Why should not an author produce a novel a year or at a certain time? The repeated animadversion is absurd; it is also in bad taste. Nor do I think that the reviewer understands fiction. Indeed I am sure he does not. He has not yet even discovered that *Mademoiselle de Maupin* is dead & quite worthless. The other reviews seem all right. But is it wise to put the quite brief reviews in the same typographical scale etc. as the long ones? Thibaudet is really excellent, much better than I thought he would be. I wish he would write as interestingly and concretely in the *Nouvelle Revue Française*. Turner is jolly. He tumbles into wild exaggerations sometimes, but he has something to say, & is decidedly on the up grade. I have my doubts about Nash. He is much more of a draughtsman than a writer; he writes costively. Sickert would be immeasurably better. Dent is as good as you will get. As regards the running title, why do you not have the right hand title the title of the article or of the section?

Hoping this will find you as well as it leaves me at present.

Yours, A. B.

121. J. C. Squire turned from editing the *New Statesman* to found the *London Mercury*, the first issue of which appeared in November 1919. The poems were by Thomas Hardy, Rupert Brooke, W. J. Turner, Siegfried Sassoon, Edward Shanks, John Freeman, W. H. Davies, Laurence Binyon, and Walter de la Mare. Robert Nichols's story was 'The Smile of the Sphinx', an allegory; for letters to Nichols see below. Edmund Gosse wrote on George Eliot. Robert Lynd (1879–1949) reviewed an edition of Horace Walpole's letters. J. C. Stobart wrote on the teaching of English. Alice Meynell (1847–1922) discussed the particles 'un', 'in', and 'less'. The fiction reviewer, anonymous, compared Frank Swinnerton's new work unfavourably with *Mademoiselle de Maupin*. Alfred Thibaudet (1874–1936), the literary critic, wrote 'A Letter from France'. W. J. Turner wrote on drama. John Nash (1893–), the painter, wrote on art. On Walter Sickert see p. 54. Edward J. Dent (1876–1957) wrote on music.

ARKANSAS / TS. / 122
(*To Frank Swinnerton*)

12B George Street
November 24th 1919

My dear Henry,

I want to arrange for Daisy Ashford to come here for tea and meet Doran again. Can you arrange it? Had Marguerite better write to Daisy? If so, what is her address? And assuming Daisy agrees, cannot the day be fixed in advance—i.e. before Marguerite writes.

Your article on me seemed to be less brilliant than your average. It was just. Nevertheless I think I could defend Act II against you with considerable success. You do not seem to see that Act II *must* be what is called 'irrelevant', for that is the whole point of it. Its irrelevance is really relevance. As regards play construction, 999 good plays out of 1000 are 'episodic'. They cannot be anything else—unless they are practically in one scene like *The Trojan Women.* I suppose people will continue to say that my plays are 'not plays', but something else. My aim is and always has been to widen the meaning of the word 'dramatic'. That is to say I was determined to prove that the interest of an audience can be held by the presentation of material generally held to be undramatic. I am not yet convinced that I have done it. I have seen the first Act of *S & P Love* when it held me. But I have also seen it when I thought it was completely wrong from a theatrical point of view and when I felt just like the critic of the *Daily Telegraph.*

Yours, A. B.

TEXAS / T.C.C. / 123
(*To George Bernard Shaw*)

12B George Street
December 12th 1919

Dear Shaw,

I saw *Arms and the Man* last night. I also saw the first performance of it blank years ago. I simply have to tell you that

122. Daisy Ashford—author of several tales written during her childhood and youth, among them *The Young Visiters* and *Where Love Lies Deepest.*

Swinnerton's review appeared in the *Telegraph* on 11 November. He did not like very much about the play.

this play wears extremely well. Indeed it improves with age. I was really delighted with last night's show, and you have got to accept my congratulations whether you want them or not. The fact is there are only three dramatists worth a damn in this country.

Yours, Arnold Bennett

STOKE / MS. / 124
(*To Hugh Walpole*)

12B George Street
12–12–19

My dear Hughie,

Marguerite has taken your letter & lost it; so I can't reply to it properly. My memory of it is to the effect that you're immensely and magniloquently booming. Go on. My benediction followeth & surroundeth thee. I don't know what you think of plutocratic society in N.Y. I couldn't stick it. I have just been to Cambridge to stay with W.H.R. Rivers, ethnologist and psycho-analyst. This fellow is one of *the* most interesting. And, your bent being what it is, he would certainly interest you. You will have to meet him. I am still doing no work,—haven't done any for 3½ months. I could work; but I won't. My next will be a play. The revival of *Arms and the Man* last night was triumphant. I greatly savoured it. The second No. of Squire's *Mercury* does not seem to me to be very promising, & it appeared 11 days late. True, I have not yet faced Squire's 300 lines on the morn. Swinnerton & Squire divide the critical field between them. I think Frank will win. He has more poise, & Squire is harming himself by most extensive log-rolling in his 'controlled press'. I really believe that, in his simple-minded purity, he has not yet suspected that he is log-rolling. I am sure he would be furious if he thought we thought he was. He is leaving the *New Statesman* at his own desire. Sharp on Squire is diverting. The War Picture show at the R.A. is opened today. This show would have been a reactionary mass of R.A. & A.R.A. muck

123. *Arms and the Man* was first produced on 21 April 1894. The new production at the Duke of York's Theatre, opened on 11 December 1919.

Bennett's third choice among dramatists was probably Barrie—though with considerable reservation.

but for Beaverbrook having the wit to leave the commissioning of pictures for the M. of I. to Masterman & me. But for Robbie Ross intimidating Alfred Mond, 99% of the credit is Masterman's & mine. (Ours are the only names that have not been mentioned in connection with it.) It is a truly great show & is having a terrific press. I have been ill and am well. Marguerite is very well. She is just now flaunting over London a fur cloak whose existence in her wardrobe is due to the cardinal fact that I must either earn money or spend it. At present I am not earning it. George Moore's *Avowals* is highly agreeable. My latest discovery is Buckle. George (Doran) & I had some great times. We discussed you all.

Our loves, Thine, A. B.

LONDON MERCURY, February 1920 / 125
(To the editor)

12B George Street
December 19th, 1919

Sir,

Your dramatic critic writes of my play *Sacred and Profane Love*, 'A writer of Mr. Arnold Bennett's eminence and great sagacity would be the last person to expect us to take this play seriously as a contribution to dramatic literature.' Only a certain ingenuousness prevents this remark from being outrageous. Of course I expect the play to be taken seriously. Your writer is perfectly entitled to condemn my play; but he is not entitled on the strength of his opinion to attribute to me an attitude which is not mine, and which, if it were mine, would render me odious in the sight of artists. Why in the name of my alleged great sagacity should I publish a play which I did not expect to be taken seriously? Did your critic perhaps imagine that he was

124. Walpole was in America from September 1919 until April 1920.

Bennett was introduced to W. H. R. Rivers (d. 1922) by Siegfried Sassoon.

The new play was *The Bright Island*, begun in the middle of January.

Robert Ross had been on the British War Memorial Committee along with Bennett and Masterman. Sir Alfred Mond—Lord Melchett (1868–1930). *The Times* reviewer said of the show that it was a 'promise of something much richer, more interesting, more spiritual than has been in English painting since the Middle Ages'. Among the painters represented were Paul and John Nash, Stanley Spencer, W. P. Roberts, and Wyndham Lewis.

Buckle—Henry Thomas (1821–62), the historian.

being charitable? One does not expect from the critics of the *London Mercury* the ineptitudes which characterise the dramatic criticism of the stunt daily Press. I mention the matter because I think that an important point of principle is involved, and because this is not the first time that one of your critics has exceeded his province. In your first number there were references to the work of Mr. Frank Swinnerton which amounted to a quite gratuitous imputation against the artistic integrity of the author.

Yours, etc., Arnold Bennett

MEWTON-WOOD / MS. / 126
(*To W. J. Turner*)

12B George Street
26–12–19

My dear Turner,

Many thanks for your letter. It is entirely beside the point. I have no objection whatever to you stating your opinion that the play is not a serious contribution to dramatic literature. What I object to is your assumption that *I* do not regard it as such. This assumption is absolutely indefensible; it has all sorts of implications; and it was one of your mistakes. You surely do not expect me to take you seriously when you say that what you mean by 'serious' was that the work must 'stand comparison with Shakespeare'. If you had said: 'Mr. A. B. would be the last person to expect us to expect his play to stand comparison with Shakespeare', I should not have demurred. I should have thought the remark inept, but I should have agreed with it. You however did not say this. You said something quite else which bears a plain meaning, & which was utterly untrue. I repeat that I have no objection to your opinion; there is an even chance that it is right. I can only hope that if you have not yet met anyone who disagrees with you in classing my work with the plays of Alfred Sutro, you will do so before you die. When I remember that after T. Hardy saw *Judith* he was so

125. The review, by W. J. Turner, in the December issue, went on to say: 'Although it is a play of modern life in the most colloquial prose, it has less reality than the wildest and most phantasmagoric drama of the Elizabethans. . . . There is nothing in this play that could not actually have happened, but it is impossible to believe in it as it is happening.'

enthusiastic about it that he couldn't sleep all night, I think that there is a chance that you may.

You say that you 'judge plays from the standpoint of a poet'. You are entitled to do so, in your private capacity, but if you do so in your public capacity, you ought always to preface your criticisms by a statement to that effect. A dramatic critic is supposed to judge dramatic literature as a dramatic critic. I always suspected that you judged plays as a poet, whereas you judge music as a musical critic. Your musical criticism is to my mind admirable, but your dramatic criticism never seems to me to show any real comprehension of what the dramatic medium is; it seems to be rather the exercises of a very talented man in a matter for which God in His infinite wisdom had not destined him.

My dear fellow, of course I had read your criticism when I last saw you. You must not suppose that a purely professional question could ever affect in the slightest degree my private relations with you. You have a public capacity; so have I. You did something in public which I think unjustifiable, & I merely asked Squire to give me the opportunity of expressing my view with an equal publicity. Your good faith is not in question: your discretion *is* in question. But that is all. Think no more of the matter. I certainly shall not—as soon as I have seen my letter to the *Mercury* in print. And come & see me.

Yours sincerely, Arnold Bennett

BUTLER / T.C.C. / 127
(*To George Doran*)

[12B George Street]
December 29th 1919

My dear Doran,

I am sending to you Dr. W. H. R. Rivers, and I enclose copy of my letter of introduction. I wish to tell you more privately that the subject of psycho-analysis is of the most absorbing interest. It is a subject which is becoming more and more prominent in

126. W. J. Turner (1889–1946) was music critic for the *New Statesman* from 1916 to 1940. He was also author of the notable play *The Man Who Ate the Popomack*. Bennett helped him professionally on occasions before and after this letter.

England and which will certainly appeal very powerfully to citizens of the United States. Rivers knows a very great deal about it. He writes very clearly and interestingly, and I think that if a small popular book could be got out of him it ought to sell well. I have not said a word to him about such a book, so that you have the field clear in case you wish to avail yourself of it.

Yours, [Arnold Bennett]

ILLINOIS / MS. / 128
(*To Jane Wells*)

12B George Street
22–1–20

Dear Lady,

The more I read of H.G.'s *Outline* the more staggered I am by it. It is about the most useful thing of the kind ever done, & it is jolly well done. Full of imagination, and the facts assembled & handled in a masterly manner. But this letter is to tell *you* that I do think the proof-reading is very faulty. I don't care to seem to be always insisting to H.G. about details. I have no exaggerated idea of their importance, & I can keep the perspective as well as most folks. But these details *have* importance, & someone ought to see to them; because H.G. never will. Quite apart from numerous easily avoided verbal inelegancies, for which H.G. doesn't care one damn (but ought), there are positive mistakes, as in phrases such as 'as big or bigger than', and acute grammatical slips such as singular verbs after collective nouns which have a plural possessive pronoun. And so on. My impression is that the carelessnesses seem to come in patches. I would do the proofs myself, if he wanted, but I can't undertake a 500,000 word business.

I don't think the footnotes by friends ought to be signed only with initials, unless a table of footnote writers with full names is given at the beginning. And the famous phrase 'op. cit.' (which many plain readers will not understand) ought never to be used for the same work on more than one page. The

127. Harcourt, Brace published most of Rivers's work in America. Doran seems not to have published anything of his.

work ought to be re-cited on every page on which it is referred to.

How the fellow did the book in the time fair passes me. I cannot get over it. It's a life work.

Yours, A. B.

STOKE / MS. / 129
(*To Hugh Walpole*)

12B George Street
23–1–20

My dear Hughie,

Thy letter received yesterday. Damned short. We heard about the Maeterlinck fiasco, & my comment was that it would react against all lecturers in U.S.A. But I hope not against you. I bet you what you like you will not return with some traces of American accent. There is no particular talk in this house except the slump in theatres, & the general & increasing badness of the *London Mercury*. I find the *L.M.* very dull & pompous. We dined at Osbert Sitwell's last night. Very good dinner & the most fantastic & hazardous service. Sickert was there. He is, I regret to say, becoming rather mannered; but his imitations of his old & intimate friend George Moore are still priceless. Wyndham Lewis also was there—in grey flannel. He left early—piqued, as some said, by remarks of Sickert. Massingham and Swinnerton also attended. I was told afterwards that my comments on things & people in general had been outrageous. Nobody minded. Osbert took us off later to Ottoline Morrell's. She has rented a house in Vale Avenue for six weeks. Many persons there, Middleton Murry, Gertler, Mrs. Aldous Huxley, the unavoidable Iris Tree (whom I cannot stick), etc. Ottoline looks younger. She is paler. Her hair is still more like a mop. She was very sweet & kind: but what a bore! Morrell walked amiably about by himself, chiefly quite silent. Quelle affaire! It was like Osbert's effrontery to insist on taking us. He marched into Ottoline's at the head of his squad with much quiet & noble pride. Well, we'll look for you on May 1st.

128. For earlier letters to Jane Wells see Vol. II. *The Outline of History* was issued in instalments beginning in November 1919.

Margaret 'joins with me in kindest regards, dear Mr. Walpole'.

Thine, A. B.

MAYFIELD, SYRACUSE / T.C.C. / 130
(*To the editor of the* NATION)

[12B George Street]
March 8th 1920

Dear Sir,

'Wayfarer' expresses the ignorance of himself and his friends about the late Charles Garvice, and for himself as a famous publicist he quite properly seems rather ashamed of this perfect unacquaintance with an outstanding social phenomenon. He brackets Charles Garvice and Mrs. Florence Barclay together. This he should not do. Charles Garvice had an immensely greater hold on the public than Mrs. Barclay, and for reasons which are creditable to both author and public. The work of Charles Garvice has little artistic importance; but he was a thoroughly competent craftsman. He constructed well and wrote clearly and not inelegantly, and he had a certain imaginative faculty. Artistically his novels are at least on a level with scores of novels which have been seriously reviewed in your columns and with some which people are seriously discussing in circles that deem themselves enlightened this very day. Further, Charles Garvice was utterly free from any sort of snobbery, intellectual or otherwise. Further, both directly and indirectly, by his own freely given energy and diplomatic skill, he accomplished a very great deal for the improvement of the conditions under which authors work. 'Wayfarer' laments the loss of 'that precious thing a common national standard of good literature'. There never was any. Good books, not excluding the classics to which 'Wayfarer' specially refers, are as highly and widely esteemed today as ever they were—probably more so.

Yours faithfully, [Arnold Bennett]

129. Maeterlinck broke short a disastrous lecture tour in America earlier in the year. Wyndham Lewis (1884–1957), author and painter; H. W. Massingham (1860–1924), editor of the *Nation* from 1907 to 1923; Lady Ottoline Morrell (1873–1938), friend of authors, and Philip Edward Morrell (1870–1943); John Middleton Murry (1889–1957), author and critic; Mark Gertler (1892–1939), painter; Maria Huxley (d. 1955); Iris Tree, poetess, daughter of Beerbohm Tree.

130. The letter was printed with negligible changes in the *Nation* on 13 March 1920.

STOKE / MS. / 131
(*To Hugh Walpole*)

12B George Street
22–3–20

My sweet Hughie,

Your esteemed epistle of the 20 Feby. reached me just after F.S. & I had returned from Portugal. We left England about 29th Jan. You must be very strong to withstand all your journeyings, lecturings, and laudations. It is about time you came back among your frank friends who ill-treat and despitefully use you. Your judgement on U.S.A., although damnably true, is not the whole truth, and is in my opinion rather severe. But by heaven I know how you feel. We are looking forward to hearing you, viva voce, on your experiences, here in this flat at dinner. The flat is now finished, & quite the resort of the beau monde. After enormous idleness I am now working again. A fantastic play. In the year 1919 I managed to collect 2 theatrical failures. But I am somewhat compensated by the apparent success of *S & P Love* in U.S.A., that benighted country. The receipts so far immensely surpass those of any other play that I ever had anything to do with. But I made a fatal error with the film rights. I sold them for £1,500, just half what I could have got. There have been revivals here, & I have been obliged to revise my views. *Arms and the Man* and *The Admirable Crichton* are both A1, & I never thought they were. *Pygmalion* is not so good. Barrie's new playlet about Karsavina is only ½ good. There have been 2 supreme books since your regretted departure. G. Moore's *Avowals* and the letters of Chekhov (Tchekoff, s.v.p.). You've probably read them. If not, read them. Not a single damn novel worth a damn since F.S.'s. This I believe to be a fact. Son, I have got an idea for a novel (which I shall write in 1921) that bangs any idea I've had for many years. Believe me! I'm dying to write it. But no. It shall ripen. In the critical world the Swinnerton camp is gradually triumphing over the Squire camp. Swinnerton and ilk flourish exceedingly.

'Wayfarer' was a pseudonym under which H. W. Massingham wrote in the *Nation*. Charles Garvice (d. 1920), journalist turned novelist, achieved a popular success that never ceased to astonish him. At his death he had a fortune twice as large as Bennett's. Florence Barclay (1862–1920) is perhaps best remembered for *The Upas Tree*.

Squire is very depressed & dull, and Shanks has completely broken down & been sent off to the continent for 3 months surcease. I am having great larks with Massingham & Murry in the *Nation*. Marguerite is off to France just before Easter. This woman with whom I live is now placidly sewing by my side. A touching Sunday night picture of the life literary. She tells me to send 'a kind message' to you. She says you must marry a young widow. . . .

Benedicite,

Ever yours, A. B.

MAYFIELD, SYRACUSE / T.C.C. / 132
(*To the editor of the* NATION)

[12B George Street]
March 22nd 1920

Dear Sir,

Mr. Middleton Murry has left the point—at any rate, my point. I objected to 'Wayfarer's' superior attitude towards Charles Garvice's work, which I maintained was no worse than plenty of work taken quite seriously by the *Nation*—and, I may add, by the *Athenaeum* and the *Times Literary Supplement*.

There is no foundation for the insinuation that I am liable to be driven to the conclusion that 'No popular taste can be a bad taste'. Mr. Murry has either not read my critical side-shows or has read them in his sleep. He did, however, note what I said of the artistic value of Charles Garvice's work.

I may be too fond of emphasizing the mechanical element in the profession of literature. But I wish to heaven some of my contemporaries would emphasize it a little more. The English,

131. F. S.—Frank Swinnerton.

Walpole reported of America that the railway system was in disarray, art ignored, the press preoccupied with murder and fornication, and the Senate senile. He thought Americans individually were 'darlings', but 'as a country it's Hell!'

Sacred and Profane Love drew £500 a week for Bennett in New York. The film rights were bought by Famous Players Lasky, and the film was produced in 1921 with Conrad Nagel and others.

Barrie's playlet was *The Truth About the Russian Dancers*, with décor by Paul Nash and music by Arnold Bax. It starred Tamara Karsavina (b. 1885).

Bennett's idea for a novel never materialized except for its death-bed scene which he used in *Lord Raingo* several years later. It was to be about Lord Beaverbrook's father. See further, Vol. I, pp. 280, 286, 296.

Edward Shanks (1892–1953) was assistant editor of the *London Mercury*, 1919–22.

however, seem to have a distaste for thorough technical competence in literature. They have not yet got rid of the Byronic attitude.

I admire Mr. Murry's courage in asserting that 'the popular writers of a hundred years ago had infinitely more artistic literary or social conscience than they have to-day'. (Mr. Middleton Murry's English—an example of what scorn of the 'mechanical' element leads to!) He specially mentions Byron, Dickens and Scott. Byron was a great genius. *Don Juan* is a terrific work. But there is scarcely a page of it which does not show that an artistic conscience was not Byron's strong point. It is notorious that Dickens, like Thackeray, often wrote under self-imposed conditions (especially conditions of haste) which made real artistic integrity impossible. The same is even more true of Scott. Nearly everybody knows this, and if Mr. Murry does not know it he should acquaint himself with literary history and so for the future avoid making generalizations which are entirely absurd.

Not long since I re-read *Quentin Durward*. What a book of hasty expedients, adroit evasions of difficulties, and artistic 'slimness'. If I wasn't so tragically addicted to money-making I would write a destructive study of *Quentin Durward*. And, incidentally, I would prove that the 'artistic, literary, or social conscience' is quite as active today as ever it was.

Mr. Murry says he can sympathize with my 'evident desire to disconcert the preciousness of the aesthete'. But when he says that things such as Charles Garvice made were 'simply not worth making well' etc., I charge him with precisely the preciousness of the aesthete. Was it not worth while to give pleasure to the naive millions for whom Charles Garvice catered honestly and to the best of his very competent ability? Ought these millions to be deprived of what they like, ought they to be compelled to bore themselves with what Mr. Murry likes merely because Mr. Murry's taste is better than theirs? The idea is ridiculous. The idea is snobbish in the worst degree. Taste is still relative. Mr. Murry, though his recent services to the cause of good taste in all the arts have been conspicuously brilliant and laudable, has probably not yet reached the absolute of taste. Charles Garvice's work was worth doing, and since it was worth doing it was worth doing well.

The attitude shown by 'Wayfarer' and Mr. Murry in these matters is, in my opinion, mischievous and perverse, and as long as I have a pen I will never cease to object to such attitudes. The pity is that these attitudinizers, whom I esteem and even love, could not put up a better defence than they did. 'Wayfarer's' performance in your last issue was remarkable only for *bravura* in the use of the red herring. It was not very clever to refer to Mr. Bernard Shaw in derision as a literary tradesman. And it was still less clever, by a long way, to cite Mr. Clement Shorter as an authority on literary taste.

Yours faithfully, [Arnold Bennett]

TEXAS / MS. / 133
(*To Lillah McCarthy and Frederick Keeble*)

12B George Street
25-3-20

My dear children,

My benediction is upon you, & your happiness will be mine. You are both experienced in the world, & therefore you have an immense start in the great happiness handicap. Be beautiful & you will be good. I could keep on in this strain for many years. But you know what I mean.

I shall be represented at the church by my special representative, Marie-Marguerite Bennett. Unfortunately I cannot come myself. But if you see a pale cloud hovering over the parson's head, it will be my soul, watching benevolently.

Yours, Arnold Bennett

132. This letter was printed with minor changes in the *Nation* on 27 March 1920, notably with the omission of the last sentence. J. M. Murry was currently editor of the *Athenaeum* and recently a reviewer for the *Times Literary Supplement*. His letter supporting Wayfarer appeared in the *Nation* on the 20th. In the meantime G. B. Shaw and others attacked him in the *Sunday Express*, and Wayfarer himself commented on these 'literary tradesmen' on the 20th, and added that he had now taken a poll among several literary friends and their knowledge of Charles Garvice was much as his own. Clement Shorter's opinion was exactly his own. For two letters from Bennett to Shorter, who was editor of *Sphere*, see Vol. II.

133. Frederick Keeble (1870–1952) was Professor of Botany at Magdalen College, 1920–7.

NEW STATESMAN, 19 June 1920 / 134
(*To the editor*)

[? Comarques]
[about 12 June 1920]

Sir,

Mrs. Mary Berenson's article on eighteenth century architecture in Spain most interestingly illustrates a principle which is capable of wide application. Our attitude towards architecture is far too much dominated by the aesthetic canons of the past. We get into a groove of taste and so miss innumerable beauties. I wonder how many of the millions of admirers of the Medici tombs at Florence have noticed that the Church of San Lorenzo visibly exists in extreme loveliness. I imagine that not one person in a hundred thousand who passes the Junior United Service Club at the corner of Regent Street and Charles Street ever notices that it is a masterpiece. But who am I to animadvert? After thirty-two years of London I noticed last week for the first time the singular charm of Stagg and Mangle's in Leicester Square! When it has raised all its school-teachers from the starvation level, the L.C.C. might usefully spend a trifle in attaching plaques to a few thousand buildings in London with the name of the architect and the date of construction displayed thereon.

Yours, etc., Arnold Bennett

BEAVERBROOK / TS. / 135
(*To Lord Beaverbrook*)

Comarques
June 21st 1920

My dear Max,

This is an example of the damned nonsense written by that man Haddon:—

From *The S.S. Tenacity.*

'Men talk about their luck with women, but when
they're in love they don't say anything about it.
With women it's just the opposite.'

. . . .

The above illuminating rumination occurred in

134. Mary Berenson was the wife of the art historian Bernard Berenson (1865–1959).

> the otherwise deadly dialogue of the Stage Society's latest exposition at the Hammersmith Lyric of the art of Continental dramatists. The Stage Society, a British institution, produces far too many foreign plays, to the detriment of native talent.

He is now giving girls' clothes and their alleged improprieties a rest, and has turned to something equally silly. If he does not know he ought to know that one of the chief aims of the Stage Society is to produce new foreign plays, so as to keep London abreast of what is going on abroad. The foreign productions, however, are not detrimental to the native author. The greatest trouble of the Stage Society is to get native plays good enough for production. Apparently such plays are not written in sufficient numbers.

S.S. Tenacity is not a great play, but it is infinitely better and more amusing than most of the stuff that Haddon is ready to praise.

I have nothing to do with the management of the Stage Society, and the production of *S.S. Tenacity* at Hammersmith had nothing to do with the London and Local Playhouse Limited, which simply let the theatre to the Stage Society.

The tennis did me much good.

Yours, A. B.

BEAVERBROOK / TS. / 136
(*To Lord Beaverbrook*)

Comarques
June 26th, 1920

My dear Max,

I enclose in this envelope a copy of the *Economic Review of the Foreign Press*. The *Review of the Foreign Press* during the war was about the most efficient thing that I came across in our line. It is still being conducted by the man who conducted it then, Captain Barber. After the war, as you probably know, the thing was taken over privately and the Treasury made certain promises which the Treasury has of course broken to bits. The

135. Archibald Haddon (d. 1942), a theatrical journalist, was on the *Sunday Express* from 1918 to 1923. *S.S. Tenacity* was translated from the French of Charles Vildrac.

Treasury in fact has done nothing. In my opinion this periodical is one of the most useful things going. It is *really* useful. Also it is quite free from political bias. Unless it is helped it will quite possibly expire, although from what I hear its prospects are pretty good if it can hold out. I permit myself to say that if a man of great means provided a relatively small amount of money for the affair he would be guilty of an act of genuine patriotism. I know the periodical very well as I have read it consistently for over three years. My acquaintance with Barber is slight, but I once told him that if he needed help and I could help him I should be glad on public grounds to do so. He has now written to me, asking whether I can suggest the name of anybody who would help. I have not replied to his letter yet, and he has no idea at all that I am writing to you. If I could persuade you to back the affair I should feel that I had done a very good day's work. I will go so far as to say that if you put money into it I also would put money into it, and that relatively to our respective resources I would put more into it than you. Of course not with the least notion of making anything, and with the robust notion of losing something.

All that I know of Barber is that he is diffident and reserved. But I am perfectly sure that the man who has run this review must be a thundering good man. I reckon to be a judge of this sort of thing.

Oblige me by replying to this distressing communication at once.

I should like to send Barber to see you.

Thine, Arnold

P.S. I was delighted to have your note. A.

IDDESLEIGH / MS. / 137
(*F. S. A. Lowndes*)

Comarques
10–9–20

My dear Freddy,

Thank you. The funeral was a most distracting affair—widow aged 26, very beautiful & powerful, & passionately

136. William Edmund Barber (d. 1958) ran the *Economic Review* until 1922, whether or not with Beaverbrook's help is unknown.

devoted to Rickards. I only got your letter today as I've been yachting. Can't something be done to buck up the *Lit. Suppl.*? It is getting duller & duller, though it always contains 1 or 2 good articles. Several friends have joined me in lamentations. They say they know Bruce Richmond but daren't tell him!

Yours, Arnold Bennett

DAVIS / TR. / 138
(*To Oswald H. Davis*)

Comarques
10th September 1920

Dear Mr. Oswald Davis,

Very many thanks for your letter and for the book, which I am glad to have. I have not yet read it. What interests me is that you have got material for three war novels. I shall be very interested in reading those novels. I do not agree with you as to Gibbs' book. It contains a few goodish things, but I am perfectly certain that human nature was never as he describes. He is incurably sentimental and inaccurate. Moreover he cannot write. I regret this, as I like him and his intentions are admirable and his sympathies sound. I have not yet seen a good war book. Doyle of course is ridiculous. I am sending you a copy of *Polite Farces* by this post. It is no good, but as you want it you shall have it.

For myself I am just going into the film business. I shall walk warily at first, but if I can make any sort of a success with a film, I shall try to do something rather new with the second one. I have already made the Lasky Company understand that sentimentality has got to be reduced to almost nothing with my first film, but I do not intend to be too revolutionary, as I do not want to frighten them off at the start. I have four plays unacted, and do not mean to write any more for a long time. My next jobs are six short stories and two novels.

I have been very unwell indeed, but at the moment I am immensely better.

Yours sincerely, Arnold Bennett

137. (Sir) Bruce Richmond (d. 1964) served on *The Times* from 1899 to 1938.
138. Davis published a book of verse in 1920, *London Pastels*.
(Sir) Philip Gibbs (1877–1962) published *Realities of War* in 1920. Sir Arthur

GIDE / 139
(*To André Gide*)

Comarques
10–9–1920

My dear André Gide,

Your letter touched me deeply. I was very sorry to have to leave so soon, and desert you. It is a remarkable thing that, if I inspire you, you most certainly inspire me. When I have seen you I always want to produce something *finer* than I have been doing—something with more taste. Je ne me sens pas assez lettré. C'est le classique qui me manque. If I could live with a small group of the *N.R.F.* for two months I should improve. But after all the greatest difficulty is to write the truth. It always escapes. I have learned something about construction and something about ornamentation. I could have taught both Dostoevsky and Stendhal something about these matters, but these 2 men had a faculty of getting so near the truth, and getting there beautifully, that I always say to myself when reading them: 'No! I could never do anything equal to that.' I have the same feeling about *Le Curé de Tours*, but about little else of Balzac's. I hear that my *These Twain* is to appear incessamment in *La Revue de Paris*. Il y aura des coupures fantastiques, j'en suis sûr. I have read 100 pages of *L. Leuwen*. It is exceedingly fine, but I don't yet class it with *La Chartreuse*. C'est toujours dans le vrai, mais pas assez élevé. When I come to Paris I will let you know.

Yours ever, Arnold Bennett

P.S. Have you read *The Pretty Lady*? It was while reading *Isabelle* that the form of this novel suddenly presented itself to me, and I began to write it at once. Yet nothing could be less like calm *Isabelle* than this feverish novel. A. B.

Conan Doyle (1859–1930) wrote an account of the European campaign in several volumes, 1916 to 1920.

On *Polite Farces*, published in 1899, see Vols. I and II. Bennett's relations with Famous Players Lasky are described in Vol. I. His first film story was *The Wedding Dress*, which was never produced. The four plays were *Body and Soul* (finished before 10 May 1920), *The Bright Island* (written January–April 1920), *The Love Match* (written July 1920), and *Don Juan de Marana* (written 1913–14). The short stories were for English and American magazines; see Vol. I, pp. 276–7, for details. The next two novels that Bennett wrote were *Mr. Prohack* and *Lilian*.

139. Gide visited Bennett briefly at the end of August, and Bennett had to leave

ILLINOIS / MS. / 140
(*To H. G. Wells*)

Comarques
15–9–20

My dear H.G.,

Much obliged for the portly volume. I have kept regularly up to date with the parts, and am now in Part 22. Such reviews as I have seen are chiefly footling. I have never read a work with a greater sense of the *achievement* of the thing. In fact for the last 12 parts I have been in a state of perpetual amazement. The affair is handled; it is done; it is accomplished; the perspective is maintained, and there is an omnipresent feeling of masterliness. Anybody who knows what a work is, & what it means in labour, presence of mind, cerebration, and grit—especially on this immense scale—will regard congratulations as extremely inadequate. The book is a majestic success, both brilliant and solid. I regret the negligences of writing, but attach only the slightest importance to them. I think you were rather casual over the Renaissance; but I haven't much else in the way of animadversion. Nobody else on earth could have done the thing one tenth as well as you have done it. You have supplied a want, and made powerfully for righteousness.

Yours, A. B.

STOKE / MS. / 141
(*To Hugh Walpole*)

12B George Street
14–10–20

My sweet Hughie,

It seems to me that I have to write to you in the same nagging strain as I do to Wells. In spite of my brotherly admonitions & my fatherly threats apropos of previous books there are at least as many grammatical slips in this one as in any. In particular

to go to Rickards' funeral. Bennett noted in his *Journal* that he had 'great book talks with Gide'. Gide wrote to him afterwards: 'Je crois que vous pouvez mal comprendre quel courage et quelle excitation mon espirit et tout mon être trouvent dans votre conversation, et même dans votre seule présence. Je vous sens posséder si pleinement et si calmement tout ce que je sens qui me manque; de quelle instruction votre exemple est pour moi!'

For other comments on Dostoevsky, Stendhal, Balzac, and Gide's *Isabelle* see Vol. II.

'anybody' & 'everybody' are followed by a plural verb at least a score times. And as regards careless writing, there are tons of it. Things like: 'She had abandoned so completely any idea that he might still come that she could not now feel that it was he.' Also there are some devilish shaky metaphors, e.g. on p. 313, the lines beginning: 'Therefore she was building.' How in hell the doors could be locked of a house of which the walls were rising, I cannot imagine. Do not suppose that I attach an exaggerated importance to these things. I don't. But I cannot understand how they could remain in a book over which you have obviously (to the seeing eye) taken such enormous pains. To my mind this is a far better book than *The Mirror*, *The City*, *The Forest*. It is more mature. It illustrates more fully than ever the extraordinary narrative gift which you undoubtedly have. Your gift in this line is Trollopian (but I am not going to accept that as an excuse for your Trollopian carelessness—I'm hanged if I do). I do not agree with all your characterisation, but your greatest enemy could not deny that these characters are immensely alive. I object to some of the stuff, which does not seem to me to have been accurately observed, but on the other hand there are lots of it with which no fault can be found. The middle of the book is the best. Round about pp. 207, 208, for instance, is the *goods*, emphatically. Some of the construction I do not understand. I can't see the constructional reason, e.g. for the Kingscote Revival Meeting. But doubtless you could produce a good reason, so I shall not insist. Dealing with the book largely, & applying to it the severest standards, I am inclined to say that the excessive power of your visualising imagination has caused you to crowd it a bit, in fact a good bit. You are imaginatively very rich, but is that a reason why you should be extravagant? I doubt not you *could* make a novel out of the history of every one of the minor characters; but need you?

And lo! a certain man went forth into the streets and spake these words:

Simplification
Austerity
Economy of material

Such, imperfectly, respectfully, & fragmentarily are my views about this history which you have so affectionately dedicated to the aged one. There are lots of questions I want to ask you about it. Will you dine Thursday 21st?

Thine, A. B.

BEAVERBROOK / TS. / 142
(*To Lord Beaverbrook*)

12B George Street
16th November 1920

My dear Max,

Many thanks. Mair's address is 34 Walpole Street, Chelsea, and no doubt letters sent there will reach him.

I am positively informed by people who should know that the Man with the Duster is Harold Begbie.

I have chucked politics because I am not sufficiently expert to deal with it, and not because I have chucked journalism. I like journalism, and shall doubtless next year continue to deal with the conduct of life.

McKenna would be no good as a leader, but he would be better than Simon, than whom there is no man in politics I despise more. I quite see that complete intellectual honesty is not only impossible but absurd in politics; also that some chicane is necessary. But between this position and 'making use of all the ammunition at my disposal' to overthrow the Coalition, there is a gulf. I should consider it merely clumsy to try to overthrow the Coalition on an issue upon which I was not in fact opposed to it. There may be some sort of a case for strict anti-dumping: but the *Daily Express* policy goes beyond anti-dumping. Nothing would induce me to support protection either actively or passively. In the Tariff Reform fight the Protectionists were argued to a complete standstill. They were shut up. You say that the dye industry is being ruined. Have you enquired about the sufferings of dye-users and public under British-made dyes? I hear a lot about it. The interdependence of nations is a thing to be encouraged. Moreover, if you keep exports out you keep imports in. Etc. etc. But you know all this far better than I do. Your last signed article 'Confidence' was *really first-class*—much better than your letter to the *Nation*.

I *want* to come to Cherkley; but I cannot spare a week-end

141. Walpole's new novel was *The Captives*, dedicated 'to Arnold Bennett with deep affection'.

now. If I take a day off I go to Brightlingsea to inspect the work on my new yacht.

Thine, A. B.

GIDE / 143
(*To André Gide*)

12B George Street
30–11–1920

My dear André Gide,

Your letter gave me the greatest satisfaction. You see, I always have the idea that French critics must regard English fiction as rather barbaric, lacking in finesse and in civilized breadth. In brief, an imperfect attitude towards life. No appreciation that I have ever received has given me such pleasure as yours. I do not except Joseph Conrad's, because Conrad is an oriental and gives praise like one. As for my new manner,—well, it is not yet materialising! I have begun a novel —true, it is only a light one—and I have not been able to get the new manner into it. After writing sixty books one cannot, I find, change one's manner merely by taking thought. However, I have hopes of my next novel after the present one. It will be entirely serious. There were, by the way, symptoms of the new manner in *The Pretty Lady*. I don't know whether you have read it. The younger men here are inclined to think it my best novel. It is not. Veinard, avec vos grandes et vos petites entrées à la bibliothèque particulière du palais de justice! Quelle chance, tout de même!

I am ill, or I should have written sooner. But I'm getting better, I'll send you a book I'm publishing in January.

142. G. H. Mair (1887–1926) was formerly in the Ministry of Information. For other references to him see below and also Vol. I. Harold Begbie (1871–1929) was an author and journalist; the reference is probably to a series of articles on religious leaders by 'A Gentleman with a Duster'; the articles were issued in book form in 1922 under the title *Painted Windows*.

Reginald McKenna (1863–1943) and John Simon (Viscount Simon, 1873–1954) both served in Asquith's Liberal government, and Simon served in several later governments. Beaverbrook was very much preoccupied with the issue of free trade, which he favoured only within the Commonwealth.

Beaverbrook's article 'Confidence', concerned with Britain's post-war problems, appeared in the *Sunday Express* on 14 November. His letter to the *Nation*, printed on 13 November, denied the charge made there that his newspapers were servants of the Coalition government.

Bennett bought his new yacht, the Marie Marguerite, earlier in the year.

My film is progressing and I am visiting the ateliers. The first film will be nothing, but when I have broken down the outer-defences of 'the trade', I hope to do something better. That man Maurice Lanoire seems to be breaking down the defences of the Paris press with my books. Grasset is to publish several. I understand that *These Twain* is appearing in the *Revue de Paris* (doubtless with the usual terrible cuts), and that *The Price of Love* is to appear in a thing called *La Revue de la Semaine* (of which I had never heard). I enclose two more articles from *The Times*. Concurrently with the former article I sent you a letter, which I hope you got. As your letters *never* deign to give an address, I am always doubtful. My wife sends you mille choses. She has just returned from a triumphant reciting tour in Scotland.

Always yours, Arnold Bennett

ILLINOIS / MS. / 144
(*To Jane Wells*)

12B George Street
8–12–20

Dear Lady Jane,

The whole Jane world (extensive, orbicular) has been shaken to its depths by this affair of yours. Happily it now has reason to recover, & is recovering, & I am once more getting the lime-

143. Gide wrote to Bennett earlier in the month about *The Old Wives' Tale*, which he had just read: 'Mon cher ami, vous êtes ce que Flaubert eût appelé "un fameux gaillard". D'un bout à l'autre de ce livre énorme, je n'ai trouvé pas une faiblesse, pas une impatience, pas la moindre diminution de clarté. Je ne crois pas avoir jamais lu roman où la réalité se présentât moins déformée. La force de pénétration de votre sympathie est prodigieuse. Je ne souffre jamais avec vous de cette sorte de supériorité qui fait que Meredith, par exemple, semble toujours se pencher sur ses personnages et les considérer de haut en bas. Vous restez toujours et maintenez toujours le lecteur, sur le même plan qu'eux. Et tout en restant particulier, de quel intérêt général devient pour nous ce médiocre et pathétique exemple de l'impossibilité du désacclimatement (excusez le néologisme) de Constance, et de réacclimatement de Sophie. Admirable.'

Bennett began writing *Mr. Prohack* on 10 October. The next novel was presumably the one about Beaverbrook's father. The January book was *Things That Have Interested Me* (first series).

Maurice Lanoire translated several of Bennett's works into French, beginning with *Sacred and Profane Love* (for serial publication) in 1912 and *Clayhanger* in 1915. The firm of Bernard Grasset published *Sacred and Profane Love* in book form in 1920 and *The Price of Love* in 1921. Grasset also published *Tales of the Five Towns*. On the French serial publication of *These Twain* see above, p. 5 n. *The Price of Love* seems to have been published in the *Revue de la Semaine* in 1921; copies of the periodical were not available.

light. Before your unhappy appearance in the pathological theatre, I was attracting a certain amount of attention by means of pyorrhea, high frequency electrical treatment, microbic injections, dentists, specialists, etc. But you wiped me off the map in one day. However, I think I can beat you in permanence of sickliness, & I am doubly glad of it. I saw H.G. yesterday. Dr. Shufflebotham, who was there, predicted he would have to stay at home today, and lo! so it is. He is immensely proud of the fact that he can make out cheques and pay bills without your help. In fact the entire club is much bored by his interminable recitals of feats in the cheque & payment line. You will have a horrible skein to unravel when you return to management. I hear you will be back for Christmas. It is the best news. We went to Edith Sitwell's reception last night. Crowds of poets, many of whom sat on the floor. Still, not tedious. The St. John Ervines were [? my standby]. At least, *she* was. We are just beginning to know them. They are my sort. Tonight, Swedish ballet. Next week Actors Orphanage Fancy Dress Ball, C. Garden. Haven't been to one for ten years. This last week you have doubtless felt within you a peculiar but enheartening *in*fluence. You didn't know it, but it was the *e*ffluence of my blessing. I hope to see you frisking soon. Marguerite sends her love. Me too.

Yours ever, A. B.

GRIFFIN / T.C. / 145
(*To Lord Rothermere*)

[12B George Street]
[about 12 December 1920]

My dear Rothermere,

I expect that you, like most of us, are concerned about the most serious question of the disabled soldier. I should be very much obliged if you would step across here one day quite soon and have lunch and meet Reeves-Smith, the managing director of the Savoy Company, and Alfred Scott and his wife.

144. Dr. Frank Shufflebotham (d. 1932), a Potteries man, was Bennett's personal physician for a time.

Of Edith Sitwell (1887–1964) Bennett wrote in 1924 that technically she was one of the two most accomplished living poets in England.

St. John Ervine (1888–), the dramatist, and his wife Leonora met Bennett earlier in 1920. Ervine's play *John Ferguson* was put on at the Lyric Hammersmith in 1920.

These people have a big plan for getting a lot of money in aid of a comprehensive scheme for consumptive ex-service men, of whom there are 35,000 at present. Reeves-Smith is an extremely able man, and Alfred Scott you know. They would not touch anything that was not sound. The plan cannot, however, be handled without the help of a powerful daily. It would cost the daily nothing and would be an enormous advertisement for it. The plan affects chiefly women, and the *Mirror* is indicated. I am not competent to explain the plan to you myself. That is why I would like you to meet the people who have conceived it. If the thing doesn't appeal to you, you have only to turn it down. But I think that your interest in the disabled soldier will be more than sufficient to persuade you to listen to it.

If you could lunch next Friday, the 17th, at 1.30, I would get the others. If that day won't suit you, will you name some other day between the 17th and the 23rd. You see I am rather counting on you!

Yours sincerely, Arnold Bennett

FALES, NYU / MS. / 146
(*To Robert Nichols*)

12B George Street
23–12–20

My dear Robert,

About ⅔ds of this play is undoubtedly very fine. I think it weakens in structure in the 3rd act. I can't see any sufficient

145. On Lord Rothermere see above, p. 53. For a letter to George Reeves-Smith see below, p. 339. Alfred Scott is not known. Bennett made several attempts to help disabled soldiers, notably in a pamphlet entitled *A National Responsibility* which was reprinted from an article of his in the *Daily News* on 6 June 1917. Nothing more is known about the present effort. On the occasion of another appeal he wrote: 'It is important to recognise clearly one great fact about the war: every day disabled and otherwise unfit men are being discharged from the army, and thrown on the world, not because the state has done all it can do and ought to do for them, but because the army has no further use for them. After being called heroes in the newspapers they are dismissed from the service of the state while the nation is still in their debt. True the state grants them pensions which may or may not be adequate. But the nation owes more to the disabled or otherwise unfit soldier than any state pension, however adequate, can pay. The nation owes it to each man that every effort should be made to render him reasonably capable of the great task of resuming his civilian existence. Until the man's individual handicap has been mitigated as far as possible by special training or treatment, and until a full and favourable opportunity for a new start in life has been offered to him, the nation must remain his debtor.'

reason why Bentley's public disgrace should necessitate the breaking off of Lois' engagement. The Lois affair is a magnificent complication, but I don't consider that you have quite brought off all the motivation. From this point the play to my mind weakens. The last act does not hang together well; it is immensely too long, and it reads much more like a draft than the finished article. *It ought to be re-written.* Such are my views. Acts I, II, & III need nothing but cutting as far as the big scene between Bentley & Lois. I only met the dedication tonight. Thanks. It is very agreeable to me. I don't know where you are.

Yours, A. B.

ARNOLD BENNETT / 147
(*To George Moore*)

[12B George Street]
December 24, 1920

[fragment]

. . . and I wish also to tell you that it was the first chapters of *A Mummer's Wife* which opened my eyes to the romantic nature of the district that I had blindly inhabited for over twenty years. You are indeed the father of all my Five Towns books.

[Arnold Bennett]

MAYFIELD, SYRACUSE / T.C.C. / 148
(*To the editor of the* DAILY EXPRESS)

[12B George Street]
24th February 1921

Dear Sir,

Touching your dramatic critic's remarks about my criticisms of dramatic criticisms. He makes dark references to the affrighting difficulties which hamper the dramatic critic, difficulties needing courage to reveal them and whose disclosure might cause the heavens to fall. He also refers to his

146. Robert Nichols the poet (1893–1944); his play was *Guilty Souls*; see below, pp. 229–31.

147. This fragment of a letter is all that is known to survive among perhaps twenty letters from Bennett to George Moore. For other comments on Moore see Vols. I and II.

thirty years of experience. I was a dramatic critic for a number of years for several papers. I have been a literary critic and a musical critic and an art critic. I have professionally advised both theatre managers and publishing houses. I have been an editor. I am familiar with the theatre from the management side, and not unfamiliar with the organisation of concerts. I have had plays produced. I have been a political writer. Guided by my own experience I assert most positively that the hidden difficulties of dramatic criticisms are no greater than, and scarcely different from, the hidden difficulties of any form of artistic criticism, or even of political or commercial criticism. They are merely the difficulties which must surround the public expression of any personal opinion in any organised society, and they can almost always be overcome by the adroit.

I quite agree that to judge a farcical comedy in a sparsely occupied auditorium is exceedingly difficult. The remedy for that, however, is very simple. Follow the continental practice and fill the house at the dress-rehearsal.

Yours truly, [Arnold Bennett]

HILL / MS. / 149
(*To Gregory Hill*)

12B George Street
1-3-21

My dear Gregory,

A lusty infant!

It is all rot about not being able to get my photo. My photo is bought by newspapers several times every week. It can be had for instance from Hoppé of Baker St. On principle I never keep photos of myself. I refuse to have them in the house. So that I cannot send you one. If I had one I would. I have no connection with Leek. But I have referred to Leek in my books under the name of Axe & also under the name of Manifold. I prefer Axe. Also I have referred to Rudyard Lake in 'The Death

148. The letter was published in the *Daily Express* on 25 February with negligible changes. On 23 February Bennett published an article entitled 'Dramatic Critics' in the *Express*, in which he attacked the critics for lack of standards. On the following day Archibald Haddon (see pp. 127–8) replied that Bennett did not mention the real difficulties facing the critics, but he did not identify the difficulties.

of Simon Fuge' & other deathless productions. This is about all.

The fact is, my dear boy, I had not really realized in my mind that you were married. As for your being a father, it startles me. I am all for marrying Dutchwomen. If I had not married a French ditto I would have done so myself. Good luck!

Kindest regards to your mother,

Yours, Arnold Bennett

DAVIS / TR. / 150
(*To Oswald H. Davis*)

12B George Street
12.3.21

Dear Mr. Oswald Davis,

Many thanks for your letter. I should have answered it before but for insomnia, neuralgia, dyspepsia: of which I am not yet quite cured, though I am better. I hope your novel will impress the right people as it might do. I am not much of a believer in First Novel Competitions, for the reason that the original 'weeding out' is not done, and cannot be done, by first-rate experts. The risk is that the best novel may not even reach the advertised judges. I once acted in a competition with Conrad and Squire. Working quite independently on a selected dozen stories, we substantially agreed as to the order of merit, but if we got the best dozen that were sent in I should be greatly surprised. I doubt whether *The April Forfeit* is a good title. I am quite sure that *London Pastels* is a bad title. The *Birmingham Post* certainly ought to have behaved better. But I wish you could read the comments of the *Staffordshire Sentinel* (Hanley) on me! I have come to the conclusion that I am no judge of my own books, that few authors can judge their own books. If I gave you my real opinions you might be scandalised. Your own opinion of *The April Forfeit* 5 years hence will be vastly more thrilling than your present opinion of it, and, if the two opinions differ, you will probably never know which one is right.

I don't now believe in settling all details of plot before

149. E. O. Hoppé (1878–) the famous portrait photographer.
'The Death of Simon Fuge' appears in the collection *The Grim Smile of the Five Towns*, 1907.

beginning to write; and I don't remember whether I ever did believe in this practice. Not long since I made a contract to produce a revised version of *How to Become an Author*; but I see no immediate prospect of executing it. I am at a period when I happen to have rather too much to do and not enough verve to do it with. In fact I feel as if I wanted to write only one more novel; and for this novel I have a great scheme. But I have neither the desire nor the power to 'produce' as I used to produce. My immediate diversion is writing an original film.

Yours sincerely, Arnold Bennett

ETHEL SMYTH / 151
(*To Ethel Smyth*)

12B George Street
30 March 1921

Dear Dr. Ethel Smyth,

Pardon my forwardness, but I must tell you I think that *Streaks* is another what-I-call-a-*book*. In fact I should say it is better than *Impressions*. You imply that the absence of shyness is a symptom of conceit. My experience is that *shyness* is a symptom of conceit. (Naturally, since it springs from the illusion that anybody's attention is monopolised by oneself!) I think that the great majority of shy people whom I have known ultimately proved to be conceited.

I do not like you using 'phenomenal' in the sense of 'exceedingly extraordinary'. Such is not its meaning, and the misuse of it comes all the worse from one who has the sense and the presence of mind to follow 'none' with a singular verb: which few even highly experienced writers do.

But what really does annoy me is the note to the effect that your thanks are due to certain editors for permission to reprint. Nothing of the kind! You sold the serial rights of your stuff to these august beings (or at any rate you ought to have done), and they have no control whatever over the volume rights or any other portion of the copyright.

Still in spite of these terrible blemishes I love your book and

150. Davis published a few novels of Birmingham life during the 1920s. There was no new edition of *How to Become an Author*. Bennett's novel is still the one about Beaverbrook's father, his film story is still *The Wedding Dress*.

am looking forward to seeing you with or without your inamorato Maurice. My wife is at present away.

Yours sincerely, Arnold Bennett

TEXAS / TS. / 152
(*To R. D. Blumenfeld*)
PRIVATE

12B George Street
1st April 1921

My dear Blumenfeld,

I am glad to see that today you give some figures to show what the coal strike is really about. The public seldom knows what a strike is about. I think it would be still better if you gave the national and the district percentages of decrease below the rates last ruling and of increase over the 1914 rates.

In my opinion there is a future for a paper which will give impartial and fully informing labour news on its news page, while expressing its opinions boldly on its leader page.

No paper gives impartial and full labour news, and the worst sinner is the *Daily Herald*.

Most papers are coloured by the personal desires of proprietors and editors. This is bad journalism surely. Most papers give the idea that strikers are idiots or criminals, and employers most reasonable beings. Whereas the facts are that morally there is not a damn to choose between them, and that one lot is just as right as the other. Take the point of the engine-men and pump-staff. How grossly disingenuous on the part of the press not to mention that the engine-men and pump-staff received notice to quit from the employers just like everybody else! Yet how many papers did mention it?

Another point. Before a strike most papers are generally too optimistic and thus they dope the public. Again and again it has happened that executives have been overruled by delegates, and notoriously the best labour leaders are conservative. Yet newspapers continue, before a strike, to take what executives and leaders say at its face value.

151. Dame Ethel Smyth, the composer (1858–1944), published four volumes of autobiography, including *Impressions That Remained* and *Streaks of Life*. She also wrote a biography of Maurice Baring, an intimate friend for many years. See below for letters from Bennett to Baring.

You don't want to learn from anybody about getting circulation. But what satisfaction can circulation give to you without prestige? You will never get prestige in this country unless you get an outstanding reputation for impartiality and fullness of news about the most controversial questions. So long, however, as the facts are given and faced you can use any headlines you please and express any opinions you please.

But before formulating a policy it would be well to consider realistically the differences between the personal interests of the average reader and the personal interests of the proprietors. These differences are vast, and some proprietors make the fatal mistake of pretending to themselves that they do not exist.

A policy of opportunism will never result in prestige. Respect is the sole foundation of genuine prestige.

The *Express* has an unequalled chance of succeeding with a policy which combines scoops and honest presentment of news with fearless expression of opinion and a contempt for opportunism. Given the personalities of the principal proprietors, this is the only policy whose results can ultimately satisfy the said proprietors. Look how much potential prestige you have lost already by a daily refusal to contemplate Ireland! Hamar can never win, and nobody with any historical sense ever believed that he could win. A truce is inevitable. Why not advocate it, and why not have advocated it long ago?

I know you could offer a million opportunist reasons in favour of modifications of the policy above suggested. But you cannot remind yourself too often of the main principles thereof.

You may get a million and a half circulation, but I tell you that neither you nor Max will be happy unless you feel that the paper has, broadly, the respect of outsiders like me. I know nothing about the practice of daily journalism, but I know that psychological fact.

We will now sing hymn No. 451.

Yours, with all apologies, Arnold Bennett

152. The coal strike came about because the owners of many of the mines were proposing to reduce wages by up to forty per cent. The *Express* printed some of the figures—weekly wages down from £5/–/– to £3/17/–, from £4/17/– to £2/17/–, and so forth. The miners believed the reductions were in the interest of greater profit. The argument of the owners, and the view of the *Express,* was that falling prices made such reductions inescapable. The strike was not settled until July, with the government stepping in to subsidize the wages of the miners.

BEAVERBROOK / MS. / 153
(*To Lord Beaverbrook*)

12B George Street
3–4–21

My dear Max,

George Moore is in France. I should however like you to come on 12th (Tuesday) at 1.15 to meet Frank Swinnerton, an extremely intimate friend of mine, & in my opinion the best all-round judge of things literary in London. He has turned Chatto & Windus from a corpse into the liveliest thing of its sort in London. . . . My neuralgia lasted till Friday. A tribute to your varied forms of entertainment that I enjoyed myself continuously at Cherkley with continuous neuralgia.

I must have women. Capt. Macheath in *The Beggar's Opera.*

This is the greatest thing ever said; & it reminds me that we must have a dance. Let us arrange one for next week. (Not this, I am full up.) If you'll have it at the Grafton, I'll bring one or two. My difficulty is to find men who dance and are not tedious to me personally.

Thine, A. B.

KEDDIE / MS. / 154
(*To E. V. Lucas*)

12B George Street
4–6–21

My dear Edward,

On Thursday night Cochran asked me to write a revue for him. I at once said that you ought to be invited to collaborate with me. He liked the idea. I don't know how you feel about it, but anyway for me this condition is an absolute sine qua non.

I really didn't attach any importance to his suggestion, knowing that all these people are alike. But the next morning he sent me a note saying he was 'tremendously keen', and inviting

---

(Sir) Hamar Greenwood (1870–1948) was Chief Secretary for Ireland, and very shortly he and the English government had to yield to Irish demands for independence.

153. *The Beggar's Opera*, adapted by Bennett, began a three-year run at the Lyric Hammersmith on 5 June 1920.

Bennett took up dancing in the twenties.

me to lunch. For political reasons I refused his invitation, and asked him to dine with me at the Garrick on Thursday 16th at 8. He has accepted. My experience is that it is always wise to keep theatrical managers hanging about a bit. I have further told him that under no circumstances can I touch any fresh work until October.

Will you come to the dinner? If the notion of a joint revue—the collaboration to be equal in every respect—appeals to you, doubtless you will come if you can. But perhaps an earlier meeting between us two would be advisable. I shall be out of town next Friday to Tuesday, & I have only one or two lunches free. Tea here is a feasibility.

Yours, A. B.

ARKANSAS / MS. / 155
(*To Frank Swinnerton*)

Yacht Marie Marguerite
8–8–21

My dear Henry,

The enclosed explains itself. Please return it. Permit me to say that, unless you have decided definitely to give your whole time to fiction, you have to bear in mind that you=a gold mine to any publisher, & that you are merely making a present to C. & W. of at least £1,000 a year. You need to realise this, & I doubt if you do, yet. Personally I was not much impressed by Butterworth during the few moments I saw him, but George seems to believe in him. I have noticed a certain hesitation on your part to say whether or not you intended to give up everything for fiction. If you do not intend to do so, then in the words of Dr. Dillon you should 'envisage the situation afresh'. No place at any publishers is worth anything to you unless you receive both a salary & a share of the profits.

(Clever chap, George! Note his use of the word 'alliance'. I bet you he deliberated over that word. Less than a partnership, more than a situation.)

All this, to quote George, 'is a delicate intrusion on my part'. When I was at the Reform last week but one I heard all about

154. Charles Cochran (1873–1951), the theatrical manager and producer. Nothing came of the proposal.

your car (from the barber). I hope it is going well. I have now been cruising for 3 months (with 2 or 3 brief intervals)! I had a week at Comarques, 3rd week in July, and found Marguerite holding a court. I have had Lillah McCarthy, Prof Keeble & Olive, for Cowes week. They were all simply fine, & they were ravished by the yacht. Racing splendid; weather [?]. Also I've been to Cornwall. Tomorrow W.P., I go to Deauville, with Shuffle and Alistair Tayler. Beaverbrook came to see me the other night. Dark. He couldn't hire anything else to come off, so he hired a motor coal-lighter about as big as the yacht. Next morn the decks were covered with coal dust. He brought with him Herbert Holt, 'the richest man in Canada'. The whole visit was hugely characteristic. But he was much impressed. I shall see him at Deauville. I've been entertaining Lady B. & her sister, & was very well satisfied with both of them. If you've got any spare time between now & Sept. 12th & could come to France, perhaps you would care to sojourn for a week. Sept. would be best.

Yours, A. B.

BIRMINGHAM / MS. / 156
(*To John Galsworthy*)

Yacht Marie Marguerite
Fowey
28–8–21

Dear Galsworthy,

I have signed & sent on the book. What a race, the American! Be not puffed up—you will only make it next time. Still, it was a feat, & I congratulate thee. I have been cruising now for 3½ months, & shall cruise for one more month. (But I have a study on board, & have already written 50,000 words therein.) I believe my wife still exists. She spent a few days on the yacht at the start, & we shall end up together in a blaze of glory at Ostend; but otherwise I see little of her during this cruising craze. She hates yachting.

Hang it. I *know* it is a long time since we saw you. I

155. Bennett spent much of 1921 sailing off the English and French coasts.
Thornton Butterworth—a publisher for some years; George—George Doran; Olive—Olive Valentine; Shuffle—Dr. Frank Shufflebotham; Hubert Holt (1856–1941), engineer and financier.

want to see you. But God knows where you are at any given moment.

My devoted homage to your wife, to whom in my Midland way I am deeply attached, & I don't care who knows it.

Yours ever, Arnold Bennett

STOKE / MS. / 157
(*To Hugh Walpole*)

12B George Street
27–10–21

My dearest Hughie,

I have seen an envelope addressed in what I took to be your handwriting to my wife. She is not here, & it has been sent on to her. I am only writing to you to guard against the risk of your having possibly invited her at the same time as myself. The very gravest trouble has arisen between her and me. She is not here, and she will not be here if I can possibly help it. I positively & solemnly desire you to say nothing about this affair, nor to hint at it even in the vaguest way, to anybody whatever at present. And I know that I can rely upon your perfect muteness. Two or three people of course know about it, as I was obliged to consult certain people who were equally intimate with both of us. You are now of the number. When something is settled I will let you know.

My affections.

Thine, A. B.

W. MORGAN / MS. / 158
(*To Frederick Marriott*)

12B George Street
5–11–21

My dear Frederick,

I greatly regret that I shall not be in tomorrow afternoon. Would the next Sunday do? Marguerite will not be here in any case, as she & I have agreed that it will be better for us to live apart, owing to certain fundamental objections made by me. The deed is not yet signed, but I hope will be very shortly,—so that the affair is not at present officially public. I hope your wife, to whom my affections—also to Menetta—is better entirely.

Yours, A. B.

BEAVERBROOK / MS. / 159
(*To Lord Beaverbrook*)

12B George Street
10–11–21

My dear Max,

I couldn't very well tell you on the telephone this morning: I have arranged that my wife & myself shall live apart, & she has already gone, though the deed of separation is not actually signed yet. The cause of this rift is a profound difference of opinion between us as to the propriety of the position held by a young Frenchman named X (whom I think you met here once at dinner) in our mutual existence. That's all. There has been a hell of a row, and the row is over. Henceforth I shall be decidedly more free. I'll come with pleasure to Cherkley Saturday 19th, & you're going to drive me down, I hope. I've no car here now.

It is a 1,000 pities the *Express* didn't get the Wells Washington stuff. His first 3 articles in the *Mail* have been absolutely tremendous. Still, Nevinson will be good.

Yours, A. B.

BUTLER / MS. / 160
(*To Edward Knoblock*)

12B George Street
17–11–21

My dear Edward,

I ought to have written you before. I do hope you are going on all right. I have not written partly because I have been laid

158. For earlier letters to the Marriott family see Vol. II.

159. The young Frenchman was in fact from the Channel Islands. There are a few references to him in Bennett's *Journal* in 1920.

H. G. Wells went to Washington to report on the Disarmament Conference. The editor of the *Westminster Gazette* wanted Bennett to go, but he declined; see Vol. I, p. 297. H. W. Nevinson (1856–1941), famous as a war correspondent, began his reports in the *Express* on 14 November.

up with a most rotten chill, & partly because I have been arranging for a separation from my unhappy wife. The cause of this separation is a young French man, named X, whom you may have met. Understand, *I am making no divorce-court allegations against her*. Only superficially the thing had become such a scandal that I had to do something. Our mutual solicitor gives her the alternative of giving me up entirely, or giving X up entirely. She chose to stick to X. I am very sorry for her, as she is the victim of an infatuation for a man whom all our friends utterly detest & despise. And she cannot be made to see reason. Everybody has failed. I am making her an ample allowance. It is absolutely tragic—or soon will be—for her. For me it is an immense relief.

At the end of the month I am going to join Bertie Sullivan on his new 109 ton yacht at Nice, for—I hope—2 months.

Yours ever, A. B.

STOKE / MS. / 161
(*To Hugh Walpole*)

12B George Street
22–11–21

My dear Hughie,

I don't know what you mean by 'romantic'. All the big realists are romantic, no one more so than Balzac or Dostoevsky or Chekhov. The only sense that I can attach to the word as you use it is 'sentimental'—meaning a softening of the truth in order to produce a pleasant impression on people who don't like the truth. It is quite possible to be romantic & truthful at the same time. All untruthful romance is vitiated. There is no opposition or mutual-excluding between romance & realism. Believe me.

Your novel shows once more your most genuine and even devilish gift for narrative. By God you can tell a story! Also the first half of the book is full of charming things, excellent bits of observation and fancy, new gleams of light on the world. But, also by God, I will not hide from you my conviction that the book does not improve as it goes on. The *invention* of the latter half is not good, & it gets more & more conventional. Some of

160. For earlier letters to Edward Knoblock see Vol. II.
Herbert Sullivan (d. 1928)—nephew and biographer of Sir Arthur Sullivan.

the critical scenes are not really 'done'. I instance round about p. 252 & p. 339; various others. I think that Victoria & Peter are well drawn. I am obliged to call the book 'pretty'—that is as a whole. The fact is that you have made the factual development too poignant for the general mood of the book.

The [?] business is not suited to it. Your instinct told you not to attempt to 'realize' the [?] scenes, and you didn't realise them; the failure to do so saved the homogeneity of the novel, & that is all that can be said for it. I am well aware that my strictures, whether you accept them or not, will cause you pain. But I would a jolly sight sooner cause you pain than insult you by wrapping up my feelings about the book in pink paper. I do not reckon that this book has come off. At first I thought it would, but the 'romantic' idea ran away with you. Don't imagine that I have any objection whatever to the 'romantic' as such. But I do not accept it as an excuse for falsification, or conventionalisation, & I maintain that a process of increasing falsification & conventionalisation goes on throughout the book. The mere details of writing I think are better than in *The Captives*.

F.S. agrees with me that your skill in narrative is diabolic—hellish.

I've just had 6 days in bed—chill.

Thine, A. B.

STOKE / MS. / 162
(*To Hugh Walpole*)

12B George Street
27–11–21

My dear Hughie,

Be not hurt! Some time before I received the invitation to your party I received an invitation to the Devonshire House Ball. I declined it, as I declined yours, for the reason that I had no expectation of being in England on the date. Ten days in bed & the complexities attendant upon legal separation from one's wife upset all my programme, & I was in England on the date. My host at the D.H. Ball was my friend Dr. F. Shufflebotham. He was on the Reception Committee of the Ball

161. Walpole's new novel was *The Young Enchanted.*

(League of Health stunt, you know, & he was also staying in my flat). Being in London, I not only *had* to go, but was under a duty to go, if there is anything in the theory of priority of invitations. This lucid explanation will, I doubt not, cicatrise your wound. Hang it, it must. But if you imagine I enjoyed the damned ball—!

I should like to have a chat with Conrad about your theories. I should be intensely surprised if we didn't agree. As for the rest of your list, its critical attitude towards anything whatever in literature has no interest for me.

Get better, brother, & hurry up with that Gothic cathedral of yours.

I leave Tuesday morn.

Thine, A. B.

SWINNERTON / MS. / 163
(*To Winifred Nerney*)

[Yacht Amaryllis]
22–12–21

Dear Miss Nerney,

As I sent coloured cards to the servants I don't quite want to send ditto to you; but I want to wish you the best wishes & to thank you very much for the extremely sympathetic & valuable help which you have given to me during recent events. I have greatly appreciated it. I dare say that my manner is often rather curt, but no doubt after all these years you understand that my feelings towards you are not precisely cold.

We expect to move on to Monte Carlo on Monday or Tuesday; but the correct postal address is the yacht, au port, *Monaco*.

Yours sincerely, Arnold Bennett

P.S. I forgot whether I told you that your salary is to be raised from the 1st Jan by 10/- a week. I have done ½ the book. A. B.

162. Walpole interrupted the writing of *The Cathedral* to write *The Young Enchanted*.

163. For other references to Winifred Nerney see Vols. I and II and above. pp. 80–1.

IDDESLEIGH / MS. / 164
(*To Marie Belloc Lowndes*)
PRIVATE

12B George Street
16–2–22

My dear Lady,

It was good of you to write me so promptly & so frankly.

I do not want Marguerite to do anything.

So far as I can judge from your letter, you seem to me to have been somewhat hasty in expressing decided opinions when you had heard only one side of the case. Indeed from some phrases in your letter I could almost think that you are among those persons to whom Marguerite has managed to tell her story without mentioning the name of X . . ., who is the sole cause of the separation. Whatever may be the physical relations between Marguerite and this unspeakable young man (who constantly accepted her bounty and who did not conceal from at least one of my friends his opinion that the proper policy of a poor ambitious young man was to attach himself to a married woman with money) there can be no doubt, & even no disputing, that, superficially regarded, their attitude toward each other became the scandal of my household and staff and even the scandal of restaurants. In the last two years preceding our separation Marguerite had £2,500 from me for her own various private purposes (in addition to an excessive sum for housekeeping), and yet she was always complaining that I was stingy with money and kept her poor. There can be no doubt that much of her money went to X. Indeed I know it did. And when they planned & carried out a sojourn in Italy together without saying a single word to me I knew that something serious must occur fairly soon. My friends (and hers) most seriously reproached me for not acting sooner. When I did act I acted under the advice of the best people I know, and of my solicitor and hers. I gave her the alternative of a separation from me or a separation from X.

It may also be news to you that at various times (at least a dozen times) since she met X Marguerite has asked me to agree to a separation. I always refused, hoping that this passion between a woman of 47 & a man of 31 would die out as such passions generally do. In the end I went to our mutual solicitor, and I imagine that she was considerably startled. But it was always she who had demanded a separation. I will not write any further details, but I should be delighted to see you.

I know more about Marguerite's fine qualities than any other person on earth, and I have always spoken of them. And nobody has ever heard me say anything against her. On the contrary to this day I am standing up for her against her own friends & mine. But it would be absolutely impossible for me to live with her again.

The Anglo-French P.S. will break up at the end of its first year. The misguided girl has smashed the Committee by insisting on the presence of X at the meetings, & the Committee has resigned. I only heard this the other day. But in any case the Society could not have survived the acute boringness of its performances. . . .

Yours, Arnold Bennett

IDDESLEIGH / MS. / 165
(*To Marie Belloc Lowndes*)
PRIVATE

12B George Street
17–2–22

My dear Lady,

Many thanks. The amazing thing is, not that deception should occur, but that Marguerite should attempt to conceal matters which are within the personal knowledge of numbers of quite unprejudiced persons. It is impossible that Marguerite can have persuaded herself that she did not desire, and had not demanded, a separation. The trouble is that, being extra-

164. Mrs. Lowndes met Bennett in Paris not long before Bennett met Marguerite, and they became good friends. In her memoirs, *The Merry Wives of Westminster*, Mrs. Lowndes recalls the separation. Marguerite came to her in great distress. 'I wrote to him, at her request, and begged him to reconsider his determination that they should have no more to do with one another. I reminded him, not at her suggestion, of how she had nursed him through three serious illnesses, and I added that but for her unselfish devotion during their early married life, he could never have written the book that had made him famous. . . . He sent me an angry letter, informing me of what had been his principal grievance against her.' In Mrs. Lowndes's opinion Bennett had a low regard for women and was obsessed by sex. For other references to Mrs. Lowndes see Vols. I and II.

ordinarily deficient in imagination, she entirely failed to realise what a separation would involve for her. And any attempts to help her realisation of this only made her very angry. If she ever goes to live in Paris she certainly will not stay there. She has *no* friends there except those she has made through me. She has no friends because she does not desire friends, and has very often said so. In London, despite various recent quarrels, she still has one or two very faithful friends (women), who know only her version of the facts and who even if they were accurately informed would still out of loyalty stand by her. Hence I think it is best for her to stay in London, which she prefers to Paris. . . . The only solution of the X problem lies in her ultimately seeing through him.

I ought to tell you that your remarks on the subject in social circles, though they were prompted by a laudable and warm-hearted sympathy for an apparent victim, have done me some temporary prejudice. It is right that you should know this, but I am not in the least troubled, because nothing can prevent a fairly correct judgment being in the end formed by the mass of our acquaintance. You were known as an old friend of mine, and accordingly the more weight was attached to your verdict against me; but even this cannot count for long.

Do come & see me. I am very busy, reorganising my existence generally, and tracassé with two plays at once. I know I ought to come to you, but if you will come here you will be extremely welcome & you will oblige me. Will it suit you to have tea here on Tuesday 22nd about 4.30?

Yours ever, A.B.

BEAVERBROOK / MS. / 166
(*To Lord Beaverbrook*)
PRIVATE

12B George Street
2–3–22

My dear Max,

I very greatly appreciate what you said to me on the phone this morning. As regards the theatre, I can get all the capital I

165. *The Love Match* and *Body and Soul* were produced in 1922.

want without you; but as things are I am in practical control of considerably more than half the capital, and so my considered opinion will prevail in any crisis; and I want this state of affairs to continue. I reckon that you, Whitburn, Richmond, Snagge, Hambro, Sullivan, & probably Rothermere would support me in any action I thought right to take, and this gives me absolute power. If I don't find it, much of the new capital would come in through Nigel Playfair & he would control it. I won't agree to any arrangement that would enable him to outvote me at a general meeting. He is a very able man, full of original ideas, & has fully justified my belief in him; but without Tayler and me he would have bust up the theatre in the first six months. The present combination is excellent. Playfair supplies the ideas, Tayler supplies the minute Scotch patience, and I supply the commonsense. But Tayler & I have all we can do to keep Playfair on the rails.

This is why I came to you for more capital. By the way Whitburn, Richmond & Sullivan have agreed to do as I ask. Snagge has declined.

Of course you may say that I might supply the capital myself. I won't, on principle. I said I would go into the thing absolutely uncommercially, and I shall stick to that. In 3 years I have received £100 for director's fees, & 15% on £100 stock, and I have supervised the whole enterprise in detail every week when in London. The confident belief of people that I am doing well out of the affair is very funny. The inability of people to believe that my sole desire is to prove that a good theatre can pay is also very funny.

I reckon that on last year's working, after paying all taxes, percentages & fees we shall have at least £5,000 net profit on a capital of under £4,000.

I shall expect your car on Tuesday at 1 p.m.

Thine, A. B.

166. Aside from Lord Rothermere, the several shareholders cannot be positively identified.

In some comments on Bennett in the *Author* a few years later, Nigel Playfair said that he was a poor judge of theatre and of acting, and didn't really know what the theatre was about. He added: 'I never met a man more sincere than Bennett. . . . Only his businesslike methods were a pose, though a nearly unconscious pose, for I don't believe he was really much of a business man.'

STOKE / MS. / 167
(*To Hugh Walpole*)

12B George Street
23.3.22.

My dear Hughie,

Thanks for your lugubrious account of Vienna. Rest assured that I am not going to Vienna unless I can enjoy more than the music. I am disappointed but it doesn't matter as next week I shall begin the preparations for the yachting season. Since your protection was reft from me I have been passing through vast tribulations. My play *The Love Match* is the greatest failure that ever was. The 1st night audience received the last 2 acts in silence; the whole of the press without exception was frankly hostile, and the public is sedulously staying away. The loss being about 100 quid a night, the piece will be withdrawn at once. My previous record for shortness of run was 36 nights. This comes of writing modern, otherwise new-fangled, plays consisting of realism delicately enveloped in wit. (The tragedy of course is that I am unteachable.) But I bet that one day that play will be revived. My previous record failure, *What the Public Wants*, is about to be revived in New York—and with éclat. I hear that Robert Nichols is about to land in this country via U.S.A. on 6 months leave. Wells is back, and in the greatest form, & is occupying himself with Ireland. Your beloved, sardonic, cruel, realistic, imperturbable, callous, ruthless, remorseless Frank is writing his new novel. Messrs. Cassells have officially informed me that they are enthusiastic about my new novel *Lilian*, but wish me to modify 2 sentences in it for serial use. These sentences are:—

(a) 'I am going to have a baby.'
(b) 'I am 7 months gone.'

It is a great world! I hope you will continue to enjoy yourself, and will speedily return.

Thine, A. B.

167. *The Love Match* opened at the Strand on 21 March. No revival of the play is known. *What the Public Wants* opened on 1 May at the Garrick Theatre in New York. Bennett wrote *Lilian* in December and January.

MANCHESTER GUARDIAN, 29 March 1922 / 168
(*To Frank Vernon*)

[12B George Street]
[27 or 28 March 1922]

Dear Frank,

Thanks for your disturbing letter. I am very anxious to please the public but I am still more anxious to please myself. Twenty-four years ago before I met you I wrote a number of plays to suit what managers told me was the public taste and not to suit my own taste. Most of them were sold, but none was produced. After eight years of this I took an oath never to write another play, but I was persuaded by the Stage Society to write plays solely to please myself. Since then I have only written plays to please myself. If they please the public I am delighted and encouraged. If they don't, they don't. The public save money and we lose money.

The intelligent criticisms which I have heard about *The Love Match* amount to two. The first is that the play doesn't end. It merely stops or it ends in the wrong way. The character of Naughty Nina (it is alleged) ought to develop to some definite conclusion. Preferably Nina ought to reform herself into another sort of woman. Second, the discovery of her adultery and her divorce constitute episodes far too powerful for the remainder of the play, which seems to peter out.

My answer is as follows:—

There is any quantity of naughty, voluptuous, pleasure-loving Ninas knocking about. I regard the Nina type as a sign of the times, and my play is meant to be an exposure of the typical Nina. I try to be fair to the enchanting creature. I let her be genuinely in love and genuinely loved.

The episodes of her detection in adultery and of her divorce are purposely made tremendous so as to give her every inducement to reform. If such experiences won't change her nothing will. Well, though she does behave heroically in a momentary crisis she does not permanently, and the truth is that nothing will change her. She has fine impulses in idle moments, but they are not sustained enough to modify her enormous egotism. Nina is unalterable. She wants everything on earth, and will give nothing but passion in return. And so she will go on till she dies. The play might plausibly and sentimentally have ended in her death. But the Ninas do not die. They are very strong; they survive in full power for amazing periods, exercising their singular fascinations long after other women have retired from the great battle of the sexes. (If an author has chosen a subject of which the essence and lesson is that it runs on indefinitely, how can he decently bring his play to a conventional 'full close'? He can't.)

It would have been easy for me to reform Nina, reintroduce her philosophical first husband at the end of the play in a scene combining comedy with moral axioms, and send comforted multitudes home with the pleasant delusion that things are not what they are. It would have been easy, but it would have been criminal. I have committed crimes and may commit more, but not that variety of crime.

I have a great respect for the public, also for you. That is why I will not alter my play. It may be bad, but if I altered it it would be worse.

Yours ever, Arnold Bennett

OBSERVER, 2 April 1922 / 169
(*To Frank Vernon*)

12B George Street
April 1, 1922

Dear Frank,

Thanks for your second strenuous letter still urging changes in my play at the Strand Theatre. As regards the examples which you give of the illustrious and great who have begun to write their plays again after finishing them, I cannot offer any opinion.

I deem it unwise to dig too deeply into the psychology of genius. But I must tell you that, though I have altered other people's plays, I have never altered one of my own. I have

168. Bennett's letter was part of a public exchange of letters with Frank Vernon, who produced *The Love Match*. Vernon's letter mentioned an avalanche of correspondence from theatre-goers who objected to the sensuality of the heroine and who wanted her to reform. Vernon concluded: 'As first producer of four of your plays, including *Milestones* and *The Great Adventure*, I claim the privilege of old friendship to ask you to reconsider an ending which my correspondents feel to be neither inevitable nor right.' For earlier letters to Vernon see Vol. II.

always cut my own plays, which is quite a different matter from altering them.

For me, the characters in *The Love Match* exist; certain things happened to them; the narrative is set down. I cannot conceivably pretend to myself that certain other and contrary things happened to my characters.

It might be amusing to pretend that Wellington lost Waterloo, or that Lord Carson loves the Lord Chancellor, but it would also be rather silly.

Yours sincerely, Arnold Bennett

YALE / T.C.C. / 170
(*To Edith Sitwell*)

[12B George Street]
4th April 1922

Dear Edith,

I am dining at Mrs. Ralph Hammersley's tomorrow (Thursday) night, and she arranged the party specially for me to meet Wilson Steer. I quite expected to get away before 11 o'clock, but last night I learnt, by accident, that she is giving a concert after dinner and that the concert does not begin until 10 o'clock. As Mrs. Hammersley is herself playing at this concert, I am very much afraid that I cannot decently depart till it is over, and I doubt if it will be over much before midnight. I am extremely sorry. I should greatly like to come to your party but it seems improbable that I shall arrive. I am sure that you will understand and pardon.

I have just borrowed a copy of *Ulysses*. It appears to me to be jolly good, and it is certainly the most obscene genuine literature ever published, not excepting Juvenal and Co.

Best wishes to you both,

Yours, [Arnold Bennett]

169. *The Love Match* ran until April 22nd. In an essay entitled 'Egotism', which appears in *Things That Have Interested Me, Second Series*, Bennett discusses the play in much the same way as in his letters to Vernon.

Lord Carson—Edward Henry Carson (1854–1935), the Ulster leader and Lord of Appeal in Ordinary, opponent of Lloyd George's government, in which Lord Birkenhead was Lord Chancellor. See also pp. 275–9 on Birkenhead.

170. Mrs. Ralph Hammersley was the widow of a prominent banker.

Wilson Steer, the painter (1860–1942).

On James Joyce (1882–1941) and *Ulysses* see p. 228 below, and see also p. 348.

TEXAS / T.C.C. / 171
(*To George Webster*)

[12B George Street]
26th April 1922

Dear Mr. Webster,

Thanks for your letter of the 26th. At the risk of seeming obstinate I must say that I do not agree with you at all. The Review in the *Daily Mail* is kind enough but it is execrably written and shows no comprehension of the book whatever. I do not see how any quotation from it would persuade anybody with any experience of other novels or reviews to buy the book. Further, no one who is interested in books cares a fig what the *Daily Mail* thinks about a novel. (I know I am exaggerating a little but you understand what I mean.)

Further, I hope that you will not imitate the extraordinary stupidity of publishers' advertisements (which are notoriously the most futile in the world) and quote the same reviews in all the papers in which you advertise. Extracts which might please the readers of the *Evening Standard* for example, would leave quite cold the readers of the *Nation*, *New Statesman*, *Literary Supplement*, *Observer*, or *Sunday Times*. No publisher within my experience has apparently ever thought of this obvious truth.

However, the question of the method of advertising has not at present much actuality. Although the book is out I have not yet seen a single advertisement of it.

Yours sincerely, [Arnold Bennett]

YALE / T.C.C. / 172
(*To Edith Sitwell*)

[12B George Street]
23rd May 1922

My dear Edith,

There are few things that I would not do in order to be agreeable to you, and so I will read this play of Mr. Hamer's, though

171. George Webster was on the staff of Methuens, who published *Mr. Prohack*. The reviewer in the *Daily Mail*, on 26 April, said that 'not for a long time has Mr. Bennett's humour played so searchingly and brilliantly over the surface of life today'.

to read it means that I must forswear myself. Not that I mind much forswearing myself. If I accepted all invitations to read MSS of other people I should do nothing else but read the MSS of other people. Hence I inform everyone that I have an absolute rule against reading the MSS of other people.

I will read *Roasted Angels* aussitôt que possible. What with the Wagnerian Ring and finishing a little book of my own, I have been having a hades of a time lately. Thank heaven they are both now finished, and I am going to sea at once on my yacht. (But not for a holiday. No! To write a play.)

With affections to you both.

Ever yours sincerely, [Arnold Bennett]

BUTLER / MS. / 173
(*To Edward Knoblock*)

12B George Street
27–5–22

My dear Edward,

This is very nice of you & I much appreciate the floral offering, which has arrived in great form.

You can arrive on the day which suits you, & if you want to finish some work of your own on the yacht, you can do that also; & I will provide you with a secretary during Whitsuntide. I shall have her for the yacht on *Wednesday*. You can either telegraph to the *yacht, Marie Marguerite, Brightlingsea* or you can inform Miss Nerney, the time of your arrival.

As regards clothes, remember that yachting in June is not absolutely sultry. When I wear flannels I usually put on 2 pairs of pants! A yachting cap is *not* de rigueur, but when you see me wearing one you will be sorry if you haven't got one yourself. That I swear.

If you have been working like hell, you will have to take a little holiday of a few days before starting again.

Thine, A. B.

172. Mr. Hamer is not otherwise known.

Bennett finished writing *How to Make the Best of Life*, the last of the pocket philosophies, on 21 May. He wrote *London Life* with Edward Knoblock in June. He was sailing off the English coast during the summer months.

GIDE / 174
(*To André Gide*)

12B George Street
28–5–22

My dear Gide,

I was very glad to hear from you, and I shall certainly be disappointed—gravely—if we do not meet this summer. I cannot, however, to my great regret, come to Pontigny in August. Pontigny is not marked in the largest and best English atlas. But I had the wit to look for it in the *Grand Larousse*. I see it is near to Auxerre, and quite inaccessible from the French coasts. Why do you have these elegant reunions in these pays perdus? I shall be in my yacht all the summer. I start on the 1st June. If Pontigny had been near the coast I would have come with the greatest pleasure for several days. I shall be frequenting the French coasts, and I most particularly desire you to come to the yacht in some port. Dieppe? Havre? Boulogne? Calais? Deauville? I will entertain you well, and you will be very comfortable. I want to listen to you, and to learn certain matters.

You remember when I saw you I told you I was determined to write a novel with a (for me) new technique. Well, I couldn't do it! And yet now that it is published everybody says that it is quite different from any other novel I have written! Is not this rather queer and disturbing? The book is *Mr. Prohack*, and the unanimous enthusiasm with which it is being received makes me think that there must be something fundamentally bad in it.

What has happened to your 'Lettres à Angèle'? Do you know what you are? You are le Stendhal de nos jours, but thank God better educated and more widely sensitive. I never tire of Stendhal, Dostoevsky, Chekhov, and A. Gide. No, never!

As for my 'nouvelles sensationnelles', do not be disturbed. It is all for the best. What a novel to be made out of it! Mais ce sacré bon goût anglais m'empêche. Si j'étais d'Annunzio.

Please let me know where I must bring my yacht to meet you. And remember me cordially to Marc Allégret. (Quel beau nom, tout de même.)

Ever yours, Arnold Bennett

174. On the literary reunions at Pontigny see Vol. II, p. 287.
Gide published several 'Billets à Angèle' in *La Nouvelle Revue Française* in 1921.
Marc Allégret, son of the Protestant minister who was Gide's tutor, was adopted by Gide.

YALE / T.C.C. / 175
(*To Edith Sitwell*)

[12B George Street]
29th May 1922

My dear Edith,

I have read *Roasted Angels* and I now return it. It is a very unusual and even a very remarkable play. It is full of wit and fancy and most admirably written. I should like to know who H. Hamer is. He, or she, must have been writing for quite some little time.

There is a railway in the Argentine that runs in a straight line on a dead level for 100 miles. The first 56 pages of the play are rather like a train on that railway. The first three acts ought to be compressed into one act. Through two and a half acts the author has forgotten that a play must be dramatic. It must state a situation at once and begin to solve the situation in some manner immediately after it has stated the situation. From about p. 56 the play improves, as a play. The scene between Papani and Nana (pp. 70–80, about) is very good. The crucifix between the breasts is a brilliant idea. And the second or major crucifix scene is also very good.

The drama of Papani's confession as to his identity (p. 83) is good.

The author, in spite of his terrific verbal skill, is extremely clumsy as a dramatist. For example, he hit on a good trick in dividing the poet into four separate images, and then practically makes no use of the device at all.

His first attempt at drama is to resort to the very oldest of stage dodges—the mistaking of somebody for somebody else (about p. 57).

You ask me what can be done with the play. Nothing except print it. It is not practicable for the stage in its present form. There are over forty speaking parts. Who do you suppose is going to pay the salaries of these actors and actresses? Most of these characters, by the way, serve no useful purpose at all in the play. They amount to a mere [?] of material.

The psycho-plasm scene would be frightfully difficult to do with any conviction. And the café scene would be equally difficult. Anyway, it would still be no good for the British stage, because it is too sinister, bizarre, bitter, cock-eyed, and nonchalant. The Stage Society might produce it. I should say that it would have a very fair chance of success in Berlin, where gargantuan trains running between 'futurist' scenery are sure of profound applause.

You have asked me for my opinion of the play. You have my opinion.

You might now tell me who wrote the thing. For he, or she, is no ordinary person, and I should like to inform him sometime that cleverness is the curse of all the arts.

Yours ever, [Arnold Bennett]

COHEN / TR. / 176
(*To Harriet Cohen*)

Yacht Marie Marguerite
4.6.22.

[fragment]
I am afloat (in the great Blackwater River) and still thinking of your musical evening, for which I did not sufficiently thank you and Miss B.H. It was great, and worth 40 concerts. I want now to know how you are going on, and if and when you are coming on to the ship. Do hurry up and settle with the Proms tyrant. When you come I'll arrange about a chaperone of sorts for you, and I'll keep out of stormy or even un-smooth seas. I can't do more, can I? No. There are as many varieties of seas as there are varieties of love, including several quite nice ones that will suit your heart, stomach, and complexion.

[A. B.]

COHEN / TR. / 177
(*To Harriet Cohen*)

Yacht Marie Marguerite
17. 6. 22.

My dear Tania,

I shall expect you on July 27th for a week. You will meet first rate people: Sir Denison Ross and lady.

176. Harriet Cohen (d. 1967) was at the beginning of her distinguished musical career. Bennett noted in his *Journal* a year earlier: 'Went to Harriet Cohen's concert. Very good playing. The modern music came out pretty well, but there was nothing first-class. I was never really "held" for more than a moment at a time. I ought to have been at the Eng. concert at Queen's Hall hearing Gustav Holst's *Planets*. All this because I liked Harriet Cohen's physical style and her playing.'

B.H.—presumably Beatrice Harrison (b. 1892), English 'cellist.

Don't fail me,
Yes, write me 'properly'.

Yours ever affectionately, A. B.

P.S. *This is the most important part.* What have you been doing to get ill again? I leave town; you fall ill. You must have been guilty of indiscretions against the laws of nature, I fear. Please let me hear that you are better. I am disturbed. A. B.

COHEN / TR. / 178
(*To Harriet Cohen*)

Yacht Marie Marguerite
12. 7. 22.

My Sweet Tania,

No. G.B.S. will not be on my yacht.

Neither will you be seasick on board. I shall see to that.

I am very disturbed by your accounts of yourself, and want to estimate the situation with my own eyes and judgment.

I hope, and doubt not, you will have a great success on Wednesday night. But I have no use for gratis playing. I mean that on your behalf I have no use for it.

Of late I have been laid aside with acute rheumatism.

The weather is lovely. I am at Poole, and return to Southampton on Friday for 24 hours.

My loving sympathy is with you,

Yours, A. B.

COHEN / TR. / 179
(*To Harriet Cohen*)

Yacht Marie Marguerite
18–7–22

My Sweet Tania,

I have looked in *The Times* every day for the advertisement of that concert of which you are to be the lightning, and haven't

177. Sir Denison Ross (1871–1940) was head of the School of Oriental Languages. Bennett met him in 1918 and described him in his *Journal* as 'a wild, very interesting person'. Lady Ross (d. 1940) was an accomplished musician.

seen it. But I suppose the demand for seats has made advertisement absurd. You won't get this before you play, and God knows where it will be posted. The weather *won't* change. We had to drop anchor last night near nowhere at all. Then ½ a gale arose and is still mounting. But it has not yet with all its efforts dislodged the circular photograph which I received (unsigned) from the place where I affixed it in front of some Balzacs. You can't be so frightfully out of sorts if this really lovely photograph is recent, as I presume, assume, and suppose it to be. I've been laid up with neuralgia. I have downed the beast, but I had to stand over it with a dog-whip lest it should leap at me again. I fully expect that the weather *will* change before your arrival. I have now had 7 weeks of it (tomorrow) with 2½ exceptional days of *fine* weather. That's all. I might ask you to join the ship at Southampton or I might ask you to join the ship at Weymouth. All my plans have been upset. I wanted to take my present cargo (to wit)

one war-widow
one war-virgin (very blonde)
one nephew

to Guernsey, but I doubt if it can be done before the 27th. Anyhow I will let you know. Also the Rosses. I hope you will like the Rosses. Which somehow reminds me to tell you that you don't mean that Shaw is all cerebral. Shaw is one of the kindest-hearted men I ever knew, and the stories of his benevolence are staggering. Further, he is a very great writer.

Is this the fifth or the sixth time I told you you will not be sea-sick? Because you won't.

Your adorable letter written at 8.30 a.m. in bed on the blank day of the blank month of God knows what year has reached and enheartened me.

Ever yours, A. B.

179. The concert may already have taken place. Miss Cohen played at the Æolian Hall a week before.

Bennett's cargo is unidentified except for his nephew Richard.

COHEN / MS. / 180
(*To Harriet Cohen*)

Yacht Marie Marguerite
5–8–22

My sweet Tania,

I was very glad to have your wire, which, I apprehend, you must have wakened early in order to send off. Things are now greatly changed on this yacht. I now kiss a niece aged 15, & the other niece, aged 21, I do not kiss. They are very nice little things, these two, & I spend my days in making them laugh. They do everything I tell them, but I never tell them to do anything, because, for a change, I want them to have perfect freedom. I have already taught the elder one to smoke and to drink brandy and stout. In fact I am doing them lots of good. It is all a most drastic change from yourself & the Rosses, with your extreme alertness of mind, artistic sensibilities, and variegated experience of the world's life. You know, I enjoyed your too short week acutely, intensely. I admit you are a handful and that you are capable of being very naughty, but you richly make up for these excitations. The one matter which disturbed me was your remark that Dodo didn't like you. There you were quite wrong. Dodo appreciated you as well as anyone. I have the highest esteem for her judgments & also for her character. But she is a reserved woman; with all her 'matronly naughtiness'. I don't see that her demeanour could have been different. She talked to you at least as much as you talked to her. And someone in a mixed company has to redress the balance of unconventionality. Moreover, if you had been in her place you wouldn't have stood [?] of speech with *your* husband a whit better than she did yours to hers. I told you to put yourself in her place, but I didn't tell you enough. I know that she likes you (& you are a pretty sturdy specimen of the artist being the artist the whole time!), and I should be upset if you didn't like her. You could not possibly have a more valuable or a more large-hearted friend. True, she is not expansive, nor does she go damning, blasting, and godding all over the place, nor does she talk about herself even to the degree which a member of an intimate group ought to talk about herself. But she is as sound a feminine creature, and as brilliant a brain, as you are likely to meet on earth. I do hope you will stick to your intention of giving that little dinner-party. I am much looking forward to that. And I am much more looking forward to more duets & dinners of two, & to the next time we meet—I mean just us two. Wear your most abandoned dress on that occasion. Will you make a definite appointment for Monday evening Sept 4th? No theatre. Just piano. My much love (which is of a very individual sort) and thank you for coming to the yacht.

Ever yours, A. B.

This is written at Yarmouth in the Solent. I expect to sail for Guernsey tomorrow Sunday morning. Weather still septic.

COHEN / MS. / 181
(*To Harriet Cohen*)

Yacht Marie Marguerite
Carantec, Brittany
14th August 1922

My sweet Tania,

I only got your excellent letter yesterday, owing to difficulties with the red tape ism of the post office in this barbaric [?village], which nevertheless is bien fréquentée en ce moment. The launch is out of order; we are about 2 miles from the village, and everything has to be fetched. Today we get water. I found all my Parisian friends here, qui adorent les yachts. The weather is extremely rotten, with a few fine intervals. It is now raining, & I hear the horrid familiar sound on the deck. I am not working at all well, but it is a great pleasure to me to see my old friends who include the most delicious feminine creatures from 23 to 45.

As regards the new dress, I much desire to see it.

As regards the accusation made against you of flirting, it depends what you mean by flirting. *I* mean to pretend to make love, or to pretend that one has amorous feelings when one has not. In this sense, I cannot offer any valuable opinion on your proclivities. At any rate I have never seen you at work on the

180. The nieces were Mary Kennerley, daughter of sister Tertia and W. W. Kennerley, and Margaret Beardmore, daughter of sister Fanny Gertrude and Frank Beardmore.

Dodo—Lady Ross.

operation. But from your own accounts of yourself I should incline to the view that you are a flirt. I always receive your recitals of the sieges made upon you with calmness, as I cannot succeed in understanding how these sieges can be maintained without your consent or even without your help. The limitations of my comprehension prevent me from understanding how, for example, R could have stayed at your flat from 3 p.m. to 11 p.m. unless you wanted him to do so. Personally I have very little use for flirting. I have never flirted in my life. What is more I have never made love to any woman in my life, at any rate in words. This must be because there is rather more of the feminine in me than there is even in most artists. Most women have been extremely kind to me. They know at once that I am interested in them, cannot do without them, and understand them. And those who read know that there is no more convinced & uncompromising upholder of the rights of women than myself in English literature today. True, I demand a great deal of perfection from them! True, I violently object to them claiming privileges without realising that privileges involve duties and responsibilities! And why not? I could go on for ever praising myself in this quiet, unexaggerated but ruthlessly egotistic manner.

I had a letter from Dodo yesterday containing the most charming references to yourself.

Now I cannot possibly come to tea during the week I shall be in London. You cannot rehearse a play and go out to tea. On Tuesday I go to the other A.B. show at the Promenade. On Wednesday, and Thursday evenings (6th, 7th Sept) I am engaged, & for the remaining evenings I may or may not be free—it depends on how rehearsals go. There remains Monday evening (4th) (apart from any happy chance that may turn up during the week) for you & me to meet. I should *exceedingly* like to spend this evening with you—and in any manner *you like*. It therefore remains for you to decide yes or no, & if you [?].

My peculiar love,

Ever yours, A. B.

181. *Body and Soul* was in rehearsal. It opened at the Euston Theatre of Varieties on 11 September.

A.B.—(Sir) Arnold Bax (1883–1953), Harriet Cohen's great friend. On 6 September he shared a Proms concert with Brahms, Vivaldi, and Sibelius.

COHEN / MS. / 182
(*To Harriet Cohen*)

Yacht Marie Marguerite
1 – 9 – 22

My sweet Tania,

Your 'vulgar' letter (all genuine artists are 'vulgar' at times—it is another way of saying that they are robust) was probably written before you got mine. I addressed mine to Swiss Cottage partly because I couldn't decipher your hell of a Welsh address, & partly because I didn't know how long you'd be out of town. [? It is] now repeated & known to you that you are expected at 12B on Monday night at 8.

We have been having the most devilish weather. When we arrived here, though the harbour is entirely enclosed & we are at least 1½ miles from the entrance, the sea was so rough that the Customs boat after 2 attempts gave up trying to come out to us. Nevertheless we had one marvellous day, & that was the day we sailed (or rather motored) from Guernsey to Swanage. Not a breath of wind. Astounding colour schemes. Constant changes. Porpoises playing round the forefoot of the ship. Shoals of mackerel. Miraculous sunsets. The voyage took 19 hours. I went to bed at 3 a.m. It was then still calm and warm, all stars working full time. 3½ hours later, when I arose again, a gale was blowing, & it was a real official job in the strict marine sense. Sailing from Swanage here we got drenched. I shall sail to Southampton Saturday & go to London Monday morn.

You do *not* think sex horrid. If you do, you ought to reconsider your whole philosophical position, having regard to the fact that sex is the most important thing on earth.

I don't know Amber Reeves, but I know a good deal about her, & I have come much more intimately into her life than she knows. Nor do I know Major Graham Pole. It is now 30 years since I reviewed *Towards Democracy* in the *Star*. (I think I might like Major G.P.) Some of the Whitman stuff in *T.D.* I used to like much.

What, however, pleases me is that you find life rosier. It means your health is better.

Your affectionate, A. B.

182. Amber Reeves—author of a few novels and some socio-economic books. Major Graham Pole (d. 1952), solicitor, soldier, and political figure.

COHEN / MS. / 183
(*To Harriet Cohen*)

Yacht Marie Marguerite
at sea
21 – 9 – 22

My sweet Tania,

I only got your letter dated 'Tuesday' yesterday. (But which Tuesday? God knows.) Anyhow I am now ending the yachting season, & I expect to reach Newhaven some time in the middle of this present night (from Dieppe). I do hope the [? burnt] finger is fully recovered, & that I shall see you in fullest form next week (some time) in London. As for the play, it was *not* a great success. I will go further & say that it is a failure. Only about 1 person in 100 has seen the point of it. The press was awful (it usually is for my plays). So was some of the acting. But Viola Tree, except she doesn't trouble to learn the words, was excellent. I agree with the general managerial conclusion that practically all young actors & actresses are amateurs & do not know their business. Nevertheless, do not mistake me. I attribute the failure of the play chiefly to the play, which with luck may be understood of the people in 20 years time as Shaw's plays will. As regards your tray table, I must *talk* to you about that.

I am alone on the yacht, owing to male men breaking promises. And quite apart from this & from the failure of the play, I am in rather a gloomy mood,—gloomy because unsettled in mind and body. I don't know how to arrange my life for the best, & I *must* know soon as I have to leave the flat. And I have no one who can throw fresh *illuminating* light on the problems. I am always gloomy when undecided.

Affectionately,

Yours ever, A. B.

Bennett's review of Edward Carpenter's *Towards Democracy* could not be found. He mentions it in Chapter IX of *The Truth About an Author* as the second piece of reviewing he ever did. The third edition of Carpenter's book appeared in 1892, and the review could not have appeared long thereafter; but what is presumed to be Bennett's first review was published in the *Illustrated London News* on 18 November 1893. See the brief comment on his early reviewing in Vol. I, p. 13.

183. *Body and Soul* was produced by Nigel Playfair, with Viola Tree (1884–1938) playing Lady Mab. It was withdrawn in September. The reviewer in *The Times* saw it as the product of a provincial mind displaying a false modernity.

COHEN / MS. / 184
(*To Harriet Cohen*)

Yacht Marie Marguerite
(Newhaven)
22 – 9 – 22

My sweet Tania,

I got your letter 'Monday' and your notelet 'Now Wednesday' about 2 hours ago on this spot. How *could* you? I mean the notelet. I wrote to you last night, but it was at sea between Dieppe & here, & the letter was not posted till this [a few words unreadable] which sight I desire to occur as early as possible & certainly next week). I will deal with all your questions & suggestions. In the meantime I positively do *not* apprehend that our relations will suddenly or even gradually dissolve. I conceive it possible that they mean more to me than you think. I'm a man of few words, as you may have observed, but I say that. Thank heaven you are an artist in affections as in other matters. I have had a very difficult time this last 12 months, for which I blame no one, & assuredly not myself. And in the six months before that I had an intolerable time. But of it, I do not, & probably shall not, speak in detail. Let it be said only that I have gone through it and am immensely relieved and enfranchised.

I had a hades of a crossing last night—dead calm (after a gale) and [?]. All on board (the skipper, crew, & I) are somewhat pale & exhausted this morning. My secretary is coming down tonight [a few words unreadable]. I shall reach London probably on Tuesday or so, when I will telephone you. I shall probably leave here tomorrow morning en route for Brightlingsea. Like Tania, I have a vast amount of work to do.

Ever your affectionate & grateful, A. B.

MAYFIELD, SYRACUSE / A.D. / 185
(*To the editor of the* DAILY EXPRESS)

[12B George Street]
[19 October 1922]

Sir,

S.P.B.M. calls my novel *Lilian* a pot-boiler.

The *Oxford Dictionary* definition of pot-boiler is 'a work of art or literature done merely to make a living'. That is to say, the writer of a pot-boiler has venally contrived something for a purely commercial end, and solely for money.

Nearly all writers write for money, Shakespeare did. But the serious writers do not write solely for money. Serious writers produce the best work they can, and hope to make a living out of it.

Literary critics seem to have fallen into quite a habit of describing as a pot-boiler any novel which they do not like. They have not the least right to do so, and in doing so they presume upon the indifference of authors. Such a description is undoubtedly libellous. Not that I should ever dream of bringing a libel action! But some day some critic with more cheek than prudence will find himself in trouble.

If S.P.B.M. knew the literary world as he should, he would know that the writing of a novel like *Lilian* involves a considerable financial sacrifice to its author, in the matter of serial rights alone. It would have been easy for me to write a novel twice as remunerative as *Lilian.* Only I wanted to write *Lilian.*

This letter is not concerned with purely literary verdicts. I am not prepared to deny that S.P.B.M. is the greatest critic of the age, or that I am the meanest of novelists.

Yours truly, [Arnold Bennett]

TEXAS / TS. / 186
(*To William Lee Mathews*)

12B George Street
1st November 1922

Dearest William,

You once supplied me with a secretary, as to whom it is sufficient to say that she is still with me. H. G. Wells sometimes puts into my hands matters which he does not feel equal to

185. The letter was printed with negligible changes in the *Daily Express* on 20 October (in early editions) and also on 21 October. S. P. B. Mais (1885–) was a journalist, novelist, and lecturer in English literature. How deeply his review rankled may be seen in the fact that a year and a half later Bennett made an unpleasant and unnecessary attack on Mais's literary style in the pages of the *Adelphi*.

According to Frank Swinnerton Bennett wrote *Lilian* as an answer to one of Swinnerton's novels. 'When he finished my novel, *Coquette*, he said "What is the end of this book?" (At the suggestion of Eugene Saxton I had deleted the last section of the book.) I told him. He said, "No, that's not the end. Should you mind if I wrote a book to show what the end should be?" I said "Do!" The result was *Lilian*.'

dealing with himself, and he has now instructed me to find him a secretary. This secretary must be of the male sex. He must have all the attributes of perfection in a secretary, and must be prepared to move about from Essex to London, and to do all the things which secretaries do and a thousand more. The salary would be all right. Do you happen to know of any mirror and exemplar of paramount-secretaryship? If so, I wish you would let me know.

Thine, A. B.

BODKIN / TR. / 187
(To Thomas Bodkin)

12B George Street
7.11.22.

My dear Thomas Bodkin,

I ought to have acknowledged your letter earlier, but I have been acknowledging the claims of the picture muse instead. I

186. For earlier letters and other references to William Lee Mathews see Vols. I and II. In 1912 Mathews wrote to Bennett about Miss Nerney: 'I have taken a very great deal of pains about your Secretary, and unless I am very much mistaken I have found you the right person. The 'X' in question is a woman. She is 26 years of age. She has done personal service for a man for 8 years, she has dealt with his stocks and shares, she has done the whole of his correspondence, she has kept his books, and she has looked after his housekeeping accounts. She has had no holiday for 8 years, except about 3 days. She has devoted herself entirely to this man's interests. The man in question is obliged to retrench, and is unable to keep her on any longer. He gives me about the finest account of 'X' that I could well get, and this is borne out by a private letter from a friend of hers, who is secretary to Lord Montague. I have had 'X' up myself about three or four times, so as to get to know exactly what she is like. I have dictated Bernard Shaw to her to take down in shorthand to test her capabilities in this respect, which are quite good. Her handwriting is also good.

Her defects are that she has rather a disagreeable speaking voice, and a Cockney pronunciation of certain words.

I like 'X' myself personally, and I therefore told her that, quite apart from anything else, she would have to take some elocution lessons, and that they would be good for her in any case. . . . She has read some of your books, and understands them. The post would be one that she would rather have than any other. She would be perfectly prepared to go anywhere that you wanted, i.e., if you wanted to take her to America, if you wanted to take her to the Riviera, if you wanted to take her to Timbuctoo, she would go. I have gone very fully into the sex question with her, and have told her that from this point of view she is simply a piece of wood. This she absolutely and entirely understands, and on these lines there would not be the faintest difficulty as to her going anywhere with you where a man would go equally.

'X' is the only applicant that I have seen who is likely to be of the faintest use to you.'

saw Colnaghi's second effort at mounting, and condemned it:—
(1) because the words at the top were over the coloured margin instead of *in* it.
(2) because they had not abolished the full stops.

I thought I was following your instructions in doing this.

Have you seen any of the [? Marees] Society reproductions? I saw some for the first time to-day, and was staggered thereby. I expect that if you had the original and the reproduction side by side you *could* distinguish between them; but the sight of the reproduction by itself produces in you the delusion that you couldn't. Of course you *could*, because the surface of the reproduction is flat, whereas the surface even of a water colour is not. Anyhow they leave all other reproductions right out of sight. I have bought a portfolio of Renoirs. 15 water colours. £9.9.0. I am amazed at the beauty of them. I don't know how they are done; there are no signs of a 'screen' on them.

You will note that I am rather excited.

I have written the first part of my novel, the heroine of which is a charwoman.

I had an evening with the L.J. I expect he's told you. I've also had Padraic and wife.

Kindest regards to Madame and yourself.

Yours sincerely, Arnold Bennett

COHEN / MS. / 188
(*To Harriet Cohen*)

12B George Street
14–11–22

My sweetest Tania,

I wouldn't worry you on the 'phone this morning. I hope you are better. I know you aren't, but I hope you are. On reflection I don't think there was anything last night that I didn't think *fine*. The least satisfactory to me was the 1st English song. But I don't call any of these things songs, they are duets for voice & pf.—anyway the way A.B. plays the piano parts. *You* had the most difficult music to play—the sonata. It is fantastic, the

187. The new novel was *Riceyman Steps,* begun on 10 October.
L.J.—James O'Connor.
Padriac Colum the author (1881–) and Mary Colum (d. 1957).

demand which this sonata makes on the audience—to say nothing of the player. At present I prefer the so-called 1st sonata. But perhaps if I heard last night's again I shouldn't. I thought you played magnificently, and as for pedalling effects, here is the  Enough! I suppose A.B. is satisfied. He ought to be. And so ought Murdoch. It was a terrific ordeal for A.B.'s genius, & he came through it A1. I say again, Enough! I suppose I shan't see you now till after Glasgow. I regret it much. See here, Mrs. Mayer asked me to dine next Tuesday. I told her I was engaged & I am, but it has struck me I could arrive at 10 p.m. Will the four-fisted sonata be over by then, & if it won't be, do you think I might suggest coming in? I don't know her spouse's initials nor where she lives, & there are 10,000 Mayers. You might cause this information to be telephoned to me.

Eugene, Leon & Cedric stopped till ten minutes to two.

I trust the other A.B. got you home safely & rapidly.

Yours constantly, A. B.

You've left some music here. Shall I send it by post?

COHEN / MS. / 189
(*To Harriet Cohen*)

12B George Street
5–12–22

My sweet Tania,

I am much touched by the floral offering, which sweetens my desk. I am not going to tell you any more about these pictures, after this. No language could be clearer than that in which I said that you were perfectly at liberty to accept or refuse. I am not forcing these pictures on you, but I am forcing you to take or refuse them, or any of them. These pictures will very probably make anything else look silly. Unless you have a store of pictures that I haven't seen, the only one of yours that would

188. On William Murdoch see p. 104.

The Mayers—presumably (Sir) Robert Mayer (1879–) and his wife Dorothy (née Moulton). Sir Robert was President of the Goldsborough Orchestra for a while.

On Eugene Goossens see Vols. I and II and below. Cedric—Cedric Sharpe. Leon Goossens (1897–), Eugene's brother and an oboist.

stand being with them is the Russian one, which is quite nice. One unsuitable picture will spoil any room. I believe in the unity of a room. I will give you a picture of mine, on the sole condition that you do *not* hang it in the music room.

Will you please ring up tomorrow morning & let me know definitely about Saturday.

Early to bed and late to rise
Makes a distinguished pianist more
beautiful and wise.

Ever yours, A. B.

GIDE / 190
(*To André Gide*)

75, Cadogan Square
S.W.1
1–1–23

My dear Gide,

I was delighted to have your letter. I have just installed myself in my new house here (near Victoria Station), but unfortunately at the same moment I was struck down by influenza, from which I am not yet fully recovered; so that I cannot write long letters. I am half way through a long novel—genre 'shopkeeper'—which I hope will be fairly good. I have published 2 novels this last year, and both have had much success, but not as much success as *La Garçonne*. Ah! I wish I could talk to you. I have been re-reading *Du Côté*. Well, it is marvellous. I have also been re-reading *Anna Karenina*. Well, it is more marvellous. I have also been re-reading *Les Frères*. Well, it is most marvellous. Das ist das.

Le cinéma est dans l'eau. J'ai eu des histoires fantasques, inoubliables, indicibles, impayables, et désolantes avec cette bande-là.

Come over and see me.

Yours ever, Arnold Bennett

190. Bennett moved into his new house at 75 Cadogan Square in December.

La Garçonne—by Victor Margueritte (1867–1942); see also pp. 181–2. On Marcel Proust (1871–1922), Leo Tolstoy (1828–1910) and Feodor Dostoevsky, see pp. 182–3, 233, and 131–2 respectively.

Bennett's difficulties with the film world are recounted in an essay in *The Savour of Life*, 1928. See also Vol. I.

BERG / MS. / 191
(*To John Middleton Murry*)

75, Cadogan Square
13–1–23

Dear Middleton Murry,

Although only an acquaintance, I must send you a word of sympathy. I know that you were attached beyond the ordinary to your late wife, & I can understand a little the tremendousness of the blow which the loss of such a woman must mean for you; and I feel for you very much. At any rate she could not have passed her last days in a more beautiful place.

Yours sincerely, Arnold Bennett

STOKE / TS. / 192
(*To A. J. Caddie*)

75, Cadogan Square
29th January 1923

Dear Mr. Caddie,

Many thanks for your letter of the 26th. I shall be very glad to come on Wednesday 7th proximo. Please give my best thanks to the Mayor and say how much I regret that I shall not be able to stay the night. The fact is that I ought to have told you that I have a regular weekly theatre directors' meeting every Wednesday afternoon, at which I preside. I have got this meeting altered to Thursday morning for next week, so it will be absolutely essential that I should return on the Wednesday evening.

Now I wonder whether you will mind my suggesting that you invite my brother Sep to the affair. I suggest this as I should like to see him, and I fear I shall have no chance of doing so except at the meeting.

While hanging my pictures in this house I have discovered two oil-paintings by local artists.

1. 'Needpath Castle' (24″×17″) by Alfonso Toft. Alfonso Toft is the brother of Albert Toft the sculptor. He is a fine painter in the best English tradition, and this, though very sombre in tone, is a beautiful thing.

191. Katherine Mansfield (1888–1923) died in France near Fontainebleau, where Bennett lived for several years.

2. 'Penkhull' ($14'' \times 9\frac{1}{2}''$) by John Currie, who lived at Newcastle for many years, and then after shooting his mistress in his Chelsea studio shot himself. This is an oil sketch, but very brilliant. It shows an expanse of fields rising up to the village, which appears in silhouette at the top.

If you care to have these paintings I shall be happy to give them to the Borough.

Yours sincerely, Arnold Bennett

P.S. I shall come by the train you suggest, and shall be pleased to see you at the station. A. B.

ARKANSAS / MS. / 193
(*To Frank Swinnerton*)

75, Cadogan Square
1.2.23.

My dear Henry,

I don't very much care for the atmosphere of your letter. You still seem to me to be not at all well. Further I cannot believe that this solitude is really the right thing for you. In fact I am disturbed somewhat. I should say that one of the things you need down there is the society of a young woman. Such is my deliberate opinion. What amazes me in the reviews of your novel is the bloody benevolence of most of them. I would sooner see you slanged as H.G. and I are usually slanged. My own novel is progressing, but God knows if it is dull or not.

Hedley L. B. is trying to arrange to publish the '12 best novels of A.B. selected by H.G.W.' The latter instantly consented to select. I was rather surprised. If a hitch occurs it will be through

192. A. J. Caddie was Curator of the Museums of the County Borough of Stoke-on-Trent from 1911 to 1923.

On Septimus Bennett, Arnold's youngest brother, see Vol. II and also below. Alfonso Toft (d. 1964), landscape painter; Albert Toft (1862–1949); John Currie (1884–1914), figure and portrait painter.

Bennett wrote to his nephew Richard of his trip: 'I had a great time in the Potteries. . . . The Mayor wore his 2 ton chain. I sat on his right. I saw all sorts of people who knew me and whom I didn't know, and whom I admirably pretended to know.' The occasion of the trip is not known.

Methuens, damn them. Hedley says I ought to make quite a lot out of the enterprise. My house is now nearly finished. The stair carpets will go down tomorrow. This is an event. I am being almost excessively social. I went down to Brighton today on theatrical business to see Dorothy Cheston play the aunt in *Magda.* I saw a rather wonderful performance of a very fine play, produced with taste & without any of the West End customary exaggeration. Mrs. Pat Camp. was superb (but obese) as Magda, & she produced the play herself. Full house. I have just come back (7.30) & am going out to dinner.

Yours, A. B.

BUTLER / T.C.C. / 194
(*To Percy Withers*)

[75, Cadogan Square]
14th February 1923

Dear Sir,

I have not read *La Garçonne* to the end. I got about half way through it and then I had to give up, not because of its indecency but because of its dullness, poorness, and badness. The indecency is only episodic, but I have never read such indecency in the work of a reputable author published by a reputable firm. I object, however, to expulsion of the author from the Legion of Honour, and I do not believe that he was expelled on account of the indecency. I believe that the motive was political more than anything else. In my opinion if a book is so indecent as to call for public action, the public action ought to be taken by the police, and by nobody else. It has also to be remembered that M. Margueritte has written, either alone or in collaboration

193. Swinnerton's new novel was *The Three Lovers.*

On Sir Hedley Le Bas see above, p. 94. His proposal came to nothing. Further details on it appear in Vol. I.

Bennett saw Dorothy Cheston for the first time on 6 March 1921, when she acted in a playlet at a party he attended. They met formally a year later in Liverpool, where she was playing one of the two leading roles in *Body and Soul.* His letters to her collected in *Arnold Bennett, A Portrait Done at Home* show the course of their developing relationship. He declared his love in February 1923. At the present time she was beginning a provincial tour of Sudermann's *Magda* with Mrs. Patrick Campbell (1865–1946). For letters to Mrs. Campbell see Vol. I.

with his late brother, several novels of genuine importance, such as *Le Désastre.*

Yours faithfully, [Arnold Bennett]

ARKANSAS / MS. / 195
(*To Frank Swinnerton*)

75, Cadogan Square
19–2–23

My dear Henry,

No, I cannot agree with your estimate of your powers. There are here & there scenes in your novels of first-rate power, scenes which remain in the mind for years. Proof enough of what you *can* do when circumstances are favourable. What is wanted is the staying quality, & my belief is that this depends largely on health (physical & moral). I wrote a fatherly letter to Hughie & told him the error of his ways & also that I didn't like *The Cath.* well enough even to say anything about it to him at all. He replied that he was *delighted* with my letter, & he evidently was! All he desires is for people to be really interested in him. And he wrote me a most intimate *confession.* Unfortunately he double & treble marked the damn thing private, so I can't say anything about it. He swears that I alone, etc etc. I don't know how true this is. But it was a most taking letter. I have now written 80,000 words of my novel. I think another 10,000 ought to finish it nearly. I had the happy idea of reading the McLauchlin trial, one of the most captivating of the Hodge series, & found it full of small useful 'sordid' details of daily life in a small house. The old grandfather (87) trying to get into bed with the servant, & refusing to go away when she wanted to make water (*after* he'd tried to murder her). A1 stuff. I have a sort of an idea that my novel is not so bad. But it is infernally monotonous. I have written on Proust, & written the preface to *Don Juan de Marana*, & corrected all proofs of *How to Make the Best of Life*, & given 2 dinner parties in this house & am about to give 3 more, & talked to George Moore, & nursed Mrs. Loraine's baby, & improved my health & sleep astonishingly by means of exercises, & got a shade thinner, & paid my income

194. Percy Withers (1867–1945) was an author and a lecturer in English literature. Victor Margueritte and his brother Paul (1860–1918) wrote several socio-historical novels together.

tax, & arranged for the next season's yachting, & engaged a rather pretty house parlourmaid; & there was something else awfully interesting; but I can't recall now what it is. Beaverbrook said he would like to meet some nice girls, so I asked Gertrude Jennings & Marjorie Gordon to dinner with him & 2 other people. Gertrude (who however is not very self-critical as to the quality of her wit) rolled him in the dust again & again; she is very witty at times. Marjorie was not far behind. He had a hell of an evening, started to go home, but returned, fascinated. *You* would have particularly enjoyed it. Look here, I've exchanged books with W. B. Maxwell, & read *Spinster of This Parish.* The opening of it is a masterly exposition of narrative—the sort of thing Hughie would like to do but can't. There is also some good South American stuff. Then it goes to pieces & gets more & more sentimental. But about 75% of it is highly readable stuff. As a whole, très disappointing. I hope your novel is going ahead, and, if I may say so, that you aren't forcing it. Many enquiries about you at the club.

Yours, A. B.

FALES, NYU / MS. / 196
(*To St. John Ervine*)

75, Cadogan Square
11–3–23

My dear St. John,

Many thanks for the book on Methuselahs. Shame to say, I've only read myself in it yet! The one point on which I would *seriously* oppose you is your statement that old people who have mannerisms always had them. Briefly, this is not so. In consideration of the generosity & insight you display in dealing with me I overlook the lapse from verity.

195. *The Cathedral* was published October 1922.

The McLauchlin trial was one of the series of 'Notable British Trials' issued by W. Hodge, Edinburgh and London.

Marcel Proust: An English Tribute, ed. by C. K. Scott-Moncrieff, and with an essay by Bennett, was published in 1923.

Don Juan de Marana was published privately in October 1923; *How to Make the Best of Life* appeared in May.

Mrs. Loraine—wife of Robert Loraine (1876–1935), the actor-manager; Gertrude Jennings (d. 1958), the playwright; Marjorie Gordon (b. 1896), an actress and a good friend of Bennett's.

For another comment on W. B. Maxwell (d. 1938) see Vol. II, p. 344.

By the way I would like to hear your defence, constructionally, of the last act of 'M.M.Q.C.' I doubt not you have one and a good one, & next time we meet you shall tell me. I much enjoyed this piece of larking.

Yours, A. B.

COHEN / MS. / 197
(*To Harriet Cohen*)

Hotel Majestic
Paris
24–3–23

My sweet Tania,

This is to warn you that [?] stay in this hotel after Tuesday morning. It was the only good hotel we could get into, but now that I am in Paris I can exercise more influence over hotel bedrooms, & I shall get what I want in the middle of the town. Dr. Rosenbach leaves for Rome on Tuesday morning. I then move also. We had an excellent journey yesterday. Rosenbach is one of the exhaustless persons. He *would* go to a music-hall last night, because of the row going on here about nude women on the stage. There is a danger of them being forbidden: so we had to see them before they were forbidden. Well, we saw them all right. Some with a frail girdle, some with nothing whatever. Then he wanted to go forth for supper, but I dissuaded him & got him home at 12.30, & this morning he thanked me heartily for that. I shan't know anything about what is *really* going on in Paris till this afternoon, when I take tea with friends. I think you would like being here in Paris with people like my Paris friends *and me*. We have a terrific apartment here, the Dr. & I. Drawing-room, 2 bedrooms & 2 bathrooms, for £3. 10/- a day. You wouldn't get it in London for twice that. But I shall leave it, because the Champs Élysées is such a hades of a length. Are you better? I hope to be back for Easter, when we ought to forgather, since you are ever in my thoughts.

Yours respectfully, E. A. B.

196. Ervine's book was *Some Impressions of My Elders*, his play was *Mary, Mary, Quite Contrary*.

197. Bennett went to Paris for several days late in March. His companion was Dr. A. S. W. Rosenbach (1876–1952), the bibliophile, whom he met in America in 1911. The letter is misdated 24–1–23 by Bennett.

FALES, NYU / TS. / 198
(*To Leonora Ervine*)

75, Cadogan Square
3rd April 1923

Dear Leonora,

I have now made enquiries about Carantec, Finistère, Brittany. I am told that the best place would be Madame Maumé, Hôtel Moderne, Carantec, and that the best arrangement would be for you to have what rooms you wanted in a private house near by, and to eat in the hotel. The advantage of this place is that you can eat under cover in a garden. The total cost would be about 20 to 25 francs per day per person. This is under 7/-. I am able to say from experience that the food is very good and plentiful, and very badly served. The houses which Madame Maumé has a call upon for her guests are clean but very primitively furnished. I am told that many English visitors have been very pleased with their stay. If you decide to go it would be necessary to write to Madame Maumé, and the sooner the better. Would you write yourself, or would you prefer me to write?

I have just returned from a most violent week in Paris which I tremendously enjoyed.

Ever yours, Arnold B.

BUTLER / T.C. / 199
(*To George Doran*)
PRIVATE AND CONFIDENTIAL

[75, Cadogan Square]
[about 3 April 1923]

My dear George,

Very many thanks for your letter re Marguerite. I did not know of her visit to N.Y. until after she had arrived there. (Not that there was any reason why I should.) I suppose that her intention is to recite, or something of the sort. I have no doubt that you will deal sweetly with her. The very last thing I desire is that she should feel anything against her old friends. I know she has said that, on my instigation, many friends have abandoned her; but the fact is that I have most strongly urged all our friends here to keep up relations with her.

I've just been to Paris for eight days and had a great time. I am in A1. health, and hope you are.

Ever yours, A. B.

MAYFIELD, SYRACUSE / T.C.C. / 200
(*To Geoffrey Lapage*)

[75, Cadogan Square]
9th April 1923

Dear Sir,

I am obliged for your letter and the enclosures. I return all the latter, together with my report and adjudication.

Let me say that in my opinion the general level of the contributions is rather high—considerably higher than I should have expected.

Believe me,
Cordially yours, [Arnold Bennett]

200. Geoffrey Lapage (1888–) was a lecturer in zoology at Manchester University, and the *Serpent* was a journal issued by the Manchester University Unions. In 1923 Bennett judged their annual literary contest. His report follows. 'Cinna' was subsequently identified as Geoffrey Bullough, who was presently to become a distinguished scholar. 'Muda' may have been Lapage himself, who later published some poetry.

'Subject is the chief thing in a work of art; treatment is secondary. See the Greeks; see Matthew Arnold. It has been said that the best question for a good plot is: Does it seem interesting when told in a few words? "A.A.D." (author of a short story to which he has omitted to give a title) has found a very good (though horrible) and complete notion for a tale, but unfortunately he has not told the story; he has merely given a résumé of it in about six hundred words; with the result that he promises and does not perform. Which proves that subject is not absolutely everything. His fault is a typical fault. Most of the contributions are too short, too slight,—hints and whispers of what they might be and ought to be. Competitors think nothing of attempting to tell the story of a whole life in a thousand words or less. It cannot be done. It certainly cannot be done by a tyro. Chekhov might have done it, but then Chekhov was too modest to try to do it. Another fault is indirectness of narration. A happens to see B and is thereby moved to tell the history of B's life to C. Why? The machinery is unnecessary and it is a serious handicap; it takes the spirit out of a tale. How much better for the author himself to tell the story of B's life direct!

On the other hand the general level of the writing is really very high. I was astonished and delighted.

It was suggested to me that the adjudicator's difficulties might be increased this year by the enlargement of the definition of the word "fiction" so as to include

BERG / TS. / 201
(*To John Middleton Murry*)

75, Cadogan Square
1st May 1923

My dear Middleton Murry,

I have your letter and your prospectus. I think you are a good literary editor. Under you the *Athenaeum* was very good, and I hope the new thing will be as good and better. But the organisation of my life will not permit me to be of active assistance to you. I am too busy with creative work to have time for other sorts. Nor have I any inclination for other sorts— unless for a whole book of essays on one subject. Moreover at the present time I have contracts to fulfil which I cannot fulfil in

---

plays and essays. Not a bit! In the first place the stories and plays are easily superior to the essays. And in regard to the stories and plays, I don't care whether a contribution is a story or a play. I have only one criterion for both. The thing that interests and pleases me most is, for that sole reason, the best. A tale is a tale, whether told in narrative or dramatic form.

The playwrights have committed the indiscretion of nearly all beginners. They have started without any clear idea of their destination. It is easy to begin, so difficult to finish. "Muda", the author of *Tommy Fiddler: A Burlesque in Six Scenes*, begins with immense gusto and goes straight ahead, but after quite a short time he might be a man unconsciously walking round in a circle in the dark. And he gets so fogged that he turns his burlesque into a tragedy and then by mere effrontery drags it back into a burlesque. This is very naughty of him. Nevertheless "Muda" has a keen sense of life; he deals with life; he has creative power, audacity and interestingness. He distances the other playwrights.

Among the story-writers "Cinna", author of more than one contribution, possesses the narrative gift in a marked degree. *From Bondage* opens thus: "John Burnham saw the woman he loved on to the boat-train and then went home to his wife." What an opening! The interest is acutely and instantly excited. *From Bondage* is an "unpleasant" affair. I doubt if the *Serpent* would print it without grave misgivings. But I cannot help that. I have to deal only with its artistic merits, which, despite a failure in convincingness towards the end, are unusual. Another good story is Miss Kate Simmonds' *The Best Policy*, and still another is "J's" *A Pedagogic Tragedy*. And a pleasing if somewhat conventional fairy-tale, with a sound moral, is "El Assed's" *The Christmas Gift*. All these four are well constructed and well written, and they hold the attention. There is nothing haphazard about them. Lastly I must mention a tiny jeu d'esprit, "T.S's" *The Mathematics of Personal Appearance*. "T.S." has wit and adroitness, and the last section of his opuscule, *The Theory of Attractions*, would not be out of place in *Punch*.

In my opinion the three best contributions, in order of merit, are:

1. *TOMMY FIDDLER* By "Muda"
2. *FROM BONDAGE* By "Cinna"
3. *THE BEST POLICY* By Kate Simmonds.

But I beg to inform "Muda" that he has had a mighty near shave of being only second.'

less than two years. I am no longer living on twenty four hours a day, and my age will be fifty six in less than a month, and although I think myself young, young people do not think I am young, and you need young people who will see in the appearance of any book or other manifesto by such as me a grand occasion for proving with ferocity that literature does not stand still. I noticed the other day that you were saying appreciative things about the work I used to do years ago. I could not do that kind of work now, and I have no desire to do it. I know that as a rule authors of my age are very dissatisfied with the work of the young generation, and are prejudiced by reason of age against it. Yet I am bound to say that in my opinion I have no prejudice against the young, rather the reverse, and yet I am looking in vain for a really good novel by that generation, and *Men Like Gods*, with all its limitations, seems to me to contain more fundamental 'stuff' than anything else I have read for a long time. I am very disappointed with Lawrence, who appears to me to have genius concealed somewhere within him. Joyce has enormous power and originality, but he lacks the balance which is essential to great work. George Moore can write the heads off any of you, and he is nearly 70. I will tell you the men you need for your paper—Lynd, Forster, MacCarthy, Tomlinson. Get them. I am not a critic. I can only assert. I can only divide the crowd into sheep and goats, whereas there are no sheep and no goats. I know that.

Come and see me. I should like to hear you talk, and I should like to make some assertions.

My life is an immense romance. It shall continue to be a romance. But I can only keep it so in my own way, and that way will not be by joining les jeunes. Tell me when it is most convenient for you to come.

Yours sincerely, Arnold Bennett

P.S. What in hell do you mean by saying there is no such thing as philosophy? You are only playing with words. A. B.

201. Murry's new journal, the *Adelphi*, began publication in June. H. M. Tomlinson appeared often in it and so did Bennett himself but with brief reviews. Robert Lynd was literary editor of the *Daily News* from 1912 to 1930. On Desmond MacCarthy see above, p. 28. On E. M. Forster see below, pp. 308–9.

Wells's *Men Like Gods* appeared in 1923.

BUTLER / T.C.C. / 202
(*To George Doran*)

[75, Cadogan Square]
14th May 1923

My dear George,

Many thanks for your letter of the 4th, which reached me this morning. I am very glad that you have finally decided to come to England twice in a year. As I told you, this house will be closed, but I shall be dispensing hospitality in my yacht. Also, if necessary, I shall come to London, but I shall have to stay at an hotel if I do.

Eric ought to have told you all about my new novel. He had the MS with him. It is entitled *Riceyman Steps*, and the scene is laid in Clerkenwell, an industrial quarter of London. Practically the whole of the novel is occupied with shop life. The principal male character is a bookseller. There are two principal female characters, the wife of the bookseller (both of them are misers) and a charwoman who becomes their general servant and even nurse. This charwoman is the heroine of the book. She is a fine person, and I hope you will like her. She is a war-widow, but at the end of the book she marries again very happily. The subject matter has very little real resemblance to that of *The Old Wives' Tale* or *Clayhanger*, but the method of narration is the same as in these books. *I* think that the story is exciting. It is, however, not in the least melodramatic. Also it has no showy personages, no material splendours, and no 'daring' sexualities. It might be put into the hands of the most young-ladyish young lady on the Atlantic coast. There are broadly speaking two themes—the miser theme and the love theme.

The book is about 100,000 words in length—rather less perhaps.

I think this is about all.

I shall go on board the yacht on the last day of May, but this address will always find me.

Affections.

Ever yours, [Arnold Bennett]

202. Eric Pinker (1891–) was now head of the Pinker literary agency. See Vol. I for his relations with Bennett. Bennett finished writing *Riceyman Steps* on 17 March. He was sailing in his yacht during the summer months.

BERG / TS. / 203
(*To John Middleton Murry*)

75 Cadogan Square
29th May 1923

My dear Middleton Murry,

Pardon a word of unsolicited criticism about your venture. I think the contents are pretty creditable, but I think that the material presentation leaves something to be desired. The page is not good, and the type is entirely without distinction. Whatever it brings in—and it cannot bring in much—the half page advertisement on the front cover detracts terribly from the appearance of the review, and as for the advertisements 'facing matter', the irritation which they produce is past words. I have never seen this in a serious monthly before. I feel sure that they will do far more harm than good. Taken as a whole, the mere look of the review is extremely disappointing—even to the sinister colour of the cover. Why don't you get it printed by some firm that understands printing? Why I should worry your worried life with these remarks I cannot imagine; but you need not take any notice of them.

Yours sincerely, Arnold Bennett

BERG / MS. / 204
(*To John Middleton Murry*)

Yacht Marie Marguerite
3–6–23

Dear Middleton Murry,

I think your opening parah is rather formless, but you got through it into the idea all right, though not without difficulty. The theme is stated. It is most admirably illustrated by Lawrence & Sullivan. I didn't think Sullivan could do anything equal to this—very highly delicate and effective. The Lawrence is magnificent. Pity he is falling more & more into the trick of repeating a word or a phrase. It irritates the reader & enfeebles the stuff. Also the connection between trees & human beings is not very strong. But really this article *is* the goods. The Tomlinson article is also magnificent. No better stuff than this is being done. The K.M. story is excellently characteristic. Mr. Joiner is good; it halts at the beginning. It is another good illustration of the magazine's theme. One or two items in the 'Club' are a bit perfunctory or are too slight to have importance. But it is very creditable, and you have put the best item first. Somebody else on board is reading the magazine at the moment, & I can't refer to it, to see whether I have mentioned every item, but I think I have—except 'Multum in Parvo', which will just do. I think the number is simply splendid—especially for a first number, & you are to be seriously & gravely congratulated upon it. I confirm what I said in my previous letter about the format and advertisements. And I am far from being alone in the opinion that the appearance of the review is deplorable.

Such are my ideas, for which you asked.

Yours sincerely, Arnold Bennett

BERG / MS. / 205
(*To John Middleton Murry*)

Yacht Marie Marguerite
Southampton
9–6–23

My dear Middleton Murry,

Thanks for your letter. I am greatly delighted at this success. It's fine. I know pretty well what advts. are worth, & I know that in suppressing the ½ page on the front you would lose money directly. Nevertheless I think it would pay you to suppress it. It looks dreadful, & must distress people. I would say almost the same for the other pages facing matter. As for the printing, it is *not* distinguished, & it might be. I shall try to send you something for the next number, but I don't know what in this world yet.

204. In his editorial remarks in the first issue of the *Adelphi* Murry said: 'The *Adelphi* is nothing if it is not an act. It is not a business proposition or a literary enterprise, or a nice little book in a pretty yellow cover; it is primarily and essentially an assertion of a faith . . . that life is important.' He remarked incidentally that Bernard Shaw was shown a prospectus and said: 'You will live either by charity or advertisement.'

The several pieces in the first issue were 'Trees and Babies and Papas and Mamas', by D. H. Lawrence; 'On Being Oneself', by J. W. N. Sullivan (1886–1937), the writer on science; 'The Estuary', by H. M. Tomlinson; 'The Samuel Josephs', by Katherine Mansfield; 'The Contributors' Club', which included brief reviews by several people, first among them Bennett; 'Mr. Joiner and the Bible', an anonymous conversation; and 'Multum in Parvo', miscellaneous comments on books and other topics.

I have a notion that I once, some years ago, sent you a sketch by a girl named Smith which you turned down. She showed me a short story this very day which I think quite first-rate of its kind. It seems to me to be absolutely the goods. I wish you would read it. I enclose it with this. I wish you would come down to Southampton the next time I am here & have lunch & tea on board. (The anchorage is secure and calm.) We could then talk.

Yours sincerely, Arnold Bennett

COHEN / TR. / 206
(*To Harriet Cohen*)

Royal Albion Hotel
Brighton
[July 1923]

My sweet Tania,

I hope you are better; at any rate less gloomy. It is a great pity you cannot be here, and that you should work and 'manage' and scheme. Still, you are independent. It is one of the chief things. We are staying at this hotel, which is the 2nd of Harry Preston's hotels, instead of at The York, where 2 football teams are staying—with their ladies (said to be mothers and sisters, je n'en sais rien). I have bought a wonderful Victorian scrap-screen for 2 guineas. It will delight you almost as much as you delight me—*no*, but something like that. There was a famous Victorian pianist named Arabella Goddard—a great star in the sixties. I think you are rather like her, except that she probably couldn't play Bach or Bax. I have also bought a wondrous pair of Victorian vases and a Victorian dessert service. In fact, I am content with my purchases. Also 2 books. I saw the screen in the window of a shop, and went in, and the old gentleman, who was reading a novel, said he was leaving his shop next week and would practically give me anything I wanted. I have a wonderful miniature edition of Byron's *Don Juan*, illustrated, for you, with a staggering Victorian preface. I am bound to say, with all my modesty, that it takes me to find these things. Anyhow you must have had a pleasant evening

205. Bennett contributed a lively article on the Sitwells to the August issue. Also in the August issue appeared Pauline Smith's 'The Pain'. Another story by her, 'The Schoolmaster', was published in October. For other references to her see below, and see also Vols. I and II.

last night with Cedric and Désirée. I hope Moeran's music will not exasperate you on Monday night. I look forward to Thursday evening. These two women with us are very nice and exceedingly well dressed, and always equable. *Wanting* to be pleased, they *are* pleased. Alistair Tayler has charge of all the material arrangements. We have been to the Aquarium and to 'Old Bill M.P.'. Maintenant je vous embrasse très affectueusement. The answer to the question you put to me on Thursday in the intervals of practising is in the affirmative. I need say no more. Your constant

A. B.

BODKIN / TR. / 207
(*To Thomas Bodkin*)

Yacht Marie Marguerite
(Southampton)
5.8.23.

My dear T.B.,

It is not an article at all. It is a romance, a drama, an epic; and puts you in the grande lignée des collectionneurs. I read it with the greatest interest, and pride in you. I shall certainly not return it. I shall keep it to astound people with. I suppose '1816' at the bottom of p. 240 is a misprint. I don't see anything the matter with the writing of it. I cannot imagine why you should persist in giving me pictures for my V. Dining Room. But if you do, I assuredly persist in accepting them. Your description of the latest gift is most alléchante. I hereby express to you my keen gratitude. Trust me to pay the carriage etc. all right. My V. Dining Room exists with additions. At Brighton I saw a 3 fold scrap-screen through a shop window. I rushed in. How much? £2. I purchased, with various other things. At Torquay, 5 weeks ago, a yachting friend of mine saw a large framed water-colour (about 24 by 18, I mean) and said 'If you'd like it for your V. dining-room I'll buy it and give it you.' I liked it. He gave it me (17/6), and since then it has been lost

206. Harry Preston (1860–1936) was manager at the Royal York when Bennett wrote part of *Clayhanger* there in 1910.

Arabella Goddard (1836–1922); Cedric Sharpe; Ernest John Moeran (1894–1950), English composer. Désirée is unidentified.

on the railway! The subject is a full length figure of a Victorian gent on a Rhenish landscape. Top hat. Kid gloves carefully laid on a boulder. I hope to retrieve it, as it is one of the most side-splitting things you ever saw, and not at all ill-painted. Now as regards your visit to Holland, please let me know the dates in due course. I do not yet know whether I shall be ashore or afloat in September. If I'm ashore you must positively come to 75 en route. I'll tell Swinnerton (not Swynnerton).

Bring the Canaletto. What a devil of a fellow you are!

I have observed that de Valera makes an ass of himself to the last. Quel monde, tout de même.

And what a moral tale, this tobacco exploit of James O'Connor's! They hadn't foreseen that the big combines would not leave them alone! Sanctissima simplicitas!! In other words, quelles cruches!!!

My kindest wishes to you both.

Yours sincerely, Arnold Bennett

TEXAS / MS. / 208
(*To Jonathan Cape*)

[? Yacht Marie Marguerite]
9–8–23

Dear Mr. Jonathan Cape,

I have just been enquiring about Pauline Smith, author of 'Pain' in the current *Adelphi*. Miss Smith is a discovery of mine. Her address is The Moors, Broadstone, Dorset. I have been trying to make her write a novel, & I think she will do so; but her health is not good & she is a very slow worker. I wish you would write to her (not referring at all to myself), & urge her to produce a *novel*. I am quite convinced of her first-rate quality, but of course its fruition depends on her health & the encouragement given to her.

Yours sincerely, Arnold Bennett

207. Bodkin's article was 'Adrien van de Venne', which appeared in *Studies* (Dublin), June 1923.

Eamon De Valera (1882–) was standing for election in the Republican opposition party, and the Irish Free State ministry arrested him, as they had before. He won easily, though the Government itself returned 39 seats to the Republican 24.

208. The letterhead address is 75 Cadogan Square, but unless Bennett made a quick trip to London he was still on his yacht, probably at Cowes.

Jonathan Cape (1879–1960) was founder and chairman of the Cape publishing house. On Pauline Smith's novel see below, p. 216.

BUTLER / MS. / 209
(*To Robert Nichols*)

Yacht Marie Marguerite
14–8–23

My dear Robert,

Well I am very glad at last to hear from you. You have owed me a letter for about ten years; & I told Siegfried I wouldn't write till you did. Your description of the Californian Scene is very alluring, but I doubt the value of your girl poet, if the pretty little fancy you quote is a measure of her. I'll tell you what I think of 'Golgotha'. I think it is a prodigious cataract of eloquence, managed with astonishing skill and verve, but too diffuse by far in its movement and somewhat naive in its philosophy. Do you realise that the main ideas in it are the ideas that dominated such as myself 25 years ago? To my mind the war has taught us rather more than you here express; and, chiefly, that hatred and scorn of the legendary 'Fat Man' (*Herald* cartoons of 1910–11–12) cut no ice whatever & are indeed too ingenuous for this time of day. A little more Sermon on the Mount is what we all need, and the clear realisation that there is no 'villain of the piece'. Withal, the narrative is very soundly handled. Such are my views. You were doubtless aware when you asked for them that you would get them naked. I think that the said views are shared by the judicious 'on this side'. If I find that I *can* be of any assistance to you here I shall infallibly be of assistance to you. What are your qualifications for an academic post in this traditional country? As for running any sort of a periodical, I don't think this is quite your job—any more than it is Siegfried's. You are too creative, temperamental, and wilful to be an editor. These high matters should be left by people like us to people like the excellent Middleton Murry. I doubt whether Aldous is picking up much in the 'plum' line from journalism tel quel; but his books are certainly selling better & better in both England & America. So much so that, the last time he was at my house, he announced to us his intention of retiring from journalism as quickly as possible. He is a fine journalist, & I thought that the best things in *On the Margin* were as good as such things could be. They were about equal to, though quite different from, the essays of that *master*, Robert Lynd. Well now, I think your instinct to return is a very sound one. You don't need to stay in Japan for the sake of Japan. Japan will struggle on all right. Apparently there is no money for you in Japan worth talking about. I hear you are happy in your marriage, so you would be happy anywhere—even in England, & England is still the centre of the Anglo-Saxon movement, I imagine. You ask about me. I am 56 and still ridiculously keen. So is Wells. So is Shaw. I doubt if John Galsworthy is,—I'm not sure. I wish I knew your wife, so that I could send her my blessing without impertinence. My newest Chinese proverb is: 'Be healthy & you will be happy.' I concoct several proverbs a month. Write me again, & count upon me as yours,

A. B.

GIDE / 210
(*To André Gide*)

Yacht Marie Marguerite
15–8–1923

My dear Gide,

Your book on Dostoevsky (for which many thanks) has made a very considerable impression upon me. And yet you say almost nothing about his technique, which interests me considerably . . . (If he had any technique!) Of course Dostoevsky is *your* author. His moral foundations suit yours. The result is A1. I notice with satisfaction that you refer to an obiter dictum of mine. I had no idea you had your eye on me! After reading what you said about *The Eternal Husband*, I read that story again. Je le trouve un peu manqué, surtout vers la fin. It ought to have been his best work, but I certainly do not think it is. It lacks power. I suggested to Chatto and Windus that your book ought to appear in English; it is by far the best thing on Dostoevsky I ever read; but they reply that there is a great 'slump' in things Russian in England just now, and that nothing Russian can be published except at a loss. However, Swinner-

209. 'Golgotha & Co' was one of the tales in *Fantastica*, published in 1923. Nichols at this time was Professor of English in Tokyo.

Aldous Huxley (1894–1963) published his collection of 'notes and essays' *On the Margin* in 1923, which also was the year *Antic Hay* appeared.

ton is reading it, with a view to further consideration. But perhaps you have yourself made arrangements for its publication in England. I've been twice over to Paris to see you, and have not seen you. Instead, I had lunch with Edmond Jaloux! I cannot read his novels. Am I wrong? I have read no good French novel for a long time, and *La N.R.F.* devient de plus en plus scie. Especially since Boissard departed. Boissard was really good. I am publishing a novel in the autumn of which I will send you a copy, as I think it is rather better than some of my novels. I am now exercising myself in the short story (400 or 500 lines). I'm writing a lot of them. I wanted to see whether I had forgotten how to write a short story.

A new monthly literary review has begun in London. The *Adelphi* edited by Middleton Murry. It has had a great success, and is not so bad. I wish I could write you an interesting letter, but I am suffering from insomnia.

Always your devoted Arnold Bennett

CALIF / MS. / 211
(*To Eden Phillpotts*)

Yacht Marie Marguerite
Swanage
19–8–23

My dear Eden,

I was delighted to have your letter, & I shall take the *greatest* pleasure in seeing you again. By this time I should have reached Torquay in the above named craft, but a storm drove us into Swanage, where we have rolled incessantly for 60 hours & the wind is still contrary! But I expect to reach either Torquay or Dartmouth in a few days. Also, as I know deeply that you won't come to London, I will come to Torquay later for a week-

210. Gide's *Dostoevsky* was published in England by J. M. Dent in 1925, with a preface by Bennett.

Edmund Jaloux (1878–1949), novelist and critic.

Maurice Boissard was the name under which Paul Léautaud (1872–1960) wrote his theatre criticism. Léautaud was an old friend of Bennett's.

Riceyman Steps appeared in October.

Some of Bennett's new stories appeared in the *Strand* from 1924 to 1927, and were later collected in *The Woman Who Stole Everything* and *The Night Visitor*.

end as you & Emily most benevolently suggest. I still reckon that you know more about constructing a novel than anybody else in this country, & I still wish to God I could invent plots as you do. But God in his wisdom has decided otherwise.

Salutations to all yours and you.

Ever yours, A. B.

ARKANSAS / MS. / 212
(*To Frank Swinnerton*)

Yacht Marie Marguerite
Poole
26–8–23

My dear Frank,

I thank you. I've been held here (& am & shall be still held) for over a week by one continuous gale. I've let the yacht from 1st to 18th Sept. & shall be in town and at the Reform shortly after the 1st. Say the 3rd. For the winter! Insomnia not gone. Neuralgia gone. A little work being done daily, but not much. I've had about enough of the yacht for this season. Not surprising, seeing that I am now in the 6th week of violent S.W. wind, generally amounting to a gale. Still, on the whole a better season than last, because warmer & less rainy. Nevertheless, a hell of a lot of rain lately. Well, there is nothing except lively sympathy to say about your suffering mother. It's very rough on both of you, & I hope you're better.

I am *not* going to America. I should like to; but I've far too much *on* here. I have a magnif. idea for my next novel. I've just had some proofs of *Riceyman Steps*. Pretty fair, I think. I gave them to Pauline Smith to read. In a quarter of an hour she was weeping. 'Here!' said I, 'what are you crying for?' She said: 'It's beautiful.' Yet believe me its the most sordid, shop-py story.

Yours, A. B.

211. After their quarrel in 1907–8, Bennett and Eden Phillpotts saw little or nothing of each other until now. For other information on Phillpotts, and earlier letters to him, see Vols. I and II.

212. The next novel was *Lord Raingo*, which Bennett did not begin writing until May 1925.

BERG / MS. / 213
(*To John Middleton Murry*)

75, Cadogan Square
3rd September 1923

My dear Middleton Murry,

Many thanks. I will strive to let you have a note about André Maurois's *Ariel ou la vie de Shelley*. It is a very bright thing.

I do not think that the magazine is as good as the first number was, but then I did not expect that it would be. The standard of the first number was very high indeed. To my mind Lawrence has gone off, and has indeed become very wild. I should say that neither himself nor anybody else could keep him in order.

You probably do not desire me to be too frank, but out of a very genuine regard for you I will risk telling you that some of the things in your own contributions cause a certain amount of embarrassment to your friends.

Yours sincerely, Arnold Bennett

BERG / MS. / 214
(*To John Middleton Murry*)

75, Cadogan Square
10–9–23

My dear Murry,

Many thanks for your letter. The answer is:—I think (and a number of others whom you would not ignore think so too) that your editorial in the September issue is a fair example, from beginning to end, of a form of *sensiblerie* which it is in a very high degree difficult to treat respectfully. Also that your note towards the end about style and K.M. is a mistake in demeanour, as likewise your previous repeated references to K.M. In brief, the view is that it would be better for you to leave the appreciation of K.M.'s unquestioned and remarkable gifts to others. My dear fellow, I realise that you are entitled to describe the above as an enormity. I try to realise the gravity of the emotional crisis through which you have passed and indeed are passing. My sympathy is yours whether you want it or not. I have ventured, perhaps wrongly, to tell you what I think, because I know that your present policy is harming you with the very

213. Bennett's review of *Ariel*, by André Maurois (1885–1960), appeared in the October issue.

soundest people that I am acquainted with. If you resent this letter I shall not complain, nor shall I allow anything adverse that you may say to alter my deep good will towards you.

I agree that *some* of the Lawrence stuff is excellent. But as a whole his contributions (except the first) have been painfully patchy, with a preponderance of wildness that simply will not bear examination.

Yours sincerely, Arnold Bennett

GIDE / 215
(*To André Gide*)

75, Cadogan Square
23-9-1923

My dear Gide,

I am delighted to hear from you and what pleases me most in your letter is the news that you have in hand a long novel. This is precisely what I most want to read. As for Pontigny, yes, I ought to go. I am sure that it would do me an immense amount of good. My crudities would shock some of your refined minds, but the benefit to me would be great. I assure you that I know nobody in London, except possibly Maurice Baring, who at once thinks continentally about literature and who has an expert creative acquaintance with literature as a craft. Baring is a wonderful man, not only reads but speaks 18 or 20 languages, extrèmement cultivé, a poet, critic, nouvelliste (no word for this in English); but not strongly creative. I dare say you know him. In the matters which interest you and me, I am really rather lonely in London. Twice have I been to Paris to see you, and twice you were not there! And I only met Paul Valéry in the Place de l'Opéra, between two Metro trains; and Larbaud not at all. Now as regards the *N.R.F.*, *am* I unjust? All I know is that under Copeau, I panted monthly for the *N.R.F.* Under Rivière, I pass a fortnight before opening it. The foregoing is fundamental and unanswerable literary criticism! Yes, I had read *Clodomir l'assassin*. It was marvellous. Inspired by

214. Murry's September editorial was a diffuse discussion of the romantic character of English literature. It made an incidental attack on an essay in the *New Statesman*. In his note on style, Murry remarked that in his opinion Katherine Mansfield 'alone among the writers of her own generation had achieved a truly original style'. His editorial the previous month described the shock to him of her death.

your letter, I searched out the Numbers containing it and read it again. It is still marvellous. In fact it is great, and gave me the very keenest pleasure. We have just had a new edition of the works of Hale White (Mark Rutherford). It is a miserable and ill-printed edition, but it exists, and I am reading him all over again. Hale White is a great writer who adopted a form which he never learnt how to use: the novel. His construction is usually naif to the point of absurdity. But he is full of great stuff, and a most genuine stylist—one of the best, I think. He is exactly *your* sort of writer; and I doubt not that you have already read him. Touching the *Old Wives' Tale*, I could never get anyone practically interested in my work in Paris, until Maurice Lanoire came along. He is a provincial, and he writes Bordelais, not French. But he was keen on translating my work and nobody else was. I gave him the right to translate all my books. He has not yet translated the *O.W.T.*, and I doubt not that some arrangement could be made with him and Grasset (Jaloux assisting), if some other translator would [?] for himself. I should love Maurois to translate it, and I am flattered that you should have it in mind. The Cinema? Rien! I could not persuade them to take anything original. At the moment another very big American firm is trying to get me; but I will see the colour of their money before I write a line. I am just about to publish a novel *Riceyman Steps*, of which I will send you a copy. Scene—London. Type: réaliste. Old-fashioned, of course. C'est plus fort que moi. We have several young novelists here who are trying to invent a form to supersede Balzac's. *They are not succeeding*. I also am trying, and almost succeeding. Still, I shall go on trying. To my mind, a really original novel was *Mort de Quelqu'un*. Balzac could not have written that. But he could have written nearly everything else. Please remember me to Marc Allégret. And please come to London.

Ever yours, Arnold Bennett

215. Gide was writing *Les Faux-monnayeurs*.

For letters to Maurice Baring and Valery Larbaud see below.

Paul Valéry (1871–1945), the poet; Jacques Rivière (1886–1925), director of *La Nouvelle Revue Française* until his death; Mark Rutherford (1831–1913), best known for his *Autobiography*.

Clodomir l'assassin, a short novel by Marcel Jouhandeau (b. 1888), appeared in the *NRF* in October 1922. *Mort de quelqu'un*, by Jules Romains, was published in 1911.

STOKE / MS. / 216
(*To Hugh Walpole*)

75, Cadogan Square
19–x–23

My sweet Hughie,

Thanks. I don't care a damn who is or isn't there on Wednesday so long as you're there. Don't listen to tattle about yourself. Most of it is necessarily untrue & all of it is reported with a malicious intent. If I took notice of a quarter of the things which you are reported to have said about me my appetite would be impaired. But I don't. I have said nothing to other people about you beyond what I have said to you, & shall probably say again.

Thine ever, A. B.

STAR, 20 October 1923 / 217
(*To the editor*)

75, Cadogan Square
19th October, 1923

Sir,

'Alpha of the Plough' based his article of yesterday on a statement attributed to me to the effect that the finest example of modern English prose is to be found in Mark Rutherford. I should like to have the reference for this.

Mr. Fisher Unwin, without asking my permission, quoted the alleged statement in his advertisements of the Rutherford novels. I asked him for the reference. He could not give it. Not without difficulty did I get Mr. Fisher Unwin to remove my name and my alleged statement from his advertisements.

I am still asking vainly for the reference.

Yours faithfully, Arnold Bennett

217. Thomas Fisher Unwin (1848–1935), founder of the Unwin publishing house.

In his *Journal* on 30 September 1923 Bennett wrote a long reconsideration of Rutherford, and remarked: 'I said some years ago that his prose was almost the finest modern prose. I still think his prose is generally very fine, but it is rather untutored.'

BEAVERBROOK / TS. / 218
(*To Lord Beaverbrook*)

75, Cadogan Square
24th October 1923

My dear Max,

re the *Standard*. This is the only evening paper that appeals even a little to educated people, and it ought to be made to appeal a great deal more to them than it does. You can't, in my opinion, get much prestige out of a yellow paper. Hence I wouldn't let it be yellow.

I admit of course that it must have a political policy, and that in the main that policy must be your own. But I wish you could have a policy of 'Do' rather than of 'Refrain from doing'. And I wish that we could see a paper that faced the music editorially every morning. Why, for example, no leader in the *Express* this morning, about Smuts's speech? Surely important enough! I'm glad at any rate that the *Express* doesn't wobble like the *Mail* does. Last week the *Mail* policy on food-taxes varied about once a day. The *Express* seems to keep off food-taxes! Your policy about retiring from Europe may be sound, but I don't think you'll get any Government to adopt it. There is a moral side to this matter that counts heavily. You might, and would, argue me to a standstill, but I should continue to think that to clear out of Europe was not right.

All this is beside the point. I should make the *Standard*'s policy positive, not negative. And I should make it less opportunist. You *must* do this if you want prestige. You won't get prestige without burning your boats, nailing colours to the mast, etc. Nobody ever did. I should preserve freedom to be cynical and critical of anybody and everybody. Surely you can afford to do this in *one* paper? I should have the whole paper well written; and especially the news stories—at present they are not interestingly written; they lack brilliance. Books, pictures, theatres and music are none of them well done at present. There is a great new public interest springing up in architecture, but I don't know any London paper that attempts to touch it.

I don't think it matters, in the making of prestige, what your policy is, if only it is adhered to and is brilliantly explained. I can see a *Standard* that every well-educated person would *have* to read, if only for pleasure, but it is not the present *Standard*.

You can't get anything for nothing, and you can't get prestige without paying for it in some way. I don't mean news prestige (which *you* can always get and have got), but moral prestige. I am assuming that in the *Standard* you want moral prestige. If you think only of circulation you won't get prestige, and if you think only of prestige you won't get circulation; but there is a middle course, with a slight inclination to the right!

There is a fellow named Peter Page on the *Daily Sketch* that I think would be better employed on the *Standard.* I don't know him personally. He has a considerable subterranean reputation in Fleet Street.

The above are just a few notions that formed themselves in my so-called mind after you left me in the rain. You can forgive me for the sermon on Friday.

Yours, A. B.

STOKE / MS. / 219
(*To Hugh Walpole*)

75, Cadogan Square
5–xi–23

My dear Hughie,

I thank thee. No. You are probably wrong & Jack Squire probably right. He does know *something* about style; you know nothing; or at any rate you write as if you know nothing. I see you believe rather in Edith Wharton, & assert that at her worst she has never descended as low as Wells & me in certain books. Innocence, you ought to see a doctor; the case is urgent. The excellent Edith is nobody at all, & she has deceived you. She never *began* to write. And what I have charged you with is not violent writing but slipshod writing. Have you ever *known* a miser personally & well? I have, and I am in a position to tell you that you are quite wrong. In fact your idea is stagey, pseudo-romantic & beautifully absurd. My miser is a real miser. Why the Lakes, my misguided friend? You will get wet through, & it is a hell of a way from London. Your touching sentimental-

218. Beaverbrook bought the *Evening Standard* in 1923 from Edward Hulton.
Smuts gave a speech at the Savoy Hotel devoted to the European economic situation, especially that of Germany and the occupied Ruhr.
Peter Page is not otherwise known.

ity has led you to the Lakes. You wanted to get into contact with Nature, didn't you? I bet you did, & of course the Lakes are the spiritual home of Nature. Never mind, my dear Hughie, I am entirely yours.

A. B.

BUTLER / MS. / 220
(*To John Drinkwater*)

75, Cadogan Square
21–xi–23

My dear Drinkwater,

You are to hear officially from Playfair. For myself, & unofficially, I want to urge you to alter Part II sc. i. You quite convinced me that such a scene was necessary & also that it was properly in the scheme of the play, & not out of key with the rest. But I strongly feel that it might with advantage be very much simplified & shortened. I am venturing to write now not as chairman of a theatre but as author to author. Further, you could easily do it. Personally I loathe altering a play, but there are times when it can be done without too much exasperation of nerves, & I think this is a time.

Lastly, it is most important to reduce the expenses. We cannot at present see how the thing can be done at all at Hammersmith without drastic reductions, & we are all very concerned.

Yours, Arnold Bennett

P.S. Were you joking or serious when you said that a copy of one of your books inscribed to me was on sale? If it is so, I cannot explain it. I have a number of your works all together on my shelves, & I should never dream of disposing of any of them. Somebody must have borrowed & pinched it; *or*, my

219. Some years earlier Bennett wrote of one of the novels of Edith Wharton (1862–1937): 'Not fine, but capable. No connection with literature.'

Bennett's chief source for Earlforward in *Riceyman Steps* (published in October 1923) is not known. But according to Edward Knoblock some details were drawn from the proprietor of a bookshop in Southampton, and others from a book that Bennett purchased there, *Lives and Anecdotes of Misers* (1850), by F. S. Merryweather. An article on the subject was published in *Modern Fiction Studies* (U.S.A.), summer 1962.

Walpole went to live in Cumberland. He replied to Bennett: '*What* an insulting letter!'

wife must have had it in *her* library (she lives apart) & it must have got away through her—but not with her knowledge I'm sure! A. B.

BEAVERBROOK / TS. / 221
(*To Lord Beaverbrook*)

75, Cadogan Square
7th December 1923

My dear Max,

It was nice of you to ask me for last night, but I was dining and concerting with Tania; and afterwards in the fog to the Reform Club, where God still reigns—I am told. Home at 2 a.m.

My objection to the policy of the *Express* of late is that I can't understand it—nor have I met anyone else who can. Therefore, however good the policy may be, the paper fails as the vehicle of it.

The matter vaguely presents itself to my mind thus. You give the effect of having conceived two policies, and of not having chosen between them. You may say that these two policies are not mutually exclusive. Perhaps they aren't; but I doubt whether it is politic to run two war-cries side by side. You have an imperial policy, and you have an anti-labour policy, and in order to back the latter you encouraged voters in certain circumstances to vote against the former.

It is possible that you have a third policy, namely at any cost to down Baldwin, with whom you are not in direct contact.

As regards your imperial policy, I do not consider that you have yet justified this in the *Express*. For example you have not disposed of the British criticism that the colonies want something for nothing, or something positive in exchange for something highly problematical. Nor have you answered the criticism (with all its implications) that Colonial preference will still leave the retail price of goods affected by it just as high as if there were no Colonial preference. Nor have you done anything to soften the British impression (doubtless false!) that the colonies are a damned grasping lot of coves.

I am well aware that you could brilliantly argue me out of

220. For an earlier letter and other references to John Drinkwater see Vols. I and II. The play in question is not known. Earlier in 1923 the Lyric produced Drinkwater's *Robert E. Lee*.

my position. But a man may be in as just possession of an argument as of a city and still be thrown out of it.

Lastly I will mention the question of your recent headlines. Considering that the immense psychological effect of headlines is largely the creation of people like yourself, Blum, and the Harmsworths, I think the *Express* might handle headlines with greater care than apparently it has been doing.

The statement that the circulation of the *Express* is rising is entirely off the point.

As for the *Daily Mail*, I can remember in the popular press no such sustained exhibition of dishonest fatuity as it has given to the world during the last fortnight.

Yours ever, A. B.

BUTLER / MS. / 222
(*To Edward Knoblock*)

75, Cadogan Square
20–xii–23

My dear Edward,

First, I am delighted very much by the success of *Lullaby*, of which there is considerable talk here. I specially heard of it from Freddy Lonsdale.

Second, I was very sorry to hear of your ear operation, & glad of your method of curing the resultant depression. I immensely appreciate what you say about *Riceyman Steps*. (Thanks about misprints.) The thing is certainly having a strange success here. Even barbers delicately mention it to me. I trust it will also go in U.S.A.

Third: Damn you! Curse you! I am sick of not seeing you. And also there is *London Life*. I enclose copy of a letter just received from Dean. You see what he says. You recall, too, I hope, that a clause of our unwritten contract (I mean yours & mine) says that you are director-in-chief, on behalf of the firm, of the rehearsals. It is a bedrock certainty that I *cannot* take your place. I have neither the skill nor the will. Further, *The Great Adventure* is positively going to be revived at the Haymarket in May. If Harrison has another play running then he is compelled by his contract to take it off. Therefore you will have to help in

221. Stanley Baldwin (1867–1947), Conservative Prime Minister.

the rehearsals of *The Great Adventure* also, & probably simultaneously.

On your recommendation I have just bought *The Dance of Life* and am reading it. It repayeth perusal, & I thank thee. (But I have been an admirer of Havelock for 30 years.)

My house is not huge, & only one room in it is Victorian, but it is not so bad in some ways. I am told that Ruby Peto has decided that *Vogue* shall publish photographs of its interiors.

I've had a whole series of trifling illnesses this autumn, but am now extremely well. Engaged chiefly in writing articles & short stories! I've written the *Prohack* play up to nearly the end, but don't like it & have put it away for 3 months. I've re-written *The Bright Island.* I've been active in assisting Donald Calthrop in his Shakespeare productions. To my mind he is a wonderful producer. I put on to him a friend of mine, Dorothy Cheston, who acted 5 years in U.S.A. but couldn't get a decent job here. On the strength of what I said he actually gave her the part of Viola, without ever having seen her act! It was a frightful risk; but I knew she would come through, & she jolly well did; & has had some great notices.

The last night (1463rd) of *The Beggar's Opera* was a function the like of which I have never seen, & shall probably never see again.

The best plays of the year here have been *At Mrs. Beam's* and *Outward Bound.*

I've sold *Don Juan.*

Now look here, I say, governor, you'd better return not later than March 31st, or I foresee trouble. And kindly remember that the future of the play in N.Y. will largely depend on its success here, & its success here will largely depend on your work at rehearsals. I say no more.

But after all the main point is that I ardently desire your society.

Yours ever, A. B.

222. Knoblock's play *Lullaby* opened in New York in August 1923. Frederick Lonsdale (1881–1954) was a more consistently successful playwright than Knoblock.

Basil Dean produced *London Life* at Drury Lane. Frederick Harrison (d. 1926) managed the Haymarket Theatre for three decades. For other references to Dean and Harrison see Vol. I For a letter to Dean see below.

The Dance of Life, by Havelock Ellis (1859–1939), was published in 1923.

ARKANSAS / MS. / 223
(*To Frank Swinnerton*)

75, Cadogan Square
22–1–24

My dear Henry,

I have just received with thanksgiving your letter from Cleveland O. Your headache was probably liver. Mine are neuralgic (greatly decreasing, owing to marriage). You must be very strong to stand what you are going through, especially by yourself. But of course you have Intellectual Resources, which I never have when travelling alone. However, the gaffes which you hear must lighten the burden of life considerably. It is good about *Felix*. I think George said he should try for 40 thou. It was either 40 or 50. I bet you it goes over 30. George also said of *Riceyman* that he would eat every copy he didn't sell up to 60,000. This boast was called forth by Flower's boast that he would sell 40. If 40 in England, then at least 60 in U.S.A., you see. Flower had actually sold 31,000 a fortnight ago. So he ought to reach 40, despite railway strikes. If anybody thinks that I am not as pleased and self-satisfied as an infant with the sales of *R.S.*, let him or her be undeceived. It is a solemnizing thought that I have never had what I call a sale. (I don't count cheap editions.) George said the other day that *The O. W. Tale* had just passed 60,000 in U.S.A. This in about 15 years. Hence, if I have made money by my pen, it is the fruit of the fact that I produce as much as H.G.W. & 3 times as much as most other people.

I cannot understand the small sale of *Felix* in this bloody country. George was in the greatest form while here; but noticeably excitable & even a bit hysterical on the subject of Hughie. He even said he meant to quarrel with Hughie. (But he won't.) Hughie told me that George was ill at the Savoy. I

'The London House of Mr. Arnold Bennett', article and pictures, appeared in *Vogue* in September 1924.

Ruby Peto is not otherwise known.

Donald Calthrop (1888–1940) produced *Twelfth Night* at the Kingsway Theatre on 3 November 1923.

The productions of *At Mrs. Beam's* (by C. K. Munro) and *Outward Bound* (by Sutton Vane) were revivals, opening 2 April 1923 and 15 October 1923 for runs of more than two hundred performances.

Don Juan de Marana never reached the stage. For other information on it see Vols. I and II.

saw George in the evening very lively. 'Hullo', I said, 'I thought you were ill. I'm glad it's over.' 'Ill? Who told you I was ill?' He was simply furious against Hughie. Said Hughie called on him at 9 a.m., in itself inexcusable, & found him dispensing castor oil & then goes about the town saying he is ill. Can't a man take a dose of castor oil? Et ainsi de suite. But George has been very witty this visit. He is improving each visit. The women, including all mine, adore him. He gave a farewell dinner, Savoy, before he left: me, Harriet Cohen & Dorothy Cheston. These creatures were in especially good form, & got on to the subject of Christ. 'You can't get anything like this in New York, Arnold.' I hear R has reviewed *Riceyman* in the something-something (International something) & I haven't seen it. I want it. From my private sources of information I may tell you that your tour *is* regarded as a success. George, e.g. spoke cautiously but *very well* of it. Tommy Wells has had the singular idea of asking me to review the whole field of English literature from Chaucer, for *Harper's*. But I don't think I shall do it, partly because I don't want to write and partly because he doesn't want to pay.

I hope you got my letter in answer to your last. It was addressed chez George.

Yours, A. B.

ARKANSAS / MS. / 224
(*To Frank Swinnerton*)

75, Cadogan Square
12–ii–24

My dear Henry,

Your breakfast-food-letter of the 15th has duly reached my pleased self. Thank God for something sensible said to me at last about *Riceyman*. I am sick of the praise of Elsie. It is an acid-test (forgive the cliché) of critics. Jack Squire has fallen into it. As if the sympathetic quality of Elsie had anything whatever to do with the quality of the book. Now what I like about Elizabeth Lewis is that she never attempts to flirt or cock-tease or anything. She has no taste, but looks nice in an

223. *Young Felix*, Swinnerton's new novel, had a considerable success in America. On the reliability of George Doran's sales figures see Vol. I, p. 126 n.

Thomas Wells was an editor at Harper's; see Vol. II for letters to him.

oriental way, & she responds to intelligent stimulus. She is the world's worst pianist (except me). I may say I seldom see her. I prefer her mother, who to my mind is no ordinary woman. The younger sister, now married, I have little use for.

I do not think that R is 'in' with Beaverbrook. B. would much sooner be 'in' with Harriet Cohen. He little knoweth that Harriet recounts to me many pleasing details (but doubtless not all) after each of their interviews. There is absolutely nothing doing there.

Desmond. What you say is true, but it must not stand by itself. He has much taste (except for the stage) & he is one of the best talkers I ever heard or squashed. George. All publishers are about as much alike as all authors are alike. George is getting far too sentimental, and comes nearer in this respect to being Hughie than he suspects. I have settled up with Eric, & the contract is executed. He said: 'By the way, of course this is private. You won't tell anyone.' 'No.' 'Not even Swinnerton.' 'Why damn it man, I discussed it with Swinnerton before I even approached you at all.' 'A dirty plot', said he semi-humorously. 'Yes', said I, 'But he doesn't know the details, & I won't tell him.' So I mustn't. But I may say I shall save 3 or 400 a year, perhaps more. (I am now negotiating direct with the *Strand* for some reminiscences.) I am also just finishing a 20,000 word story about the adored Elsie. I have got a new idea for this, & shall finish it on Friday. I am also finishing my series of articles for the *Royal*, & with half of them I am ill-pleased. But when the *Royal* wrote to Eric to say that they were not what it wanted or expected & Eric asked me to send him a letter to show to the *Royal*,—well I wrote a letter which pleased Eric intensely. Immediately afterwards the *Royal* wrote to me to say how pleased it was at my conviction & how valuable it was. Etc. 'Laf! I thought I should ha' died.' I will emulate you & say all editors are alike. Did I tell you George was in a blue funk about the repercussion of a Labour government on U.S.A.? He had quite lost his head, & couldn't be talked to. 'Come, Arnold', said he, '*You don't want to be governed by Fred* (my butler, if you remember).' At the Lyric we have recently been rehearsing *The Way of the World*. I never comprehended the plot, and still don't. I announced publicly that it was bound to be a complete frost, the plot being silly and the dialogue far too subtle for any public. I convinced everyone in the theatre that we were in for a perfect frost. Well, it has made a perfect furore. The cars of the high-brows throng our slum. The booking far exceeds that for *The Beggar's Opera*. (Of course it won't last, but it now is terrific.) Edith Evans in it is the finest comic show I ever saw on any stage in the wide world. The gallery nightly 'eats it'. You should have seen all the highbrows together on the first night. Clive Bell, St. John Hutchinson & Co., Duff Cooper, Lytton Strachey, the Viola Trees, the Goossens—all side by side! By the way I have been getting much more intimate with Viola lately. She is a most charming creature, & I love her—after Dorothy, Harriet, Marjorie, & Pauline. Do you know that the barber at the Reform has been very ill? He is quite changed. He always asks after you. I gave your love to the gang. Mrs. Clutton-Brock has written to me once or twice for advice about Arthur's literary remains. Richmond Temple is quite coming out, & has at last acquired some small-talk. I have been all over the working parts of the Savoy Hotel & was much impressed. I helped Sybil Thorndike . . . to judge the costumes at the Hassan Ball, & was interfered with by the other judges Lady Terrington (a bitch) & G. Frankau (another). I hope you will continue to conquer. I am well (except ill-sleeping) & much stronger. I think the Knoblock-Bennett play may be done at Drury Lane.

Yours, A. B.

224. Elizabeth Lewis was the daughter of Sir George Lewis (1868–1927) and Lady Marie Lewis.

Desmond—Desmond MacCarthy.

Bennett's negotiations with Eric Pinker on their new contract appear in Vol. I.

The *Strand* did not publish any reminiscences at this time, but they did publish twelve stories from 1924 to 1927. See Vol. I. 'Elsie and the Child' was published in *Storyteller* in September 1924; see Vol. I for other details.

The *Royal Magazine* published a series of ten long articles, beginning in November 1923. For Bennett's letter to Eric Pinker see Vol. I, pp. 330–2.

The Way of the World opened on 7 February 1924, with Edith Evans (1888–) as Mrs. Millamant. Clive Bell (b. 1881), the writer on art and literature; St. John Hutchinson (1884–1942), a barrister; Alfred Duff Cooper (Lord Norwich, 1890–1954), at this time M.P. for Oldham; the Viola Trees—presumably including Viola Tree's husband, Alan Parsons (1888–1933), dramatic critic and journalist.

On Arthur Clutton-Brock see Vols. I and II.

The Hassan Ball was presumably in celebration of the long run of James Elroy Flecker's play. Sybil Thorndike (1882–) was presently to be seen as Joan of Arc in Shaw's play. Lady Terrington was the widow of Lord Terrington (d. 1921). Gilbert Frankau (1884–1952), author and journalist.

GIDE / 225
(*To André Gide*)

75, Cadogan Square
25 February 1924

My dear Gide,

I ought to have answered your letter of 29th January before, but I have been absorbed in a 'nouvelle' (20,000 words) which I have just finished, on the subject of the heroine of *Riceyman Steps*. Of course the chief news in your letter is the news of your *first* 'roman'. This excites me, especially the 20 first line characters! Yes, I need time in order to read this. No doubt you are well aware of the sensations which one has when one knows suddenly that a work is being written which is bound to thrill one. I am very much obliged for *Intentions*. Marc A. very kindly said he would send me the succeeding numbers containing *M. Godeau*. I should very much like to have them. This Jouhandeau has *real* originality. It is rather wonderful that you, at your age, should suddenly become intimate with du Gard, to the point of showing him your work as you do it. This is a rare phenomenon. Now I never show my work to anyone: I couldn't: I never ask advice about it: I scarcely ever talk of it even to the women I know well, and if I am asked about it, I avoid answering. Moreover, I write it only once and never alter it. I say: 'What is done is done, and I have several more works urgently demanding my attention!' By the way, du côté 'carrière', the publication of *Riceyman Steps* has been very interesting. I was undoubtedly, with H. G. Wells, falling under the whips of les jeunes. In fact every book was the signal for a general attack (Wells suffered more than me). Also my bourgeois public was considerably disgusted by those very innocent works *The Pretty Lady* and *Lilian*. So that I was being counted as a back number. *Riceyman Steps* has altered all that, and I am suddenly the darling of the public—not because of the excellence of *Riceyman Steps*, but because the heroine thereof is a sympathetic, *good*, reliable, unselfish and chaste character! She is a domestique, and all London and New York is wishing that it could find devoted servants like her! 'Psychologies des foules'! I want you to tell R. M. du Gard how highly I esteem *Barois*. When I first bought it, ages ago, I was so impressed by it that I had it charmingly bound, and I often read *in* it again. I am not yet in a position to speak definitely of his latest novel. There is no literary news in this town, except Shaw's bad plays (I publicly slept at one performance). And at our Lyric Theatre we have produced Congreve's *The Way of the World.* I thought it would be much too subtle for the public; but it is a tremendous success, et on refuse de l'argent tous les soirs ('turn money away'). It is a wonderful play. Why have they printed that Russian story in the last number of the *N.R.F.*? Ça m'a l'air passablement médiocre. I am very pleased with *Amants, heureux amants,* especially the last story; Valery's best work, I think. Oh! And I want your advice, please. *I have escaped from the contract with Lanoire for translating my works*; *The Old Wives' Tale* and other things are now free for me to do as I like with. What do you suggest I ought to do? Your portrait by Roger Fry hangs in my hall and is much remarked on.

Ever your devoted Arnold Bennett

VICHY / MS. / 226
(*To Valery Larbaud*)

75, Cadogan Square
8–iii–24

My dear Valery Larbaud,

I ought to have written you before about *Amants, heureux amants,* which you were so kind as to send me. It is, in my opinion, a very fine book, highly distinguished, and certainly your best work. I enjoyed it immensely. Especially the last story, which throws light on many things—including yourself. (I wish I could enjoy travelling as you do, could feel it in quite the same romantic-realistic way. I seldom travel now, except in my yacht, which, for me, is the very finest mode of conveyance known to man.) All my congratulations.

Only I should like a longer book.

We have no new young novelists in England. D. H. Lawrence is the best, & he is very uneven; also he is growing older. Of

225. *Monsieur Godeau intime,* by Marcel Jouhandeau (see pp. 200–1), was appearing in *Intentions,* a short-lived French journal.

Roger Martin du Gard (1881–1958) published *Jean Barois* in 1913; Valery Larbaud published *Amants, heureux amants* in 1923.

The Shaw play was *Back to Methuselah,* which had just opened at the Court Theatre.

course there is Joyce. Your study of him was very useful to me when I wrote a review of *Ulysses* some time ago. I think that he also is too uneven ever to be quite first-rate. But his best chapters amount to genius.

When are you coming to England? It is time you came again.

Ever yours, Arnold Bennett

BUTLER / MS. / 227
(*To Edward Knoblock*)

75, Cadogan Square
20–3–24

My dear Edward,

Here are my views, with respect, & for what they are worth.

I think that considered as a melodrama the piece is all right. It might be cut in the 1st act, & also in the scene where the innkeeper tells Conch that he is selling her to the Captain. Also, the sailor gets over that wall once too often. I think that the Captain might set his men to guard that wall, & the sailor might come in by the door, & surprise them. This would be a new stunt.

Conchita is not to me satisfactory. She is too monotonous. After her gowning, she is too ladylike. She scarcely suggests her mother's daughter—insufficient abandon & Spanishity. Nor does she suggest sufficiently her mental disturbance & grief at the murder of the innkeeper. The latter is just chucked aside & forgotten entirely save when people want to go to the cellar or to speak with him.

The sailor should surely show some sign of his Spanish blood in *his general demeanour*. He shows it sufficiently in his actions!

The barber & the innkeeper were 90 per cent *inaudible* & both to my mind thoroughly unsatisfactory. They both misconceived their parts. The Cuban lover was not bad.

Impossible to judge Harding on this first night.

I certainly think that the trussing & gagging are too prolonged & detailed, & done too far downstage & too prominently.

226. Larbaud published an article on Joyce in the *NRF* in April 1922; it was reprinted in the *Criterion* the following October. On Bennett's review of *Ulysses* see p. 228.

As for the lovers sitting on his body, no audience will ever remain serious through that performance. I thought La Rubia was very good. Ditto the negress. If the last act was reconsidered in the matter of interpretation I think it would go all right. Last night ribald laughs were positively asked for. *I see nothing wrong with the play itself that couldn't be altered in 2 minutes.*

With the moon invisible, & therefore rather high in the heavens or behind the audience, I do not see how the audience could possibly see its reflection in the water, nor any reason why the reflection, if seen, should be a narrow furrow instead of a general light.

Yours, A. B.

TEXAS / TS. / 228
(*To Jonathan Cape*)

75, Cadogan Square
22nd March 1924

Dear Mr. Jonathan Cape,

Re Miss Pauline Smith's work. She is not very well, and as she lives in the country she has put all her literary affairs into my hands. I have a collection of 8 short stories of hers, all, in my opinion, fine. Middleton Murry would have published them in a small volume, but his publishing enterprise has not come to anything. I have been wondering whether you would care to publish them. They are undoubtedly very unusually good work, and I think that they would make a considerable stir among a really educated public. I ought to mention that Miss Smith is now at work on a novel, which, so far as I have read it, is at least as fine as the best things in the short stories. If you published the stories I should of course see that you had the first refusal of the novel.

Yours sincerely, Arnold Bennett

227. Knoblock's play *Conchita* opened at the Queen's Theatre on 19 March, with Tallulah Bankhead as Conchita and Lyn Harding (1867–1952) as Don Pablo. The critic of *The Times* found the play laughable too, and it was withdrawn in April.

228. Miss Smith's stories were published by Cape in February 1925 under the title *The Little Karoo*, with an introduction by Bennett. Cape published her novel, *The Beadle*, in September 1926.

BERG / MS. / 229
(*To John Middleton Murry*)

75, Cadogan Square
2.4.24.

My dear Murry,

Certainly. Rely on it.

I doubt if your observations upon George Moore escape being ridiculous. They certainly do not escape bad form. For myself I think G.M. is a pretty great writer: but my opinion is beside the point. If he sells his books in limited editions that is a very pardonable caprice in an old man. The reason is not that his work has been caviare to the general. Some of his books have had very large sales. *A Mummer's Wife* was in its 20th ed. twenty five years ago. It still sells. *Esther Waters* had an immense sale. The first edition of *Evelyn Innes* was 12,500 copies. I consider G.M.'s final verdict on Hardy absurd, & I have told him so. But in *The Confessions of a Young man* (published before you were born), he put down some criticisms of Hardy which are unanswerable. *Esther Waters* is not a pattern of 'grammatical correctness'. Have you read it? It is studded, like all the earlier works of G.M. (in their original form), with incorrections. G.M. took about 30 years to learn to write even correctly. All the younger generation owe a lot to G.M., who fought for a freer code & established a certain freedom which you & others now enjoy—in a deplorable ignorance of how you came to enjoy it. At any rate he is now over 70; he has always been absolutely unvenal; he has cared for nothing but literature; & I think that he is entitled to some respect from serious persons—even if they are young. However, it doesn't matter; because if G.M. chooses later to deal with *you* in return, we shall see some fun.

Yours, Arnold Bennett

BUTLER / T.C. / 230
(*To Basil Dean*)

[75, Cadogan Square]
3rd April 1924

My dear Dean,

Thank you for your letter of yesterday. I assume that the phrase 'last night' is a mistake for 'last week'.

229. Murry wrote a long piece for the *Adelphi* comparing George Moore unfavourably with Thomas Hardy.

We have strengthened both the scenes. In fact we have done all that you suggested. I quite appreciate that you have much at stake in this matter. So have we. Indeed I am inclined to think that the fate of this play inaugurating a new regime at Drury Lane may have some slight influence on the immediate future of English drama. At the same time we must be careful not to fall between two stools, and to my mind the principal thing is to have faith in the public, whose intelligence I am convinced is generally underestimated. (I would have betted 100 to 1 that *The Way of the World* would be a failure.) After all, as you probably know better than I do, plays far more subtle than *London Life* are often produced with success in continental theatres at least as large as Drury Lane, in cities far smaller than London.

You may rely on the authors doing everything that they feel themselves able to do to help the chances of success.

I think it would not be a bad plan if Knoblock and I came to see *Good Luck* before the run concludes. It would doubtless be a terrible ordeal, but we might face it.

Yours sincerely, [Arnold Bennett]

BEAVERBROOK / MS. / 231
(*To Lord and Lady Beaverbrook*)

Hotel Concha-Miramar
Juan Jauregui
Fuenterrabia
(Marina)
28–4–24

Dear Max & Gladys,

This is to state that I still live, though no longer with you. I should like to thank you adequately for the royal progress in which you enabled me to take part: but, being a man of few words, I cannot. I will be content to say that it was the greatest pilgrimage I was ever in, and executed throughout with the finest munificence. So that's that. I wish I could have rivalled Tim in the vast business of putting champagne out of sight, and

230. Bennett and Knoblock hoped that *London Life* would provide the sort of spectacle that Drury Lane audiences looked for and at the same time be a fairly substantial play. *Good Luck* was a sporting drama by Seymour Hicks and Ian Hay.

Tom in the treatment of enigmatic maladies. But I could not do that either. I feel I must use up some of the stuff gathered, in the making of short stories. The pity is that I could not put in much of the *real* stuff, as it would be recognised. I would certainly get Pendriga into something had I not accepted his hospitality, or di Libour had I not a certain feeling for his wife & her father. Tim of course is sacred; but what an epical figure for a story—at the stage of his 3rd whisky in his train-bed! You have realised for me one of my ambitions. I am now realising for myself another, if a smaller one; to wit, to see the Basque country. There can be nothing quainter in Spain than Fuenterrabia, & no Spanish landlady younger, darker, more beautiful than the landlady of this hotel. They also have processions of images here, & they have thought of something in the idolatrous line that even Seville has not thought of. On Good Friday night they have an articulated Christ with moveable limbs nailed on a cross in the church, & they do a realistic descent from the cross with him. I wish I'd seen it. 300 motor cars brought starers to stare at it at Easter, so I was told. The country here is heavenly, the Pyrenees are just over the roof, & it seems to me to be nearly as hot as Seville. It is a relaxing place, & makes me sleep nearly as well as Tim & far better than Tom. Curious, you should have had Tim & Tom. My name ought to have been Dick or Harry instead of Enoch. I take it you are now on the way to London where I shall soon join you.

Ever yours, A. B.

GIDE / 232
(*To André Gide*)

Hotel Concha-Miramar
30–4–1924

My dear André Gide,

I have been without an address—travelling in Spain—Madrid, Toledo, Seville, and—surtout—Fuenterrabia, and without an address. So I only got your letter of the 21st last night. I am

231. Bennett went on a trip to Spain with the Beaverbrooks early in April. Timothy Michael Healy (1855–1931) was the first Governor-General of the Irish Free State. Thomas Horder (Baron Horder, 1871–1945) was later physician to George VI.

delighted that you will come to the yacht. (1) About the 1st of July will suit me very well.

(2) You can work on the yacht (while she is at anchor). I will give you a cabin with a table.

(3) Stay as long as you like. I expect you won't want to stay for less than quinze jours.

I want you to understand that the 'Marie Marguerite' is *not* a *big* yacht. She has a salon, une salle de bain, et 3 cabinets (W.C.s). She is lighted by electricity. She is about 20 metres in length and six in breadth. Now you can judge, a little. I am very anxious to have some talks with you. Whom shall I ask to meet you? Would you like any of the Godebskis? Let me have all your ideas.

Your affectionate and admiring confrère.

Arnold Bennett

P.S. Bring Marc, if you like, I shall be glad to have him.
P.P.S. The food and the service and the drinks will be quite as good as on land.

You will join the yacht at *Southampton* (via Havre).

ILLINOIS / MS. / 233
(*To H. G. Wells*)

75, Cadogan Square
1–6–24

My dear H.G.,

Well, 2 unfortunates have been pushed out of the stalls into the dress circle for you. The tickets will await you at the box-office; but there is bound to be a great crush at the box-office before the performance, & if I were you I should send up for them in advance. You will have to pay for them. Drury Lane is run by a 'Board'. I have had to pay for some of my own seats. Please understand that this play is merely a *tactful* attempt to break with Drury Lane traditions & to seduce the Board. The

232. Bennett spent most of the summer sailing off the English and French coasts. The Godebskis were a Polish family living in Paris who had been friends of Bennett's for many years—Cipa (a painter) and Ida, parents of Jean (a sculptor) and Mimi.

latter part of the attempt has already failed. Not a single member of the Board (except Dean) believes in the play, & one of them is so certain of failure that he has resigned in advance.

Thine, A. B.

BUTLER / MS. / 234
(*To Edward Knoblock*)

Yacht Marie Marguerite
at sea
20–6–24

My dear Edward,

Thank you for your cards. I am very sorry indeed to hear that you are still not well, & I do hope that Marienbad will do you good. I joined the yacht at Salcombe last Friday; but I shall have to be in London again on July 3rd for the 1st night of the new show at the Lyric Hammersmith. There is a flying matinée of *The Great Adventure* at Portsmouth next Wednesday & I deem it my duty to be there on the yacht! I doubt if Dean's 'waits' are the whole explanation of the apparent failure of *L.L.* Yet I could have sworn on the night we saw it that the public would like it. I don't think now that the public really does like it, & I wish we had stuck to the Queen's, where it would have been less expensively produced & where the same number of people per night would perhaps have gone to see it & it would have run longer. However, this is what the stage is! I am very busy on board writing short stories, & between June 13th & July 3rd shall have earned £1,200 and enjoyed myself to boot, and been idle most of the days. This is better than writing & producing plays, & far more satisfactory.

If thoughts will cure your ill-health you are cured.

Ever thine, A. B.

P.S. I particularly desire to know of your return. A. B.

233. *London Life* opened at Drury Lane on 3 June. For other details see Vol. I, pp. 337–8; the date of opening is given there incorrectly as 4 June.

234. The new play at the Lyric Hammersmith was Clifford Bax's *Midsummer Madness*. The revival of *The Great Adventure* opened on 5 June at the Haymarket.

TEXAS / MS. / 235
(*To Maurice Baring*)

Yacht Marie Marguerite
Southampton
28–6–24

My dear Maurice,

I offer you my sincere & almost violent congratulations on *C.* I have been greatly impressed by it. It held me throughout its immense length. The fact is, it lives. I think that some of the later literary conversations lack point & seem rather casual; but this is about the only criticism I would make—& I make it with diffidence. You keep pretty calm in the first half of the book, but in the last third there is *great emotional power*. The latter half is better than the first: which doesn't often happen in novels. I think it is all highly original, delightful, moving, and authentic. I think it is an important work, and so I am proud of you.

This said, I want to make a minor animadversion—nothing to do with the book's quality. That slip containing 8 errata is really rather comic. There are scores, if not hundreds, of misprints & lapses in the book. (I mean this.) Even proper names are misspelt (e.g. 'Lenbach'). French words are misspelt. 'Ressembler' is spelt wrong every time. The adjective 'undefinable' occurs about a million times. In the first place '*in*definable' is the correct word, I think; & in the second place is not 'indefinable' rather a queer word for a novelist to use habitually? Is it not a confession of inability to do the job . . .?

Then I think that, though your style is admirable, it is sometimes marred by negligences. What do you think of this? 'C. must be looking *forward* to such a possibility at the *back* of his mind.' (p. 660)

Also lines 2 to 6 on p. 88 cannot be defended.

Also your indulgence in clichés. Well, Maurice, we all must use clichés—I admit it. But I do draw the line at 'plunged in medias res,' in a novel by you. There are others, many.

I have only mentioned a very few things. I don't want to be tedious, or to seem carping; so I stop there. I attach the slightest possible importance to such minuscule details. But I wanted to mention them to you, with all deference & respect. Forgive me if you think I am hypercritical. I'm all right really.

Thine, Arnold B.

P.S. Curious how minor felicities strike one! I think the description of the projected novel (pp. 78–9) is simply masterly. It is very funny & yet it is touching. A. B.

TEXAS / T.C.C. / 236
(*To Hubert Griffith*)

[75, Cadogan Square]
31st July 1924

My dear Griffith,

I have now read *Tunnel Trench*. The copy which you kindly gave me got lost—I don't know how, but I obtained another one. I think that taking it page by page it is very good indeed and I thoroughly enjoyed reading it. My view is that you ought to be, and will be, a playwright. Of course the play is not 'nice' reading, and of course we who never went to the front in a fighting capacity hate to be reminded by those who did so go that there ever was a war. But all that does not matter. My criticism of the play, or of myself, would be that I cannot quite find the central moral idea upon which it is based. I can see a very fine moral idea in the speeches of Brunnhilde, an original idea too, but I would not call it the central idea of the play. Further, I do not gather the significance of the last scene. I suppose that I ought to read the play again. I think that in your place, having obtained the Brunnhilde idea, I should have made a great deal more of her and of it.

The drama is to my mind excellent. It is thoroughly well *nourrie* and *serrée* and you are to be congratulated upon it.

I expect that you think it is a bit thick that one should take months to read the play which must have meant so much to you. The world is like that.

Always yours sincerely, [Arnold Bennett]

235. Maurice Baring (1874–1945) and Bennett had been friends since 1913 or before. See Bennett's description of him to Gide on p. 200. *C.* was published in June 1924.

236. Hubert Griffith (1896–1953) was a dramatic critic and journalist. See further, pp. 235–6.

YALE / TS. / 237
(*To Richard Curle*)

75, Cadogan Square
5th August 1924

Dear Mr. Curle,

Many thanks for your letter of the 4th, which is very touching. I fear that I shall not attend the funeral, wherever it may be. I have a strong objection to large funerals, and my view is that funerals ought to be confined to the members of the family of the deceased.

I saw Conrad very little of late years. I had some talk with him at a dinner party in London about a year ago, and I found him simply magnificent. He wrote to me from time to time, and in one of his letters he said to me that 'the light of sunset' was over the pages of *The Rover*. I did not think from his appearance that he would live very long. He has lived, which is something.

Yours sincerely, Arnold Bennett

TEXAS / TS. / 238
(*To J. B. Priestley*)

75, Cadogan Square
5th September 1924

Dear Mr. Priestley,

Many thanks for so kindly sending me your book. Of course I read the essay on myself when it appeared in the *Mercury*. (One never misses these things.) Equally of course I did not agree with all of it; but at any rate I thought it very able and I agreed heartily with all the praise; also I thought that some of the animadversions were rather good. However, like all authors, I feel deeply convinced that I am not understood as completely as my amazing merits deserve. An editor who wanted a free article from me once came along and said: 'You are the greatest writer that ever lived—or *could* live.' That is the nourishment we require.

Yours sincerely, Arnold Bennett

237. Richard Curle (1883–1968) was the author of several books on Conrad. *The Rover* was published in 1923.

238. J. B. Priestley (1894–) published a long article on Bennett in the *London*

BEAVERBROOK / MS. / 239
(*To Lord Beaverbrook*)

75, Cadogan Square
26–9–24

My dear Max,

Of course I regard the whole thing as a monstrous piece of bad taste on my wife's part. It is not as if she is short of money. She lives quite simply, & I give her £2,000 a year free of income & super tax; so she must be saving quite a lot. When I told you to do as you liked I argued thus: The thing is bound to be published somewhere; it is bound to be regarded, generally, as a piece of self-advertising concocted by me with my wife. But if it is to be published I would sooner have it published by a friend upon whom I can absolutely rely to cut out anything that is offensive or indiscreet. And so make the best of a bad job. I shall naturally inform all my acquaintances what my attitude is. I've written to Doran to look after U.S.A.

Thanks very much for telling me about it & leaving the decision to me.

Yours, Arnold

ARKANSAS / T.C.C. / 240
(*To George Doran*)
PERSONAL

[75, Cadogan Square]
27th September 1924

My dear George,

Beaverbrook rang up last night and said: 'Arnold, I want to tell you. The *Daily Express* has been offered a biography of you written by Mrs. Arnold Bennett. It was offered through Curtis Brown. It is 15,000 words long. I have read a lot of it and I think it is pretty good. It contains nothing offensive or indiscreet so far as I have read, and my editor says he would not object to having anything said of himself during his lifetime that is said in this biography about you. I should like to buy

---

Mercury in February 1924, and reprinted it in his collection *Figures in Modern Literature*. Priestley discerned three Bennetts: the tipster of the pocket philosophies, the engaging innocent of the light novels, and the compassionate and pessimistic author of the major novels. He thought Bennett would produce greater work if he could combine the qualities of *The Old Wives' Tale* and *The Card*.

it for serial publication in the *Express*, but of course I shall not do so if you have any objection.'

I reflected upon the matter, and then told Max that so far as I was concerned he could do as he liked, and I therefore assume that he will buy it.

My reason was as follows: Marguerite is bound to get the thing published somewhere, and I should prefer it to be in the hands of someone who will take care to cut out anything which might be offensive.

Of course I should never be surprised at anything that was done in that quarter, but I must say it seems to me rather outrageous that Marguerite should write and sell this little book without consulting my wishes in any way. Probably it has never even occurred to her that I should find anything objectionable in a biography by my wife being published during my lifetime. Comparatively few members of the public are aware that she and I are separated, and those of the majority who possess any decent feeling will certainly consider that both she and I are guilty of a grave offense against good taste. However, things are what they are and it cannot be helped.

The book is certain to be offered in America, and I shall therefore be obliged to you if you will make it known viva voce that the book has been written without my knowledge and consent and that I very strongly object to it, but have no power to stop its publication.

It must be full of inaccuracies.

I do not know who has helped her to write it. She could not possibly have written it alone.

Ever yours, A. B.

MANCHESTER / TS. / 241
(*To A. N. Monkhouse*)

75, Cadogan Square
2nd October 1924

My dear Monkhouse,

Many thanks for your letter of yesterday. In the first place I hope you are better. In the second place I have to thank you

240. Mrs. Bennett's reminiscences began appearing in the *Daily Express* on 19 November 1924. They were published in book form the following year under the title *Arnold Bennett*. A. M. Philpot was the English publisher, Greenberg the American.
Curtis Brown—the literary agent (1866–1945).

for one or two very appreciative articles about me which I think I am right in attributing to you in the Manchester press. This is the sort of stuff I like and am grateful for.

With regard to your suggestion, I regret to say that I cannot accept it. I believe that the *Manchester Guardian* is honestly out of touch with the literary market. Be it known unto you, my dear Monkhouse, that I have rather more journalistic work than I can do at the rate of 2/- per word, or £200 for 2,000 words. My price was until recently 1/6d. a word, but I have put it up, with the sole result of an increased demand. The *M.G.* offers me rather less than 2½d. a word, and it will not do. At least I can conceive no valid reason why I should make to this wealthy journal a present of £180 over one article. You may be able to think of a reason, but I cannot.

Swinnerton is all right, and I like his second wife very much indeed.

My very best wishes to you in every way,

Always yours sincerely, Arnold Bennett

BUTLER / T.C.C. / 242
(*To Jonathan Cape*)

[75, Cadogan Square]
17th October 1924

Dear Mr. Cape,

Do you know that someone on your staff has been very naughty and ought to be crucified? In your advertisement of *A Portrait of the Artist as a Young Man* in the *Times Literary Supplement* this week you attribute words to me that I have never written about this book.

What I have written about the book is as follows:

> 'But in the horrid inaccessible thickets of my mind I heard a voice saying: "On the whole the book has bored you." And on the whole it had; and with the efflux of time I began to announce this truth. There are scenes of genius in the novel; from end to end it shows a sense of style but large portions of it are dull, pompous, absurd, confused and undirected. The

241. A. N. Monkhouse was on the staff of the *Manchester Guardian*. For earlier letters to him see Vol. II.

author had not quite decided what he was after, and even if he had decided he would not have known how to get it. He had resources but could not use them. He bungled the affair.'

This is a little different from stating a doubt whether I had ever read anything to equal this novel. What you make me say is absolutely preposterous.

The words you make me say were written about one [some words missing].

[Arnold Bennett]

W. MORGAN / MS. / 243
(*To Frederick Marriott*)

75, Cadogan Square
18–10–24

[no salutation]

Frederick, you are a great judge of a play; but I am exceedingly angry with you all the same. For well thou knewest, and knowest, that it would have given me real pleasure to send you whatever seats you desired for that great birthday occasion. However, God is love.

A. B.

SHAW / TS. / 244
(*To E.V. Lucas*)

75, Cadogan Square
31st October 1924

My dear Edward,

Many thanks for your letter of yesterday.

The six novels which you mention would do very well. I am not at all keen on having either *The Gates of Wrath* or *Teresa of Watling Street* included in the set. I always regard *Teresa* as the world's worst novel.

242. Bennett himself was confused as well. His comments concerned *Ulysses*, not *A Portrait of the Artist*. The Cape advertisement for *Portrait* in the *Times Literary Supplement* on 16 October quoted his opinion of the last chapter of *Ulysses*: 'I have never read anything to surpass it, and I doubt if I have ever read anything to equal it.' Bennett's review appeared in *Outlook* on 29 April 1922.

243. The Marriotts apparently saw *The Great Adventure*, which was just ending its run at the Haymarket.

I should say that 10/6d would be a very proper price for the incomparable work on the Five Towns.

When you and I have settled the main points I shall of course leave the details of the contract to Eric Pinker. You and I have more important affairs.

Yours sincerely, [Arnold Bennett]

TEXAS / T.C.C. / 245
(*To George Bernard Shaw*)

[75, Cadogan Square]
7th November 1924

My dear Bernard Shaw,

Many thanks for your letter of today's date. I daresay that there is a great deal in what you say, but I have definitely arranged with the Stage Society to do the play, and I shall now let them do it. Moreover the bother of having the thing turned into a comic opera and the impossibility of getting it produced after it had been so turned, would be too much for me. I have no hope of making any money out of the play. I have already made £500 out of it, from forsaken options, and that has paid for the typewriting. When I wrote the play about 7 years ago I thought it was very good, and God knows what I shall think of it when I see it performed.

Ever yours, [Arnold Bennett]

FALES, NYU / MS. / 246
(*To Robert Nichols*)

75, Cadogan Square
17–11–24

My dear Robert,

I saw your play last night. Your father, brother, sister, Henry Head, were there. All most flatteringly excited. Curse you, Robert, why didn't you take my advice & shorten the last act?

244. E. V. Lucas was on the staff of Methuens. Nothing came of the proposal.

245. The Stage Society produced *The Bright Island* on 15 February 1925. Shaw wrote to Bennett of the play: 'humanity cannot stand one hundred and fifty minutes' unrelieved scoffing, no matter how witty it is. There must be refuges for the affection, the admiration, the detestation of the audience; or else you must fill the gaps with refuges for its concupiscence and ferocity. . . .' The play was written little more than four years before, and then revised.

All that I said was sound. In the last act, effect after effect was made—& then frittered away! The curtain *wouldn't* fall. It fell at 11.30. Nevertheless the play is full of meat. The first long scene between Vyson and Bentley in the 3rd act was *most* impressive. So were lots of other bits. One felt how courageous & how original the play was. The audience was exasperated, exhausted, but impressed deeply. The play has both nobility and power. I sat just in front of Agate (*Sunday Times*) & George Mair (*Evening Standard*) two old friends, and men of considerable parts. They were both deeply impressed. Technically the play is very jejune. The first act is far too long, too loaded with futile detail, too realistic. *All* the machinery of the play creaks, & much of it is too complicated. I call it a romantic play, in the grand manner, weighed down by its physical garment, ill-fitting, [?] and coarse—I mean the garment. The producer did not understand the play. Also, *his* technique was surprisingly bad—for him, because he is no fool. Ernest Milton did not play Vyson well, but he played it *romantically*, which was what I liked. Claude Rains played realistically. So there was conflict. Rains got everything over by main force; but I didn't like him. I must say that Agate & Mair both liked him very much. Muriel Pratt was A1 in the first act, but less good afterwards. She did the seduction stuff fine, but not the rest. Dorothy Holmes. She didn't know what she was doing; the part was beyond her. The solicitor's clerk was awful. Rupert was awful—indeed he was silly. Still, the play held together. I think you have the dramatic instinct, but you treat it very badly. You won't realise the limitations of the medium of the stage. You are too uncompromising. Think of Shakespeare, my headstrong boy. You certainly have creative power. Don't squander it. Use it. I think that if you have an idea for another play you ought to write it. It would be received with all respect.

As regards your last (long) letter, it shows even cruder political thinking than the previous one. All your arguments have already occurred to us, my child. They leap to the eye. But you think you are indicting a system, whereas you are only indicting human nature. However, I won't write further on this, except to point out that you yourself are a parasite of the system you condemn. So am I.

Yours ever, A. B.

The Lois renunciation business is not well motivated, & is a grave blot. A. B.

BIRLEY / MS. / 247
(*To Margaret Kennedy*)

75, Cadogan Square
5–12–24

Dear Miss Margaret Kennedy,

I think the *C. N.* is fine. It is bound to make you respected among those whose respect alone is a comfort in moments of depression. For myself, I have been more impressed by it than by any novel from a new writer for years. I wish I had been still 'Jacob Tonson',—I would have written about it and made people sit up. I am glad to hear that the book is now being demanded. What I ask from a novel is emotional power and an individual attitude towards things. The *C. N.* has both in a high degree. Having them, it is bound to have what *I* call style. The musical stuff is splendid. I cannot imagine how you got hold of it. I've lived with & among musicians, creative and interpretative, most of my life, and it beats me. Nor can I imagine how you got hold of the sexual stuff, all of which is authentic—or what I call the goods. Of course it is very 'free', & I rejoice in that. I doubt if the bourgeois characters are quite as good as the artists, but they are very good. The first scene between Miss Churchill & her papa seems to me to be a bit conventional beneath its realistic surface. I've lent my copy, so I can't refer to the pages which I marked for comment. But that doesn't matter, because I know I had only two things to criticize of any moment. I think the second quarter (about) of the story hesitates or lacks direction. And I think that you are uneconomical of material. To my mind, over half of the Sanger children serve no real purpose in the plot. They exist all right,

246. Nichols' play, *Guilty Souls*, was produced by the 300 Club at the Royal Academy of Dramatic Art on 16 November, with Ernest Milton (1890–), the actor-manager, as Paul Vyson, Claude Rains (1889–1967), famous later for his film roles, as Oswald Bentley, Muriel Pratt (d. 1945) as Clara Bentley, Dorothy Holmes-Gore, daughter of the actor Arthur Holmes-Gore, as Lois Forster, and George Blackwood as Rupert Adderley. James Agate (d. 1947) reviewed for the *Sunday Times* for many years. G. H. Mair (see above, pp. 134–5) served briefly as dramatic critic for the *Evening Standard*.

(Sir) Henry Head (1861–1940), the neurologist, was a great friend of Nichols'.

but not usefully to *you*. This seems to me to indicate something wrong in the necessary *artifice* of construction. Also, why should Miss Churchill have an uncle as well as a father? When the father (the more interesting of the two) might have served every purpose? The last scene is A1, the extraordinary perfectly unconscious callousness of Dodd. This scene is sound in every line. But I don't know why Tessa had to die. I don't in the least mind her dying if I could see the reason for it. That death strikes me as facile, as an event finishing the book. I am just going away for about six weeks. When I come back I hope I may see you.

Yours sincerely, Arnold Bennett

BODKIN / TR. / 248
(*To Thomas Bodkin*)

Excelsior
Napoli
8.1.25.

My dear T.B.,

See here! What does James want with a title! I was delighted to have your letter, and I reciprocate, to you and your wife, all your good wishes, enhanced. It is a pity about the panel; but the album of cartes de visite is fine. I'm ever so grateful. I haven't seen it yet, as my Secretary very wisely did not forward it. Only letters ever arrive in Italy. I shall be in London on 15th. I've had perfect weather for 3 weeks. This hotel is on the edge of the Bay of Naples (of which you may have heard). Vesuvius sits opposite about 10 miles off, and is 3,600 feet high and doesn't look it. One sits at the open window on Xmas morning and so on every morning and has breakfast in contemplation of Vesuvius, Sorrento and Capri. It will be a great relief to you to know that Naples (with environs) which I had not previously seen, meets with my approval. I don't reckon that Pompeii is so very great, and I am sure the Pompeians were a rotten lot, with 2nd rate taste, but Baia and the region thereof is marvellous—not only humming with classical tradition and thick with remains; but absolutely lovely. I have seen nothing so thrilling

247. Margaret Kennedy (1896–1967) had recently met Bennett, and they became good friends. *The Constant Nymph* was her second novel.

and pathetic in all my life. Also this hotel is very good, and I am staying here incognito (under my real name E.A.B.......tt)! I hope you are all right and that you are soon coming to London.

Always yours sincerely, A. B.

JOHNSON / TS. / 249
(*To L. G. Johnson*)

75, Cadogan Square
20th January 1925

Dear Mr. Johnson,

I venture to write a very few words about your book on me. It has given me great pleasure. Both your appreciations and your animadversions are full of interest, significance—meat! The book is incomparably better than Darton's—at any rate than the first edition of Darton's. I never read the second. (I was once introduced to him in the street and he said that he felt ashamed of his work!)

With regard to your criticism of *These Twain*, I will only say that the restriction, the 'narrow-down', was intentional and deliberate, and part of the scheme as a whole. Compare the much more drastic narrowing down into domestic life at the end of *War and Peace*. I cannot remember whether I read *War and Peace* before or after I planned *Hilda Lessways*, which I consider to be quite inferior to *These Twain*. Frank Swinnerton calls it a 'tour de force' and this is my view also. Whereas I have received the most *passionate* testimonies to the authenticity and force of *These Twain*.

You mention *Sacred and Profane Love*, and would apparently put it above *The Pretty Lady*. I do not think that it is to be mentioned in the same day as *The Pretty Lady*.

I doubt if I have any other serious differences with you.

Always yours sincerely, Arnold Bennett

248. Bennett was in Italy from mid-December to mid-January.
James O'Connor was made a King's Counsel (English Bar) in 1925.

249. L. G. Johnson (1894–) was born on the fringe of the Potteries and, as he says, 'in a way . . . grew up with some of Bennett's characters'. His early work was in literary criticism; later he was senior lecturer in the Department of Economics at the University of Leeds. His book, *Arnold Bennett of the Five Towns*, is mainly concerned with the Five Towns novels. On Harvey Darton see Vol. II.

COWARD / TR. / 250
(*To Noel Coward*)
PRIVATE

75, Cadogan Square
25.1.25

My dear Noel,

I only want to say that your performance was *masterly*.

As regards the play, first act very good as an American imitation of an English comedy. But for the rest—

Christ!

Yours, A. B.

TEXAS / TS. / 251
(*To William Lee Mathews*)

75, Cadogan Square
18th February 1925

Dearest William,

I have been in bed ever since Sunday with something that may be either a cold or 'flu—I don't know which. I had been sickening for this since the middle of last week.

Is the play really dramatic? As I watched it, I doubted. Certainly there were parts which seemed to me to drag, but this may have been due to groping for words all the time.

I was very pleased indeed with Komi's production.

I thought all the playing was good except Harlequin's. Whoever chose this gentleman for an important part ought to be compelled to go and see *A Midsummer Night's Dream* at Drury Lane every night for a month as a punishment.

Of course the play was under-rehearsed. It would be impossible for anyone to produce this play satisfactorily in 2½ weeks, even if he had full control of all the artistes. Komi did wonders—really wonders. It was a great scheme of yours to get him.

Thine, A. B.

250. Noel Coward (1899–) played the son in his play *The Vortex* at the Royalty Theatre.

251. Theodore Komisarjevsky (1882–1954) produced *The Bright Island* on 15 February. For other information on Komisarjevsky see Vol. I, p. 367. Harlequin was played by Alan Trotter.

TEXAS / T.C.C. / 252
(*To Hubert Griffith*)

[75, Cadogan Square]
25th February 1925

Dear Hubert Griffith,

Thank you for your letter. I quite understand the difficulty of the *Observer*. Of course they cannot pay my price. My ordinary regular price is £100 for 1000 words. When they asked me to criticize the Wells-Ervine play I screwed them up to £25 for the article, but not easily. You had better tell them that if they would like me to do the article on your play, I will make them a present of it. I do not want to be paid anything for it. But of course they may not want me to do it at all.

With regard to your criticism of my play, what troubles me is not the reception of my play but the general state of dramatic criticism in London—quite apart from its relation to myself. I showed what I thought of my play by asking the Stage Society to produce it. My opinion of the thing remains what it was. I consider that bits of it are undramatic, but otherwise I do not blush for it. I have been glad to learn that many people were delighted with the play. The only dramatic critic in London that it is possible for me to take seriously—P. P. Howe of *Truth*—was undoubtedly very pleased with the play and said so. His pleasing final comment was that the play ought to be revived before a more intelligent audience. I have been preaching the solitary virtues of Howe (who is the author of the big book on Hazlitt, and of a book on contemporary dramatists) for years, and if *he* had damned *The Bright Island* I might have been disturbed in my mind. However, he did not. The rest of the press, apart from the occasional expression of personal regard for my other work, treated the play just as they treated *The Monkey House*. Some critics even suggested that I ought to be forcibly restrained from writing such plays. There is something humorous in all this. It is also humorous to turn over the slashing criticisms of, e.g. *The Great Adventure*, in the very papers which now say that if only Mr. B. would write as he did then.

All this is nothing. What is important is the *nullity* of current dramatic criticism, and the very low estimate in which it is held—practically all of it—by people of taste. Dramatic criticism seems to have no standards of taste. It seems to have nothing but weariness, negativeness, and a morbid hatred of anything that is not like everything else. I thought that your Hamlet article was far more deplorable than your article on me. I might conceivably agree with all your criticisms of the Hamlet production, and still call the article deplorable, because of its utter lack of balance, of any perception of the fine positive qualities of the production. I thank God that your play is very much superior to your criticism. Otherwise I would not have ventured to offer to write about it.

Yours, [Arnold Bennett]

TEXAS / T.C.C. / 253
(*To George Bernard Shaw*)

[75, Cadogan Square]
26th February 1925

Dear Bernard Shaw,

I saw *Man and Superman* last night. It must be a pretty good play which can survive such an awful performance as I had to witness. I seriously think that it was one of the very worst performances of any play that I ever did see. I have always understood that you are very autocratic about your productions, settling everything yourself, and refusing productions unless your demands are complied with. Indeed I have had personal experience of this excellent trait of yours. Why, then, this ghastly show at the Chelsea Palace? If these performances were even decent you would fill the theatre for months instead of for weeks. I liked the *play* rather more than ever.

Ever yours, [Arnold Bennett]

252. Bennett reviewed the Wells-Ervine play, *The Wonderful Visit*, in the *Observer* on 10 January 1921.

Griffith said of *The Bright Island* in his review on 22 February that it was 'the worst play written by a celebrated man for a long time past'. Percival Presland Howe, author of several books on literature and drama, liked its 'malice and wisdom'. *The Monkey House*, by Walter T. Ellis, opened at the New Oxford at the end of January. Griffith condemned the John Barrymore *Hamlet* on the same page that he condemned *The Bright Island*.

253. Shaw's play was produced at the Chelsea Palace on 25 and 26 February.

DAILY EXPRESS, 13 April 1925 / 254
(*To the editor*)

[75, Cadogan Square]
[about 10 April 1925]

[no salutation]

In his leading article on my article of last Monday the Editor of the *Daily Express* put to me three questions to which he demanded a simple negative or affirmative. He cannot have a simple negative or affirmative, for the reason that all three questions confuse the issue. The first question was:—

Is it true that there is not one serious contemporary play in the West End of London which does not deal with 'sex' either in the form of infidelity or seduction or decadence?

The answer to this is that ninety-nine serious plays out of a hundred, in the present age as in all previous ages, deal with 'sex' either in the form of infidelity or seduction or decadence (whatever decadence is).

The second question was:—

Is it true that the theatrical managers openly state that they dare not produce anything now but a comedy, a musical show, or a sex play?

The answer to this is that modern theatrical managers have always openly stated that they dare not produce anything but a comedy, a musical show, or a sex play.

The third question was:—

Is it true that the stage, in its present condition, is a mirror held up to reflect life?

The answer to this is that the stage in its present condition is as much a mirror held up to reflect life as ever it was.

In reply to other editorial remarks, I will say that there is certainly not 'always a profitable market for indecency'. And, further, that indecent plays are just as liable to fail as any other sort of plays, and pay no better than any other sort of plays.

I was not, however, discussing indecent plays. I have seen very few indecent plays in London, generally to the accompaniment of music. But there is no indecent line or situation in any of the three plays with which I dealt. Mr. Hannen Swaffer says that in order to defeat me he would have to ask the *Daily Express* to print things that he cannot ask it to print. Perhaps Mr. Hannen Swaffer will communicate to the Editor privately a few specimens, from the plays under discussion, of what he considers to be unprintable; and perhaps the Editor, if he does not consider them too shocking for my perusal, would pass them on to me, so that my eyes might be opened to the mentality of Mr. Hannen Swaffer. I feel very sure that no publisher of plays would refuse to publish these plays on the score of indeceny.

The whole situation may be reduced to this. Some people maintain that certain phenomena which are a commonplace of life, of talk, of the newspapers, and of novels ought to be forbidden to dramatists. And if one or two dramatists happen once in a while to touch these phenomena, these people immediately begin to cry out hysterically about 'decadence', 'filth', and 'a rush of indecent plays'. Other people would give the same liberty to dramatists as is given to journalists and novelists, and they regard the outcry as merely foolish. I belong to the latter class.

Mr. Knoblock in his admirable article—assuredly the best of the series—pointed out that, while serious dramatists are persecuted, facetious musical operators are given complete freedom. Dozens of musical comedies and farces have concerned themselves mainly with the twin themes of fornication and inebriety, but I do not remember that Sir Gerald du Maurier ever came righteously out against them with locutions such as 'filth', 'hell', 'cad', 'bestial', 'pornie'. (What is 'pornie'? It is not English. If resentment necessitates the manufacture of new offensive epithets, they should at least be coined with some respect for the language.)

Sir Gerald, however, is too emotional a controversialist to be taken seriously. He cannot even object to shingling, in an age when five women out of six are shingled, without casting a slur on the morals of all women who shingle. He cannot reply to me without suggesting that I wrote what I did for a commercial purpose. This kind of dialectics is either silly or base, or perhaps it is merely an error in deportment. In either case the tu quoque, to Sir Gerald, would be so easy, and so devastating, that I forbear to employ it.

[Arnold Bennett]

254. On 6 April in the *Express* Bennett had a front-page article entitled 'Is Real Life Worse Than the Stage?' It was apropos a court case concerning a play that depicted debauchery among the upper classes. The justice found occasion to attack Frederick Lonsdale's *Spring Cleaning* and Coward's *The Vortex*, and Bennett admitted in his article that the unchaste mother and the drug-taking son in *The*

BEAVERBROOK / MS. / 255
(*To Lord Beaverbrook*)

75, Cadogan Square
18–4–25

My dear Max,

I don't know what your interviewing is apropos of; but don't please try to get away with any wrong ideas about insomnia—especially mine. And don't try to twist facts to support any theory you may have. After 30 years devoted to insomnia I know something about it. Such elementary considerations as the possibility of having been asleep when you thought you were awake have long ago been carefully studied by me. But I don't reckon I'm asleep when I'm walking about a room, or smoking or drinking, or reading. Of course I *may* be, but I don't reckon I am. Whenever there is a *chance* of my having been asleep I count it as sleep. At the suggestion of my masseur, who has taken oath he can cure me, I keep a record of my sleep. Recently it has slightly improved. In the last 7 days the average is actually 6.2 hours! Not counting my afternoon doze of .3 hours. I feel frightfully well.

After the singular feebleness and misleadingness of your leading article in reply to my first article, I had to make some retort; also it was advisable for me to reply to Gerald du Maurier, who is capable in moments of depression of being an ass. Gerald's article was really written by Viola Tree. She told me. She was dining here & left early in order to try to destroy me over Gerald's signature.

Yours ever, A. B.

P.S. Nor is my best work always done early in the morning. Most of the fundamental cerebration is. But I can do goodish work between tea & dinner. A. B.

Vortex were characters he had never heard of in real life. Also on the 6th appeared the three leading questions addressed to Bennett. Hannen Swaffer (1879–1962) was a dramatic critic for many years and especially notable for his help in closing the promenades of the old music halls. For other references to Sir Gerald du Maurier (1873–1934) see below and see also Vol. I.

COLLINS / TR. / 256
(*To G. K. Chesterton*)

75, Cadogan Square
28.4.25.

Dear Gilbert Chesterton,

In your issue of the 11th you had some comments upon Lord Beaverbrook's social policy. Lord Beaverbrook has got hold of the idea that these comments were meant to have a personal application to himself—which would mean that he was practising miscellaneous fornication on the one hand and on the other opposing birth-control, etc. Certain Canadian papers have already interpreted your remarks in this sense. Beaverbrook is a close friend of mine; he is an absolutely clean-living man. This, however, is not the point. The point is whether you intended to be personal. Of course I have assured him positively that his idea to this effect is utterly wrong, and that you would not dream of being personal. To be brief, he asked me whether I would ask you. I am now asking you. If you care to reply, I will show him your letter.

Yours sincerely, Arnold Bennett

BEAVERBROOK / MS. / 257
(*To Lord Beaverbrook*)

75, Cadogan Square
12–5–25

My dear Max,

Yes. We forgot Shaw. His income must be rising. He is now the most popular world-dramatist writing. With stalls at 16/- (gold value) in Berlin, he must be making a lot. I should estimate that his plays average 4,000 or 5,000 performances a year, at least. (I have had 2,000 in a year myself, & even in a rotten

256. G. K. Chesterton (1874–1936) edited *G. K.'s Weekly* from 1925 to 1936. In his 'Notes of the Week' he attacked Beaverbrook's advocacy of Empire free trade. One can't run one half of the world and ignore the other half, he said, and added: 'So he [Beaverbrook] wishes to have the most respectable marriage with the most reckless divorce; he wishes to eat his wedding-cake and have it. So he wants to have uncontrolled sexuality and uncontrolled birth-control; to eat his birthday cake and have it.' Chesterton seems to have replied graciously to Bennett's letter, for in a few days Bennett wrote a brief note of thanks to him. For other references to Chesterton see Vols. I and II.

year have 400.) Shaw's income cannot be less than £20,000. As regards Oppenheim, I know that 2 years ago he made £20,000. There are films. I don't think Oppenheim's income is falling. It takes a long time for an established author's income to fall. Authors' incomes are as a rule grossly exaggerated. My own always is. And very few authors keep even the state that I keep—what with the maintenance of a wife, a morganatic ditto, & a yacht. Yet I have never made more than £18,000 in a year (after paying agents fees) & I have made as low as £10,000. (This is private.) Until the last 6 or 7 years Wells never made more than £12,000. An odd author or so will sometimes make quite a bit (Hutchinson made over £100,000 out of *If Winter Comes.*) But they don't keep it up. They can't. Authors cannot make what I call *money*. Musical composers can—a few of them. Puccini really made money. So do Wagner's heirs. And authors can only make a fair income if they have a great deal to say—like Shaw, Wells, & me—and are incurably industrious, as we are. And they can only make it even then by not trying to make it. Shaw & Wells have always said: Be damned to popular taste. And I have given popular taste a miss for many years now. I never made any money out of 'popular' books. Hall Caine is a very able man, with big ideas and a crude mind. *No* play of his has *ever* failed. He has had huge sums for film-rights. Newman Flower (Cassells) told me that his firm had sold over 1,000,000 copies of H C's books in the last 3 years. He told me this last week. And Cassells by no means handle all H C's books.

Withal, thanks to agents & Authors Society, the economic position of authors has greatly improved in my time. I remember when we were all thrilled at the news that Stanley Weyman was getting 6d. a word for serial rights. Then Stevenson got 1/-, & we thought it couldn't possibly last. Tennyson got £300 from the *Nineteenth Century* for *The Ballad of the Revenge*. He said: 'It was worth £500.' *He* didn't really think it was; but in fact it was. I am told that the sale of Kipling's works is increasing. God knows why! There is quite a lot of meat in this letter.

I see you are still harping in the *Standard* on my incredibility as a witness about my own sleeping. But you have made no attempt to answer the argument in my letter to you. God, what an article I could write on this subject!

R

Max, you must forgive me if I want to trouble you again soon about my novel.

Yours, A. B.

BODKIN / TR. / 258
(*To Thomas Bodkin*)

75, Cadogan Square
22.5.25.

My dear Bodkin,

Your essay is excellent, but too kind. Your discovery about the shade *desolates* me utterly. You may not know it, but you are going to the 1st night of *The Cherry Orchard* at Hammersmith on Monday night. You will kindly give me the pleasure of your company to dinner at 6.50. A friend of mine, Miss Dorothy Cheston, will be present. We shall go all of us to the theatre together, but you will sit with Miss D. C. in the stalls, as I have to be in the directorial box, where I never allow ladies.

Yours ever, A. B.

BEAVERBROOK / TS. / 259
(*To Lord Beaverbrook*)

75, Cadogan Square
26th May 1925

My dear Max,

Hastings in this morning's *Express* calls Chekhov's *Cherry Orchard* 'fatuous drivel'. Anybody is entitled so to describe a play which after twenty years is accepted by the instructed in every European country and in America as a masterpiece. But I doubt whether anybody holding such an opinion, especially after seeing the play three times, is entitled to be a dramatic critic. And even if he is entitled to be a dramatic critic, he ought

257. E. Phillips Oppenheim (1886–1946), A. S. M. Hutchinson (1879–), Hall Caine (1853–1931), Stanley Weyman (1855–1928). Robert Louis Stevenson was nearly starving to death in the early 1870s and by 1887 he was receiving offers in America of £200 apiece for short articles. Rudyard Kipling's rise was even more sensational. For other references to both Stevenson and Kipling see Vol. II. See Vol. I, especially pp. 195n. and 411, for details on Bennett's income.

Bennett published an article on insomnia in the *Evening Standard* on 27 May.

Beaverbrook was giving Bennett information for the political side of *Lord Raingo*, which Bennett began writing on 13 May.

certainly to express his idiosyncrasy with some regard for the consideration due to the immense artistic prestige of a writer like Chekhov.

Although I personally had one of the greatest theatrical evenings of my life last night, I can quite comprehend that the play might baffle and exasperate a certain type of mind, but I perceive in this no excuse for such language as Hastings employs. If he had been content to say that he could not make either head nor tail of *The Cherry Orchard*, he would have been within his rights, and would have inspired nothing but compassion.

What disturbs me is, not that he makes the play look ridiculous, for this he cannot do, but that he makes your paper look ridiculous.

I have seen only two other criticisms, *The Times* and the *Daily News*. If you will read them you will notice rather a different attitude. I met the *Observer* man last night, and he was so enthusiastic he could scarcely speak.

Thine, Arnold

GIDE / 260
(*To André Gide*)

Yacht Marie Marguerite
Falmouth
13–6–25

My dear Gide,

I have not written earlier, because I have been waiting for the remainder of the proofs of *Les Faux-monnayeurs*. I have so far received only 'placards' 1 to 27. There must evidently be a lot more. Perhaps the rest has not yet been printed, or corrected. Anyhow I cannot offer any opinion worth having about the book until I have read it all. I am only writing now because I fear you will shortly be leaving for Africa. So far I think the book is very beautiful and 'entraînant'. I have not yet realised quite why you call it your 'first novel'. It has of course a more 'romantic' quality—especially in the management of the intrigue: there are some lovely bits of invention here—and the 'machinery' of the presentation is of course more varied and even slightly capricious (in the manner of Edouard) but the

259. Basil MacDonald Hastings (1881–1928), dramatist and journalist.

essential YOU is just the same,—nor do I suppose that you would wish to have it altered! The boys are admirable, and the 2 children are even more admirable. I want more of Lilian! I cannot help thinking—to judge by the part which I have read—that you have brought in the discussion about fiction, and the notes in the 'Journal' about fiction, more because you are interested keenly at the moment in the technical and philosophical questions than because the discussion is necessary to the furtherance of the plot. But I admit that I am not in a position to judge yet. If you have any doubts about the artistic success of the first 27 placards I desire with great respect to ask you to discard such doubts. I have read it all with the greatest eagerness and admiration. In the way of criticism I would only say that I have not perceived the raison d'être of some of the earlier extracts from the 'Journal'. Perhaps you will be able to send me the remainder of the book soon. I hope so.

I am writing this at sea (where you ought to be) in heavy weather, with sunshine and a nice breeze, and have beautiful young women on board. In two hours I shall be in Falmouth harbour.

Ever your devoted friend, Arnold Bennett

Mille choses à Marc.

ARKANSAS / TS. / 261
(*To Frank Swinnerton*)

75, Cadogan Square
3rd July 1925

My dear Frank,

I do not know sufficient about Villiers de l'Isle Adam to advise you. His best known book is *L'Eve Future*. I have read half of it twice, but could never get to the end of it. However, I will not say that it is not good. It is certainly full of ideas. *Axel* (play) is another famous book of his but I have not read it. His short stories are very renowned indeed. *Contes Cruels* and *Nouveaux Contes Cruels*. I have read all these. I should say that they were pretty wonderful fifty or sixty years ago, but what

260. Bennett was sailing off the English coast from about 3 to 20 June.

they would look like in a translation I cannot predict. On the whole I should say 'No' to your question.

Yours, A. B.

TEXAS / T.C. / 262
(*To Francis Hackett*)

[Salzburg]
22.7.25

[no salutation]

Now my sweet Francis I have read your book in this Alpine district. I wish you had begun to write novels earlier. This one is too mature for a beginner. It lacks crudities, which a first novel ought to have. It doesn't show many possibilities in technical improvement, and as for emotional improvement—can this come after 30? How old are you? Perhaps it can. There is not, *really*, much fault to be found with *T.N.Y.C.* It is well-constructed; *and the pace is maintained*; I mean it doesn't flag. Some parts are a bit flat (in my opinion), but that is due I should say to selection of material sometimes which has not made a special appeal to you. You thought it ought to be in and constructionally it ought, but you didn't somehow get your teeth into it. (I am well aware that all this is like my cheek, so don't tell me.) Constructionally I would say that the only fault is the introduction of the Democratic Convention, which, taken by itself, is about the most brilliantly felt and realised thing in the whole book. But what in hell bearing has it on the story? You have tried, towards the end, to make it have a bearing, but I doubt if you have succeeded. On the other hand I think you have left out parts which you might well have included, e.g. the beginning of the partnership between Beale and Madigan. Also the final reconciliation between Beale and Eleanor. It is all very fine to show this by showing two pairs of boots outside a bedroom door, but this device does not clear up several fundamental points. Also I do not know what is the moral of the story. All great stories have morals. Further in the way of criticism (I am no good at praise), there are various descriptive passages which seem to me to lack point, e.g. the description of the dubious party on pp. 310 to 311. These people come and go

261. Philippe-Auguste Villiers de l'Isle Adam (1838–89).

and are forgotten, and I think the guests ought to have been 'synthetised' instead of being particularised. In my opinion the descriptions of the appearance of people seldom are effective. Oh, and I was forgetting, in another connection I think the letter on page 310 about Sally is a bit forced. In the matter of writing I somewhat resent your brightness. Has it occurred to you that this book is a perfect orgy of simile and metaphor and cruelty to words. Why should a girl 'wheel' her head instead of turning it? Why should a book 'loll' on a lap instead of lying there? What in God's name is a 'spineless voice'? Some passages of this kind of thing—complicated working out of a metaphor or simile are very brilliant indeed. But I see no reason for a whole book of them. The great masters seldom, indeed never, indulge thus. Stendhal, Tolstoy, Dostoevsky, Hardy. They are not *bright*. They do not try to put a glitter on to the page. I am a great believer in being 'spired by the great masters and not by the little ones. You can do the 'bright' business far, far better than Michael Arlen, but I honestly don't want you to do it at all. No, I think you can be better than bright. Have I made myself understood? Of the characters I think Beale is better than Eleanor, and Mrs. Byrd and brother-in-law better than either. The Convention is the show chapter. But for the initiated there are passages of synthesis which are finer, e.g. the description of society at Long Point (apart from the brightness thereof) on p. 233. This is about as good as it could be and amounts to sociology lifted into poetry. There are others. I could write lots more but shan't. I doubt if you will be able to decipher even this. You may object to some of my notions. But I am in an impregnable position; you asked for them. The book is better than you had a right to be able to do, as a beginner; much better. It has the geniune narrative gift. But I am incapable of being satisfied. I'm like a woman, in that. I want more emotional force in the next book, and less brightness.

Kindest thoughts and best wishes to you both.

Yours, Arnold B.

262. Bennett was in Austria until 11 August.

Francis Hackett (1883–1962), Irish-American author and critic, published *That Nice Young Couple* in 1925. When Hackett was a critic in Chicago he reviewed *The Old Wives' Tale*, and Bennett wrote to him to say that of all the reviews he liked Hackett's best. The two men became friends in the twenties. Michael Arlen (1895–1956) had recently published his best-known novel, *The Green Hat*.

BODKIN / TR. / 263
(*To Thomas Bodkin*)

Salzburg
29.7.25

[no salutation]

I hear the address of my oculist has been sent to you. Sorry about the eyes. I read the accounts of the Sargent sale in *The Times*. They *staggered* me. I am quite sincere in saying that if I had one of those water colours, I would not hang it. I would sell it. I had a dreadful time in Sargent's [?] studio some years ago, when he showed me a considerable number of these aquarelles—they were lying about the floor, even—& I could not think what in hades to say to him about them! Salzburg is fine. I shall be in London August 12 for a few days.

Best wishes to you,

Yours, A. B.

BUTLER / MS. / 264
(*To Edward Knoblock*)

Yacht Marie Marguerite
26.8.25

My dear Edward,

I enclose 2 brief notes about your 2 stories. There is not the slightest doubt in my mind that you can produce *excellent* saleable stories. I have practically no fault to find with these technically. The narrative style and the plots are admirable—quite surprisingly so, unless you have had a lot of practice which you have concealed from me! But I think that, for the market, you will do well to have less fornication in the tales. I should advise you to go to an American agent direct. Brandt is the best one. If you don't know him, you will only have to mention me. I am keeping the stories here till you arrive. You will almost certainly have to come to the Hook of Holland, via Harwich. I will wire you on Saturday what station you shall be

263. The sale of John Singer Sargent's paintings upon his death in 1925 broke all records for the sale of modern paintings.

met at on Tuesday morning. The Rosses will no doubt come by the same steamer.

I think you can make your mind easy about short stories.

Thine, A. B.

FALES, NYU / TS. / 265
(*To R. D. Blumenfeld*)

75, Cadogan Square
15th September 1925

My dear Blumenfeld,

In the matter of distribution, the following extract from a letter from a relative in Liverpool may be of interest to you, and perhaps of value:—

'Round about 6.30 p.m. (after working overtime) I visited the newsagents and asked at each for the *Daily Express*. Each one replied "Sold out". I said to the fifth (W.H.S. Lime Street): "Why is the *Express* sold out?" In a non-committal way he replied: "You won't find an unsold copy in Liverpool". So I drove him to it and again said "Why?" His reply was:—"There is an article by Arnold Bennett." Such is fame. Such is bad distribution.'

Yours sincerely, Arnold Bennett

P.S. I note that the Bishops have darned little to say to me this morning. A. B.

264. Bennett was sailing on the inland seas of Holland from 16 August until the end of the month.

Knoblock started to write fiction in the mid-twenties. He published a novel, *The Ant Heap*, in 1929.

Carl Brandt (1889–1957) was the New York associate of the Pinker firm.

265. Bennett's article, 'What I Believe', published in the *Daily Express* on the 14th, was the first of a series in which eminent persons stated their beliefs. The articles were published in book form later in the year under the title *My Religion*. Bennett confessed himself unable to believe in the divinity of Christ, virgin birth, heaven, hell, the immortality of the soul, or the divine inspiration of the Bible. But he admitted the greatness of Christ as a teacher; he wasn't prepared to assert there *isn't* a hell; he believed in God in the respect that he could not help believing in a first cause and a source of order in the universe; and he thought the presence of conscience in man suggested divine implantation. Christianity was failing because Christians did not follow Christ, and he imagined that any new religion would have to be based upon kindliness. The reply of the bishops was mainly to the effect that in denying historic Christianity, Bennett was denying the ladder up which he himself admittedly climbed.

ILLINOIS / MS. / 266
(*To Jane Wells*)

75, Cadogan Square
17.9.25.

My dear Jane,

This was very disturbing news about Frank. I hadn't the least idea he'd been ill. Remember me to him. I suppose there is no sort of doubt, now, that he has come through. But these things are terrible while they are on. You have all my retrospective sympathy. I was once nearly dead myself once, & very annoyed about it.

I noticed strangely few misprints in *C. A.'s Pa*, though I had my malicious eye open for them. I like Preemby better than Lewisham, Kipps, or Mr. Polly. He is a very distinguishedly-conceived character. The book is urbane.

Well, I like Frank much: but then I am much attached to the whole H.G. family. Thank H.G. for his letter, & yourself for your kind message to Dorothy. She is 34, & a very hefty wench.

Ever yours, A. B.

FALES, NYU / MS. / 267
(*To E. V. Lucas*)

75, Cadogan Square
29.9.25

My dear Edward,

Thanks for sending me the observations from your correspondent. I think that perhaps he has not quite understood me, in my use of the word 'believe'. I am using it in the full sense, as if I was saying: 'I believe that 2 and 2 make 4.' On such a kind of belief a man can base something. Surely I am entitled to say that 'I am *inclined to accept* the theory of a future life' without saying that 'I believe in the immortality of the soul'. I see no contradiction here. I had no intention of trying to pacify anybody: and I think that on reflection C.M.E. will be 'inclined to accept the theory' that my intentions were of the best, even if he cannot entirely 'believe' it.

Yours, A. B.

266. Frank Wells (1903–), Wells's younger son, became a film editor and production designer.

Christina Alberta's Father was published in September.

DAILY EXPRESS, 2 October 1925 / 268
(*To the editor*)

75, Cadogan Square
[about 1 October 1925]

Sir,

I do not propose to write anything further about Christian dogma. I was asked to state my religious views, and I stated them, as briefly and plainly as possible. That they should arouse resentment was inevitable: that people should find in my articles arrogance and inconsistency I regret. I have no pretension to be an expert on religious dogma. I have no desire to force my views on others, much less to 'float' a new religion.

Arnold Bennett

FALES, NYU / TS. / 269
(*To R. D. Blumenfeld*)

75, Cadogan Square
3rd October 1925

My dear Blumenfeld,

I am beginning to suspect a certain amount of hanky panky in the selection of the letters about Christian dogma for publication. I will tell you why. I have received quite a number of letters from people who are all of my way of thinking, and who complain that they have not been able to obtain publication of their letters to the *Express*. On the other hand I have not received a single letter from dogmatists complaining that their letters have been suppressed by you. Secondly, the number of letters from dogmatists published far exceeds the number of letters from anti-dogmatists published, whereas I have received many more favourable letters from anti-dogmatists than unfavourable letters from dogmatists. Wherever I go I am acclaimed as the saviour of society, and complete strangers stop me and supplicate for the honour of shaking my hand. How is this? I do not *charge* you with jockeying the correspondence to suit what you imagine (quite wrongly) to be the popular view, but I *suspect* you of this nefarious act. And indeed

268. Bennett's first article elicited several sermons the following Sunday and a large number of letters to the *Express*. He wrote a second article, 'The Dilemma of Christianity', which was published on 29 September.

I consider that the man who made me strike out from my article references to the Immaculate Conception, the Virgin Birth, etc., would be capable of any dialectical iniquity.

Ever yours, Arnold Bennett

BEAVERBROOK / TS. / 270
(*To Lord Beaverbrook*)

75, Cadogan Square
5th October 1925

My dear Max,

I return the typescript of your book.

You asked me to tell you whether I thought it was interesting.

It is very interesting, and it is all interesting.

But of course it is barefaced propaganda on behalf of the two *Expresses*. If you intend it to be this and are prepared for it to be stamped as such by every newspaper which notices it (not all of them will notice it, I think) well and good.

I have made a number of notes here and there. They are in pencil, and only your familiarity with my handwriting may enable you to single them out from other pencil alterations.

The mere writing (phrasing) is a bit loose, and needs careful revision throughout. I have made some emendations in the earlier chapters. Then I thought I was wasting my time in doing so, as it would all be revised. Do not mistake my meaning: the fundamental quality of the style is excellent. But many details of expression are in a literary sense maladroit.

I cannot see how the chapter on eating and drinking enters into the scheme of the book.

I suggest that Chapter VII might advantageously be divided into two.

You can say that you can get a very large sale for the book, and I think you can. But I doubt whether the book has the sort of interestingness that will appeal to a very large public. Its main appeal will be to people who read it with at any rate some inside knowledge of, or enlightened interest in, the events with which it deals. For these it will be a feast.

You will be attacked on account of it, politically, but I do not see how the attacks can be honestly maintained.

You will be accused of self-advertising, and cannot rebut the accusation. All you can say in reply will be: 'Churchill has advertised himself at much greater length.'

Thine, A. B.

TEXAS / TS. / 271
(*To Maurice Baring*)

75, Cadogan Square
17th October 1925

My dear Maurice,

Please excuse typewriting and candour. I have received your booklet. I am very grateful to you for sending it to me. I read the last one with immense admiration, and I expect this one will meet the same fate at my hands. But I have not yet read it. I am in the midst of a long novel of my own, and I dare not embark on the vast enterprise of reading yours until I have got to a certain safe point in my own, which is at present entirely absorbing me. The recent journalistic stuff of mine which you doubtless have *not* been reading was written long ago.

Kindly let me know whether you are likely to be in town for a few weeks, as I wish to ask you to dinner. Your luncheon some time ago was a wonderful event.

Yours ever, A. B.

COHEN / TR. / 272
(*To Harriet Cohen*)

[75, Cadogan Square]
4–11–25

My sweet Tania,

I had your second letter yesterday. Thank you. No; I should say that your present illness is partly due to your persistent ignoring of the counsel of your friends. But, of course, I can't be sure. It is no part of perfection to seek after perfection unduly. You have worked unduly hard—and that is all there is to it. For myself, my child, I read little. I can't both read and write.

270. Beaverbrook's book, *Politicians and the Press*, was published later in the year. (Sir) Winston Churchill (1874–1965), then Chancellor of the Exchequer.

271. Baring's book was *Cat's Cradle*, published in October 1925. Bennett was still working on *Lord Raingo*.

I have new books by Maurice Baring, Sylvia Lynd, and W. Gerhardi lying unread and they are all coming to dinner on the 17th inst.! and I shan't have read anything of them by that time. I only read in bed, and before napping in the afternoon. . . . I dined with Dame Nellie Melba and Knoblock and young Beverley Nichols (a nice creature) at The Ivy. Rotten dinner. Melba is 64. She is a great partisan of modern music, but not of modern singers. Says there is no singing nowadays. The usual jeremiads! Otherwise she is a great lark and full of go. We went to see her sold and dismantled house in Mansfield Street. Very fine. She was to be up at 6 a.m. next day to catch 9 a.m. to Paris, where she is going to settle. I expect boredom is the secret,—she is trying to run away from herself. However, I liked her. I had only met her once before. . . . Re the Holst Symphony. I haven't yet found anybody who speaks up for it. But *I* now speak up for the Beethoven choral. What a work! I hadn't heard it in full for about 20 years. My work is now over ½ done, and by far the hardest ½. I suppose you will be back in England before we are. When we are all back you must meet W. Gerhardi. You will adore him and he you (I hope). So no more at present from your affectionate young friend

A. B.

BEAVERBROOK / MS. / 273
(*To Lord Beaverbrook*)

75, Cadogan Square
9–11–25

My dear Max,

I can't tell you how relieved I was to hear what you said on the telephone this morning. I was *tremendously* afraid that you might have found the political stuff all wrong in the 'feel' of it. I trembled when I was told you were on the 'phone.

Neither can I tell you how delighted & *thrilled* I am by your praise: which, especially on such a subject, means more to me than anybody's.

272. Sylvia Lynd (1883–1952), poet, novelist, and wife of Robert Lynd, published *The Mulberry Bush, and Other Stories* in 1925; William Gerhardi (1895–) published *The Polyglots*; Beverley Nichols published a youthful autobiography the following year. For other comment on Dame Nellie Melba see Vol. II, pp. 87–8. Gustav Holst (1874–1934).

Neither can I tell you how grateful I am to you. Of course without you I could not have *begun* to do the book.

There are 3 or 4 more chapters (which I shall finish today) completing Part I of the book. These I shall send to you in about a week. After this politics cease in the book. Part II is devoted to Raingo's illness and death done (I hope) in the grand, deliberate manner, and lightened by the falling in love of Raingo's son with Delphine's half-sister. Part II begins with the discovery of Delphine's suicide. Part I ends with Sam's triumph at the great Press-banquet.

Thine, Arnold

GRIFFIN / MS. / 274
(*To Harriet Cohen*)

75, Cadogan Square
27–11–25

My sweet Tania,

I've been expecting to hear from you. I hope the reason I haven't is that you're enjoying yourself, or improving your mind, so industriously that you haven't had time to write. The papers are now full of Spahlinger and cows. He was to be here, but I think he isn't. The *Manchester Guardian* is saying that his treatment ought to have a full & proper scientific show and 'Lens' in the *New Statesman* is enthusiastic about him. Lens has been to see him. I've begun the 2nd part of *Lord Raingo*. The four people (or five—including Max) who have read Part I are *very* enthusiastic about it. So I'm pleased & much relieved. I've been writing an article about crime, which appears in the *Express* tomorrow, Saturday, & which may cause trouble. My articles generally do. On Sunday next Max is giving another grand party, at Stornoway House, this time, & Dorothy & I are going to the same. She is very well. I have made the

273. Bennett wrote in his *Journal* earlier in the year: 'On Friday . . . I had my first long serious detailed talk with Max Beaver about political material for my novel *Lord Raingo*. It lasted just 1½ hours. He was marvellously effective and efficient. He didn't need to be told what sort of stuff I wanted. And he gave way at once when he was on the wrong tack—for me. He has exactly the right sort of imagination, and a very powerful and accurate one. He can invent pieces of plot to fit certain incidents, and is just as interested and as effectual in the matter of women as in the matter of politics. I got an immense amount of stuff.'

acquaintance of her mother, who has drunk my champagne & I hers. And Dorothy has made the acquaintance of my sister Tertia. And all is smooth. I had a dinner here last week which was most uproarious. I had to rap the table to obtain order. The Rosses, Jane Wells, Dorothy, the Lynds, Geoffrey Scott (I doubt if you know him. Author of *The Story of Zélide*—ex Foreign Office & a neurasthenic, stuffed with brains, dark, romantic, soft spoken). Dorothy is having numerous small parties. The new piece at the Lyric is a considerable success. *Juno and the Paycock* (jolly Irish) is fine. *Hay Fever* frothy. Dorothy & I went to a Sunday afternoon League Concert 12 days ago—Cortot and Thibaud—and it was one of the most satisfactory concerts I ever heard. They beat it last Sunday with Cortot, Thibaud, *and* Casals! But we couldn't attend. Had to go to Brighton to drink mamma-in-law's champagne. So that was that. I think we'll take a cottage (with a grand piano) at Amberley for May & June. I want to know how you are. My youngest brother has got a touch of [?your] mischief, in both lungs, & has to go into a Home for 3 months. (He hasn't a cent & his business will go to wrack.) The doctors say his cure is a certainty. Well, I think it is. Thank God Ethel Sands is back; but various persons whom I need, including you, are obstinately away. Especially Lady Colefax, who has gone to America to see her son! New York will certainly ring with her. We are [?set,] off for Rome on Monday 14th. E. V. Lucas is already there. Maurice Baring is going. George Doran will arrive (for a few days) the same day as us. And I think the Sullivans are going, and perhaps Lillah McCarthy. So we shan't be cut off from all high-browism. A young woman named Hughes, whom I know slightly, writes that she sees and loves you. *Her father* is a *great* friend of mine. Fred's baby has been ill, and there was a hell of a commotion, because this infant had *never* been ill, or cross, for an hour. God has mercifully restored her. The day before she fell ill, I said: 'That baby looks ill.' The parents pooh-poohed such an absurd idea. The next night Fred was running for the doctor. That's me, isn't it? My sweet child, all my affection, and Dorothy's.

Ever your devoted A. B.

274. M. Spahlinger was head of a tuberculosis clinic in Geneva. Harriet Cohen was tubercular.

COHEN / MS. / 275
(*To Harriet Cohen*)

75, Cadogan Square
13–12–25

My sweet Tania,

You say 'Not very well'; but it isn't clear whether this applies to your practising or your health. Which is it? I wonder whether you got a letter I wrote you *before* I received your last letter written from Geneva. Anyhow I hope you got it. Dorothy is exceedingly well. She had a bit of a turn-up early in the week, but the gynaecologist, on visiting her, said she was absolutely all right. She is. She has made a most useful conquest of the gynaecologist, who has now got to the state of putting off other appointments in order to attend to her. (I hope it will end all right.) He is a most charming man. Frank [?] by name. I have a chill. Indeed I have had 2 distinct chills in a week. As we leave tomorrow [?morn] I am taking great care of myself. I don't want flu. My child, I reck little of V. Woolf. This is putting it mildly. I have had trouble with Dorothy over this authoress. But Swinnerton & I *know* we are right about her. . . . Pauline Smith is ill again. She had a major throat operation which was intended to cure her. But she isn't cured. This virgin is a terrible responsiblity for me. Do you know that I write to her, chiding & encouraging, & counselling, about 3 times a week? Her novel isn't finished yet. I could have written 3 novels with less expense of energy than I have dissipated in making her write one novel—& that not finished! My own novel *Lord Raingo* is going to appear serially in the *Evening Standard*, I hear. Which surprises me, for it is all compact of

---

Bennett's article on crime could not be found.

For other comments on Bennett's sister Tertia see Vols. I and II. His youngest brother was Septimus; see pp. 179–80 and below.

Geoffrey Scott published his notable biography *The Portrait Zélide* earlier in 1925.

Lionel and Clarissa, Charles Dibdin's opera, was produced at the end of October, Sean O'Casey's play was at the Royalty; Noel Coward's was at the Criterion.

Alfred Cortot (b. 1877), Jacques Thibaud (1880–1953), and Pablo Casals (1876–) formed their famous trio in 1905.

Ethel Sands was a cultivated American woman who lived in London. Janet Hughes was the daughter of George Reeves-Smith. See below for a letter to Reeves-Smith.

Fred—Fred Harvey, Bennett's butler. His daughter Winifred was born in 1925.

fornicatory passages. *I* didn't sell it to the *Standard*. Cassells had bought the serial from me long ago, & paid for it, and they, shy of it, have unloaded it on to the *E.S.* No, I am not sleeping well—far from it. But my health is curiously fine, & the novel is proceeding all right. I must now close, as I am most damnably rushed, besides having a chill. God keep you till I see you—and later. Dorothy sends all her fond love.

Ever your affte. A. B.

BODKIN / TR. / 276
(*To Thomas Bodkin*)

Hôtel de Russie
Rome
28.12.25.

My dear T.B.,

I hear from my Secretary that your gift has arrived in safety. What it is, I know not, and shan't know till March. But I know it is fine, and I am very much indebted to you, and have a sense of unworthiness. Well, I look forward to *The Approach to Painting*. I know it will be original. Here in Rome, despite the pictures therein, sculpture reigns. My God! I've been to Rome twice before, but I'd never grasped till now what a terrific monument it is. I shouldn't now, were it not for the tireless resistless enthusiasm of Dorothy (she sends you warm messages). I drove along the Appian Way yesterday afternoon—all among the tombs and other ruins, with hills in the distance and aqueducts in the half-distance. *Never* have I had such sensations! No, never! I'm finishing my novel.

275. Bennett and Virginia Woolf (1882–1941) attacked each other's writing on more than one occasion, Mrs. Woolf notably in her pamphlet *Mr. Bennett and Mrs. Brown*, published in 1924, and Bennett in an article in the *Evening Standard* on 2 December 1926 and reprinted in 1928 as part of the essay 'Young Authors' in *The Savour of Life*. On 1 December 1930 they attended a party together. Bennett wrote to his nephew Richard: 'Last night I was at Ethel Sands' and had a great pow-wow with Virginia Woolf. (Other guests held their breath to listen to us.) Virginia is all right.' Mrs. Woolf described the occasion in her *Diary*: 'I do my best to detect signs of genius in his smoky brown eye'; and then she drew Lord David Cecil into the conversation, 'and we taunted the old creature with thinking us refined'.

Lord Raingo began appearing in the *Evening Standard* on 20 September 1926.

My very best wishes to you both, and again many thanks for this unseen gift.

Ever yours, A. B.

COHEN / MS. / 277
(*To Harriet Cohen*)

[Hôtel de Russie]
4–1–26

My sweet Tania,

I don't think I've heard from you at any length, but still I never make bargains about correspondence. If people don't write to me they still hear from me. I am now in full work & the novel is approaching completion. Dorothy is also working —on a journal! I haven't read any of it yet. She is getting into a bit of a nervous condition: which is not surprising. However, she has discovered a dressmaker here. The said couturier came this afternoon with 6 frocks, &, after her buying 5 of them, all Dorothy's ills departed from her as if by magic. She said she hadn't a thing to wear, and in a fortnight's time she will be saying she hasn't a thing to wear. You are all alike: this is not an easy generalisation but a fact. I've finished Baring's *Cat's Cradle*. 770 large pages. Well, it isn't so bad, though highly curious in technique. We drove out in the Campagna the other day to Frascati and Albano. My dear, what views, landscapes, distances, atmospheres, vestiges, gaudy peasants' carts, wine, bad roads! Unforgettable sensations. But the finest sensation is produced by a drive (or rather, jolt) along the Appian way— desolation, tombs: I've never experienced anything so acute! It would make you cry. I'm now reading Stendhal's *Promenades dans Rome*. Tomorrow night we're going to the opera. . . . Among other people encountered here: old Frankie Schuster, the amateur of music, & giver of musical parties. He has a heart of flint, but is very agreeable company, & a pleasing

276. Bennett and Dorothy left England on 14 December to go to Italy and France for three months.

Bodkin's book, *The Approach to Painting*, was published in 1927 by G. Bell (London).

talker. We've asked him to dinner. Look here, sweet child, how the hell *are* you? Dorothy sends her love.

Ever your affectionate, devoted A. B.

TEXAS / MS. / 278
(*To Maurice Baring*)

Hôtel de Russie
8–1–26

My dear Maurice,

I read *C. C.* very carefully in a fortnight: about 50 pp. a day. It held me all right, though not quite so strongly as *C.* As with *C.*, *C. C.* is strongest & best in the last $\frac{1}{4}$ or $\frac{1}{3}$. I think it is very good, but not so good as *C.* I've tried to find my objection to it, & I think my objection is that (à mon idée) it isn't sufficiently poetised, lifted up. It seems a bit too matter-of-fact, as if it had all actually happened. This is praise on one plane, but dispraise on another. I think there is too much detail in it (e.g., about people going away, letting houses, taking houses, etc.), and I feel sure there are too many characters in it. Impossible to keep track of so many characters, or for you successfully to visualise them to the reader. Tolstoy didn't succeed in doing it in the 1st part of *War & Peace.* I wanted the whole thing simplified, sublimated, and *conventionalised.* I've been seeing a lot of classical sculpture these days, & the experience has made me see how modern fiction is too realistic and un-simple. I think the best parts of the book are the last passages with Blanche's first husband (very dramatic and eerie), and the last chapters of the book. Both husbands are admirably realised. Blanche is good. Nevertheless is Blanche, as a character, strong enough to weld what is really two stories into one story? I rather doubt it. You'll say that this is all blame. It is. But I wanted to criticise adversely, in order to explain why, to my mind, the book being so good is not more grandly imposing than I think it is. I've lots of praise for it, & all the praise is summed up in the words: 'It held me.'

My boy, you may have made 70 corrections in the new edition, but there are plenty more to make. You've even left

277. Frank Schuster (d. 1927), the great friend of Elgar.

'Wood Norton' in at least two places. What a strange aberration for a man like you to use 'Wood Norton'! And how well I know these aberrations!

Ever thine, A. B.

P.S. In the way of mere machinery, I think you might have done better than have an overheard conversation followed by an 'over-read' letter. A bit thick, this, say I. A. B.

UNWIN / TR. / 279
(*To Stanley Unwin*)
PRIVATE

[Hôtel de Russie]
20.1.26

Dear Mr. Stanley Unwin,

I have now read *Mr. Moffatt.* If the author is very young I regard it as a pretty sound book, fundamentally true throughout, with a good plot well constructed and improving as it goes on. What I think it lacks is originality of observation and attitude, and emotional power—though there *is* emotional power in the latter half of the story. As for lack of originality, take e.g. the section 'Taxi', beginning on p. 129. I fail to see any point in this. It throws no new light on a taxi-journey in the given circumstances: indeed it seems to me to be entirely commonplace and of no help to the story. Also it has no power.

As for the alleged originality of technique, I cannot honestly agree that there is any. James Joyce has already done the 'running accompaniment of thought' business far more elaborately, realistically, and brilliantly than Mr. Cobb. And Joyce is already responsible for a school. A great deal of *Mr. Moffatt* appears to me to go back to Zola. It reminds me of the enthusiastic Zola disciple who said that he would write a novel about a man going away from Paris, and the first volume should deal with the journey to the Gare St. Lazare! Mr. Cobb may produce a superficial effect of originality by missing out about ten thousand verbs, but even here he has been forestalled.

Still, I think there is something in the book, and I am glad to

278. 'Wood Norton'—a misnomer; the name is 'Norton Park' in the first pages of the novel.

have read it. I wish Mr. Cobb had let himself go more. He is too disciplined for a very young writer.

Yours sincerely, Arnold Bennett

KEDDIE / MS. / 280
(*To E. V. Lucas*)

Hôtel de Russie
27–1–26

My dear Edward,

Thanks for your letter & *The Polyglots*. I regret not to be able to agree with you as to the latter. I have read it, & though it is loose & contains some merely silly pages, I much enjoyed it. I think it is an original and diverting work, with power in many places, and un peu touchant.

I wish you were here, so that I could take you to Alfredo's. I esteem the cooking here *extremely* good. Among restaurants which we have visited & which pass muster I beg to mention Ranieri, Costaldi, & Bucci (Fish market). Umberto leaves me cold, & San Carlo tepid.

Novel finished yesterday. 130,200 words. I hope yours is being printed.

I might write an article on Rome. Weather, Dorothy & I are well.

Respex to all yours.

Thine, A. B.

ARKANSAS / MS. / 281
(*To Frank Swinnerton*)

Hôtel de Russie
4–2–26

Cheers,

Glad to receive p.c. I had sworn I wouldn't communicate until I was communicated with—unless of course I wanted something from you. 20,000 is good. You can't complain. I also doubt the 30. I desire that Hutch's accursed '4th' should change to '5th' when I wasn't looking. I suppose the new novel is now

279. (Sir) Stanley Unwin (1884–1968), chairman of George Allen and Unwin; Chester Francis Cobb (b. 1899).

nearly finished. . . . I finished *Lord Raingo* on 26th at 5.30 p.m. 130,200 words. The *Sat Eve Post* will buy it if they like the last part, but I know they won't like the last part. £3—4,000 gone to pot through my damnable artistic integrity. (But I know it pays in the end: that's why I keep it up.) We are very well. Dorothy particularly so. But she now likes to have seats near the door in large dining-rooms! I now have *new* material for 40,000 novels. But nothing for that mystery novel which I am determined to write. George was in the greatest form here, & revelled in the undersigned. Well, he is no fool, generally speaking. I found myself in a headline of the Continental *Daily Mail*. Then trouble began. Journalists. Photographers. One woman wrote to me: 'I have met Mr. Locke through the good offices of Mr. James Milne. Cannot I meet you, so that you may tell me just how you work? Can you not give me an half-hour on some golden afternoon at an hour to suit you?' Pretty good. But I have met one very sound female: Miss Baskerville. Rome correspondent of *N.Y. World*. She is the stuff. Lots of friends and acquaintances here. On 14th we move hence, because Dorothy wants to get ½ the journey over. We shall be at Pisa on 15th & Genoa 17th and arrive at Mentone (Grand Hôtel d'Orient) 18th. All D.V. Stay there about a fortnight. Then Paris. I have nothing to do except 6 short stories, 4 articles, and a mystery novel. What I say is: There is no place like Rome. 13 years since I was here first, and I'm only just beginning to see what Rome is. I must admit Dorothy has a passion for archaeology. . . . Tell me what kind of a hotel yours is. Are there private bathrooms?

My benedictions are on you both.

Yours, A. B.

P.S. My youngest brother (50) is apparently dying of consumption.

281. The reference to Hutch is unexplained.

Swinnerton's novel was presumably *Summer Storm*, which was published later in the year.

The *Saturday Evening Post* did not buy *Lord Raingo*. The mystery novel very likely emerged as *Dream of Destiny*, the novel that Bennett left unfinished at his death.

Locke—W. J. (1863–1930), popular author. James Milne (1865–1951), journalist and author.

Septimus Bennett died in 1926.

COHEN / TR. / 282
(*To Harriet Cohen*)

[Hôtel de Russie]
[8 February 1926]

[fragment]

. . . Two or three weeks ago we heard that French conductor René Baton who has just been to London and was castigated by the critics, including E. N. *We* thought he did very well—he certainly conducted *Heldenleben* jolly well. But the only item that aroused the 2,500 audience in the Augusteo concert hall to demand an encore was Handel's 'Largo'. Tut-tut! Yesterday Godowsky played Beethoven's 4th concerto and Franck's *Symphonic Variations*. Fine. I hadn't seen him for years and decades. He is getting bald, and looks quite as old as we, and far shabbier; and he has cultivated an amiable nonchalance of demeanour which fascinates women (I believe). His photographs, however, show that he could be a devil if he wanted. These Sunday Augusteo concerts are wonderful things for a city the size of Glasgow. It is very difficult to get seats for them. The building was originally the tomb of Augustus or some such thing. The sizes of things here are very upsetting; I climbed (with Dorothy) to the cupola of St. Peter's the other day and calculated that the cupola is the size of an average hotel—such as the Rembrandt or Rubens. I began a new novel this morning.

Our loves,

Yours, A. B.

ILLINOIS / MS. / 283
(*To Jane Wells*)

Winter Palace
Menton
1–3–26

My sweet Jane,

This is most nice of you & H.G. Only we shan't be in London until March 21st anyhow, & moreover Dorothy will not be in a very going-out mood then. So we couldn't accept.

282. René Baton (Rhené-Baton, 1879–1940), French conductor and composer; Ernest Newman (1868–1959), music critic; Leopold Godowsky (1870–1938), Russian-American pianist.

The new novel was *The Strange Vanguard*.

I shall be 'about' after March 21st or so. I think we shall stay at Claridges for a week or so until Dorothy goes into retirement. I hope you'll call. Good about H.G.'s novel. I finished my long novel Jan 26th & I began another one shortly afterwards & have written one-sixth of it already. Dorothy is very well. Me too. We leave here next Sabbath & go by easy stages to Paris & thence to Calais & London. . . . All is well, except that my youngest brother is dying of consumption in North Wales. He is 49 or so.

We have had, on the whole, simply marvellous weather (8 weeks in Rome). Dorothy conveyeth love unto you.

Ever yours, A. B.

P.S. Respex to the Franklet.

NERNEY / MS. / 284
(*To Winifred Nerney*)

[France]
[March 1926]

[no salutation]

Many thanks. I have told Dorothy, who is much obliged & will count on you. . . . We shall get to London about Sunday or Monday 21st or 22nd. I am arranging, through Temple & [?] to go to Claridges for about a week so that I shall not sleep at home till about the end of the month. I think this is best. Ida Godebski called yesterday & she told me she had seen Marguerite, who said to her that she would not on any account agree to a divorce, as she had nothing to lose as she was. This is what I expected. If you read the 3 letters from Tertia you will read some wonderful realistic family documents.

A. B.

ARKANSAS / MS. / 285
(*To Frank Swinnerton*)

75, Cadogan Square
[13 April 1926]

[no salutation]

Girl. Vast. All right. 7.50 a.m. 13th April.

A. B.

283. Wells's novel was *The World of William Clissold*, published later in the year.
284. Temple—Richmond Temple. On Ida Godebski see p. 220.

BUTLER / MS. / 286
(*To Reginald Turner*)

75, Cadogan Square
15.4.26

My dear Reggie,

Thanks for yours of 12th. All is going on very well. The kid (Virginia) is enormous (I'm told). Anyhow it is getting less repulsive every day. Dorothy is progressing finely, & everybody is most polite, affectionate, flower-giving, and generally all right.

I admit *Cat's Cradle* is a bit long; but *I* read it, my boy.

Very busy.

At work at 6.40 this morning. It is now 8.15 a.m. D. sends her love.

Thine, A. B.

COHEN / MS. / 287
(*To Harriet Cohen*)

75, Cadogan Square
20–4–26

My sweet Tania,

Your telegram was delivered at Dorothy's bed in less than 2 hours from its despatch by you: it gave great satisfaction to the recipient. Now your letter this morning! Her name is Virginia Mary. Sandra is a good name; but we don't want no fancy names. Needless to say that the infant is the most wonderful that ever sprang from God's creative thought. This—after Dorothy swearing in advance that she would never be an ordinary mother! Miss Nerney inspected the kid yesterday & returned flushed & enthusiastic with the information that the other babies in the Home were like monkeys compared to V.M. Dorothy is going on very well indeed. Good God! You don't mean to say you had never read Marie Bashkirtsev! I have always thought you were very like M.B. I remember telling you so once. The comparison is most interesting and close. The French reading is all to the good. But you needn't read Henri Bataille who is quite 2nd rate, M. Coppée, who is 3rd rate. I very much doubt if you will get through *Chérie*. It seems very old fashioned now. Still, there is stuff in it. I only know one

286. Reginald Turner (?1869–1938), author and wit.

'Bernard'—a painter & not a great one. Barrès is all right sometimes. The *Jardin de Bérénice* is his best work. You ought to read Charles Louis Philippe's *Bubu de Montparnasse*. And Roger Martin du Gard's *Jean Barois*. These books will hold you. I should suggest also Colette's *Chéri*, only I gravely doubt if you would be able to follow its very difficult colloquialisms.

I am wearing a Lanvin necktie, which, however, she did not give me.

Roulette is a bit of a lark, but very dangerous. See the diary of Madame Dostoevsky on the subject of Feodor's gambling mania. It is appalling. Still, I certainly wouldn't say don't gamble at all. Can't you also get to know people in Geneva? Of course its climate is Calvinistic, and so are its people. Perhaps that is why it has the finest brothel in Europe (so I've always been told). I've never been to Geneva myself. I am now getting interested in being a father. Of course it is a damned nuisance in some ways, but these ways don't count. If I hadn't been one I should never have known what an ass I should have been not to have been one. Dorothy was deeply hurt at first because V.M. was not male. Now she is developing a passion for the child. The Maternity Home is efficient & kindly, but sidesplitting. D's nurse is fine (Irish), but so ingenuous. She said the other day: 'No, I stayed in on my afternoon off, & read a lovely book, a lovely naughty book—*Gerald Cranston's Lady*.' I said: 'I've written far naughtier books than that: in fact too naughty for you.' She said: 'I *love* naughty books.' So I'm giving her *The Pretty Lady*. I await the sequel of this act. Well, my sweet dear, don't give way to the disinclination to write. Write to all your best friends. I shall tell Dorothy to write to you. She sits up a lot now. Her room is like a conservatory, for flowers. And applicants for permission to visit her have to be allotted times. I suspect her of being inordinately proud.

Love,

Your devoted A. B.

287. Marie Bashkirtsev (1860–1884), Russian painter and diarist; Henri Bataille (1872–1922), author of popular psychological dramas; François Coppée (1842–1908), poet and dramatist. On Edmund de Goncourt (author of *Chérie*), Maurice Barrès, and C. L. Philippe see Vol. II. Colette (1873–1954) published *Chéri* in 1920; Bennett wrote of her in 1928 that she had 'more finesse and more genius than any other woman-novelist'. *Gerald Cranston's Lady* was by Gilbert Frankau (see above, p. 212).

W. MORGAN / MS. / 288
(*To Frederick Marriott*)

75, Cadogan Square
1.5.26

My dear Frederick,

I was particularly sorry not to see you the other day. But I was rushed with work & couldn't, without grave risk. Also looked I in vain for you yesterday at the Private View.

I wanted to tell you something. Since Marguerite departed I have formed another affection, of which you may have heard, as it is public property & accepted by everybody whom I constantly see. Marguerite has so far refused to divorce me. I might have perhaps divorced her 5 years ago, but I couldn't bring myself to have her watched. The lady's name is Dorothy Cheston Bennett (Bennett is her real, legal name). The point is that she now has a daughter (16 days old) & named Virginia Mary. I felt that whatever you thought about it or had already heard about it, you ought to have this news direct from me as one of my very oldest & best friends. The family has accepted it very well—except Emily, who is a bit cross because she wasn't told earlier.

Love to all,

Yours ever, A. B.

COHEN / MS. / 289
(*To Harriet Cohen*)

75, Cadogan Square
13.5.26

My sweet Tania,

Delighted to hear from you. We are all three very well. Dorothy is now living here & ordering the meals, & the nurse is very good indeed. So far all is going very smoothly. The infant cries one hour before meals. She is of great size & the wonder of the world (I am told). We have come through the strike very well, and I think that the bad effects of it are likely to be exaggerated in the papers. [?We] have walked about twice as much as usual. Lots of callers. Your intimate enemy George Doran called here on Tuesday afternoon, motoring on

288. Dorothy Cheston took the name Bennett by deed-poll.
Emily—one of Bennett's sisters (1871–1953).

his way from Southampton & the Aquitania to the Savoy Hotel. He is dining here tonight. So are Squire, Maugham, Duff Tayler, Gertrude Jennings, & Philip Nichols. The last has just returned from Mexico and he is (I believe) rather melancholy. I cannot think who Lord Alington is. 'It' may be 'serious' on his part, but certainly won't be on yours. Dorothy's recovery entails for me a new course of hated theatre going. I've been free of it for over a month. I'm sorry to say that I've had neuralgia pains for a fortnight—all owing, I think, to the weather, which will *not* improve. [The rest of the letter is unavailable.]

[A. B.]

BODKIN / TR. / 290
(*To Thomas Bodkin*)

Amberley
Sussex
27.5.26.

My dear T. B.,

For days I've been meaning to answer your benevolent letter of the 11th. But haven't. I came down here, following Dorothy, daughter and nurse, on Friday last. And have had neuralgia almost continuously ever since. I've had it for a month in all. It has now at last gone. The daughter is A1. But I won't tell you about her hair yet—it's too soon. Please let me know in advance of your visit to London. We shall *perhaps* be still here. Not certain. If we are, either you will give a day to seeing us here, or I must come up to town. I shall be glad to hear that your book is finished. Who publishes it? You are *always* picking up some picture or other. Despite neuralgia I've written 5,000 words of my new novel in 5 days.

Dorothy sends her remembrances, and wants to see you.

All kind thoughts to Mrs. T. B.

Yours, A. B.

This house belongs to an artist. His pictures abound, and they are the filthiest you ever saw. Name of Stratton. A. B.

289. The General Strike of 1926 saw Bennett's views swing sharply to the right. On Gertrude Jennings see above, p. 183; Duff Tayler—i.e., Alistair Tayler; (Sir) Philip Nichols (1894–1962), brother of Robert, and in the Foreign Service for many years; Lord Alington—presumably Napier George Henry Sturt (1896–1940).

290. Bennett and Dorothy were in Amberley until early July. Fred Stratton was an oil and watercolour painter.

COHEN / MS. / 291
(*To Harriet Cohen*)

Amberley
29–5–26
9.20 a.m.

My sweet Tania,

All right. I have burnt it. I had an evening with Max about 10 days ago. He was most agreeable. No reference to you. There usually *is* some reference. As soon as you get back to work, thoroughly, you will recover from this fancy of yours for plutocrats. If you didn't, and it was realised, I should be acutely sorry for both you & the plutocrat, especially the latter. I am very glad that you are so happy. But platonicism, when carried on at close quarters & daily, never lasts. Although I write this in London, I am really staying at a cottage as above. I came up yesterday for a *New Statesman* Board meeting, & to see George Doran, who leaves today. He & I & H. G. Wells dined amiably together last night. I leave the house for Amberley in ten minutes. Mother & babe are in the greatest form & shall be duly hugged. The cottage is small. But landscapes and [?food] are excellent. I am working. . . . After having ascertained through her relatives & friends that my legal wife would not agree to a divorce, I wrote to her & formally asked her. She then formally refused—on the ground of her still-continuing professed affection for me! So that is that. Our relations (by correspondence) are always most amicable.

Well, continue in happiness.

All affections, & let me know when you return.

Your devoted pander, A. B.

FLOWER / MS. / 292
(*To Newman Flower*)

[Amberley]
9–6–26

My dear Newman,

Many thanks for yours of the 7th. What is the matter, in my opinion, with picture-covers is not the nature of the design but its quality. I have rarely seen one which, considered as an artistic work, was not to be disdained. I think you want a good artist. Given a good artist, I would suggest, not a picture design, but a conventionalised design (in the style of Kaufman who does the best designs for the Tube posters) or a striking pattern in bright colours. I should say that what is wanted is something to draw attention to the book, not something to illustrate it.

Thine, Arnold

FLOWER / MS. / 293
(*To Newman Flower*)

Amberley
29–6–26

My dear Newman,

Many thanks. I return the two rough sketches. I don't care much for either of them. The window-scene, even altered, really conveys nothing, & it is old-fashioned. The cubist design, though better, and more striking, is also very old-fashioned. Cubism has been old fashioned for ten years. But what I object to more than the *nature* of these designs, is their *quality*. They are (to my mind) mediocre and they quite lack distinction. The thing that I am after is real distinction of design. I think that I personally should prefer a pattern, & not a scene. Have you ever noticed the jackets of Virginia Woolf's last 2 books *The Common Reader* and *Mrs. Dalloway*? These, though on the quiet side, are in my opinion rather distinguished. Both you and I want this jacket to be striking. Much strikingness might be achieved by the mere colour of the paper. There is lots of scope for originality in jackets yet. Nearly all jackets are fundamentally alike,—& therefore serve little or no purpose!

Our friend Ernest is booming H.G.'s new novel with some skill!

I'll expect you at 1.15 at the Garrick on the 15th prox.

Yours, Arnold

292. The proposed cover was presumably for *Lord Raingo*. E. McKnight Kauffer (not Kaufman; d. 1954) did illustrations for limited editions of *Elsie and the Child* and *Venus Rising from the Sea*.

293. Sir Ernest Benn (1875–1954), chairman of the firm of Ernest Benn, published *The World of William Clissold* in the autumn.

BUTLER / MS. / 294
(*To Edward Knoblock*)

75, Cadogan Square
16–7–26

My dear Edward,

Glad to hear from you. But very sorry to have the news about your play. I understood that you had definitely sold it. But of course with these fellows nothing is certain till the contracts are exchanged.

You *must* write a novel.

I have finished my novel. And in the 7 days immediately following the finish, I not only removed to London but wrote £600 worth of articles (all sold) for the Daily Press. *Some* going! This is largely due to the exercises in *The Culture of the Abdomen*. They are *marvellous*. Thank Gertrude for me. Within a few days of starting them I began to feel different. For six weeks I have had no neuralgia. Think of it. In May I had neuralgia all day on eleven days of the month. I am also dieting (in accordance with a book entitled *Eat & Grow Thin*) to reduce my weight, & have clearly diminished myself by ½ a stone.

It is most important that I should see you soon, or get your advice, about introducing a young niece of mine (aged 19) who has a perfect passion for dressmaking, & a very marked talent for it, and a unique industry & force of character. I want to get her into some good house as a worker. Whom can you introduce me to? Not Victoire, please. My niece, which her name is Mary Kennerley, would be invaluable to any firm, even from the beginning. Also she is quite used to dressing plays for amateur performances, & she can direct other people with much authority.

As regards the Haymarket, Watson wrote me that he had complete & unfettered authority & that things would go on as usual. No reference to *Prohack*, however. I had written to condole with him.

Dorothy came back to her old flat on Wednesday. It is not suitable for her, baby, & nurse, but she must stay there a few weeks while the re-arrangements of various rooms are being made here. The baby is fine. Dorothy is not very well. Muscular pains (perhaps caused by hay-fever sneezing) and intestinal poisoning. She is in the hands of doctor & dentist. I do not think it is anything serious.

Eric Pinker has done a wise thing. He has taken Mrs. Dagnall into his office to have charge of the dramatic section thereof.

Edward, I wish thee well, but damn & blast thee for being out of London.

Dorothy can't send messages as she isn't here: but she would if she were. All respex to Gertrude.

Thine, A. B.

ARNOLD BENNETT / 295
(*To George Doran*)

[75, Cadogan Square]
5th August, 1926

[*fragment*]

. . . You do not seem to be altogether optimistic about the American sales of *Lord Raingo*. We can only pray to God and hope for the best. I am never surprised when my books do not sell and always surprised when they do sell.

As regards another novel, how many novels of mine do you want? I have just finished another one. It is in the vein of *The Grand Babylon Hotel* and *Hugo*.

I can tell you about *Lord Raingo*, that politically and medically it is impervious to criticism. The political part was carefully vetted by Beaverbrook, and the medical part was carefully vetted by my own doctor. And I will tell you another thing—unimportant perhaps, but interesting. The mutiny of German regiments at Brussels really did occur, as I have described it. But Lloyd George would not believe a word of it, and so no use was made of it.

[Arnold Bennett]

294. Bennett finished *The Strange Vanguard* on 8 July.

F. A. Hornibrook's *The Culture of The Abdomen* was published in 1924, *Eat and Grow Thin: The Mahdah Menus* in 1921.

Gertrude Knoblock, Edward's sister (d. 1964) was an artist.

On Mary Kennerley see pp. 168–9.

Horace Watson (1867–1934) took over the management of the Haymarket upon the death of Frederick Harrison. Bennett and Knoblock collaborated in the dramatization of *Mr. Prohack*. Most or all of the joint work was done in December 1924–January 1925.

Evelyn Dagnall was the widow of T. C. Dagnall, the theatrical manager. For letters to her see Vol. I.

ARKANSAS / MS. / 296
(*To Frank Swinnerton*)

75, Cadogan Square
30.8.26.

My dear Henry,

Thank you. I am now a little less pressed. Dorothy is going on all right, & the baby is fine. We leave tomorrow morning. I've read 200 pp. of *Clissold*. Formless & wordy, I agree (introductory note foolish); but so far I think the book is very good. It is full of brains, & very provocative & stimulating, & I enjoyed it. If you want to realise how positively *good Clissold* is, read a bit of *The Silver Spoon*. But I know you won't. Coward! I quite expect to be back *before* the 15th, but you shall hear from me. Unless I am not back in time, it will not be you who will give the lunch, it will most certainly be me. But you can secure Jane for me. She asked us down to E. G. for the weekend, but we couldn't go. Too busy. Venetianising ahead.

Loves from both to both.

Yours, A. B.

COHEN / MS. / 297
(*To Harriet Cohen*)

75, Cadogan Square
15–9–26

My sweet Tania,

I am just back from Venice, which I like, for a holiday, better than any other place I have ever been in—provided it is not raining. We had about 1 hour's rain in the daytime, & 2 night-rains. Marvellous weather. Dorothy was not too well; she will *not* take herself seriously [as] an early-to-bed convalescent. I left her there on Sunday morning, & reached here Monday afternoon, & on Tuesday morning had a cable that her pleurisy was not improving, then another cable to say that what she took for pleurisy symptoms were really Venetian fever symptoms. Very

296. On 12 September Bennett wrote in his *Journal*: 'I read Galsworthy's *Silver Spoon* most of the day. . . . It held me, and I thought it very good in its own limits. I think most of the press criticisms are too severe. The criticisms of Wells's *Clissold* are much too severe.'

E. G.—Easton Glebe, the Wells's home in Essex.

The Bennetts went to Italy for two weeks on 31 August. The Swinnertons went on a trip to America.

slight. She leaves Venice today for Milan, & someone will probably have to meet her somewhere; but I think Miss Nerney will go, as I have serious affairs to keep me here. I was looking forward to a complete change for a fortnight, & have nothing but worries (not grave). *Raingo* is being launched serially with terrific advertisements. *Great Adventure* is being produced in Berlin. The manager is in London. [A few lines unreadable here.] attended the 1st performance of *The Constant Nymph* last night. The first act is marvellous—an astonishing rendering of the book itself. Other acts not so good. Literature was brilliantly represented by Wells, Maugham, Galsworthy & me. Walpole also ran. I saw & had speech with the authoress, who had brought her papa, mamma, and husband. What Mamma really thought about the simply madcap fornications in her daughter's play I cannot say. But I rather liked the old lady. 'The first act is damn good', said I to Margaret over the front of her box after the 1st act. 'This is my mother', said Margaret. 'Sorry I said "Damn"', said I to mamma. Pauline's novel, *The Beadle*, is out tomorrow. My physiog is on the walls of London, horribly revolting. Max is spending £5,000 on launching the *Raingo* serial. I went with him & Jean Norton to *Blackbirds* at the Pavilion on Monday night. This is a wonderful show. Packed house. Applaudissements frénétiques. How are you, my girl? I really want to know. I sent the autograph to Master Landsberg.

Ever your devoted & affectionate A. B.

ILLINOIS / MS. / 298
(*To H. G. Wells*)

75, Cadogan Square
27–10–26

My dear H. G.,

Thy letter is most impressive & appreciated, & I am full of satisfaction therein and thank thee. I meant to unfold myself the other night about *Clissold II*. I was, as thou knowest, firmly held & much impressed by *Clissold I*. But *Clissold II* is decidedly

291. The German manager was Rudolf Kommer; see below, pp. 306–7.
Margaret Kennedy's book was dramatized by herself and Basil Dean.
Jean Norton was well-known in social-political circles. *Blackbirds* was a revue by Lew Leslie.

better. The women are very well done indeed and it is all keyed up more, livelier, more resilient than *C.I.*, which nevertheless had the qualities denoted by the above adjectives. This is an *original* novel. My novels never are.

Thine ever, A. B.

BUTLER / T.C.C. / 299
(*To Beverley Nichols*)

[75, Cadogan Square]
20th November 1926

Dear Mr. Beverley Nichols,

In reply to your letter:

1 The main details of the plot are clear in my mind before I begin. No story ought to be allowed to develop itself.

2 I begin at the beginning and go right on till the damned thing is finished.

3 I never dictate fiction. I never make a draft. I never write anything twice over.

Yours sincerely, [Arnold Bennett]

DAILY MAIL, 24 November 1926 / 300
(*To the editor*)

75, Cadogan Square
Nov. 23 [1926]

Sir,

In his interview with your representative printed today, Lord Birkenhead said:

> 'When Mr. Arnold Bennett wrote a novel called *Lord Raingo* it was widely stated—and he did not contradict it—that the principal character was modelled on a member of the Coalition Government. What right has Mr. Arnold Bennett to suggest that his imaginary puppet was modelled from an actual statesman?'

The answer to his question is that I never suggested such a thing. The character of my Lord Raingo was modelled on no statesman, and is the result of no attempt at portraiture.

I have said so in private ten thousand times, but it is not my custom to deny misstatements about my books in public. If it was, I should have to give my life to the business.

299. On Beverley Nichols see above, p. 253. Bennett did a lot of re-writing of his plays, notably *Mr. Prohack* and *Flora*, but not of his novels after *A Man from the North*, *Anna of the Five Towns*, and *The Ghost*.

As regards the deceased statesman whom doubtless Lord Birkenhead has in mind, I may say that I never had the slightest acquaintance with him.

It is apparent from his concluding remarks that the author of *Famous Trials* was for some undisclosed reason getting a bit cross. His emotion led him to the use of certain vituperative clichés. The vituperation one can excuse and enjoy; but the clichés will afflict the lettered.

Arnold Bennett

DAILY MAIL, 30 November 1926 / 301
(*To the editor*)

[75, Cadogan Square]
[29 November 1926]

[no salutation]

I said in my letter to the Editor of the *Daily Mail* published on Tuesday:

'The character of Lord Raingo was modelled upon no statesman and is the result of no attempt at portraiture.'

And I will now say further that so far as I know there is in the whole of my novel only one unusual incident which is related to fact.

Lord Birkenhead replies: 'I do not accept his assurance.'

Possibly not. It would be inconvenient for Lord Birkenhead to do so. With characteristic impulsiveness he got himself into an impossible position, and to refuse to accept my assurance was his only way out of it.

300. In an interview published in the *Daily Mail* on 23 November, Lord Birkenhead (F. E. Smith, 1872–1930) commented on the recent publication of scandalous memoirs, and he took some note of the political novels of Bennett and Wells. At the end of the interview he said: 'I make my profound objection to the reproduction in books of private, or alleged private, conversations, to the dissemination of lying slanders about living and dead statesmen, and to the overweening conceit of novelists, puffed out by the advertisements of the publishers of their imaginative efforts, as arbiters of public men's actions and characters.' Serial publication of *Lord Raingo* had been advertised by large posters which asked the question 'Who is Lord Raingo?', and the novel itself portrays political England in the last years of the war. As Louis Tillier has shown in *Studies in the Sources of Arnold Bennett's Novels*, considerable detail about Lord Raingo's life was drawn from information that Beaverbrook gave to Bennett about Lord Rhondda (D. A. Thomas, 1856–1918). Other detail came from other sources, and Raingo is doubtless more nearly a portrait of Bennett himself than of anyone else.

The controversy ought properly to end here. But Lord Birkenhead goes on to make more misstatements and also to ask me several plain questions. I will stretch a point to answer his questions and to correct his misstatements.

He says: 'I cannot directly prove him wrong—as otherwise I very easily could—because to do so would be to repeat his offence.'

This is not so. He could not prove me wrong. Even if both of us were at liberty to mention names and to write freely, he could not prove me wrong; but I could prove myself right.

He says: 'Messrs. Cassells say: "Set in the period of the late war, this story centres round a number of Cabinet Ministers and other prominent politicians, Samuel Raingo (a millionaire, afterwards made a peer) being the principal figure."'

This statement as to my novel is perfectly accurate. My novel is chiefly about a number of Cabinet Ministers and about one in particular. How else should the novel have been described? As a story about tinkers?

He says further: 'The *Evening Standard* in an editorial article said (and they should have known, for they were Mr. Bennett's employers): "A leading reviewer who has read the novel has declared that the central character may easily be identified." Mr. Bennett has refused to express agreement or disagreement.'

'A leading reviewer' may well have made the remark attributed to him.

I may point out in passing that the *Evening Standard* were not my 'employers', any more than Lord Birkenhead would be the employer of the department store from whom he might buy a safety razor. Lord Birkenhead should really give attention to the meaning of words. Nor, even, did I sell *Lord Raingo* to the *Evening Standard*. Until the *Evening Standard* had decided to buy the serial rights of the novel I was unaware that the serial rights (which I had sold long before to a great firm of magazine publishers) were in the market.

Lord Birkenhead quotes further a statement from the *Daily Express*: 'The book is the story of the life of an ex-Cabinet Minister holding office during the late years of the war. The woman in the case was well known at one time in the popular dining-rooms and the fashionable dancing clubs, which she visited nearly every night.'

And as to this, he invites me to answer four questions:

(1) Did he see it when it appeared?

The answer is Yes.

(2) If he did, knowing it to be untrue, why did he not contradict it?

The answer is that Lord Birkenhead should read again my previous letter.

(3) Did he perhaps think that this kind of scandalous suggestion about his forthcoming book (for he has told us now that it was scandalous) would increase its circulation; and did this consideration lead him to remain silent?

The answer is No. (Incidentally, I have not said that the suggestion was scandalous.)

(4) How could he, on any other conceivable view, as a conscientious artist have remained silent?

The answer is that my duties as a conscientious artist are confined to my work in my book. It is not my business, and I should conceive it as an impertinence, to attempt to teach the conductors of some of the most brilliant newspapers in this country how they ought to run those newspapers and how they ought to deal with their own goods.

I am glad to note that in his second communication Lord Birkenhead has thought well to modify the polemical excesses of his first. Only my warm personal regard for him induced me to answer his first communication at all. I must, however, animadvert upon his continuing innuendoes about pecuniary advantage. The tu quoque to the author of *Famous Trials* and of numberless journalistic articles would be too easy, and might be too devastating. The imputation of unworthy motives rarely helps an argument and nearly always weakens it.

[Arnold Bennett]

BEAVERBROOK / TS. / 302
(*To Lord Beaverbrook*)

75, Cadogan Square
3rd December 1926

My dear Max,

Many thanks. Since you suggest that I should suggest alterations, I return the memo with certain alterations suggested.

But I have no objection to the memo being printed as you wrote it.

I met Birkenhead last night at the Other Club. He was extremely friendly. So was I. He said, as I was leaving: 'I knew you would not take offence, my dear fellow.' Masterman was very cynical about the affair. He said the *Mail* had either insisted with a pistol that Birkenhead should start the stunt, or that they had paid him. I replied that they certainly paid me—something over £100. I do not see that I could have done otherwise than I did. Birkenhead said one true thing last night: 'I thought this was one of the controversies that ought to be closed, so I did not reply any further.' That was what he did think.

Thine, Arnold

BEAVERBROOK / TS. / 303
(*To Lord Beaverbrook*)

75, Cadogan Square
10th December 1926

My dear Max,

Thank you for your letter of yesterday.

The history of the affair is as follows:

I first suggested to you about a year ago, when you told me that you intended to enlarge the *E.S.*, that I should write book articles *under a pseudonym*.

On the 9th December 1925 you wrote to me thus:

> 'I also mentioned to Thompson our conversation about a weekly article on books. He says he would be glad to take the

302. The memo was a private one drawn up by Beaverbrook, and it recorded that some days before he wrote his article, Birkenhead asked Beaverbrook if Raingo was a portrait of himself, Birkenhead.

On 25 November the *Mail* published an article by Bennett that made some of the same points as his letter of the 29th; and after he wrote the letter of the 29th, in response to a second attack by Birkenhead in the *Mail* on that day, he learned from Miss Nerney that the *Mail* wanted a second article instead, 'so I crossed out the Sir, and Yours truly, and called it an article and charged £60 for it' (*Journal*). On the next day he noted: 'When I opened the *Daily Mail* this morning I found that Birkenhead had made no further answer to me; so the incident is now, I suppose, closed. The press has been very generally in my favour. I had prepared some heavy artillery to kill him if he had continued the fight.' The article of the 25th is reprinted in the collection *The Savour of Life*. Bennett adds some further remarks in his introductory note to that book.

article over your signature and would pay "Arnold Bennett" rates. If the article is to be anonymous, he loses all the benefit of your name. In such circumstances, he would pay the rates you would expect him to pay to W. J. Locke.'

I replied saying that we need not discuss terms as I had offered you the anonymous articles for nothing, and that we would leave the matter to Thompson.

The matter then fell into abeyance for a long time. When I was at Cherkley in the autumn you asked me to write articles under my own name. I said I would think it over.

When you came to this house for lunch, I told you that I had thought it over and that I would write articles under my own name.

Nothing was said by either you or me about payment, and I did not think that anything had to be said, in view of the explicit statement in your letter of the 9th December 1925 as to what Thompson had said about payment.

We are going away on December 29th for about six weeks, to Cortina. During my absence I am relying on God to watch over you.

Thine, Arnold

P.S. I avoided the big Asquith banquet at the Reform Club last night, only to meet Guthrie, Violet and Bonham Carter at dinner! A. B.

BEAVERBROOK / TS. / 304
(*To Lord Beaverbrook*)

75, Cadogan Square
16th December 1926

My dear Max,

Sorry to hear that you have been filled up with anxiety.

The rate of 1/6d a word will be quite satisfactory to me. It has always been the *Standard* and *Express* rate for me. I have no

303. Edward Raymond Thompson (1872–1928) was editor of the *Evening Standard*.

On Asquith see above, p. 34. Lady Violet Bonham Carter (1887–1969), his daughter, wife of Sir Maurice Bonham Carter (1880–1960), for some years Asquith's private secretary. Guthrie is unidentified.

The Bennetts did not go to Cortina until late January.

quarrel with it. But I do not want anybody round your way to go and talk about it, because all other papers pay me 33⅓rd per cent more.

Thine ever, Arnold

BODKIN / TR. / 305
(*To Thomas Bodkin*)

75, Cadogan Square
25.12.26.

My dear T. B.,

The stuff arrived duly this morning. What I appreciate quite as much as the mats is the Xmas Card which is perfect dans son genre. I am very greatly obliged. The mats will be on the dining table. They fit it. Dorothy is not permitted to have opinions re dust traps. All our good wishes go with this to you both. I wish I gave Xmas presents. But I never do—except cheques to my family. And I'm too old to change. Never mind, my heart is in the right place.

Ever yours, A. B.

BODKIN / TR. / 306
(*To Thomas Bodkin*)

Hotel Savoy
Cortina d'Ampezzo
(Belluno)
Italy
29.1.27

My dear T. B.,

What a pity! We are touched by your attention and your invitation. But it took us 4 days to get here, with terrible privations en route. So we remain here for the present! 4,200 ft. up. Billions of tons of snow. Continuous sunshine throughout the day. The Aldous Huxleys are here. Very agreeable companions. If I were you I should tell your publisher to go to hell, and refuse to make a single alteration in the book. I liked the Flemish affair, but of course it is all the same old business over again. Ever since I saw the Breughel landscapes in the Doria

304. The rate worked out at £3,750 a year, and the series began on 18 November and continued until Bennett's death. It bore the same title, 'Books and Persons', as his *New Age* column of 1908–11, and was equally successful.

Palace at Rome last year I have thought him a great landscape (or sea-scape rather) painter. I was sitting in front of 2 of his seascapes at the R.A. when Laurence Binyon came up to me and without preliminary notice exclaimed: 'Don't you think these are the most enchanting things in the world!'

All messages from Dorothy to you, and from me to you both.

Yours, A. B.

KING'S / T.C.C. / 307
(To Edward Garnett)

[75, Cadogan Square]
7th March 1927

Dear Edward Garnett,

I have not been able to reply earlier to your letter of the 16th February. I only returned home last night after an absence of six weeks.

I have never thought very well of the work of Bunin. I say this with the greatest respect for your opinion, and I admit that you are much more likely to be right than I am. *A Gentleman from San Francisco* I thought very crude indeed, and I could not get on with *The Village*. I was, however, talking to André Gide the other night, and he thought well of Bunin, especially *The Village*.

All this is beside the point. If you wish Bunin to be helped, he must be helped. I enclose my cheque for £5 towards the enterprise. This is all I can do.

Yours sincerely, [Arnold Bennett]

TEXAS / MS. / 308
(To Maurice Baring)

75, Cadogan Square
27–3–27

My dear Maurice,

. . . I should have acknowledged your letter earlier but I've been blasted busy on my return home. What people don't understand, though I expressly pointed it out, is that I don't

306. The Bennetts were in Italy and France until early March.

Laurence Binyon (1869–1943), poet and art critic.

307. For earlier letters to Edward Garnett see Vol. II. Ivan Alexeyevich Bunin (1870–1953) won the Nobel Prize for literature in 1933. At this time he was living destitute in Paris.

really believe there *are* 12 best novels. Indeed the idea is absurd. I was only writing 'in a manner of speaking'. But I don't agree with you as to Dickens. And I would read Stendhal anywhere. I only heard the other day that Jim Atkins was dead. What a disaster!

Thine, A. B.

COHEN / MS. / 309
(*To Harriet Cohen*)

75, Cadogan Square
27-3-27

My sweet Tania,

We were charmed to get your letter. Sorry to hear of 3 flu's, & alarmed by the news of your liaisons & the fickleness of your heart. I should have liked to go to Algiers & Tunis. I went through all Algeria 24 years ago, when travelling was not so good as it is now. Never to Tunis. We've been to Innsbruck, Cortina (3 weeks), Milan, & Paris. Cortina was fine. Dorothy did much ski-ing. Weather magnif. Paris was most exhausting, & French plays poorer than ever. Dorothy has just arisen from a week in bed. She had to have an operation for hemorrhoids, last Sunday. This affair has been hanging over her for a long time. Cecil Burnham, the surgeon. Admirable, shabbily dressed man. I am working, & a bit harder than ever, so as to feel more free to go for a month's cruise to the Aegean, Athens, Crete, Smyrna, Dalmatian coast, Venice, etc. with Otto Kahn, in the big yacht 'Flying Cloud', which Otto has hired from his Grace of Westminster. An exclusively male party. Otto says that when women are about men are always stupid. How true! Dorothy has persuaded me to buy a car. It is a Rolls Royce, second hand, but re-conditioned & done up. We expect to get hold of it Saturday next, & Dorothy is extremely excited about it. To me, who have had a truly great car (Lanchester) many years since,

308. In the *Evening Standard* on 17 March Bennett observed that the twelve finest novels are all Russian. Start to count them: *The Brothers Karamazov*, *Crime and Punishment*, *The Idiot*, *The House of the Dead*, *Anna Karenina*, *War and Peace*, *Resurrection*—there are seven already that it would be impossible to leave out of anyone's list; and the only author whose work you might dream of substituting is Stendhal. But then you have to reckon with *Torrents of Spring*, *Virgin Soil*, *On the Eve*, *Fathers and Sons*, and *Dead Souls*. 'That makes twelve', says Bennett. See Vol. II for some adverse comments on Dickens. Baring preferred Dickens to Stendhal.

Jim Atkins was the son of Bennett's friend J. B. Atkins (see p. 101 n.).

it is less thrilling. The infant Virginia is in the finest form, and indeed quite grown up. Six teeth! Can say 'dada' like hell! At present we have 2 nurses in the house, hers, and Dorothy's. G.B.S. & Charlotte are coming to lunch Thursday next. Dorothy has him in tow. He never takes his eyes off her. You had better look out. So had Charlotte. So had I. There is one play playing which you would *love*: *Broadway*. Not much else. I have written ⅔rds of a new novel, later than the one which begins serially in the new *Pall Mall Magazine* at Easter. We lunched with Max a week ago yesterday, & studied the plans of his grand new yacht. Our fondest loves, my dear. Dorothy kisses you. Me too! Your devoted

A. B.

CALIF / MS. / 310
(*To Adelaide Phillpotts*)

75, Cadogan Square
28–iii–27

My sweet niece,

Be not vexed that I have only just read *Akhnaton*. Of late months I have had so much in the way of absolutely imperative perusal that I've got frightfully behind. I am still six behind with friends' books. I think *Akhnaton* is a fine scheme for a play, well structured, and *very* effective in the biggest scenes. It has that fundamental 'nobility' which I found in the previous play of yours that I read, & it is vastly better done than that other one. I like the verse less than the play itself. You have, like Shakespeare, written scenes of the play in prose, & personally I would sooner have had it all in prose. Well, no! I think the last scene & the epilogue are better as they are. You previously had the gift of great ideas for drama. Then you acquired technique in construction. What I now desire in you, sweet niece, is

309. Cecil Burnham (1887–1965), later consulting surgeon to the Star and Garter Home, Richmond.

The cruise with Otto Kahn (1867–1934), the American banker, lasted from mid-April until late May.

Charlotte Shaw (d. 1943).

Broadway, by Phillip Dunning and George Abbott, was having a long run at the Strand Theatre.

The Strange Vanguard began appearing in the *Pall Mall Magazine* in May.

a more distinguished style. Yes, I do. Damn it, you have the decency to tell me what you really think of my work; so why shouldn't I have the decency to tell you what I really think of yours?

Your characterisation, I think, shows much progress.

Dorothy sends affectionate greetings.

I know you *hate* going out, for you told me so at Eltham. Still, perhaps you might call one day.

Your devoted uncle, A. B.

BODKIN / TR. / 311
(*To Thomas Bodkin*)

75, Cadogan Square
9.iv.27

My dear T. B.,

Charmed to hear from you. I had already got a copy of *The Approach*: I think it was very nice of you to give yours to Dorothy, who was much flattered by the attention. I haven't read & cannot yet read *The Approach*, because I'm engaged in the theory of Relativity, for the purposes of an article in the *Standard*. This, with my 'tasting' of books for the said paper, & my own private reading, just about fills me up. Books now come into this house in stacks, & most of them I don't look at. Don't because can't. Also I've been writing hard. 115,000 words this year. On Good Friday I'm going yachting in the Eastern Mediterranean (with Otto Khan), but I have to go to Sicily by train in order to join the yacht. Dorothy isn't going. She has been indisposed, but is all right again—if only she won't be too energetic for a few weeks. Virginia is cutting teeth all over her mouth, & yet is in the greatest form. Personally, I have never had such good health as now. I've abandoned all my old suits, which hung around me in folds, & go about arrayed much more slimly. I say, this will be fine about the National Gallery, although the salary is inadequate. I hope the job won't cramp you as a collector. I hope to be here in June. In fact, I must be. I saw a Hondecoeter birdpiece the other day. I wanted it for an American friend, who loved it but finally refused it because it

310. Adelaide Phillpotts, daughter of Eden Phillpotts, published *Akhnaton* in 1926.

had a peacock in it, & his aged mother thinks peacocks are unlucky. What a country! They asked £50 & they were ready to take £25. But I didn't keep it for myself. Dorothy & Virginia salute you affectionately, & we reciprocate the kind messages of your wife.

Yours, A. B.

GALLUP / T.C.C. / 312
(*To T. S. Eliot*)

[75, Cadogan Square]
June 3rd 1927

My dear Eliot,

I have not acknowledged your letter of the 30th April earlier for the reason that I have been out of England without an address until last night. I should very much like to see you. I have often wondered what happened to that Jazz play.

I am sorry that you did not send the letter to the *Standard* as it is full of sense. I am afraid that the time for its insertion has now passed. I did not learn until after the article was delivered that the *Criterion* was to be turned into a monthly. The news is good. If I get a chance to refer to the *Criterion* soon, I will mention the points in your unpublished letter. I would like to send you a contribution, but I am really afraid of doing so. I should have to take so much care over it! My articles, especially those about books, are rather slapdash. I am also handicapped by an intense ignorance. Indeed my life-long regret is that I have no exact knowledge on any subject on earth. I always envy scholars.

Come and see me, will you?

Yours sincerely, [Arnold Bennett]

311. 'Einstein for the Tired' appeared in the *Evening Standard* on 21 April 1927, and was reprinted in *The Savour of Life*. Bennett disagreed with Einstein on the theory of curved space.

Bodkin became Director of the National Gallery of Ireland in 1927.

The picture by Melchior de Hondecoeter (1636–95) was for Messmore Kendall (see pp. 7–8). Bennett used the episode in his story 'The Peacock' (*The Night Visitor*).

312. Part of T. S. Eliot's jazz play (*Wanna Go Home, Baby?*) appears in the *Complete Poems and Plays* as *Sweeney Agonistes*. A portion of it appeared in the *Criterion* in January 1927. The *Criterion* eventually published some extracts from Bennett's journal. For other references to the *Criterion* see Vol. I.

BUTLER / TS. / 313
(*To Edward Knoblock*)

75, Cadogan Square
14th June 1927

My dear Edward,

Charmed to have your cable with the news that we shall soon see you. Or that you 'hope' we shall soon see you. It is time you returned. Believe me, we had a great cruise in that yacht, and all the members of the party were very agreeable and easy to get on with. I wish that you had been there. During the voyage I wrote a whole (little) book about the voyage. While other people were playing bridge.

I am in full work and very well. So is Dorothy. Virginia blooms. I trust that things are going excellently with you.

Our loves, Yours ever, A. B.

GALLUP / T.C. / 314
(*To T. S. Eliot*)

[Royal Victoria Hotel]
[St. Leonard's-on-Sea]
1.9.27

My dear Eliot,

Many thanks for the brochure. Yes, I am studying it, and am grateful.

I have just written an introduction to a posthumous work of George Sturt's (who generally wrote under the name of George Bourne—very good, I mean really). In order to write it I read through all the letters I received from him in the course of about 28 years. These letters are almost exclusively given to the craft of literature, and many of them are highly interesting. In fact, fine reading. I think I could later on arrange to select and edit 5 or 10 thousand words from them for you to print in the Heart-Cri, if you choose. This is only a suggestion.

Yours sincerely, [Arnold Bennett]

P.S. I'll send you the introduction to read if you like, when I have a proof of it.

313. Cassells issued *Mediterranean Scenes* in November 1928.

314. The Bennetts were on holiday at St. Leonard's-on-Sea from 28 July to 4 September.

BERG / TS. / 315
(*To G. T. Bagguley*)

75, Cadogan Square
5th September 1927

Dear Mr. Bagguley,

I am now exercised about my diary for next year. The present one, which you have bound, is rather too big for travelling. What I should like is one bound in four volumes, quarto size, limp binding. But I do not know where to get a satisfactory diary for you to work on. Practically, all those I have seen are on rather poor paper, with bad letter-press at the top of the page, etc., etc. Also the cash lines are generally printed so close to the binding edge of the page that you cannot use the pence line comfortably. All this is very distressing, and I have been wondering whether you could give me any advice and help. I must have a page to a day. On the whole I prefer an unruled page, but I do not absolutely object to a ruled page.

The matter is, to me, somewhat important.

The MS of *The Old Wives' Tale* is being reproduced in facsimile in a limited edition by Benn Ltd. When their manager happened to see the original MS, he at once insisted that he must be allowed to reproduce it. The reproduction is pretty good, I think. There can be no doubt that that MS has caused an immense stir among people who are interested in that sort of thing, and I have come to the conclusion that it ought to be rebound. I should like to know whether you have any ideas on this subject, and what the approximate cost of executing them would be. It is in 2 volumes.

Kind regards,

Yours sincerely, Arnold Bennett

George Sturt died on 4 February 1927, and later in the year *A Small Boy in the Sixties* was published with an introduction by Bennett. Almost all the letters known to survive from Bennett to Sturt are printed in Vol. II, along with several from Sturt. No letters on Bennett's side are known from the years after 1907, though the two men wrote to each other until 1922. In 1916 Sturt had a stroke, and in 1920 a second one. In his last letter to Bennett he said: 'I can scarcely move across the room now . . . and an hour's chatter reduces me to mumbling. But I giggle a good deal; keep cheerful; and am enjoying life intensely.' In the thirties, when Bennett himself was dead and his fame sinking low, one or two of Sturt's books began to acquire the status of minor classics. Eliot did not publish any of his letters, but a few of them appeared in the *Countryman* in 1934–5.

315. In one margin of his journal Bennett kept account of his daily expenses, in

BODKIN / TR. / 316
(*To Thomas Bodkin*)

75, Cadogan Square
21st September 1927

My dear T. B.,

Are you in the Dail? If you are not too busy you might perhaps do me a very great favour and write, as roughly and disconnectedly and disorderly as you like, some information about Irish affairs. Real truths about the election. Character sketches of the principal actors therein. Who are the *real* principal actors therein? Anything that is of interest to you. I want the stuff for an article which I am going to write about the state of the world generally. You may divine that any stuff you gave me would be used with a certain discretion.

If you feel you have no time to be worried by the importunities of a journalist, don't be.

All greetings to you both. . . .

Yours, A. B.

S.A. / TS. / 317
(*To G. Herbert Thring*)

75, Cadogan Square
8th October 1927

Dear Mr. Thring,

I have demanded contributions for charities from certain firms who have asked permission to use a short article of mine for commercial purposes. I have received the sum of £25 in all. I enclose my cheque for this amount, and shall be glad if you will allot it to whatever part, or parts, of the Authors' Society's charitable work you think best.

Yours sincerely, Arnold Bennett

---

the other of his daily production of words. On the facsimile edition of *The Old Wives' Tale* see Vol. I. The firm of Ernest Benn, whose manager was (Sir) Victor Gollancz (1893–1967), published it in 1927. The title page of the second volume of the manuscript is reproduced in Vol. II.

316. In 1927 Bennett became Associate Editor of *World Today*, and for eight months wrote an article on 'Men and Events'. In the issue of April 1928 appears a column on Irish affairs.

317. G. Herbert Thring (1859–1941) was Secretary of the Society of Authors.

YALE / T.C.C. / 318
(*To Louis Golding*)

[75, Cadogan Square]
14th October 1927

Dear Mr. Louis Golding,

Thank you. You surely need no introduction to me. I received your book some time ago, from the publishers.

My life is made terrible by my *Evening Standard* article. When I took the job on it was clearly understood that I should be absolutely free to review or not to review, just as I chose. I cannot read all the books which I ought to read, nor even 10% of them. Often I am so puzzled how to be fair that I ignore a whole lot of books and write about some general subject. It is a way out.

I shall be delighted to see you. I am odiously busy, trying to look after the production of two plays at once, write a monthly review of the world, and indulge my natural idleness, so that I have to suggest odd times for appointments. Can you possibly come on Sunday next about 6.30? If not, I will suggest another date, or you will.

Yours sincerely, Arnold Bennett

BEAVERBROOK / T.C. / 319
(*To Lord Beaverbrook*)

[75, Cadogan Square]
Nov. 5, 1927

My dear Max,

I took Charlie out for a drive this afternoon. Before starting his wife said to me 'He is in a very queer state, don't take any notice of what he says'.

He said

He has only £200 in the world.

His memory is gone. He cannot even read much less write.

His father was insane, and he himself is going mad.

He cannot sleep.

His wife is worn out.

Bottomley is bringing a libel action against him which he

318. Louis Golding (1895–1958), author and lecturer, published *Day of Atonement* earlier in the year. Bennett's play *Flora*, written in March 1925, opened in Manchester on 19 October. *Mr. Prohack* opened at the Court on 16 November.

cannot defend. He will have to go bankrupt. He will be morally ruined as well. No newspaper will ever buy another article of his.

He and his family will starve.

No use trying to comfort him as like all people in his case he loves his despair more than anything.

He would not admit that physically he was better but I think he is a bit better. Anyhow he has lost 3 stone.

I said that he would not starve and I would give him money. I also said I would get your views about the whole situation. I suppose that something ought to be done.

Yours, Arnold

U.C. / T.C.C. / 320
(*To Roger Fry*)

[75, Cadogan Square]
5th November 1927

Dear Roger Fry,

You know everything. May I ask you to advise me, without taking undue advantage of your good nature? I have written a small and quite unpretentious book of travel in Greece and the Greek Isles, and I want to get some decent photographic illustrations for the same. I have some photographs of archaic sculpture from the Acropolis Museum. Can you tell me where I can get *good* photographs of scenes and sites and such places as Mycenae, Milo, Delos, Corfu, Argos, Ithaca, Crete, Sparta, —in fact all round about? I never saw any really good ones while I was away. Nor do I know a good photograph shop in London.

But the following is more important in my mind. I thought of having some reproductions of pictures of idealised classical life. Such as Poussins. Are there any others? If so, where are the best photographs to be had in this city?

I have no right to worry you. But I fear that I pass my life exceeding my rights.

Always yours sincerely, [Arnold Bennett]

319. Charles Masterman died later in the month. The obituary notice in *The Times* spoke of heart failure following internal complications. Horatio Bottomley (see above, p. 56) was a long-time enemy of Masterman's.

320. Leigh Ashton of the Victoria and Albert Museum supplied some of the photographs for *Mediterranean Scenes* and advised on others.

ARKANSAS / TS. / 321
(*To Frank Swinnerton*)

75, Cadogan Square
10th November 1927

My dear Henry,

Thank you. I will be at the Reform on Wednesday for lunch. Till then I shall be having a warm time.

Hughie was here yesterday. He is going to have all his teeth out on Wednesday, and my first night is on Wednesday. He said: 'Arnold, you think of me on Wednesday morning and I will think of you on Wednesday evening. Just give me a thought. Just let us give each other a thought.'

Loves.

Thine, A. B.

ROCHESTER / T.C.C. / 322
(*To Edward Knoblock*)

[75, Cadogan Square]
17th November 1927

My dear Edward,

Here are a few random notes on the production of *Mr. Prohack*.

I was not at the first performance. I got there just as the curtain was falling. There were six curtains and everybody seemed very pleased. Laughton had a great triumph as Mr. Prohack, after being very bad and wrong at all the later rehearsals. I learnt that the second act did not go well. I think that this was rather the fault of the production than of the play. The third act undoubtedly went very well indeed. All the playing was good, except Scott Sunderland's. He is a very stiff actor, but he can be heard and understood. Mr. Sidney Bernstein (the film man) one of our directors, had not cared much for the play when he read it, but he was positively enthusiastic about it when he saw it performed. There were, I am told, very many laughs throughout the play, which all got over except bits in the second act. The advance booking so far (4 p.m. Thursday) is very bad, but I do not see how it can be anything else. I think that the play will take some time to reach the public consciousness, but I think that it will succeed in doing so. Anyhow we shall keep it on for the present whatever happens to the returns.

The set of the first act is one of the most charming things you ever saw. Komi shows the hall as well as the dining room, and the hall effect of 'callers' going in and out is obtained in a perfect home-like manner. The set of the third act had to be altered at the last moment, as I objected to it. Though beautiful it was rather too restless in its profusion of ornament and glitter, and would have completely distracted the attention of the audience from the players.

One or two of the morning notices were bad, especially that of *The Times*, but some of the others were decidedly good, and the rest decent.

The notices in the three evening papers are all admirable. The *Star* says (speaking of Laughton's work as Prohack): 'In the dazzlement of this fine, humorous and genial piece of work every other effort seemed lessened, but it would be very unfair not to praise the excellent work of Carl Harbord, Hilda Sims and Dorothy Cheston.' Some good notices of Dorothy.

As a fact Laughton got away with all the notices. I am told that he was made up to look like me and that he copies some of my gestures etc. Whether this is true or not I do not know. It is in nearly all the papers. He took care not to do this at rehearsals.

I have seen Sidney Howard and like him. As for Clare Eames, she is a friend of mine now.

When the devil are you coming back to London?

Dorothy sends her best love.

Thine, [A. B.]

ILLINOIS / MS. / 323
(*To H. G. Wells*)

75, Cadogan Square
22.11.27

My dear H.G.,

A week or two before he died, Charlie Masterman wrote a pencil memorandum (I've seen it) in which he suggested that

322. Charles Laughton (1899–1962), beginning a notable career; Scott Sunderland (b. 1883), associated for some years with the Birmingham Repertory Theatre; Sidney Bernstein (1899–), theatre, film, and television producer; Komi—Theodore Komisarjevsky, see p. 234; Carl Harbord, an actor active in the twenties and thirties; Hilda Sims—not otherwise known; Sidney Howard (1891–1939), the American playwright; Clare Eames (1896–1930), Howard's wife.

in case of death or insanity certain of his friends (you among them) might be asked to consider the question of the education of his children. There are three children: Margaret 17, Neville 15, & Dorothy 13. First two said to have much talent.

A close connection of the family's, Reginald Bray (son of late Lord Bray) with a reputation for practical sagacity and knowledge of affairs, has gone into the matter, & he estimates that if about £4,000 were raised now, it would suffice to finish the education of all three children in the manner Charlie strongly desired. The fund would be put into an ad hoc trust.

Do you feel like contributing? There are 8 or 10 names.

Mrs. Masterman will have just enough to live on (about £350 p.a., it is hoped) provided she earns something by her pen, as she will.

I've had a long talk with her.

Hommages à Madame, Yours, A. B.

BERG / MS. / 324
(*To Richmond Temple*)

75, Cadogan Square
23.11.27

My dear Richmond,

I hear with regret that you are much hurt by an alleged caricature of yourself in a play which you have not seen.

There is no caricature, or any sort of portrait, of yourself in the play. The character of Morfey is taken from the book. I admit that his profession would not have been what it is in the play if I had not heard of that profession from yourself, who happen to be the chief exponent of it, so far as I know. Still, as the profession exists, it cannot be barred from imaginative literature. In my judgment no offence whatever can be found in the play. Morfey is even a more sympathetic person in the play than in the book. He comes out on top every time, & gives

323. Lucy Masterman edited the diaries of Mary Drew (Mary Gladstone) in 1930, wrote a biography of her husband (1939), and wrote *London from the Bus-Top* (1951). Earlier she did some of the journalistic writing that was published under her husband's name. Sir Reginald Bray died in 1923; the son is not otherwise known. Wells contributed £50 to the fund.

'Madame' is Odette Keun (?1900–), the authoress, friend of Wells. Jane Wells died in October 1927.

a lesson in manners to the Prohacks every time. He is beautifully played by Frederick Cooper. The person or persons who have given you to understand that there *is* offence are not only misleading but malicious. I am very cross with them & would cheerfully break their heads, & I don't care who they are.

So far as I am concerned, their proceedings are a matter of indifference; but I do strongly resent mischief-making between you & me. You know my feelings for you. Those feelings have not altered. The notion that I was putting a portrait or caricature in the play only occurred to me when I saw some reference to it by that ass Swaffer in Sunday's *Express*! I have never mentioned, & hardly thought of, your name in connection with the character. I don't think I need say any more, except to suggest that you see the play and judge for yourself.

Yours, Arnold B.

BUTLER / TS. / 325
(*To Edward Knoblock*)

75, Cadogan Square
2nd December 1927

My dear Edward,

The theatrical season is supposed to be rather bad (it always is). However, the Court is doing pretty well. The play is being very much talked about and the returns, on the small scale of the Court, are sound. We paid off more than £100 last week of the cost of production. And this week we shall pay off at least £150. The total cost of production is about £500. This has nothing to do with the authors, but I thought that it might interest you. House full boards out last Saturday. The reception of the play is enthusiastic every night. Dorothy had pharyngitis yesterday and could not play, but there was an excellent understudy. I went to see how she got through and was extremely pleased with her.

The trouble is that we have only got the Court until January

324. In *Mr. Prohack* Oswald Morfey is the publicity agent for the Grand Babylon Hotel, as Temple was publicity agent for the Savoy group of hotels. Bennett describes Morfey as 'nervous, mincing, intelligent; very much groomed, eyeglass, gardenia, and all'. The friendship between Bennett and Temple was not restored by this letter. Frederick Cooper (1890–1945) also played in the dramatization of *Riceyman Steps* in 1926. On Hannen Swaffer see pp. 337–9.

6th, and that then, if my hopes are fulfilled, it will be necessary to transfer. I am told that there will be no difficulty whatever about this, but I am not sure. Jackson will not let us have the theatre after January 6th, as instead of getting his rent safely from us, he prefers to pay it himself and to lose money on one of his own productions! I am bound to say that he is an exceedingly nice fellow.

Laughton as Prohack has been praised to the skies by the entire press, and in my opinion over-praised considerably. I think his performance is rough, and it certainly is not a faithful representation of Prohack as we conceived him for the purposes of the play.

When the devil are you coming home?

Dorothy sends her love,

Thine, A. B.

CALIF / T.C.C. / 326
(To J. B. Priestley)

[75, Cadogan Square]
28th December 1927

Dear Mr. Priestley,

I have read your novel, and as you were kind enough to send it to me, I hope you will not mind me giving my opinion of it.

I certainly think it is a much better book than *Adam in Moonshine*, which appeared to me to be not the work of a novelist. *Benighted* seems to me to be the work of a novelist. It strikes me as having an original plot and atmosphere which are both very fully and adequately exploited—except at the end, which seems unsatisfactory, or rather uncompleted. There is a lot of new observation about the relations of men and women—what I believe is called psychology. I still think that there is too much fancy in your fiction, but this time imagination is present in abundance and in good quality. My only other objection is that nearly all the characters seem not only to talk in your own idiom but to possess your particular brand of fancifulness. The

325. Sir Barry Jackson (1879–1961) took over the Court Theatre in 1924. Bennett was unable to get the play transferred, and it had to close. See Vol. I, pp. 366–8, for other details.

state of affairs between Philip and Margaret is admirably rendered.

I feel after all that in writing you my opinions about a good book in this way I am guilty of butting in. Please excuse me.

Yours sincerely, [Arnold Bennett]

P.S. Hugh Walpole promises to bring you to see me. But apparently he has not done so.

DAILY EXPRESS, 17 January 1928 / 327
(*To the Editor*)

75, Cadogan Square
[15 or 16 January 1928]

Sir,

The arrangements for the funeral service of Thomas Hardy in Westminster Abbey seem to deserve examination. It was stated: 'No tickets will be issued by the Abbey authorities.'

On inquiry, I found that all invitations, other than those sent privately by Hardy's family or its representatives, were absolutely in the hands of Hardy's publishers, Messrs. Macmillan and Co.

I have no personal complaint against Messrs. Macmillan and Co., who, on my request, courteously sent me a ticket for Poet's Corner; and I am sure that they issued invitations to the best of their ability and with a full desire to be fair to all parties concerned.

Thomas Hardy was a professional author. So far as I know there is only one important association of professional authors, namely, the Society of Authors. It has a very large membership, which includes practically all authors of any repute in this country. The names on its general council enjoy a literary prestige which no other collection of British names could approach.

It has acquired an official position, and watches over the interests of authors not only with the Legislature but in foreign countries. In a word, it stands for modern authorship. Incidentally, Thomas Hardy was its president.

326. *Adam in Moonshine* and *Benighted* both appeared in 1927.

Only two tickets were issued to the Society, one for its chairman and the other for its secretary. It had no influence in the distribution of tickets, and was obliged to refer applicants to Messrs. Macmillan and Co. Thus many authors who would have wished to be present at the funeral, and who had a moral right to be present, could not be present.

In my opinion (which, like this communication, is completely unofficial) a certain number of tickets ought to have been confided to the principal, if not the only, association of Hardy's professional contemporaries, for allotment among its members. I consider that the Society should have had precedence over all other bodies, local or general.

There was, however, no need to enter into questions of precedence. The south transept would comfortably have held a hundred more people than were shown into it; and thus nobody would have been inconvenienced if twenty-five tickets had been placed at the disposition of the Society of Authors.

Further, it appears to me that the Dean and Chapter cannot properly divest themselves of responsibility for the organising of the national funeral of a great man of world-wide reputation. They are not entitled to say to a private firm: 'We have consented to the interment in the Abbey. Take the Abbey and ask whom you like. We leave it to you.' The interment was a solemn ceremonial of national significance.

It is no argument to say that the arrangements were necessarily hurried. All funeral arrangements are necessarily hurried. An organisation ought to exist for the right arrangement of national funerals at the Abbey.

Lastly, I must point out, with regret and much respect, that not a single member of the Royal Family was personally present at the funeral. One of the main functions of the Royal Family is to represent and symbolise the feeling of the country. As a rule it admirably fulfils the function. But in this instance a telegram to Mrs. Hardy from the King, though a suitable and sympathetic gesture, was not enough.

Hardy was a citizen of the very highest consequence. Had the funeral been a military funeral of similar importance, half the male members of the Royal Family would have attended as a matter of course.

Arnold Bennett

BERG / TS. / 328
(*To John Freeman*)

75, Cadogan Square
18th January 1928

Dear Mr. Freeman,

I am glad to hear from you. According to my information, Hardy had a pretty good idea that he might have to be buried in the Abbey. Naturally, even if he did not want to be buried in the Abbey he could not say: 'I do not want to be buried in the Abbey'. As to the excision of the heart, I regard that as merely outrageous.

I like your work.

Yours sincerely, Arnold Bennett

DAILY EXPRESS, 19 January 1928 / 329
(*To the editor*)

75, Cadogan Square
[18 January 1928]

Sir,

In reference to the replies of the Dean of Westminster and of the Receiver-General and Clerk to the Abbey Chapter to my criticism of the arrangements for the funeral of Thomas Hardy I have to say:—

1. My criticism was confined to the arrangements in the south transept, which was reserved by ticket for the use of those with special claims to attend the funeral, and in which alone the interment could be witnessed.

2. It is indisputable that many authors of repute were unable to obtain tickets. It is indisputable that by far the most important, and by far the largest association of authors in the country, the Society of Authors, received only two tickets for the ceremony, could not get more tickets, and was obliged to inform its members that it was unable to help them to obtain admission.

When, at the suggestion of the Society of Authors, I applied to Messrs. Macmillan for a ticket, the message sent to me was

328. John Freeman (1880–1929), poet and author of books on Hardy and other literary figures. Hardy's heart was buried in the churchyard of Stinsford, the Mellstock of *Under the Greenwood Tree*.

that they had little hope of being able to supply me with a ticket, but they would try. They tried, and succeeded. It is indisputable that whereas the Society of Authors had only two tickets, a private firm of publishers had four tickets.

3. It is indisputable that, with all this, there was plenty of room to spare in the south transept. After the doors had been closed I was officially asked to move from a back bench up to the front, where were a number of empty seats. I declined, because I was sitting with friends.

4. The Dean may have been 'satisfied' with the arrangements. Many other people had the best reason for not being satisfied. Plainly, either the arrangements were grossly mismanaged or the arrangers were wanting in good will.

5. I did not suggest that there ought to be a 'national organisation to arrange Abbey funerals'. The idea to my mind was that the Dean and Chapter should have such an organisation within the Chapter. If their answer is that such an organisation already exists, then I would say that it is in the most serious need of reform. I fully agree that the Dean and Chapter must be in control of their own cathedral. Part of my case is that at Thomas Hardy's funeral they were not.

6. Surely one of the first duties of the Dean and Chapter was to inform the public through the Press where and under what conditions tickets for the south transept could be obtained. This elementary act of courtesy to the public was neglected.

7. I did not suggest that the King ought to have been present at the ceremony, I fully realised that his Majesty, for various reasons, could not be present; and, in any case, such a suggestion from a private citizen would have been gravely out of place.

I only permitted myself to express a respectful regret that no member of the Royal Family was present, and to say that a military funeral of similar importance would not have lacked the presence of royalty. As to this, I have received letters of abuse, mainly anonymous, but I maintain my position, and I know that in maintaining it I have the support of a large number of citizens.

Arnold Bennett

BEAVERBROOK / TS. / 330
(*To Lord Beaverbrook*)

75, Cadogan Square
20th January 1928

My dear Max,

Thank you for your letter of yesterday.

I was not aware that you had a conscientious objection to a Trust Fund. When I first mentioned the matter to you after dinner at the Vineyard towards the end of last year, you merely said that you preferred to pay for the education of one of the children. I could not discuss the pros and cons in the presence of others. You certainly did not give me the idea that you would have nothing to do with a Trust Fund.

I have examined the affair at length with two old and intimate friends of the Masterman family (Reginald Bray and John Buchan), and we all agreed that a Trust Fund (terminable of course, and power given to the Trustees to use the capital as time goes on) was the best method. One of the chief reasons for having a Trust is the extremely unbusinesslike character of Lucy Masterman. She is an excellent woman, but has no notion of money or even of paying bills when she has money.

The money required has all been collected, except yours, and the Trust has been formed, and I think that it will work very well. It will assuredly work far better than any other scheme.

I thought that the understanding between you and me was perfectly clear. While in my study, in reply to my question, you said that you would give me a free hand. You did not say a free hand subject to any condition; you said a free hand. In order to make quite sure I repeated the question to you at the front door and you repeated your answer. I know that you had much more serious matters to think about, but that cannot be helped.

Afterwards, I found that all the other contributors were in favour of a Trust Fund. I could not consult you, and you said that you would be away for several months. I had to act and, assuming that I had full authority to speak for you, I did act.

However, I should not dream of trying to involve you with your conscience, or of trying in any way to insist on a promise which you gave, very good-naturedly but evidently without due consideration, in circumstances which were extremely difficult for you.

On the other hand I cannot possibly go back on what I have said to the Trustees. I have already given £190 to the Fund. I shall now increase the amount to £1190. Dismiss the incident from your mind. It's all right.

Yours ever, Arnold

COHEN / MS. / 331
(*To Harriet Cohen*)

75, Cadogan Square
16.2.28

My sweet thing,

Why in the hell have you got the cafard? I suppose it's due to travelling by yourself. Well, that's one of the inevitable drawbacks of the life of an international solo artist: Que voulez-vous? God keep you. We returned last night from a week-end in Paris. Party of 4, including Cynthia Noble, and young Alfred Beit (aged 25) son of Sir Otto, & extremely keen on music. We saw 4 plays in 5 days, and *he* went also to the opera, *Salome*, & said it was a rotten performance. I warned him it would be. We went to see a great play, *La Parisienne*, at the Théâtre Français, & it was one of the worst performances of any play I have ever seen. The Français is certainly the worst theatre in the world. Packed! We saw lots of people. Went to night haunts, and one morning we went to bed at 5 a.m. Still, though exhausted, I remained in fine health. Dorothy enjoyed herself enormously. She is today dead with fatigue. *I* have to work. We had a rough journey home. Small French steamer. Upper deck washed from stem to stern. Dorothy seriously thought she would be drowned. However, the boat was only 15 minutes late, & Dorothy was not ill. Most people were very ill. The wireless operator let us into his cabin on the upper deck. We have a lunch today, but I'm damned if I know who's coming. . . . We heard the [?] the other night—opus 131. Hall not nearly full. This work is the goods, most emphatically. Utterly classical & lovely. My dear, there is only Beethoven, after all. The rest are nowhere. Really. We saw several good plays in Paris & 3 fine performances. Things are looking up there. Also the food is good. It is not so dear as in England; but

330. Beaverbrook paid his £1,000. On John Buchan see p. 79.

it is dear. I am now about to begin a most marvellous play, the idea for which enthralls me. Have you had successes? I hope so. I think so. But I hope no more successes with men—for the present. Take a rest from the seduction business. It rained *all* the time we were in Paris. It is blowing like hades here, and it is raining. And I can't yet proceed with my play because I'm clearing up the prodigious arrears of the week-end—including you.

Our loves,

Toujours votre dévoué A. B.

BBC / TS. / 332
(*To the Assistant Controller of the BBC*)

75, Cadogan Square
3rd May 1928

Dear Sir,

Referring to my letter of the 21st April (to which I have as yet received no reply) I must report to you about the behaviour of the instrument which you installed here, and for which you ask me to pay the sum of £60. Last night, as regards the performance of the Second Act of *Die Walküre*, we found it absolutely impossible to get an uninterrupted transmission of the opera. Another programme, and perhaps two other programmes, kept breaking in with more or less comic music of a violently anti-Wagnerian character, and no amount of adjustment would prevent this. Also a long speech. The Wagner would go on excellently for a few minutes, and then, for no apparent reason, it would be drowned by something else. Any further attempt at re-adjustment only resulted in whistling and various other strange noises.

This receiving set is admirable within certain limits, but I consider that the limits are far too narrow. An instrument which will neither get Continental stations, nor a Daventry station without mingling with it London or some other place, must surely be classed as extremely unsatisfactory.

Yours sincerely, Arnold Bennett

331. Cynthia Noble, daughter of Sir Sexton Noble and now Lady Jebb; (Sir) Alfred Lane Beit (1903–).

Salome, the one-act opera by Richard Strauss; *La Parisienne*, by Henri Becque. Bennett began writing his play *The Return Journey* on 7 February.

SYRACUSE, CARNEGIE / TS. / 333
(*To Sinclair Lewis*)

75, Cadogan Square
7th May 1928

My dear Sinclair,

All congratulations. I shall certainly come to the lunch to which you so nicely ask me. Sinclair, my boy, I have been trying to get to see you, but I have not been able to. This is just my busiest time. I am doing a play and a film, and also it is the period of the month when I have to do my *World Today* article, in which article I survey the world—no trifling job. Shall you be free on Saturday night?

All good messages to Dorothy Thompson.

Thine ever, Arnold Bennett

SYRACUSE, CARNEGIE / TS. / 334
(*To Sinclair Lewis*)

75, Cadogan Square
8th May 1928

My dear Sinclair,

I fear that in my unholy haste yesterday I did not make my suggestion to you about Saturday quite clear. When I said 'you' I of course meant you and Miss Thompson if she happens to be free. Possibly you could one or both of you dine here at 8 o'clock.

My wife is unfortunately away in Paris and will not be back till the middle of next week. But I am very capable of entertaining alone.

I was finishing the third act of a play yesterday, and therefore utterly careless of all human ties.

Yours ever, Arnold Bennett

333. Sinclair Lewis (1884–1951) was at the height of his literary fame. He married the journalist Dorothy Thompson (1894–1961) on 14 May 1928.

Bennett wrote his film story *Piccadilly* in May. The film had its first showing on 30 January 1929. The story was published in March 1929.

BEAVERBROOK / TS. / 335
(*To Lord Beaverbrook*)

75, Cadogan Square
18th May 1928

My dear Max,

These are what I am credibly informed, by the other actor in the affair, to be the facts about Asquith's book.

Asquith had refused for years all offers to do a war book. One day my informant went to see him about another matter, and handed him a draft contract for a war book. 'What is this?' asked Asquith before opening the document. As he opened it a cheque for £2,000 (payment on account) fell out. 'So this is your bait', said Asquith.

He reflected in silence for about five minutes and then swallowed the bait.

He had a lot of help in getting his material together.

The thing was typed from MSS etc., prepared by himself, but he did not revise the typescript, nor did he see the proofs. By that time he was too unwell to do such work.

The book was revised and passed by Bonham Carter—with the occasional assistance of Vivian Phillipps.

The first MS which Asquith delivered (not yet published at all—it will form the first volume of the two volumes which are to be published in the autumn) was thought by the publisher to be too mild and reticent. The publisher gave his view to Asquith personally: and the result was that the next lot erred on the other side. Much cutting, it appears, was done by Bonham Carter.

Yours ever, Arnold

P.S. I deeply enjoyed Newmarket Heath. A.

335. Asquith published *Fifty Years of Parliament* in 1926 and *Memories and Reflections* in September 1928. On Maurice Bonham Carter see above, p. 280. Vivian Phillipps was Asquith's private secretary in Asquith's last years.

Beaverbrook had a house at Newmarket, and Bennett visited him on 14–15 May.

BERG / TS. / 336
(*To Reginald Pound*)

75, Cadogan Square
6th June 1928

Dear Mr. Pound,

With reference to my article, which appears this morning, I am glad that you did not put any cross-headings to it, but I do most solemnly exhort you, if you ever print any other articles of mine, not to diversify them with varieties of type. I am like another of your notorious contributors in my objection to this kind of emphasis. All the emphasis needed is supplied by me in the actual writing.

Yours sincerely, Arnold Bennett

BUTLER / TS. / 337
(*To Rudolph Kommer*)

75, Cadogan Square
14th June 1928

My dear Kommer,

The contents of your letter were so agreeable that I at once forgave you for the delay. I am exceedingly relieved to get your verdict on the play. I quite agree with you about the question of names. My only reason for using them was to give the British playgoer—who is a perfect ass—and the British critic—who is much the same—some sort of guide to the nature of the play. I should be very willing to alter them. I hope to finish the piece by the end of this month. Du Maurier is terribly keen to see it. He even offered to buy it without seeing it; but I would not allow him to do this.

As regards Salzburg, I will let you know about this later. I do not at present know how I shall be fixed—with regard either to plays or to films. It is quite possible that I might be compelled to remain in London. We are going to Le Touquet for a month on July 1st.

Will you please return the play to me. I want another copy of

336. Reginald Pound was literary editor of the *Daily Express* for some years, and later wrote Bennett's biography.

it. I should be delighted if you would translate it into German.
Dorothy sends her love.

Ever yours, Arnold Bennett

ARKANSAS / MS. / 338
(*To Frank Swinnerton*)

75, Cadogan Square
19.6.28

My dear Henry,

In reply to your sad tidings, for which thanks:— George was certainly unwell, & markedly depressed, on the night before he left. I had no idea of strained relations between him and the Doubles, except that he said he wouldn't go back on the same ship with old Double, & that he seemed cross with old Mrs. Double in showing satisfaction that she had refused his invitation to lunch. I should think old Double, from what I know of him, must be a bit barmy now. For months I have been saying to the other barmy one, Chalmers Roberts (these 2 own the *World Today* between them equally), that the *W. Today* couldn't go on as it was, & that in particular the *price* must be altered. The reply always was that old Double was prepared, & preferred, to persevere, that everything took time etc., etc. Also old Double wrote to me from Nassau, entirely off his own bat, that my stuff was the 'livest' they had had for 20 years. Then old Double arrives & at once announces to Roberts his decision that the *W. Today* must be merged with *Personality*. I was very relieved myself, because I should never have been able to do anything with Roberts (who thinks consistently in terms of 'Frontier Stories' etc.); but it seems no way to run a magazine. I ain't going to make any more contracts with Damned Damned & Co. till the situation is clarified.

I'll be at Reform between 7.30 & 7.40 Thursday.

If I don't hear, I won't dress.

Loves,

Yours, A. B.

337. *The Return Journey* has as its chief characters Dr. Henry Fausting, Marguerite Maider, Satollyon, and Richard Young. On Rudolf Kommer see above, p. 274, and see also Vol. I.

338. The firms of Doran and Doubleday merged in 1927. F. N. Doubleday (1862–1934) had been president of the Doubleday firm since 1900. Chalmers Roberts is not otherwise known. Further details about Doubleday-Doran appear in Vol I.

TEXAS / MS. / 339
(*To Maurice Baring*)

Grand Hôtel
Le Touquet
10–8–28

My dear Maurice,

Thank you. Yes, I expect I was too hard on A. Lang, & I agree that the temporary loss of prestige of a name should not influence me. I, however, never cared much for Andrew. I accuse him of having the lowest of human qualities (not defects)—cleverness.

We are coming home on Tuesday. Dorothy's greetings.

Thine, A. B.

U.C. / T.C.C. / 340
(*To Radclyffe Hall*)

[75, Cadogan Square]
28th August 1928

Dear Radclyffe Hall,

Thank you for your letter of yesterday. Yes, it is quite true that I objected to the phrase which you mention. I still object to it. I told Forster that I was prepared to stand absolutely for both the merits and the decency of the book. He persuaded me to agree to the phrase remaining in because it enables certain other, more timid, persons to sign.

I do not think that Forster's enterprise will result in anything. It is now rather late, and the difficulty of getting hold of signatories at this time of the year is extreme. Nor do I see how anything else can be done. I was asked to write an article for the *Nation* on the matter, but it was absolutely impossible for me to do so, as I was, and am, so terribly busy with rehearsals of a play and the 'shooting' of a film.

Yours sincerely, [Arnold Bennett]

339. The Bennetts spent most of July and the first half of August in France on holiday.

Andrew Lang (1844–1912), poet, journalist, folklorist.

340. Radclyffe Hall (d. 1943) published *The Well of Loneliness* in July. It was the subject of police prosecution. E. M. Forster (1879–) was active in the defence of the book, and Bennett remarked in the *Evening Standard* that it was 'honest, convincing, and extremely courageous'. He also thought it was badly written.

The Return Journey was in rehearsal, and *Piccadilly* was being filmed.

BERG / T.C.C. / 341
(*To E. M. Forster*)

[75, Cadogan Square]
1st September 1928

My dear Forster,

Thank you. I certainly would not sign such a letter as she suggests, even if the co-signatories were all the swells in the world. You had better leave the thing. You have behaved in a noble manner, and she will perceive this later on, when she gets a bit calmer.

Yours sincerely, [Arnold Bennett]

BEAVERBROOK / TS. / 342
(*To Lord Beaverbrook*)

75, Cadogan Square
4th September 1928

My dear Max,

This is very nice of you. It's like this. Swaffer some time ago said something personal about Gladys Cooper which (I believe) he ought not to have said. Gladys said to Gerald du Maurier: 'Gerald, you will swear never to admit that man to one of your first nights.' Gerald replied: 'I swear.' When Gerald related this to me I told him that to attempt to dictate to a big newspaper what individual it should or should not send to a first night was childish. Gerald said: 'But I am a child.'

I agree with you that the incident has no importance. I do not believe that notices affect the fate of plays. No play of mine has ever had a good press, except *Mr. Prohack*. There are not, literally, three dramatic critics in London whose opinions have the least interest for me. I hate the stage, but I cannot help writing a play now and then. These plays are always a damned nuisance to me after they are written. This new play would never have been produced by Gerald if he had not overtaken me crossing a street and said: 'If you go on like that you will be killed.' I said: 'I know exactly what I am doing, and I have only the appearance of mooning. I am thinking out a play.' He said: 'It's for me. I must have a play by a great man.' I said: 'You cannot have it. It's not your sort of play at all.' He sent Viola Tree to see me and under her blandishments I promised that he should have the first sight of the play. I then refused to go on with it, as I could not see the last act. He then said: 'I will buy it in the dark.' I declined to let him buy it in the dark. By this time he had an absolute obsession about the play. When I had at last finished it, I said to him: 'You must say Yes or No in 48 hours.' He bought it in 24 hours. I must say that he is perfect to work with.

God may know whether the play is any good. I don't. I merely know that nine critics out of ten have shown no understanding of the play whatever. This is usual.

Thoroughgood's notice of Wells's book was deplorable. For one thing the book is magnificently written. To me it is the best novel Wells has written for years. Being a member of what are called 'The Big Four' I make a rule of never dealing with the work of the other three myself. It would not be becoming of me to do so. Moreover I could not possibly say what I think of Galsworthy.

I much appreciate your letter, Max.

Yours ever, Arnold

P.S. I am going today to Annecy to write a film. I return in a fortnight.

BEAVERBROOK / MS. / 343
(*To Lord Beaverbrook*)

Imperial Palace Hotel
Annecy,
Haute-Savoie
9.9.28.

My dear Max,

Thanks for yours. I never admired Haldane as a writer, whether of 'minutes' or anything else. But I shall want a devil of a lot of persuading that he was [not] in the first rank of our

342. Gladys Cooper (1889–), actress and film star. She played Mrs. Cheyney in 1925 under the direction of Sir Gerald. *The Return Journey* opened at the St. James's on 1 September, with Sir Gerald playing Fausting.

Horace Thoroughgood (d. 1962) was on the literary staff of the *Evening Standard* for many years. Wells's new book was *Mr. Blettsworthy on Rampole Island*.

Bennett's film story was *Punch and Judy*. It was never produced. See Vol. I for further detail.

war-secretaries. After all, who initiated and watched over & corrected the organising of the E.F.? Whose was the creative mind? Has everybody been wrong about Haldane? Haig may have been ingenuous; but he must have had a certain competence, and his recently published laudation of Haldane (coming with double effect from a man so little addicted to superlatives) struck me as being authoritative and not more than just. I agree that Haldane was at his worst pen in hand.

Yours ever, Arnold

P.S. We're coming home in the fourth week of this month. I want to see you.

MEWTON-WOOD / TS. / 344
(*To W. J. Turner*)

75, Cadogan Square
29th September 1928

Dear Turner,

Thank you for your letter and the letter from Sharp. It is certainly very interesting. Before sending it to me I hope you got his permission to do so. I was already in possession of some of Sharp's views about your article, as he had written me on the subject. (I had not approached him in any way.)

I myself should very much like to know where I insisted that 'the amount of money a writer makes is the measure of his work as a writer'. You must be hopelessly inaccurate to attribute any such saying to me. A journalist who is capable of such an enormity of wild negligence is bound to get his paper into a mess, and he must expect severe editorial castigations from time to time.

I should not violently disagree with Sharp's estimate of my defects. I have long been aware that some of the younger generation despise me. (The feeling is not mutual.) One does what one can. I always do the best I can, and let it go at that. I seem to get on very well with the younger generation when I meet it, which is often, except when it expresses its scorn of

343. Richard Burdon Haldane (Viscount Haldane, 1856–1928), Lord Chancellor, 1912–15, and organizer of the British Expeditionary Force; Douglas Haig (Earl Haig, 1861–1928), Field Marshal in the First World War.

Wells, who in my opinion is worth the whole younger generation put together—and more. My criticism of the younger generation is that it seriously lacks both power and application. I do not blame it for that. It does what it can, like myself. There is no critic of the younger generation at all comparable to MacCarthy. There is not one, except yourself, whom it is a pleasure to read for the sake of reading. There are not four critics, young or old, whose views on my work have any interest for me. Not one man in a thousand can judge contemporary work. I should not be surprised if my productions proved ultimately to be worthless. On the other hand I should not be surprised if some of them proved to have life in them. For me the point is not material. The sole material point for me is that my work is honestly the best I am capable of.

I return Sharp's letter. He appears to agree with me about your ignorance of life.

Yours sincerely, Arnold Bennett

MEWTON-WOOD / TS. / 345
(*To W. J. Turner*)

75, Cadogan Square
1st October 1928

My dear Turner,

I have just received your letter. You seem to be incapable of learning. You ought to be perfectly well aware that I have never judged poets by the number of cylinders in their cars, or said anything resembling what you apparently attribute to me. Either you are mischievously dishonest or mischievously inaccurate. Or perhaps it is only your fun. God knows!

At the same time I am strongly in favour of poets having 6 cylinder cars. So are poets. For I notice they always get them when they can. The country in which poets customarily had 6 cylinder cars would be a better country than ours.

That, without the writer's permission, you should send a

344. Turner reviewed 'Mr. Arnold Bennett's *Faust*' in the *New Statesman* on 22 September. He thought that Fausting had no soul to sell: Bennett had sold it long ago. '*The Return Journey*, as the work of an author of reputation, is really shocking. It reveals him as a man who, if he ever did think, has now ceased to think.'

On Clifford Sharp see above, p. 25.

letter in which another man is frankly discussed to that man, shows the sort of *enfant terrible* you are.

Yours sincerely, Arnold Bennett

MEWTON-WOOD / TS. / 346
(*To W. J. Turner*)

75, Cadogan Square
3rd October 1928

Dear Turner,

Thanks for your letter of yesterday. I have not read Muir, but I am absolutely certain that he does not quote me as saying anything 'similar' to what you said I said. If you want to know my views on the subject read the last part of my book *The Author's Craft*. You will then know. At present you don't know. You have never seen anything in the *Standard* on the lines of what you attributed to me. I have never said that 'success' was a criterion of 'value'. I have said, and I shall always say, that, if success means the sharing of his ideas or emotions with the public, an author does not succeed until he is read, and that in proportion as he is read he makes money, unless he is dead.

Yours sincerely, Arnold Bennett

BODKIN / TR. / 347
(*To Thomas Bodkin*)

75, Cadogan Square
13.10.28.

My dear T. B.,

Well, be sure to advise us in time of your appearance in this city. As I am only just recovering from a slight infliction of flu, I cannot reply to you on the subject of *The Return Journey*. All I can say is that when I saw it for the first time in front of an audience (a fortnight after its production) I said: 'This play cannot run'. And it won't, though business has been very good so far. I thought the last act was too harrowing. Also I felt that the audience failed to get contacts. I've no notion whether the play is good or bad. G.B.S. & H.G.W. think highly of it. Dorothy doesn't, though she admitted that it was only at the

346. Edwin Muir, the author (1887–1959).

3rd visit that she appreciated the points of the last act (which I think is the best act). I'm just beginning a new film. I've received the book, thanks. I lay you 2 to 1 you don't get your wife to London. We are all well, except me, and I am rapidly mounting in strength. We are charmed to hear from you.

All greetings to Madame.

Yours ever but feebly, A. B.

BUTLER / T.C.C. / 348
(*To Jonathan Cape*)

[75, Cadogan Square]
10th November 1928

Dear Mr. Jonathan Cape,

On the conclusion of the *Well of Loneliness* case, I propose to devote an article to it in the *Evening Standard*. I need not tell you that I am anti-police.

I wish you would give me some information. *Of course I should not use any of it without your permission.*

1. Why did you ask for trouble by sending the book to the Home Secretary, on the mere menace of a quite ridiculous article?

2. What was the nature of the communication of the Home Secretary to you? Could I possibly see his letter? Did the letter bind you to secrecy? If so, why?

3. What power was the Home Secretary exercising?

4. At the hearing yesterday, why did your Counsel not put it to the magistrate that as he had allowed a police witness to express an opinion he should in fairness allow you to call witnesses in rebuttal of the police witness's opinion? The police witness expressed nothing but an opinion. There can be no question of fact except the seizure of the books. The magistrate himself can after all only give an opinion. His finding can in no circumstances be a finding on facts.

5. I am told that in a book of Sir Chartres Biron there is a passage against book censorship. Can you give me the reference to this passage? So far as I know Biron has published only one or two books. One of them is entitled *Pious Opinions*. I have it.

Yours sincerely, [Arnold Bennett]

348. On 16 November Sir Chartres Biron (1863–1940) declared *The Well of Loneliness* obscene. He was Chief Magistrate at Bow Street from 1920 to 1933. In

BUTLER / T.C.C. / 349
(*To Jonathan Cape*)

[75, Cadogan Square]
13th November 1928

Dear Mr. Jonathan Cape,

I am very much obliged for your letter of the 12th and the enclosure. It tells me all that I want to know. I still think that in your place I should have taken the risks of ignoring Douglas's article.

I have read *To the Pure*, in the American edition, and I brought it into an article for the *Standard* which I wrote and delivered before the summons was taken out. As the summons preceded the day for publication of the article, the article of course had to be held over. I shall embody the substance of it in another article which will appear as soon as Biron has delivered himself. Unless I hear from you I shall assume that I may use the correspondence between you and Jix.

Yours faithfully, [Arnold Bennett]

P.S. If *To the Pure* has not yet been despatched to me please do not send it as I have a copy. If it has been despatched, I will return it to you at once.

---

his opinion the question of literary merit was irrelevant, though he did not hesitate to say that he thought some of the writing in the novel was deplorable. Nor was he concerned that it depicted perversion. The test was whether it made perversion seem attractive and unblameworthy, and here he thought the novel succeeded and was therefore obscene. *Pious Opinions* (1923) is a collection of essays on eighteenth- and nineteenth-century literary figures. The other book, *To the Pure*, is not known. Sir William Joynson-Hicks (1865–1932) was Home Secretary from 1924 to 1929.

In *Just as It Happened* Sir Newman Flower commented on the case. He recalled that Bennett 'was very much annoyed with me . . . because we refused to publish *The Well of Loneliness* by Radclyffe Hall. We had published her two previous books —a fine brace of novels. But my refusal to publish this particular book, and, still more, the attack made on it by another member of our club which led to the book being withdrawn, owing to the intervention of the authorities, made Arnold furious. He told me openly that he would like to have the critic killed. Yet two months later he said he thought we had acted quite rightly about it . . .; he realized that it was not a book for Cassell's.'

349. It was apparently some comment by the critic James Douglas that brought Cape to withdraw *The Well of Loneliness*. On 29 November Bennett published an article entitled 'Who Shall Select Books for Censorship?' in the *Evening Standard*. He did not mention the *Well of Loneliness* case, but merely argued against book censorship and supported his argument with apt quotations from *Pious Opinions*. He identified Sir Chartres Biron as the author at the end.

'Jix'—Sir William Joynson-Hicks.

BERG / TS. / 350
(*To Esmé Percy*)

75, Cadogan Square
16th January 1929

Dear Esmé Percy,

Last night you received my criticisms of the production with such good nature that I feel inclined to make one or two more remarks, though I have no right whatever to do so.

I want to repeat what I said of your own performance. It was magnificent and very impressive, and it is bound to add to your reputation. I venture to make about it only two small observations.

First. You have, to my great satisfaction, shown in your rendering of Byron that there is always something feminine in the creative artist. I think that this is a most important point, neglected by every other actor that I have seen in the role of a creative artist. But I have a suspicion that some uncomprehending people may say that you stress the characteristic a little too much (in gestures).

Second. In the epilogue you employ, with immense effect, a large variety of tone. I could wish that you would employ this variety of tone throughout all the previous scenes.

As regards the play itself, to my mind it is not a good play as it stands. It is not well constructed. All that one can say of it is that it contains a lot of fine dramatic material.

As regards production.

Act I, sc.i. I think that this would be improved by cutting. The scene is not dramatic. It merely establishes Byron's environment. Of course an opening scene *ought* to establish the environment, but it should be dramatic as well. The defect is incurable now. It can, however, be softened by shortening.

The scene was under-lighted last night.

There is a portrait of somebody hanging on the prompt wall. This portrait looks quite modern. Nobody could possibly accept it as a portrait of the period. It clashes with all the rest of the set. Would it not be better to cut it, and to cut any lines which refer to it?

Act I, sc.ii. The entrances of the guests appear to me too protracted. Could they not be shortened?

Also, the miscellaneous chatter of the crowd is too loud, and interferes seriously with the speeches of the principals.

Throughout the play there are a number of speeches delivered up-stage and therefore not heard.

I think that the production of this scene is rather loose and confused, weakening the drama.

Act II. Music in the house next door seemed to me to be too loud. It did not sound to me in the least like music heard through a wall.

As I told you last night, I think that the positions of yourself and Anabella in the big scene are much too far apart. The scene nevertheless is superb and superbly acted by both of you.

Act III, sc.i. Anabella's final exit is absolutely ruined by the comedy bow of Mrs. Minns. There need be no bow at all, and if there is to be a bow, it should not be a comedy bow, but a straight bow. Mrs. Minns obviously plays it for a laugh, which she gets, but the price of the laugh is the disaster to the exit of Anabella.

(By the way, your own exit in Act III sc.ii was absolutely ruined last night through it being masked by two guests.)

I feel strongly that the scene should end on the throwing away of the glasses. There may be beauty in what comes afterwards, but it is an anti-climax and quite spoils the effectiveness of the scene. The throwing of the glasses would be a splendid curtain.

Act III, sc.ii. If this scene could be omitted entirely, so much the better. It is wrongly conceived and ineffective.

If it is omitted entirely the excellent section between you and Caroline might be brought into Act III sc.i *before* the throwing of the glasses. This would be easy to do.

If Act III, sc.ii is to stand I should drastically cut it, and I should also simplify the movements and the grouping of it. It has the same air of confusion as Act I sc.ii.

I think that there is not sufficient contrast between the Prince Regent's demeanour towards Byron in this scene, and his demeanour in Act I, sc.ii.

My considered opinion is that if the epilogue stands as played last night it is certain utterly to kill all the chances of success. I cannot put this too bluntly and plainly. No play could survive that epilogue. I should cut it down by more than half. All necessary explanations could be done in a few words. The scene is the scene of Byron's death, and nothing else is of the slightest importance. I am convinced that the scene did not really hold the audience last night. The Suliots should only just enter and then be ordered to retire. Both Major Parry and the doctor were in my opinion thoroughly bad, and I do not see any need for either of them. They would cause laughter on the first night. I should also take out the line about the length of time Byron takes in dying. This is a dangerous line for a first night; and, further, it is a misquotation. What the King said was: 'an *unconscionable* time'.

From all I can hear, if you leave the final decisions about alterations to the authoress, the result is likely to be a calamity. If I were in the place of yourself and Mrs. Wheeler I should take the matter into my own hands, and confront her with a fait accompli—for her own sake as well as yours.

Lastly, if Miss Mona Limerick's conception of the individuality of Augusta is correct I have been wildly wrong about Augusta all my life.

You are extremely busy. Please therefore do not trouble to acknowledge this letter. And please do forgive my intrusion. I cannot defend it.

All good wishes,

Yours sincerely, Arnold Bennett

BERG / MS. / 351
(*To Gwladys Wheeler*)

75, Cadogan Square
24.1.29.

My dear Gwladys,

Thank you for your letter. I have the greatest sympathy with you. I don't regard the play as 'dead' yet. It might pick up. You have been handicapped by a very stupid & obstinate author. But you have only been going through the usual experiences. The same things have happened scores of times before. The play was chosen, not because of its qualities, but solely because an actor happened 'to see himself' in the leading

350. Esmé Percy (1887–1957), actor and director, was especially notable in the twenties for his performances in Shaw's plays. *Byron*, by Alisa Ramsay, opened at the Lyric on 22 January. Lady Byron was played by Dorothy (under her stage name, Dorothy Cheston), and Augusta was played by Mona Limerick, the first wife of the producer Iden Payne.

role. This is generally a bad reason. When I first read it, I said that though it was a very bad play, it was not a bad specimen of its kind (which is a very bad kind). I have now seen it 3 times, and each time I see it I think worse of it. But that is no argument against it succeeding. The pity is that the obviously necessary alterations which are now being made, were not made before the 1st night. But here again is a thing which I have seen occur again & again. The play might have been made, & might still be made, melodramatically effective, were it not for the blind obstinacy of the author. I agree in the main with Hannen Swaffer's notice. The play is well staged but badly produced. Percy is a man of experience, but he certainly is not experienced in West End production. He is an extremely talented and resourceful actor, well suited for the part: but this kind of acting, at this date, is only justifiable when the construction of the play allows it to succeed: which is not the present case. Again, some of the casting is perfectly rotten. Far better artists could have been got for the same money. I refer especially to Augusta, to Milbanke, and Minns, and the doctor, who are all terrible & a terrific drag on the play. I know nothing about Percy except that I like him very much indeed. In fact I like him enormously. But you are further handicapped by his reputation. For anything I know, this reputation may be utterly false. Such reputations often are. I hear from my youngest sister, who for some reason known only to herself went into the gallery on the 1st night, that Percy was simply adored by the gallery. (I know he was adored by the 1st row of the stalls.) My sister enjoyed the play. After the next rehearsal or two [you] can't do anything else, except sit tight and wait. The rehearsals ought to include a change in the end of the last act before the epilogue. This change is quite easy to bring about—especially if the author could go to a nursing-home for a week. I think that you have worked splendidly, & that you have exercised strong commonsense so far as the author permitted. I think that Mrs. Patrick Campbell has been invaluable. I have not shown your letter to Dorothy. I would love you to dine with me one night next week. Will you? Wednesday or Saturday?

Ever your devoted A. B.

COHEN / MS. / 352
(*To Harriet Cohen*)

75, Cadogan Square
8.ii.29.

My sweet Tania,

Well, this was the first firm address I've had from you. You say nothing of health or of applause. Why? We hope confidently for the best. Dorothy has had a bad bronchial cold, & spent 2 days in bed. But we hope to go to Paris tomorrow. Dorothy (mustn't / won't) go to the Schnabel recital tonight. So I must get someone else. I heard Schnabel play the Emperor the other night. It was magnif. Goossens' opera is to be done twice at Covent Garden. I have appeared on the stage as a public singer, & thereby created an *immense* stir in London. I brought down a house full of stage professionals, just because I am, really, a born comedian! My film *Piccadilly* is a great success at the Carlton Theatre. I'm not doing much work. Is this enough news? Anyhow, there isn't any more at present. There may be some more after Paris (Hôtel Matignon till Wednesday next—D.V.). God keep you. We send our loves, darling Tania.

Ever your devoted A. B.

GIDE / 353
(*To André Gide*)

[75, Cadogan Square]
11th March 1929

My dear Gide,

I am very happy if I can be of any service to you.

I have read a lot of *The Vatican Swindle* and also *The School of Women*.

I see in the course of a year a large number of American translations, and I have not yet seen one which was not extremely inferior to Madame Bussy's translation of you. She

352. Artur Schnabel (1882–1951).

Eugene Goossens's opera *Judith*, with libretto by Bennett, was produced on 25 June.

Piccadilly had its first showing on 30 January 1929. For other details see Vol. I.

certainly writes the English of an educated person with a feeling for words. The rhythm of your sentences could not possibly be rendered in English, but I do not know any translator who would fail with more distinction than Madame Bussy. I know only one translator who would be likely to do better; Scott-Moncrieff. But Scott-Moncrieff would allow himself more freedom than Madame Bussy allows herself.

It is just conceivable, but it is highly improbable, that you might get a better translator than Madame Bussy, and my advice to you is most decidedly to keep her. She is *vastly* better than the average translator.

At the same time she is not always accurate or elegant. So that you may see the sort of small slips which (in my opinion) she makes, I will give you one or two examples from the first, second and third columns of the first page of the translation of *The School of Women*:

Column I. 'How have I remained so long without perceiving this?'

More literally: 'Why have I taken so long to perceive this?'

Column II. 'She could not *admit* that marriage ought to confer all the prerogatives on the husband.'

More literally: 'She could not *accept* marriage if it was to confer prerogatives on the husband.' (not *all* the prerogatives).

Column III. 'made her able' is a clumsy phrase.

'Enabled' would be much better.

'very likely'. This adverbial phrase has been added by the translator. It is not in the original at all. It is quite unnecessary, and it impairs the significance of the word 'might'.

I could give other examples of slight mistakes, but these are characteristic, and you can judge for yourself from them how trifling such errors are. (Also, I have no doubt that the translator could defend them.)

I return the translation of *The School of Women* for your reference.

Ever yours sincerely, Arnold Bennett

353. Madame Simon Bussy (*née* Dorothy Strachey, sister of Lytton Strachey and wife of the French painter) was the chief translator of Gide's works into English. C. K. Scott-Moncrieff (1889–1930) was the translator of Proust.

CALIF / MS. / 354
(*To Adelaide Phillpotts*)

75, Cadogan Square
12–3–29

My dear Adelaide,

I tried to see you last night, but I didn't succeed. I must tell you your play is in my opinion too subtle for the general understanding; also not dramatic enough. True, ironic, full of a sense of character, but lacking in dramatic movement. It wasn't till the 3rd act was well on that I comprehended, really, what you were driving at. And you *have* a nerve, too, to put 3 tea parties into one play! The satire amounts to cruelty, and is, I imagine, a shade overdone. I thought you were very well served by the players; but not by the producer. Among other faults, the producer seemed to have no idea of giving life by means of variety of tone, etc., to mere discussions—of which there are so many in the play. The people seemed to say what they had to say by rote—regular rise & fall, regular rise and fall, for ever & ever. As for the positions & the movements which he allotted to the people, the less said about them the better. I admit that you set him a devil of a task in manoeuvring 16 or 18 people on that small stage & with about 40 intimate tête-à-tête to contrive! Withal, I would only charge you with one *real* fault—lack of drama. We were both extremely interested. The thing is full of originality & of just observation.

Dorothy sends you nice messages.

Ever yours, Arnold Bennett

P.S. 'The Mayor' is a promise of a better play. A. B.

MAYFIELD, SYRACUSE / A.C. / 355
(*To the editor of the* EVENING STANDARD)

[Antibes]
31.3.29.

Dear Sir,

In his article of last Wednesday on my pamphlet, *The Religious Interregnum*, Dean Inge would like me to say whether in religious controversy I have been assailed by coarse abuse,

354. *The Mayor* was produced at the Royalty on 11 March 1929.

imputations of disgraceful conduct, and personal insults. The answer is Yes, many times. A few weeks [ago] a priestly religionist started a public controversy with me which I publicly declined to proceed with because of the insulting tone of my would-be opponent.

The Dean asks why I chose to 'sample Christianity' in an ugly dissenting chapel. (The dissenting chapel was no uglier than thousands of Established churches.) For two reasons. One, I am very well acquainted with dissenting chapels. Two, I wished to show that very fine spiritual experiences can be and are obtained by worshippers even in ugly dissenting chapels—those conventicles for which prelates of the Established Church too often in their lamentable spiritual pride, exhibit so much scorn.

The Dean wonders that I should write about religion. He says: 'I have never given to the world my views about Beethoven and Bach.' If the Dean had been half as interested in Beethoven and Bach as I am interested in religion he would, I think, have given to the world his views about Beethoven and Bach.

However, I wrote my pamphlet at the express invitation of the Bishop of Liverpool, who came to see me and urged me to contribute to his series of *Affirmations*, in such terms that I could not decently refuse his request. I warned him that he probably would not find my ideas very sympathetic, and that anyhow they would be misrepresented and myself made the object of sneers and contumely. He said, Never mind. I did not mind.

The Dean's article contains various inaccuracies about me and my books, doubtless the result of imperfect knowledge on his part. I need not catalogue them.

In conclusion, let me express the opinion that, if the popular religious press is any guide, the dogmatic beliefs of the average Christian are much less 'advanced' than the Dean, who has done his able best to demolish dogma, imagines them to be.

[Arnold Bennett]

355. The Bennetts went to France for a month on 26 March.

Bennett's letter was published with negligible changes in the *Evening Standard* on 3 April.

Dean Inge (1860–1954) was Dean of St. Paul's for many years. *The Religious Interregnum* was published in March 1929.

BERG / MS. / 356
(*To Cedric Sharpe*)

75, Cadogan Square
24th May 1929

My dear Cedric,

I have not the slightest objection to you selling the MS of *Anna of the Five Towns*. But also I have not the slightest idea what it is worth in the market. I know that I have just refused an offer of £3000 for the MS of *The Old Wives' Tale* because I think that the prices of my MSS are going up and that in a few years it will be worth £5000.

If you could get it into a sale of modern MSS at Sotheby's it would have a better chance. Or you might advertise it. Or you might write to one of the big secondhand booksellers such as Maggs Bros, or you might write to Sotheby's yourself. The value of my MSS is bound to go up, like the value of my first editions. Only two or three years ago, a first edition of *The Old Wives' Tale* could be had for £1. The other day I signed a copy for which the owner had paid £50, and it was not a very good copy either. At an auction the other day the MS of one of my short stories—10 pages, of no particular interest—was sold for £40.

This is about all I can say. Anyhow, do not sell the thing in a hurry.

My blessing is joined to that of God upon you and yours.

Ever yours, A. B.

TEXAS / T.C.C. / 357
(*To Jim Tully*)

[75, Cadogan Square]
6th June 1929

Dear Jim Tully,

Many thanks for your letter. I shall be delighted to make your acquaintance, and the introduction from George Doran, though of course agreeable, was quite unnecessary. At the moment I am exceedingly busy and ruthless, finishing a work, but if you

356. In 1936 in the middle of the Depression *The Old Wives' Tale* was bid up to £1,250 at Sotheby's, which was below the reserve price. The manuscripts of *Clayhanger* and *Imperial Palace* sold for £100 and £200.

could come and have tea with me here on Tuesday next at 4.30 I should be glad.

I have always understood that you are celebrated, among other things, for your interviews. I just want to tell you that I am never interviewed, that I absolutely refuse to be interviewed, or to talk in any way except for the strictly private annoyance of the person to whom I am talking.

Yours sincerely, [Arnold Bennett]

COHEN / TR. / 358
(*To Harriet Cohen*)

Celtic Hotel
[St. Cast]
28.7.29.

My sweet Tania,

Charmed to hear from you, though your letter was undated. Anyhow I got it only yesterday. We've been motoring incessantly, & I only got the epistle last night. Now I have a big mail to deal with, & can't get on with my own work till this is cleared. I'm going to Russia on the 8th August with Beaverbrook & a party. But who is in the party I haven't asked & don't know. So I shall be leaving here on the 7th. What are all these comparisons between G.B.S., Cunninghame Graham & me? I don't understand what 'The Music Cure for a Talkie' is. Anyhow you wouldn't like it. I've never heard of Bates, & it will be too late for me to deal with Bates on my return. I finally reach home on August 31st. (D.V.) We had a great time on Lake Garda despite the enervating heat (which I enjoy despite enervation). You live in a continuous perspiration: which carries off all toxic matter. Very convenient. Garda indeed is heavenly, & pretty well unspoilt. Also cheap. We went twice to Verona, & had other excursions. Garda is the largest Italian lake. The hotel is a pension & is 1st rate, but we had it to ourselves as the season is not begun. [A few lines unreadable.]

Ever your devoted A. B.

357. Jim Tully (1888–1947), pugilist and author.

358. At the end of June the Bennetts went to France and Italy for six weeks. R. M. Cunninghame Graham (1852–1936), traveller, scholar, and author; H. E. Bates (1905–), prolific author, then just beginning to be known.

EDEL / TR. / 359
(*To Leon Edel*)

[Celtic Hotel]
29.7.29.

Dear Sir,

In reply to your letter, I will not trust my memory. Also I have no idea why Alexander brought on H.J. I don't think for a moment that the gallery was anti-American. The gallery in my opinion had merely been bored. I can't remember just what Alexander said, but I clearly remember my feelings of resentment against Alexander, and I think that his remarks amounted to a sort of apology to the audience for having produced the play! I cannot even remember what I wrote in my short essay on James. Nor can I refer to it, as I am away on holiday. I fear this letter will not help you much.

Yours sincerely, Arnold Bennett

359. Professor Leon Edel (1907–) was just beginning his long labours on Henry James. The first night of *Guy Domville*, produced by Sir George Alexander (1858–1918) at the Haymarket in 1895, was very likely the most ignominious in James's life. Bennett attended the performance as a critic for *Woman*. Shaw and Wells were there too. In an article on James in the early twenties Bennett remarked: 'I know I felt sympathetic towards the play; but it had a fatal fault; it was not dramatic. The house was full of votaries of the cult, and the reception as a whole was very favourable. The gallery behaved roughly; but in those days there was nothing at all unusual in that. The gallery booed Henry James. Of course this was sacrilege, but the gallery didn't know it was sacrilege. The gallery had probably never heard of Henry James until that night. My memory is not clear for details, but I have a kind of recollection that George Alexander made a speech which annoyed me far more than the behaviour of the gallery—a speech somehow apologising for the play and admitting that it was a mistake. . . . The whole of the first night, and especially its culmination, was horrible torture for the sensitive James. But if he had known thoroughly the technique of the drama he would have saved himself the torture. Part of the technique of a thoroughly equipped dramatist is never to go to his own first nights. Having failed to make money out of plays—and not, according to his own account, having failed to write a good play, James abandoned the drama. This also I think was pretty bad. I must further point out that James once for commercial purposes altered the ending of a play from sad to happy. Tut-tut!'

GIDE / 360
(*To André Gide*)

R.M.S.P.
Arcadian
Leningrad
21–8–29

My dear Gide,

No letter about my work has ever given me so much pleasure as yours, and I thank you for it very warmly. I am exceedingly grateful to you and du Gard and Coppet and the others. It seems to me that your labours have been entirely altruistic. I hope you will convey my sentiments to the others. I have certainly kept the letter you wrote me about *The Old Wives' Tale*. When I get home I will send it to you. If you *do* write a preface for the translation, you will still further increase my obligations to you. Such a preface would of course be the making of the book. I think it very doubtful indeed that I shall be able to come to the Midi. I am just starting a long novel, and I fear I shall not be able to leave it. I wish I could write short novels like your completely admirable *L'Ecole des Femmes*. But I can't. I have seen Leningrad and Moscow. The effect of the spectacle is overwhelming—half desolation and half hope.

Ever yours, Arnold Bennett

HARVARD / MS. / 361
(*To William Rothenstein*)

75, Cadogan Square
3–9–29

My dear William,

You are a charming fellow, a fine letter-writer and a most pleasing critic. Yes, I am all for la bonne peinture—and no ornaments. Hence ces ânes say that I have no style. (Perhaps I haven't, but not for their reason.) Your epistle delighted me,

360. Bennett returned briefly to Cadogan Square in early August, and on the 10th went to Russia with Beaverbrook until the end of the month.

Gide wrote an enthusiastic letter to Bennett about the French translation of *The Old Wives' Tale*, which he and R. M. du Gard were revising from the original work of Marcel de Coppet (b. 1881), then Governor of the Tchad. See p. 136 n. for part of Gide's earlier letter about *The Old Wives' Tale*.

Bennett began the actual writing of *Imperial Palace* on 25 September.

and Dorothy too. I've just returned from a glance at Leningrad & Moscow, & my articles on the Soviet régime begin in the *Daily Express* tomorrow. I started out to be sympathetic, but am now hostile, to the Soviet régime. I've been out of England—Italy, France, Baltic, Russia—for two months. Too long!

Our special greetings to you & all of you.

Yours ever, A. B.

P.S. I address this to your esteemed residence because I can't be sure of the first word of your address, & I don't know whether Tirol is in Austria or Italy. A. B.

BERG / TS. / 362
(*To Wilfred Hardie*)

75, Cadogan Square
30th September 1929

Dear Sir,

Thank you for your appreciative letter. I am glad to have it. I did not say that *A High Wind* would be the best book of the autumn. As for Powys, he is a friend of mine, but I could not get on with his book, and so I have said nothing about it. I think that you have touched its weak spot in saying that it is too abnormal. I do not consider that Powys has a real narrative gift. He is, however, a very remarkable man.

Yours sincerely, Arnold Bennett

STOKE / TS. / 363
(*To Hugh Walpole*)

75, Cadogan Square
21st October 1929

My dear Hughie,

You have no doubt heard of the 'little theatre' which calls itself the *Playroom Six*. This organisation, in which by the way I am interested only artistically, is on the point of taking new and

361. Sir William Rothenstein (1872–1945) was Principal of the Royal College of Art from 1920 to 1935.

Bennett published four articles on the trip to Russia. For other comment on it see Vol. I, pp. 396–7.

362. Wilfred Hardie is not otherwise known. Richard Hughes (1900–) published *A High Wind in Jamaica* in September, John Cowper Powys (1872–1963) *Wolf Solent* in July.

much larger premises. It can obtain the necessary capital, but it wants some vice-presidents. I suggest that you should be a vice-president. The situation will involve you in no responsibilities, no duties, and no expense—unless of course you decide, as you probably would, to see a show now and then, in which case a ticket would cost you about 4¾d. I have been acquainted with the organisation for several years. I have lately held a pretty full enquiry into it, and I am prepared to answer for the aims and the sincerity of the managing group.

Thine, A. B.

BUTLER / T.C.C. / 364
(*To George Doran*)

[75, Cadogan Square]
9th November 1929

My dear George,

Many thanks for your letter and the Russian stuff. The latter is very interesting indeed, but I read it with a certain amount of reserve.

There is an American author named Faulkner who wrote a novel entitled *Soldiers' Pay*, and another called *Mosquitoes*, and another (just out I believe) called *The Sound and the Fury*. I should be greatly obliged if you would cause these three books to be sent to me, debiting my account with the cost thereof.

Is it still true that you are to arrive here in November?

All is well here.

Ever your affectionate, [Arnold Bennett]

HARVARD / MS. / 365
(*To William Rothenstein*)

75, Cadogan Square
15–xi–29

My dear William,

Very many thanks for this most distinguished collection of people. I know naught of the technic of cellotyping, but I like

363. Bennett wrote a similar letter to G. K. Chesterton, who accepted a vice-presidency. The organization is not otherwise known.

364. Bennett read two of the three novels of William Faulkner (1897–1962), and wrote of him in the *Evening Standard*: 'He has inexhaustible invention, powerful imagination, a wonderful gift of characterization, a finished skill in dialogue . . .; and he writes, generally, like an angel.'

these portraits, & especially Einstein; and I am charmed to possess them. Dorothy too is grateful for the loan of the Ellen book. I will tell you a tale about Ellen. I was once sitting in the stalls of a theatre, & I heard a fussy, restless woman behind me. Then a hand was put on my shoulder. Ellen Terry said: 'Mr. Bennett, you don't know me, but I know you.' I blushed.

Our gratitude & our loves to all.

Ever yours, A. B.

TEXAS / T.C.C. / 366
(*To Eugene Goossens*)

[75, Cadogan Square]
22nd November 1929

My dear Eugene,

Thank you for your letter of the 13th, to hand this afternoon. As soon as I heard from you last I gave instructions to Doubleday, Doran & Co., that a copy of *Don Juan* of some sort should be sent to you, and as I had no further news I thought that this had been done. I am now making further efforts to get a copy for you. I have unfortunately no copy of the play here. I seem never to have copies of my own works. Personally I think that you might find material in *Don Juan* for an opera.

Reading Berlioz's *Soirées de l'Orchestre* the other day I found that an opera on the Aztec subject was actually written and composed in Berlioz's time. I suppose that it would be possible to get hold of this and see what the libretto is like. I infinitely regret to say that at present I cannot do any real creative work on a libretto as I am involved in a novel which is not yet by any means finished. I dare not leave it. But if I had an old libretto I could manage to modernize it without disturbing my work on the novel.

I am delighted to hear about the Philadelphia production.

All good luck, my dear boy,

Ever yours, [A. B.]

365. Rothenstein's *Twelve Portraits* was issued in 1929. On Ellen Terry, who died in 1928, see Vol. II, pp. 87–8.

TEXAS / T.C.C. / 367
(*To Eugene Goossens*)

[75, Cadogan Square]
24th December 1929

My dear Eugene,

Many thanks for your letter of the 12th. You have made yourself perfectly clear, and I agree with what you say. I fully understand that the convention of an opera is very different from the convention of a play. I can adopt all the suggestions which you make. There is no reason why the opera should not end with Juan's death if you prefer this. Personally I am not sure that this would be a good thing, but you know better than I do. There is no reason why the nun should be an organist. But there is a reason why she should have the character which I have given her. She must be more smoothly lyrical than the other heroines. It is she who by her humility really defeats Juan. As regards the dialogue, I also agree. I could do this in a proper style.

The only trouble is that I am in the middle of my novel, and it would be impossible for me to do the work until after the novel is finished, which will be about the third week in April. Could you not do some other opera, with a libretto by another hand, in the meantime, or perhaps some orchestral work, and then do the Don Juan later on?

All good wishes,

Ever yours, [A. B.]

HARVARD / TS. / 368
(*To William Rothenstein*)

75, Cadogan Square
25th March 1930

My dear William,

I am returning your Memoirs.

Technically they have practically no faults, except those of the typist. A few slips in writing I have marked here and there. And also one or two places where I think a little cutting might

367. Bennett did not finish writing *Imperial Palace* until July, and he did not begin the libretto of *Don Juan* until September.

be done. As regards the opening, I am as a rule against recollections of childhood. They are always the same and I doubt if they are really interesting. Your childhood's recollections are not very long, but in your place I should be inclined to shorten them a bit, though they are as interesting as such souvenirs can be.

In my opinion the whole book is very interesting indeed. It does not want any re-casting, re-shaping, or anything of that sort. I thoroughly enjoyed it. I think that on the whole you are apt to be rather too kind. I should have liked more harshness. It gives salt to a book. Why not?

The mere writing is excellent. (*pp. 209–11* I think that there is too much about a drawing here.)

pp. 31–40 These are missing.

There was a letter among the leaves. I have not disturbed it.

I suppose that you have the right to use the Conder letters, and others. The copyright of a letter does not belong to the recipient, but to the sender. Only the actual document itself belongs to the recipient. Pardon me if I am teaching my grandmother to suck eggs. . . .

Finally you need have *no* qualms about the book, either technically or as to its interestingness. As a fact you write a damned sight too skilfully for a painter.

Last week Mrs. William was kind enough to send to Dorothy particulars of a house near you. This was very kind of Mrs. William and we are grateful. But we have decided to take two flats in the very latest block of flats—top of Baker Street, and join them together. The total length of the abode is 185 feet. I say this solely in order to impress you.

Let me know if you want any further remarks about your book.

Our loves,

Yours ever, A. B.

P.S. The total length up to now is about 115,000 words, at a rough estimate. If the whole book is 140,000 or 150,000, it will be long enough for two volumes. A. B.

368. Rothenstein published *Men and Memories* in 1931–2. A third volume followed.

Charles Conder, the artist (1868–1909).

YALE / T.C.C. / 369
(*To John van Druten*)

[75, Cadogan Square]
31st March 1930

My dear John,

I witnessed *After All* last night, and found it continuously interesting. The dialogue is admirable, so is the character drawing. The acting was good, and the production more than good.

But I wanted to know: 'What is this play *about*?' I was of course aware that it was about parents and children, but I could not define to myself the theme of the play. A play such as this sets out to illustrate a proposition by means of a clash. What was the proposition?

One further point is that I think that the first business of a play is to be dramatic. This is my antique notion. Hence, it seemed to me that the apparently long stretch of discussion in the final scene, though excellently true and interesting in itself, was out of place, and aroused a slight feeling of impatience, holding up the action. I doubted the wisdom of introducing two new characters who really had nothing to *do*; they have only to *be*. Is this enough?

Such are my views of your play. You have not asked for them. Mais que voulez-vous? Here they are.

I really enjoyed the thing. It has distinction throughout.

Yours, [Arnold Bennett]

BUTLER / TS. / 370
(*To James Hanley*)

75, Cadogan Square
4th April 1930

Dear Mr. Hanley,

I have now read your story. I return it herewith. I think that it is very well done. Of course one has read so much of the same kind of horribleness that one's reactions are not as sharp as they otherwise would be. At any rate you can congratulate yourself that you have set up a new standard of horror. Your story—I

369. John van Druten (1901–57) was already launched on his highly successful dramatic career. *After All* was produced at the Arts Theatre on 30 March.

should call it rather an episode than a story—is certainly the most acutely frightful that I have read. The level of its technical accomplishment is high.

Yours sincerely, Arnold Bennett

SUMMER'S LEASE / 371
(*To John Rothenstein*)

75, Cadogan Square
10 May 1930

My dear John,

In reply I will be frank. I should be delighted to read your novel, but one cannot read and criticize a novel in less than a day, and just now I am exceedingly busy on a little affair of my own amounting to 240,000 words. The affair will not be concluded until the end of June. Until it is concluded the Empire, my relatives, my child, my friends may go to the devil so far as I am concerned. But of course you rightly want it to be handled at once. Have any of your people read it? If so, send me a certificate that it is a remarkable work and I will give you a special introduction to a good literary agent. . . . Have I made myself clear, and am I sure of the continuance of your affections?

Yours, Arnold Bennett

BUTLER / TS. / 372
(*To James Hanley*)

75, Cadogan Square
19th May 1930

Dear Mr. Hanley,

Thank you for your letter of the 24th April. I have not been able to answer it before as I am exceedingly occupied with my novel, which I hope will be finished by the end of June, when I shall go away for a holiday. Personally I think that all cities are

370. James Hanley (1901–) was just at the beginning of his literary career. The story in question was probably *A Passion Before Death*, which describes the last hours of a condemned man. It was published in a limited edition in 1930.

371. (Sir) John Rothenstein (1901–), son of Sir William, later became director of the Tate Gallery. His novel, *Morning Sorrow*, was duly published, and Bennett said in the *Evening Standard* that the author exhibited 'many of the qualities of the born novelist'.

equally conventional. I certainly did not think that *Journey's End* was 'sloppy'. I do not regard it as a very good play, but sloppy is the last adjective I should apply to it. I think that *Nine to Six* was immensely superior to the average play, and that the end was unusually true. I agree with you that the majority of people in London streets seem rather bored; but the tragic, grasping expression of Frenchmen in Paris is, to me, much more unpleasant. You could not possibly substantiate your assertion that from Bedford Place to Kensington the whole place seems to stink of scent. Because it just doesn't.

No! You have not bored me.

Always yours sincerely, Arnold Bennett

BEAVERBROOK / TS. / 373
(*To Lord Beaverbrook*)

75, Cadogan Square
17th June 1930

My dear Max,

Thank you for your letter. No, I certainly do not think that you are unduly anxious about your possessions. (But I cannot recall that you have ever told me about this before.) On the contrary I think that your lack of interest in your possessions is sometimes quite touching, and I like it. As regards the extract in the *Journal* I merely recorded the episode as it presented itself to me. I also recorded your exact words, with their implication.

I wish to inform you that I have very little pretension to be able to read character. I am constantly meeting people who have the air of judging characters at once, and positively. I just cannot do it. To me character is so complex that I never hope to do more than give a few hints about it.

Ever yours, Arnold

372. *Journey's End,* R. C. Sherriff's famous play; *Nine Till Six,* by Aimée and Philip Stuart.

373. Beaverbrook was apparently perturbed by one of the first entries in Bennett's *Journal, 1929,* which had just been published. The entry mainly concerns the mentality of people who bet on horses, and turns at the end to an incident at Beaverbrook's stables in Newmarket (though Beaverbrook is not identified). A colt, valued at £30,000, injured itself, and Bennett and Beaverbrook walked out into the field to see what had happened. Bennett concludes the entry: 'The host suddenly remarked: "All possessions are a mistake! All possessions are a mistake!" We returned to the house and had a melancholy tea.'

MAYFIELD, SYRACUSE / T.C.C. / 374
(*To Louis Jouvet*)

[75, Cadogan Square]
17th June 1930

Dear Mr. Louis Jouvet,

Thank you for your letter of the 31st ultimo, and the enclosure. I return the enclosure, and I send with this a note for your prospectus in England. If this note is not just what you require, please let me know quite candidly, and I will alter it or write it again.

Believe me,
Cordially yours, [Arnold Bennett]

STOKE / S.TR. / 375
(*To an unidentified person*)

[Rod Meadow]
[Trewoofe]
[St. Buryan]
[Cornwall]
[about 15 July 1930]

Dear Sir,

I am not a man from the North, and never was. The period of three years in which I reviewed 1,000 books belongs to the

374. Louis Jouvet (1887–1951), actor and producer, was with Jacques Copeau and his Vieux Colombier until 1922, and then set up his own theatre. Bennett's note read:

'Good plays, and many of them, are presented on the Boulevard, but the theatre of today and of tomorrow finds a fuller expression on stages which are not on the Boulevard. And chief among these is the Comédie des Champs Élysées, directed by the youthful Louis Jouvet, an artist who, in addition to producing plays, can and does act in them with much distinction. On my visits to the Comédie des Champs Élysées, extending over several years, I have reached the conclusion that the aim of Louis Jouvet is to combine the ancient spirit of French comedy with the new. The French comic tradition, like all sound classical traditions, lends itself to evolutionary development, and Louis Jouvet has richly proved this. He is no iconoclast, no seeker after notoriety by means of eccentricity. He is at once respectful to the old and welcoming to the new. He does not, however, welcome the new merely because it is new; but only when it happens also to be good. In order to secure admission to his stage, a play must exhibit artistic excellence in addition to novelty of matter or manner or both. His productions have the characteristic of simplicity. He never forgets that the play itself comes first, the casting second, and the setting third. He has given to Paris more than one play that has the air of being a masterpiece. He is now to submit the leading items of his répertoire to the British public. I have enjoyed, and learnt from, his productions in the Champs Élysées, and I hope to repeat the experience at home. Let me end by saying that, not Louis Jouvet and his company, but ourselves, will be on trial during his tour.'

far distant past. I should not be surprised to learn from people other than yourself that your books are very good. But I must tell you that I receive lots of letters from authors written in exactly the same strain as yours, and containing the same statements about themselves as you make about yourself. For anything I know to the contrary all these statements may be true. Your controversial style does not coincide with my ideal, but I wish you good fortune, and when your next book appears I may come across it. One never knows.

Yours sincerely, [Arnold Bennett]

GIDE / 376
(*To André Gide*)

Rod Meadow
Trewoofe
2 August 1930

My dear André Gide,

Delighted to have your letter. Please make your visit as late as possible. I don't expect to be able to be back in London definitely until the 12th September.

I was in Berlin 20 months ago. I stayed at the Adlon, which is an absolutely first-rate hotel, as good as the London Savoy. I was very pleased with Berlin and I find that most English people are. I shall be very interested to see Marc's film.

Moby Dick. The present vogue of Herman Melville is mainly due to two English novelists, Frank Swinnerton and myself. We both of us have great opportunities for publicity, and 8 or 10 years ago, in the Reform Club, we decided to convince the world that *Moby Dick* was the greatest of all sea-novels. And we did! There is a lot more of Melville that you ought to read, if you have not already read it. Some of the 'Piazza Tales' are wonderful. And the novel *Pierre*, though while mad and very strange and overstrained, is really original and remarkable. Some of the still stranger books I have not yet read or tried to read. The trouble is that the esoteric books can only be obtained in the complete edition of the works. Happily I possess it. I believe that the original editions of *Typee* and *Omoo* are much better than the current editions, which have been expurgated.

375. The Bennetts went to Cornwall for six weeks in the middle of July.

Please note I think that *Evan Harrington* is better than *Beauchamp's Career* and *The Woodlanders* better than the *Mayor of Casterbridge*.

I shall be at the above address till the 30th August. After that I have to fulfill a longstanding engagement with a friend for a short cruise in his yacht.

I have not yet received the two books which you mentioned in your last letter.

I look forward most eagerly to seeing you, and I will try to make your visit to London as pleasant as possible.

Ever yours, affectionately, Arnold Bennett

STOKE / MS. / 377
(*To Hugh Walpole*)

[Rod Meadow]
[Trewoofe]
29.8.30

My dear Hughie,

It was, I think, an error of discretion on your part to say in the *Herald Tribune* that my novel is about the Savoy. Even if I mentioned to you the Savoy in connection with the novel, such a private remark was obviously not to be used journalistically, and its divulgation in print might easily lead to trouble with a large number of people. I shall therefore be glad if you will recall your dread statement in your next article. It is quite true that I have obtained a very large part of my material from the Savoy people, who were all told that I wanted the stuff for a novel. But the novel is not about the Savoy. It is about a larger and a different hotel, situate in Birdcage Walk, a hotel with a history of its own: The Imperial Palace.

Ever yours, A. B.

376. Marc Allégret was making a film at the UFA studios.

Bennett bought his edition of the works of Herman Melville (1819–91) in 1926. For other comments on George Meredith see Vols. I and II.

Bennett went for a brief cruise with A. E. W. Mason at the end of August.

GRIFFIN / MS. / 378
(*To George Reeves-Smith*)

75, Cadogan Square
17.9.30

My dear Reeves-Smith,

My hotel novel was designed to be 150,000 words in length, & to be written in 6 months. It is 243,000 words in length, & took me nearly ten months. Thus I was thrown late for the autumn publishing season, and thus it was impossible for me to submit the typescript, or even the proof, to you. I have not had one single day to spare. I am now sending to you a rough early copy of the book (without the latest corrections), just for you to look at. I said I should dedicate it to you, & I have done. The material which you so good-naturedly gave me, and enabled me to get hold of, was enough for a dozen novels. I have had the greatest difficulty in controlling it, and subduing it to the background of the tale proper. Much of it I have had to leave out. You will receive in due course a copy of the special limited edition in two volumes, with all my apologies. I do hope that none of your staff will take any character in the book as a portrait, or any incident as personal. The principal members of the staff of a hotel must be defined in the usual way. Thus there must be a grill-room manager. In my book he is very human (like the rest of the characters). Mr. Manetta *might* say to himself: 'A.B. got his material from the Savoy; I am grill-room manager at the Savoy, hence I am the character "Ceria" in the novel, & I don't like it.' He might say these things unto himself, but I feel sure that he won't. Similarly with other characters, and especially the Managing Director, who had a regrettable liaison with an English girl in Paris!

I won't say anything as to the novel qua novel, except that both the English & the American publishers are extremely excited and enthusiastic about it. Poor dears, they know no better!

As for my gratitude to yourself, you are aware of it. It persists.

Yours sincerely, Arnold Bennett

378. (Sir) George Reeves-Smith (d. 1941) was managing director of the Savoy group of hotels for forty years.

GIDE / 379
(*To André Gide*)

[75, Cadogan Square]
22nd September 1930

My dear Gide,

C'est trop fort, et je suis désolé. I counted absolutely on your arrival in this city and on the pleasure of long talks. However, I am a philosopher and I shall await your coming with what calm I can.

It was very good of you to oversee the progress of *The Old Wives' Tale*. You will receive my new book about the middle of October. Les épreuves m'ont terriblement éprouvé. However, they are all finished. I look forward to your *Œdipe*:—though I have but little idea what it is.

A very fine book indeed, recently published, is Siegfried Sassoon's *Memoirs of an Infantry Officer*. I thought that I could never tolerate another war book, but this one, after the first 30 or 40 pages is really extremely distinguished. It has style, wit, beauty and truthfulness.

Ever yours, Arnold Bennett

BUTLER / T.C.C. / 380
(*To George Doran*)

[75, Cadogan Square]
1st October 1930

My dear George,

Many thanks for your letter written from the Savoy. I hope you have had a good voyage and are absolutely well.

Miss Leonard brought me on Monday morning the dust-jacket for the American edition of *Imperial Palace*. It was extremely ugly, and it was also an unmistakable picture of the Savoy—entirely unmistakable. This in spite of the fact that 5 or 6 weeks ago I had got Miss Leonard to cable D. D. & Co. that no mention or hint of the Savoy must be made or given in the publicity for *Imperial Palace* in America. No American who had ever been to London could possibly fail to see that the hotel was the Savoy. Further, in the novel I had given a description of the façade of *Imperial Palace*. The illustrator totally ignored this.

379. Gide finished writing his *Œdipe* early in 1931.
On Sassoon and the *Memoirs of an Infantry Officer* see above, p. 37.

I was furious. I really was. I got Miss Leonard to cable; I got Ralph to cable; and I cabled myself, insisting that the jacket should be withdrawn.

Last night I saw Nelson at Maugham's play. He told me that the idea for the jacket was solely yours, and that you had given detailed instructions for the design of it. Was this one of Nelson's astutenesses?

It was absolutely monstrous of D. D. & Co., after my specific warning in August, to have allowed the jacket to go through. You of course were in no way responsible for this, as you must have left the firm before Miss Leonard's urgent cable was received.

You will guess that I am still not quite calm about this incident.

I shall be perfectly recovered by the time of your return, which I hope will be soon.

Ever your affectionate [Arnold Bennett]

STOKE / TS. / 381
(*To Hugh Walpole*)

75, Cadogan Square
4th October 1930

My dear Hughie,

I do not know any cure for insomnia. I am convinced that most insomnia is due to some poisoning of the system, usually either from indigestion or from teeth. Dr. Haydn Brown, of 53 Bedford Square, says that he can cure insomnia, and that he has already cured many cases. So far he has only begun on my case, so that I cannot speak personally as to results. He is a very interesting man and I have had long talks with him. He has the merit of having got into trouble with the British Medical Council.

I think that a good way of dealing with the symptoms of insomnia (not the causes) is to get resolutely up when one cannot sleep and *do* something—for instance, Hornibrook's

380. Mary Leonard was a Doubleday, Doran representative in London. Ralph Pinker (1900–) was now in charge of the London office of the Pinker firm; see further, Vol. I. Nelson Doubleday (d. 1949) was the son of F. N. Doubleday. Doran parted company with the Doubleday firm to join the Hearst organization.

exercises, which at once improve the circulation. Also something can be done by going to bed early and quietly, consciously tranquilizing the mind beforehand.

This is all I can say.

Ever yours, A. B.

TEXAS / T.C.C. / 382
(*To Eugene Goossens*)

[75, Cadogan Square]
7th October 1930

My dear Eugene,

I now enclose my draft of the last Act, together with the typescript of the original Act of the play. Please return both to me in due course.

This Act is shorter than any of the others. If you think it is too short you might restore some of the cut passages from the play. But I do not think that it is too short, seeing that you will need opportunities for purely musical effects.

By the way, it is essential that the play should end tragically. The whole opera is a tragedy, and from the very beginning of the work the tragedy is being prepared.

I hope that I have now made some slight amends for my previous delay.

Our loves,

Ever yours, [A. B.]

ARKANSAS / TS. / 383
(*To Frank Swinnerton*)

75, Cadogan Square
13 October 1930

My dear Henry,

Thank you. I had already asked Jo to dinner here for tonight. I will ask him to lunch at the Reform on Friday, one o'clock, as you suggest.

381. Dr. Haydn Brown (d. 1936), neurologist, interested in spiritualism. On 2 and 9 January 1927 Bennett published two articles in the *Sunday Pictorial* attacking the medical profession: 'What the Doctor Knows' and 'Can the Doctors be Cured?'.

382. Bennett wrote the libretto for *Don Juan* from 20 September to 3 October. The opera was produced at Covent Garden on 24 June 1937.

What am I to do in the clash between my favourite critics? Desmond has no use for Violet, but admires Gracie. You have no use for Gracie, but admire Violet. I ought to tell you that in my opinion Gracie did say quite a few interesting things, and that the Paris affair was intended *not* to be passionate.

Bruce Richmond has written to me apologising for the opening paragraphs of the review in the *Lit. Suppl.* And I expect a general apology for Bruce Lockhart's grossly inaccurate article in the *Standard.* There may be some secret history behind that article. If there is I will

Relate the same
For the delight of a few natural hearts.

Our loves,

Yours, A. B.

BEAVERBROOK / TS. / 384
(*To Lord Beaverbrook*)

75, Cadogan Square
15th October 1930

My dear Max,

Thank you for yours of yesterday. I must tell you that I was delighted to see you again—and to see you looking so well. I have not seen you in such apparent good health for ages.

Feeling myself under the necessity of keeping my end up on a trifling matter, I wrote to Gilliat last Friday, and incidentally mentioned your name. Today he writes asking whether he can show the letter to you. Well, of course he can. Does he suppose that I write letters to your editors that I would not care for you to see? Good God!

383. Jo Davidson (1883–1952), the American sculptor, was doing busts of several authors for Doubleday, Doran. He did one of Bennett in the autumn.

On Desmond MacCarthy and Bruce Richmond, see above, pp. 28 and 130. The review of *Imperial Palace* in the *Times Literary Supplement* began by imagining Bennett saying to himself, 'Well, if So-and-so is attracting the public with interminable novels at 10s. 6d. net I can do the same with one hand tied behind me'. (Sir) Bruce Lockhart (b. 1887) was on the editorial staff of the *Evening Standard* for several years. He objected to the profusion of factual detail in the novel. He was also amazed that Bennett should think that newspapers would suppress a story about an accident to an ocean liner for the sake of advertising revenue. Bennett based the accident to the *Caractacus* in the novel on one that occurred with the S.S. *Majestic*, the German boat taken over by the British after the war.

I shall give Mrs. Carswell a miss.

I saw Nicolson yesterday at a dull lunch given by Ernest Benn to Henry Ford. Nicolson said that I should be very angry with him when I read his article on Thursday. I said I should not. This gave me the opportunity to inform him that I thought that his remarks on Galsworthy last week were very ill-mannered. (Not that I have any use whatever for Galsworthy's later work. I have none.)

I think more highly than ever of Henry Ford. I learnt yesterday that as soon as he read it he bought 500 copies of *How to Live on 24 Hours a Day* to give to his friends. Some admirer, that!

Technically, I venture to think that your Bulletin No. 2 today is very good. As for the merits of the case I have no opinion, and I am not entitled to an opinion. But the technique of these affairs always interests me greatly.

Ever yours, Arnold

GRIFFIN / MS. / 385
(*To Harriet Cohen*)

[75, Cadogan Square]
22.10.30

My sweet Tania,

I was charmed with your letter from Chicago. (A few days before I received it, I had written to you.) And to write such a letter immediately after your 'opening': This was something! I'm fearfully & wonderfully glad that the concert was a great success. Now, of course, the others will be. And now you may accomplish Gilbertian marvels in U.S.A. It's a relief that you really like the book. I must disgustingly say that, though I remember well the occasion, I have no memory of your saying to me at Claridges: 'Be still, etc.' I got that phrase about a year ago, through my habit, then, of reading the Psalms daily.

384. George Gilliat was editor of the *Evening Standard.*

Catherine Carswell (1879–1946) published her *Life of Robert Burns* in 1930. It was reviewed unfavourably in one of the Beaverbrook papers.

(Sir) Harold Nicolson (1886–1968) was on the editorial staff of the *Evening Standard* in 1930. His comments on Bennett and Galsworthy could not be found.

On Sir Ernest Benn see p. 270. Henry Ford (1863–1947), American automobile manufacturer.

Beaverbrook's 'Bulletin' was a front-page statement on his favourite subject of Empire free-trade.

I came across it, and I thought: 'My God, this is the greatest thing ever said!' I agree: Gracie is not a first-rater; simply because she was incapable of marshalling her faculties. In the main, the reviews of *I.P.* have been excellent. But it is curious that 2 out of 3 of Max's papers were excessively rude about it, the third (*Sunday Express*) was fulsome. I wrote privately to the Editor of the *Standard* pointing out grave misstatements in fact in Bruce Lockhart's article on it. He could offer no defence whatever. Similarly I protested to the editor of the *Times Lit. Supplement* about its assertion that I had been imitating Priestley's fashion of length, for the sake of gain. The editor replied with a full and unreserved apology. As if *I* had not set the fashion of long novels before the excellent Priestley began to write at all! Enough about me. Well, anyhow there have been some grand reviews—especially Ivor Brown's. I haven't heard about the sales yet—I shall hear tomorrow—but the *talk* about the book is loud. I am now beginning another novel, in the intervals of helping Dorothy to organise the egression from 75 and the ingression (T. Browne's word 'ingression into the shadow of God') into 97 Chiltern Court. I think we actually move about Nov. 7. It is a complex business. . . . First Courtauld concert. Rather disappointing. I [? reck] little of Flesch, the fiddler. [? Nor did I immensely] care for Beethoven's triple concerto for pf cello & fiddle. Afterwards we went to Lil Courtauld's supper & saw many persons. What a *fantastic* bore U.G. is! Our seats at the concert were next to the Courtaulds, and Geoffrey Russell was with us, so she asked him to supper too. Whereat he was much satisfied. I am still in the hands of the dentist. My upper jaw is still totally uninhabited. Friday next the population is to flock back. They flocked back once about a week ago; but they would not stay put. And in the middle of a lunch with Henry Ford they simply hooked it. Some presence of mind is needed in these major crises of existence. The tooth problem has a slightly wearing effect on the nerves. Pauline Smith was so surprised by *Imp Pal.* that she became somewhat hysterical. Ditto Thorpe, dramatic critic of *Punch*. A bit trying for the [? immodest] author! As a fact, there is no news. We had a dinner on Monday at which the hostess was flanked by H.G.W. & Somerset Maugham—to her contentment. Maugham's *Cakes & Ale* is 1st rate. But *easily* the finest of *all* recent novels is

D. H. Lawrence's *The Virgin and the Gipsy*. Nothing else exists by the side of it. Believe me. It is marvellous, truly.

Love et caresses from

the e.d. A. B.

GIDE / 386

(*To André Gide*)

75, Cadogan Square
29th October 1930

My dear Gide,

Many thanks for your letter of the 27th. When you have read *The Virgin and the Gipsy* you might get the volume of stories called *The Woman who Rode Away* and read the title-story. After that *The Rainbow*—if you can get it. It was suppressed here by the police and I have no copy. Some unprincipled friend has stolen it from me.

I am delighted that you enjoyed *Evan Harrington*.

As regards *The Old Wives' Tale*, I quite understand your argument about the preface. I myself always refuse now to write a preface for any book. Nevertheless I shall be very sorry if you renounce your project of printing your old letter to me at the beginning of the book.

You are taking an immense amount of trouble over this translation, and I am more than ever grateful. The Tauchnitz edition of this book is 30,000 words shorter than the English edition. Perhaps this version, which I made myself, might suit one of the monthlies.

385. Gracie Savott in *Imperial Palace* is beautiful and passionate and interested in the Psalms. Ivor Brown (1891–), author and critic, wrote in the *Observer*: 'The book is not the one I should have chosen for Mr. Bennett to write: but, oddly, this author, in his wilful way, has kept for himself the choice of what books to write. And he has achieved, not a mere technical triumph, but a triumph of techinque.'

Bennett began the actual writing of *Dream of Destiny* on 25 November.

Lilian and Samuel Courtauld sponsored the Courtauld-Sargent concert series in the thirties. At the second concert, Carl Flesch (1873–1944), Artur Schnabel, and Gregor Piatigorsky played the Beethoven triple concerto. Geoffrey Russell was an attorney who did some work for Bennett at this time.

Thorpe is not otherwise known.

Cakes and Ale appeared in September, *The Virgin and the Gipsy* in October.

About the title. I suppose that you know that 'an old wives' tale' is a proverbial phrase in English, and that it means a silly old story that no one believes. I have of course used it in an ironic sense for my book. No foreigner can properly appreciate the general effect, with all its implications, of a French title. But I must say that I thought that 'Le Conte des Vieilles Epouses', though it entirely misses the significance of the English title, was not altogether an unpleasing title. Is there not some French proverbial phrase which is the equivalent of my English proverbial phrase? There must be, surely.

I agree with you that *Memoirs of an Infantry Officer* is an even better book than *Memoirs of a Fox-Hunting Man.*

Ever your grateful friend, Arnold Bennett

P.S. I am coming to Paris for a few days at Christmas. A. B.

TEXAS / TS. / 387
(*To Lillah McCarthy*)

97, Chiltern Court
Clarence Gate, N.W.1.
24th November 1930

My sweet Lillah,

Alas, it is not at all certain that I shall be able to come to your recital, much though I should like to do so. I am in the hands of the doctor (heart) and I have to lie very low. It is absolutely certain that Dorothy cannot come, as she 'opens' on Wednesday next at the Fortune Theatre. For myself, I shall come if I am allowed to do so.

Dorothy sends her special love to you both. So do I.

All our best wishes,

Ever your devoted, Arnold B.

P.S. Max would never come. He never goes to anything unless it is occasionally a theatre, very occasionally. A. B.

386. *The Old Wives' Tale* was published in France in 1931 under the title *Un Conte des bonnes femmes*. It apparently had no preface by Gide.

387. The Bennetts moved into their new flat on 9 November.
Dorothy played Cecilia Flinders in *The Man from Blankley's*.

GIDE / 388
(*To André Gide*)

Hôtel Matignon
Paris
9–1–31

My dear Gide,

In further reference to my first letter, asking you if you would sit to the American sculptor, Jo Davidson, a friend of mine, for a portrait bust to form part of an exhibition of busts of modern authors in London and New York, I saw Davidson yesterday, and told him that you were unwell at Lavandou. He said that he would go to Lavandou, or anywhere else to do the bust, and would incommode you as little as possible. I told him that I would inform you of this fact at once. I hope that your convalescence is favourably progressing.

I made the acquaintance of James Joyce yesterday. Quel drôle de type!

Ever your devoted Arnold Bennett

ARKANSAS / TS. / 389
(*To Frank Swinnerton*)

97, Chiltern Court
26th January 1931

My dear Henry,

I appreciate greatly. But no, I am certainly not going to bring you up to town and make you waste a day, just in order to see me. With all thanks, and with all respect for human nature, I think I shall give Blanche a miss. I will attend you at the Reform on Friday 6th February, wishing it were sooner.

George was pathetic the first time he came, but a little more perky the second time. He was to have come a third time (Sunday), but he telephoned to say that something else had turned up, and he did not come. So we had Aldous alone.

My 'flu is now over, but I am very weak. I dressed in my

388. The Bennetts were in France for three weeks from 29 December.

ordinary clothes today for the first time, and walked in the street for five minutes.

Ralph is coming to see me this afternoon.

Loves,

Yours, A. B.

CALIF / T.C.C. / 390
(*To Jo Davidson*)

[97, Chiltern Court]
26th January 1931

My dear Jo,

All our acute thanks for all your and Yvonne's various good-naturedness to us during our stay in France. And we hope that you have fixed up wife and boy satisfactorily in the unsatisfactory south. Also that that young man is getting on as well as he ought to get on in health. Give her and him our best.

You will be disgusted with this letter. George Moore, who is still ill, definitely refuses to sit for any portrait of any kind. He writes me from a nursing home that he took oath to this effect some time ago.

I should have written earlier, but I have had 'flu from the moment we arrived home, and I have got up for the first time this afternoon for a few hours. Somewhat annoying.

Let me know beforehand when you are coming to London.

Ever yours, [Arnold Bennett]

FLOWER / TS. / 391
(*To Newman Flower*)

97, Chiltern Court
26th January 1931

My dear Newman,

Many thanks for your kind invitation for the 3rd prox. Of course we would not miss such an affair for anything, and we

389. Blanche—Blanche Knopf, wife of the American publisher, Alfred A. Knopf; George—George Doran; Ralph—Ralph Pinker. For further details about the break between Doran and the Doubledays see Vol. I, pp. 404–10.

Bennett returned home from France with what was diagnosed as an attack of influenza.

390. Yvonne Davidson (d. 1934).

shall therefore certainly be present. We came back from Paris last Tuesday. And I have had 'flu ever since. I am now almost reestablished.

Ever yours, Arnold

TEXAS / T.C.C. / 392
(*To Francis Hackett*)

[97, Chiltern Court]
26th January 1931

My dear Hackett,

Your most kind and welcome letter found me just emerging from the dark tunnel of influenza, so that at present I am writing nothing with my own hand.

I think that you have diagnosed *Imperial Palace* excellently well, and it was extremely good-natured of you to sit down and write to me. When you are in London next, please let me know. If your next book is as thundering a success as your last, you are made for life; which after all is something, isn't it?

All good wishes to you both,

Yours sincerely, [Arnold Bennett]

TEXAS / T.C.C. / 393
(*To Maurice Baring*)

[97, Chiltern Court]
27th January 1931

My dear Maurice,

The letter which you mentioned to me on the ship reached me last night. Very many thanks. Nothing could be more satisfactory to me, and I thank thee.

Ever since I saw you on the main I have been laid up with 'flu, but I am now beginning to get better. Still, I do not at present write my own letters.

Ever yours, [A. B.]

391. The occasion was the wedding of Desmond Flower. Bennett attended the reception at the Savoy, and said there that he felt 'wretchedly ill'.

FALES, NYU / TS. / 394
(*To R. D. Blumenfeld*)

97, Chiltern Court
29th January 1931

My dear Blum,

I have not been able to acknowledge your letter of the 13th earlier as I have been away, and I am now barely convalescent from an attack of influenza, which has made me savage.

I very much fear, my dear Blum, that I cannot do as your Reuter's Young Man desires. I will give you some details when I see you at George Doran's lunch at the Savoy on the 5th. In the meantime you can, with your customary skill, temper the wind to the shorn lamb.

Ever yours, Arnold B.

BEAVERBROOK / TS. / 395
(*To Lord Beaverbrook*)

97, Chiltern Court
14th February 1931

My lord,

Mr Arnold Bennett wishes me to write and thank you for your enquiries, and to say that he would much like to see you but his doctor, Sir William Willcox, absolutely refuses to allow him to have any visitors at present. He sends his love to you.

Yours faithfully, Winifred Nerney
Secretary

395. Sir William Willcox (1870–1941). Bennett's apparent recovery lasted from 26 January to 3 February. The illness was then identified as typhoid fever. He died on 27 March.

INDEX